Seventh Edition

The Little, Brown Workbook

Donna Gorrell
Saint Cloud State University

LONGMAN

An imprint of Addison Wesley Longman, Inc.

New York • Reading, Massachusetts •Menlo Park, California • Harlow, England
Don Mills, Ontario • Sydney • Mexico City • Madrid • Amsterdam

Senior Editor: Patricia Rossi
Development Editor: Tom Maeglin
Supplements Editor: Donna Campion
Marketing Manager: Ann Stypuloski
Project Editor: Brigitte Pelner
Design Manager: John Callahan
Desktop Coordinator: Jim Sullivan
Cover Designer: Kay Petronio
Production Manager: Valerie A. Vargas
Manufacturing Manager: Willie Lane
Electronic Page Makeup: Stratford Publishing Services, Inc.
Printer and Binder: Maple-Vail Book Manufacturing Group
Cover Printer: Coral Graphic Services, Inc.

For permission to use copyrighted material, grateful acknowledgment is made to the copyright holders on pp. 569–570, which are hereby made part of this copyright page.

Please visit our website at http://longman.awl.com

ISBN 0-321-01217-8

45678910—MA—0099

Contents

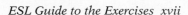

■   ▲   ●

II   GRAMMATICAL SENTENCES *131*

■ ▲ ●

IV   EFFECTIVE SENTENCES *353*

■ ▲ ●

VI   MECHANICS 465

■   ▲   ●

VII   EFFECTIVE WORDS *491*

ESL Guide to the Exercises

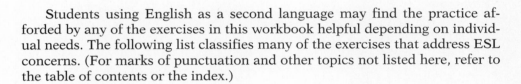

Students using English as a second language may find the practice afforded by any of the exercises in this workbook helpful depending on individual needs. The following list classifies many of the exercises that address ESL concerns. (For marks of punctuation and other topics not listed here, refer to the table of contents or the index.)

Parts of the Sentence

Prepositions

Pronouns

Sentences and Clauses

Verbs

Vocabulary and Spelling

Preface

This seventh edition of *The Little, Brown Workbook* closely parallels its companion *The Little, Brown Handbook* in organization, approach, and guidelines for writing, making it useful as either an instructional supplement to the handbook or an independent text. As in the past, this new edition aims for understanding of rhetorical and grammatical concepts by concentrating on thorough instruction as well as extensive exercises. The explanations have been praised as clear and the tone friendly.

The arrangement of the book, from whole paper to word, reflects current rhetorical theory in a format accessible to today's college students. An introduction covering critical thinking, reading, and writing sets the stage for college writing that is proficient and perceptive. Part I focuses on composing processes, featuring discussions and exercises on prewriting, thesis development, drafting, revising, paragraph composition, and support for arguments—all of which aim to encourage students in exploring and developing their own ideas. Part II shifts to grammatical sentences, with Chapter 5 giving a rapid overview of the English sentence and the remaining chapters in the section explaining principles in greater detail. Parts III through VII cover sentence problems, ways of constructing effective sentences, and then punctuation, mechanics, and diction. Part VIII provides instruction on a short documented paper. The entire book has been examined to include material on the increasingly common practice of composing at a computer.

The format of the book allows teachers to use parts according to their own teaching styles and the needs of their students. Some may choose to use the parts sequentially, from whole paper to sentences to individual words. Others may choose to use the book as a reference guide, applying Part I to classroom instruction and referring students to the remaining chapters for individual study. Most of the exercises are adaptable to cooperative group work.

We have continued some of the changes initiated in the sixth edition: streamlining the text, gathering the exercises together at the ends of chapters, and keying sections of text to related exercises both within the chapter and in other chapters. With this edition we have gone the next logical step and keyed the exercises (especially in the longer chapters) to the related text. We have also altered most of the exercise titles to represent first the subject and then the task. Thus, "Using the -*s* Forms of Verbs" has become "The -*s* Forms of Verbs: Rewriting a Text."

Exercises continue to have connected discourse wherever feasible. The contexts are mainly those common to academic settings across a variety of disciplines; they avoid concentration on a single field or culture and the overuse of personal experience. A few feature student writing. As in past editions, the exercises also represent a variety of approaches: sentence patterning or combining, controlled composition, original composition, analysis, sentence completion, plus identification and correction wherever necessary. Exercises specifically directed toward the use of English as a second language augment exercises that deal with similar concerns of students for whom written English functions often as a second dialect. Exercises that address ESL concerns have been classified under "ESL Guide to the Exercises" on pages xvii–xx.

The final chapter, "Writing a Short Documented Paper," has been revamped to reflect the shift toward electronic research. The text gives some guidance in the use of this new medium, and the new student paper illustrates both print and electronic sources. The sample MLA documentary forms reflect the fluidity of styles and probably differ from those found in some handbooks. My goal is to represent a style that is as clear as possible and provides as much as, but no more than, is necessary for source location. Exercises give practice in the skills associated with using sources.

A continued feature of this edition is the highlighted boxes corresponding to those in the handbook, making readily accessible the main elements under discussion. Accessibility is also maintained with the extensive index and the cross-references to related sections of the text. Another continuing feature is that the exercise answer book is still available to students at the instructor's option and without charge.

I am indebted to the following reviewers for their assistance in making this seventh edition a reality: Robert L. Giron, Montgomery College; Cathy Horne, Wilson County Technical College; Terrialee Lankford, Laramie County Community College; Andy J. Moore, Baylor University; Craig Payne, Indian Hills Community College; Brian K. Reed, Bethune-Cookman College. I also wish to thank Tom Maeglin, and Donna Campion, Brigitte Pelner, Patricia Rossi, and Jim Sullivan at Longman for their work in the production of this book.

DONNA GORRELL

The Little, Brown Workbook

Critical
Thinking,
Reading,
and Writing

Introduction

Critical thinking is essential for getting along in the world—in school, in work, and in life. It is a questioning attitude that is fundamental to both reading and writing. In reading, it allows us to understand better what a writer is saying; in writing, it helps clarify our thinking. This introduction helps you be more adept at all three: critical thinking, reading, and writing.

I1　Fostering a critical perspective

Critical thinking is a healthy skepticism that doesn't accept everything at face value, that looks at puzzling situations as problems to be solved, and that analyzes the unknown in order to understand it better. This skepticism is not necessarily negative and disapproving; more often it is discriminating, comparing something new with what you already know, examining the parts of the new thing or idea to see if they fit with what you know, so that you can make a judgment or an interpretation of the facts.

You already take a critical perspective in much of your life. If you wanted to buy a used car, for instance, you would select a dealer with care, carefully examine a number of cars for the sound of the engine, the condition of the tires, the presence of rust spots, and so on. If you have never bought a car before, you might consult with someone more knowledgeable than you. You wouldn't allow an overeager car dealer to sell you something you didn't want.

The same should be true with reading and listening in school: don't be sold an idea without examining it closely and asking questions. What does a speaker or writer mean? How does the idea compare with what I know is true? What else can I read or who else can I consult about this idea? You can think critically about almost anything.

I2   Thinking and reading critically

Critical thinking is most fruitful, most accurate, in subjects you know well. If you have read extensively about capital punishment, for example, you are better able to judge arguments on one side or the other. But you can increase your knowledge with a questioning attitude, by reading critically and applying the following techniques.

Techniques of critical reading

- **Writing:** making notes on your reading throughout the process (I2-a)
- **Previewing:** getting background; skimming (I2-b)
- **Reading:** interacting with and absorbing the text (I2-c)
- **Summarizing:** distilling and understanding content (I2-d)
- **Forming your critical response** (I2-e)

  Analyzing: separating into parts

  Interpreting: inferring meaning and assumptions

  Synthesizing: reassembling parts; making connections

  Evaluating: judging quality and value

You won't apply all these techniques every time you read, but the more you want to increase your understanding of the text (any piece of writing), the greater the number of techniques you will apply. For studying, you may apply them all; for reading a popular magazine, maybe only one or two. Apply as many techniques as necessary to achieve your purpose in reading.

Writing while reading

You are probably familiar with note taking for the purpose of using the material later in writing, such as in the short documented paper discussed in Chapter 35. Another reason for writing while you read is to help you get more out of the text. By making notes, you relate what you read to what you already understand about the subject. You are not only reading more closely but making connections as well.

Some people choose to write directly in the margins of their books, thus making their notes readily accessible for later review. Others make their notes in separate notebooks or reading journals, linking them to the reading with page numbers. Still others, who like the convenience of notes in their textbooks but don't want to write on the pages, use self-stick removable sheets for attaching notes at appropriate places.

 ## Previewing the material

You can greatly improve your comprehension of what you read by doing a little preliminary work. Skim the chapter or article, trying to grasp the context from headings, beginnings of paragraphs, illustrations, and so on. And as you skim, formulate questions that you can seek answers for as you read.

 ### Questions for previewing a text

- **Length:** Is the material brief enough to read in one sitting, or do you need more time?
- **Content clues:** What do the title, summary or abstract, headings, illustrations, and other features tell you? What questions do they raise in your mind?
- **Facts of publication:** Does the publisher or publication specialize in a particular kind of material—scholarly articles, say, or popular books? Does the date of publication suggest currency or datedness?
- **Author:** What does the biographical information tell you about the author's publications, interests, biases, and reputation in the field?
- **Yourself:** Do you anticipate particular difficulties with the content? What biases of your own may influence your response to the text—for instance, anxiety, curiosity, boredom, or a similar or opposed outlook?

 ## Reading

To understand the material you read, plan to read at least twice. The first time through, read fast, not taking notes, just trying to get an overall idea of what the writer is saying—enjoying it, relating it to your own experiences, maybe marking places you don't understand. The second time through, read slowly—making notes, asking questions, looking up unfamiliar words, flipping pages backward and forward as you attempt to relate parts.

See Exercise I-1.

Summarizing

To think critically about what you read, you need to understand precisely what the writer has said. Writing a summary helps. Using your own words, condense the main points of a text, in this way seeing its strengths and weaknesses. Summaries of short pieces of writing are generally no more than one-fifth the length of the original, whereas summaries of longer pieces, such as books or chapters, are shorter proportionately.

In the box below is a procedure for summarizing. Note that your completed summary begins with an overall summary sentence and then adds supporting summary sentences. These sentences are not the original sentences; rather, they are sentences that you formulate to encapsulate the meaning of the original. You may find yourself using some of the same words the original writer used, but do not write your summary by selecting sentences or phrases from the original.

Writing a summary

- Look up words or concepts you don't know so that you understand the author's sentences and how they relate to each other.
- Work through the text paragraph by paragraph to identify its sections—single paragraphs or groups of paragraphs focused on a single topic. To understand how paragraphs relate to each other, try outlining the text (see 1g-2).
- Write a one- or two-sentence summary of each section you identify. Focus on the main point of the section, omitting examples, facts, and other supporting evidence.
- Write a sentence or two stating the author's central idea.
- Write a full paragraph (or more, if needed) that begins with the central idea and supports it with the sentences that summarize sections of the work. The paragraph should concisely and accurately state the thrust of the entire work.
- Use your own words. By writing, you re-create the meaning of the work in a way that makes sense for you.

An important aspect of summaries is that their sources are cited. A common way of telling your reader what you are summarizing is to mention the author and title in the first sentence. Other publishing information can be included in parentheses at the end of the summary or in a note at the end of your piece of writing. (See Chapter 35 on documenting sources.)

The paragraph below is followed by a summary of it. Compare the summary with the original and note the objectivity, completeness, conciseness, and source citation.

Years ago when I was a high school student experiencing racial desegregation, there was a fierce current of resistance and militancy. It swept over and through our bodies as we, black students, stood, pressed against the red brick walls, watching the national guard with their guns, waiting for a moment when we would enter, when we would break through racism, waiting for the moment of change, of victory. And now even within myself, I find that spirit of militancy growing faint; all too often it is assaulted by feelings of despair and powerlessness. I find I must work to nourish it, to keep it strong. Feelings of despair and powerlessness are intensified by all the narratives of black self-hate that indicate that those militant 1960s did not have sustained radical impact—that the transformation of black self-consciousness did not become an ongoing revolutionary practice in black life. This causes such frustration and despair, for it means that we must return to this basic agenda, that we must renew efforts at transformation, that we must go over old ground. Perhaps what is worst about turning over old ground is the fear that the seeds, though planted again, will never survive, will never grow strong. Right now it is anger and rage at the continued racial genocide that rekindles within me that spirit of militancy. (bell hooks)

SUMMARY

bell hooks, recalling the racial militancy of her 1960s school days, senses a need for a renewed revolutionary outlook that will replace the feelings of hopelessness that seem to characterize black consciousness today ("Overcoming White Supremacy," *Zeta* Jan. 1987: 26–27).

 Forming your critical response

Critical reading requires you to go beyond understanding what authors of texts say to determining what they don't say, where additional meaning may lie. A poem about a road not taken, for example, is really about the poet's choices in life, and an essay about vegetarianism may really be an expression of the writer's opinion about animals' right to life. Critical thinking and reading consist of four overlapping operations: analyzing, interpreting, synthesizing, and (often) evaluating.

ANALYZING

You *analyze* a text by examining its parts or elements. Who is the writer, for example, and for what readers is the publication intended? How is the text organized? What is its thesis, and how does the writer support that thesis? Is the vocabulary technical, professional, or common? What tone or attitude does the writer assume? What does the writer not say? If the writer uses long sentences and obscure words, is it to deliberately conceal meaning; if so, why?

INTERPRETING

As you analyze, you also *interpret*, trying to understand why the writer made particular choices. What assumptions does the writer make about the audience? What values and beliefs are promoted through the writer's position on the subject? Keeping in mind the evidence of the text, what conclusions can you draw? Be careful about allowing your own biases to cause a misinterpretation of the text or undue attention to a minor point.

 Guidelines for analysis, interpretation, and synthesis

- What is the purpose of your reading?
- What questions do you have about the work? What elements can you ignore?
- How do you interpret the meaning and significance of the elements, both individually and in relation to the whole text? What are your assumptions about the text? What do you conclude about the author's assumptions?
- What patterns can you see in (or synthesize from) the elements? How do the elements relate? How does this whole text relate to other texts?
- What do you conclude about the text? What does this conclusion add to the text?

SYNTHESIZING

With interpretation, you put the pieces back together—you *synthesize*. For example, try to relate the writer's choice of words and selection of facts and examples to the purpose for writing. Relate the tone of the piece to who the writer and audience are. Make connections between the organization and the kinds of examples and other support the writer draws on. By making connections among parts, you arrive at a new understanding of the text. A synthesis is evidence of your mind working on another text.

EVALUATING

At times your critical reading may require an *evaluation*—a judgment about the quality, value, or significance of the work. Evaluating what you read may be something you don't commonly do. Who are you, you might say, to judge the quality of work by an expert? That's a good question. The answer is that when you are asked to evaluate something you read, you need to judge it according to your own experience and knowledge. Here are some guidelines that may help.

General guidelines for evaluation

- What are your reactions to the text? What in the text are you responding to?
- Is the work unified, with all the parts pertaining to a central idea? Is it coherent, with the parts relating clearly to each other?
- Is the work sound in its general idea? In its details and other evidence?
- Has the author achieved his or her purpose? Is the purpose worthwhile?
- Does the author seem authoritative? Trustworthy? Sincere?
- What is the overall quality of the work? What is its value or significance in the larger scheme of things?
- Do you agree or disagree with the work? Can you support, refute, or extend it?

See Exercise I-3.

 I3 Writing critically

Critical writing results from critical reading and critical thinking. It is more than a summary or a report of another text. It is your analysis, interpretation, synthesis, and perhaps evaluation of that text. You will find it useful in arguments, reviews of literature, and research writing.

To write a critical analysis of another piece of writing, use the notes and ideas you acquired as a result of your critical reading. First state your main point about the text and name the author and title. For support, use your analysis, interpretation, synthesis, and evaluation, concentrating not only on *what* is said but also on *how* it is said. Summarize as necessary for clarification, but don't limit yourself to summary. (See also Chapter 35.)

See Exercise I-4.

EXERCISE I-1

Reading for Understanding (I2)

Working in pairs or small groups, read the following passage, first applying the "preparation for reading" questions, then reading twice, first quickly and then more carefully. In your second reading, mark the words you want to look up in a dictionary, and write notes and questions in the margin that might help if you were to review the passage later. Compare notes with your classmates or discuss the notes with groupmates in class.

THE PROBLEM OF CHOICE

1   Teachers very often say to me, "Suppose we tell kids that they now have the freedom to choose what they are going to study, and how and when they are going to study it, and they don't choose anything, don't do anything? Then what do we do?" A good many teachers who have tried to open up their classrooms, usually in a junior high school or high school, have said that this has in fact happened.

2   We should try to see this situation through the eyes of the student. For years he has been playing a school game which looks to him about like this. The teacher holds up a hoop and says, "Jump!" He jumps, and if he makes it, he gets a doggy biscuit. Then the teacher raises the hoop a little higher and again says, "Jump!" Another jump, another biscuit. Or, perhaps the student makes a feeble pretense of jumping, saying, "I'm jumping as high as I can, and this is the best I can do." Or, he may lie on the floor and refuse to jump. But in any case the rules of the game are simple and clear—hoop, jump,

biscuit. Now along comes a teacher who says, "We aren't going to play that game anymore; you're going to decide for yourself what you're going to do." What is the student going to think about this? Almost certainly, he is going to think, "They're hiding the hoop! It was bad enough having to jump through it before, but now I have to find it." Then after a while he is likely to think, "On second thought, maybe I don't have to find it. If I just wait long enough, pretty soon that hoop is going to slip out of its hiding place, and then we'll be back to the old game where at least I know the rules and am comfortable."

3   In short, if we make this offer of freedom, choice, self-direction to students who have spent much time in traditional schools, most of them will not trust us or believe us. Given their experience, they are quite right not to. A student in a traditional school learns before long in a hundred different ways that the school is not on his side; that it is working, not for him, but for the community and the state; that it is not interested in him except as he serves its purposes; and that among all the reasons for which the adults in the school do things, his happiness, health, and growth are by far the least important. He has probably also learned that most of the adults in the school do not tell him the truth and indeed are not allowed to—unless they are willing to run the risk of being fired, which most of them are not. They are not independent and responsible persons, free to say what they think, feel, or believe, or to do what seems reasonable and right. They are employees and spokesmen, telling the children whatever the school administration, the school board, the community, or the legislature want the children to be told. Their

job is by whatever means they can to "motivate" the students to do whatever the school wants. So, when a school or teacher says that the students don't have to play the old school game anymore, most of them, certainly those who have not been "good students," will not believe it. They would be very foolish if they did. (John Holt, *Freedom and Beyond;* New York: Dell, 1972)

EXERCISE I-2

Summarizing (I2-d)

The first two paragraphs below are each followed by two summaries. Judge which is the better summary of each paragraph, indicating your choice with a check mark in the space to the left. Summaries should begin with an overall summary statement, have supporting summary statements as necessary, and name the source. For the third paragraph, write a summary on separate paper.

1   During the year 1903 a forty-year-old Detroiter named Henry Ford, having left the employ of the little Detroit Automobile Company with the idea of going into the manufacturing business for himself, designed and built a big and powerful racing car. Why did he do this? He had no great interest in speed; his idea was quite different: he wanted to make a small, light, serviceable vehicle. The reason he built a racing car was that he wanted capital, and to attract capital he had to have a reputation, and in those days when automobiles were thought of as expensive playthings in which the rich could tear noisily along the dusty roads, the way to get a reputation was to build a car that could win races. (Frederick Lewis Allen, *The Big Change;* New York: Harper, 1952, p. 109)

_____ a.   According to Frederick Lewis Allen, Henry Ford built his first automobile, a powerful racing car, in order to gain a reputation with the wealthy as an automobile builder. Once he had attracted capital, he would build the kind of car he wanted to build: a small, practical one (*The Big Change;* New York: Harper, 1952, 109).

_____ b.   In 1903 Henry Ford built a big and powerful racing car. He didn't want to do this; instead he wanted to build a small, sensible car. But in order to get the capital he needed, he first had to have a reputation, so he cleverly built the race car to get the attention of the rich and famous people who drove cars like that and had the money to invest in building them (*The Big Change;* New York: Harper, 1952, 109).

2   The early Sagas spoke, too, of the abundant fruit of excellent quality growing in Greenland, and of the number of cattle that could be pastured there. The Norwegian settlements were located in places that are now at the foot of glaciers. There are Eskimo legends of old houses and churches buried under the ice. The Danish Archaeological Expedition sent out by

the National Museum of Copenhagen was never able to find all of the villages mentioned in the old records. But its excavations indicated clearly that the colonists lived in a climate definitely milder than the present one. (Rachel L. Carson, *The Sea Around Us;* New York: Oxford, 1951, p. 180)

———— a.   There is evidence that the climate of Greenland used to be milder than it is today, according to Rachel L. Carson in *The Sea Around Us*. Old records tell of colonists successfully raising fruit and cattle and of villages located where glaciers now stand (New York: Oxford, 1951, 180).

———— b.   In the past, says Rachel L. Carson, abundant fruit and cattle were raised in Greenland. There were settlements in places that now would be at the foot of glaciers. Eskimos tell of houses and churches buried under the ice, and the Danes found in their archaeological expeditions that the climate of Greenland was once milder than it is today (Rachel L. Carson, *The Sea Around Us;* New York: Oxford, 1951, 180).

3   Even where it has long been entrenched, democracy has not proved invariably hospitable to women. Despite the growing number of women entering politics in the U.S., the country is just beginning the journey toward full equality. In the West, women like [former] British Prime Minister Margaret Thatcher and former Norwegian Prime Minister Gro Brundtland have had to struggle against the traditional demands of gender in order to impress their visions on national policies. For decades the Communist states of Europe boasted of political egalitarianism, making a show of filling token government posts with women. But revolution has torn down the facades, revealing just how cosmetic was the "power" shared by the East's women. Now the emergence of a new order is challenging women to show themselves both willing and able to take on real responsibilities. (Johanna McGeary, "Challenge in the East," *Time* Special Issue Fall 1990: 30)

Name _____   Date _____

EXERCISE I-3

Reading Critically—Analyzing, Interpreting, Synthesizing, Evaluating (I2)

Working in pairs, individually, or in groups, read the following paragraphs critically. After your initial reading, work with your partners in analyzing the paragraphs for unstated meanings, making notes for possible critical essays that relate the paragraphs to life today. Apply the "General guidelines for evaluation" (in I2-e) to evaluate the paragraphs from the experience and knowledge you and your partners share.

1   Appearance is a symbolic means of self-expression. In the United States clothes are practically a language because there is so much emphasis on how people look, what they buy, and how they package themselves. Over the past decade there have been several revolutions in clothes styles, hair styles, and general personal appearance: boots, levi's, sandals, and military uniforms have replaced pennyloafers, polo shirts, and pegged pants; Madison Avenue types and orthodontists sprout mustaches and sideburns; the suit-and-tie business uniform is embellished with (if not discarded for) wide wild ties, colored shirts, cut and flared jackets, and turtlenecks; women wear pants, their skirt hems are at the extremes of floor and crotch, and the underwear industry may go out of business. Restaurants have nearly given up excluding women in pants and men without jackets or ties. Employers, with rare exceptions, no longer try to control the hair growth—facial or cranial—of their employees. (Jean Strouse, *Up Against the Law: The Legal Rights of People Under 21;* New York: Signet, 1970)

2   When in the course of human events it becomes necessary for one people to dissolve the political bands which have connected them with another and to assume among the powers of the earth the separate and equal station to which the law of nature and of nature's God entitle them, a decent respect to the opinions of mankind requires that they should declare the causes which impel them to the separation. We hold these truths to be self-evident, that all men are created equal, that they are endowed by their Creator with certain unalienable rights, that among these are life, liberty, and the pursuit of happiness. That to secure these rights, governments are instituted among men, deriving their just powers from the consent of the governed. That whenever any form of government becomes destructive of these ends, it is the right of the people to alter or to abolish it, and

to institute new government, laying its foundation on such principles and organizing its powers in such form as to them shall seem most likely to effect their safety and happiness. (Thomas Jefferson, *The Declaration of Independence,* 1776)

3   The maids and doormen, factory workers and janitors who were able to leave their ghetto homes and rub against the cold-shouldered white world told themselves that things were not as bad as they seemed. They smiled a dishonest acceptance at their mean servitude and on Saturday night bought the most expensive liquor to drown their lie. Others, locked in the unending maze of having to laugh without humor and scratch without agitation, foisted their hopes on the Lord. They shouted loudly on Sunday morning at His goodness and spent the afternoon preparing the starched uniforms to meet a boss's unrelenting examination. The timorous and frightened held tightly to their palliatives. I was neither timid nor afraid. (Maya Angelou, *Gather Together in My Name;* New York: Bantam, 1974)

© 1998 Addison-Wesley Educational Publishers Inc.

EXERCISE I-4

Writing Critically—Analyzing, Interpreting, Synthesizing, Evaluating (I2-e)

Write a short essay based on your critical reading of one of the paragraphs in Exercise I-3. Follow the guidelines on page 6.

Developing an Essay

Chapter 1

Writing is full of opposites. Sometimes it's easy and sometimes it's difficult. Sometimes we enjoy it; at other times we hate it. Sometimes we know before we begin exactly what we want to say and how we plan to say it; at other times, we may begin by exploring a topic that interests us even though we have no idea where our exploration will take us or what form our writing will take. We are discovering and developing ideas as we write. But if writing could be described only in opposites, our understanding of it would be easy. We neither love nor hate writing; we are likely to experience both—even within the same project. Similarly, writing is both easy and difficult—often at the same time: easy in spelling our words perhaps, but difficult in finding the right words. And so parts of our writing projects may be more or less routine while at the same time they require the difficulty of discovery and exploration.

The process of writing is as varied as our reasons for writing. Writing an essay is not necessarily something that begins with an outline, continues with a draft, and then ends with revision and correction. Neither does the process necessarily begin with a broad topic and end with a narrow one, nor does it always begin with an idea, a purpose, or an organizational plan. Essays are not necessarily 500 words or five paragraphs long. There is no right way of writing an essay; there is no single right essay. How a person carries out that writing assignment varies with what the assignment is, who the writer and the audience are, and what the audience knows about the subject; it depends also on what the writer's purpose is and many other factors.

17

1a The writing situation and the writing process

We can talk about an essay as *the communication of an idea—from some-one, to someone, for a purpose.* In any writing situation, ideas may start out broadly but become narrowed as the writer proceeds to write, or they may start out as a loose collection of details that must be held together by a unifying idea yet to be discovered.

Also bear in mind that a *writer's role* changes according to the assignment. You may be a computer expert when describing a program you've written, an investigator when proposing a research project, and an interested observer when describing a fight that broke out after the soccer game.

Every writing situation takes into account the *audience,* too: the person or persons who will read the communication—perhaps a teacher, classmates, a newspaper's subscribers, a client, a business associate, and so on. An audience has a particular relationship to the writer and to the subject based on experiences and knowledge, and this relationship determines what details the writer must communicate, what vocabulary and types of sentences he or she decides to use, what attitude he or she takes in communicating the idea, and so on. As an example, a newsletter to professional ornithologists will be written on a different level from one to members of an amateur bird-watcher's society; the language of the professional publication will be more technical and the explanatory information less detailed.

Overriding all considerations is *the purpose for writing.* If the writer has no purpose, then there is little to say. The purpose determines the subject matter and the writer-audience relationship. It influences the tone of the writing as well as its length, organization, details, and style. The purpose must always be more than meeting a deadline. Just as a newspaper columnist meets an imposed deadline, so do student writers. But the newspaper columnist has something else in mind while writing, and so should a student. The way you write depends on whether you are writing a paper for your history teacher or a report for your biology professor, or whether you are exploring a new idea or reporting something you already know.

But the processes of carrying out formal writing tasks do have some things in common: **development** or **planning,** when writers explore ideas and gather information; **drafting,** when they write their ideas down in rough, preliminary form; and **revising,** when they rethink and rework their drafts. Although we must separate these processes for the purpose of discussing them, they are not separate and distinct parts of writing: writers revise while drafting and even while planning; they continue to plan as they write and sometimes as they revise. Both experienced and inexperienced writers vary in how much of the process appears on paper or on the screen: some do much of their planning in their heads, whereas others make extensive notes or make many changes on the screen.

This chapter and the next will assist you in understanding how you write and how you might adjust your process of writing to suit your varying assignments. Experiment with the procedures discussed in the following sections: finding a topic, defining a purpose, developing ideas, shaping ideas, considering an audience, developing a thesis, organizing, drafting, revising, and editing. As you use these procedures in a variety of writing tasks, you will find which ones work for you.

1b Discovering and limiting a subject

You may be assigned a subject for an essay, or you may be required to invent one from your own store of experiences. Discovering your own subject usually requires some conscious effort. This section discusses some techniques that might help.

 Pursuing your interests and experiences

Sometimes you can discover a subject by looking within yourself to find out what interests you—something that you know about and can share with others. If you don't already know what interests you, you might ask yourself these questions:

- What have I read recently (books, newspaper articles, magazines, Web documents)?
- What have I seen recently on television that I had at least a moderate reaction to?
- Have I seen any good—or bad—movies lately? If so, what made them good or bad?
- Have my attitudes toward local or national issues changed in the past year? What issues? What brought about the change?
- What is the most challenging idea I've heard in the past two weeks?
- What is my most important goal? What am I willing to do to achieve it? How did I become convinced that this is a worthy goal?
- What person do I most admire? Why?

 Matching subject and assignment

While pursuing your interests and experiences in your effort to discover a topic, use your assignment as a guide to your selection. Not all your experiences will suit the requirements of the specific writing situation. To ensure a close fit, ask questions like these:

- Does the assignment contain task-specific words like *describe, report, interpret, explain, define, argue,* or *evaluate?* (See 1c.)
- Is the audience specified? If so, who will that audience be? (See 1d.)

19

- Does the assignment require additional reading? If so, what might that reading be?
- How long should the paper be, and when must it be completed? Am I required to bring rough drafts to class for peer or teacher review?

▲3 Limiting the subject

Once you have a subject, make sure it's narrow enough for you to develop with specific details. Many freshmen, for example, like to compare high school with college, two things they certainly know something about; however, their essays end up being too general because the topic covers too much ground. Better would be a comparison of the high school library with the college library or the high school computer course with the college computer course.

Here are some examples of narrowing a subject to a manageable topic, that is, to a limited, specific essay subject:

BROAD SUBJECT	SPECIFIC TOPICS
Tradition	Holiday dinners
	Weddings
	Comparison with habit
Cooking	How wok cooking promotes creativity
	The difference exact measuring makes
	Teaching a child to bake chocolate-chip cookies
Football	Playing football in the snow
	The role of the nose tackle
	The purpose of the Heisman Trophy

To narrow your subject to manageable size, try these techniques:

- Put yourself in the role of reader and ask yourself what would interest you about this general subject.
- Discuss the general subject with two or three classmates or friends outside of class. Find out what specific interests they have.
- Practice one of the techniques for developing a topic listed in Section 1e to discover narrower aspects of your broad subject.

See Exercise 1-1.

1c Defining your purpose

While you're trying to decide what subject interests you enough for writing an essay, probably at the back of your mind is also some kind of purpose for writing.

Purpose is the chief reason for communicating something to a particular audience. You might have one or a combination of four main purposes: (1) to entertain readers, (2) to express your feelings or beliefs, (3) to explain something, or (4) to persuade readers to agree with your opinions. You might want your readers to laugh, to get angry, to know something, or to change something.

 The purposes for writing

1. To entertain readers
2. To express yourself
3. To explain something to readers (exposition)
4. To persuade readers to accept or act on your opinion (argument)

1d Considering your audience

It's impossible to talk about purpose in writing without also discussing audience. That's because, as noted in 1a, both purpose and audience are part of the rhetorical situation. If you have a purpose for writing, you also have an audience. If your purpose is to persuade, there is someone you want to persuade. If you want to entertain, you probably have someone in mind that you want to entertain. Sometimes when you write you have in mind a real reader—someone you know. At other times you create your readers; you don't know exactly who will be reading what you write, and so you imagine the type of reader who would be interested in this kind of writing. Again, purpose is integrally involved.

Even if you don't give much thought to your audience when you start writing, you certainly must do so as you revise. You need to consider whether the details are adequate and appropriate for the audience, whether the vocabulary and sentence style are right, and whether your controlling idea (**thesis**) is clear.

To communicate effectively with your readers—your **audience**—you must consider their interests, purposes for reading, and information needs as you select a topic, develop an attitude toward it, and decide what specific details to use to express your view.

1 Knowing what readers need

In thinking about what your readers might need as they read your writing, consider these needs of a reader:

- The *subject* is connected with the reader's own experiences.
- The *content* has a natural and predictable flow.
- The *information* provided is clear, concrete, interesting, and convincing.
- The *opinions* expressed reflect the reader's values and beliefs, background, and intelligence.

21

- The writing reflects the true *voice* of the author.
- The writing has no distracting *inaccuracies* or *ambiguities*.

2 Writing for a specific audience

When selecting what details to include, a writer must consider reader interests. A student writing about the school library may be addressing an audience of other students, perhaps freshmen who are not yet entirely familiar with the campus. But the writer might also be an architecture student addressing other architecture students, a librarian addressing other librarians, or a student senator writing to the Board of Regents. Freshmen want to know where the library building is and how they can use its materials, but architecture students are interested in traffic patterns and sources of light. The specific information in an essay would differ in each case. Much of the writing done for college courses is directed at a **general audience,** college-level people who bring their own interests and purposes to their reading.

 ## Questions about audience

- Who are my readers?
- Why are readers going to read my writing? What will they expect?
- What do I want readers to know or do after reading my work, and how should I make that clear to them?
- What characteristic(s) of readers are relevant for my topic and purpose? For instance:

  age or sex

  occupation: students, part-time workers, professional colleagues, and so on.

  social or economic role: adult children, car buyers, potential employers, and so on.

  economic or educational background

  ethnic background

  political, religious, or moral beliefs and values

  hobbies or activities
- How will readers' characteristic(s) influence their attitudes toward my topic?
- What do readers already know and *not* know about my topic? How much do I have to tell them?
- If my topic involves specialized language, how much should I use and define?
- What ideas, arguments, or information might surprise readers? excite them? offend them? How should I handle these points?
- What misconceptions might readers have of my topic or my approach to the topic? How can I dispel these misconceptions?

- What is my relationship to my readers? What role and tone should I assume?
- What will readers do with my writing? Should I expect them to read every word from the top, to scan for information, to look for conclusions? Can I help with a summary, headings, or other aids?

 Deciding on an appropriate role and tone

Your role in a given writing situation depends on your purpose, your subject matter, and your audience. As you write, your role will be evident not only in *what* you say but in *how* you say it—your tone. The **tone** of your writing comes from the use you make of ideas, words, and sentence structures, and it will influence how your readers react to what you say. If you want to be seen as serious and thoughtful, you will use formal words and sentence structure and will develop sensible, well-supported assertions. If you want to adopt a light attitude toward your subject, you may want to use an informal sentence structure, a conversational vocabulary, and a humorous approach. Or you may want to sound angry, sad, cynical, sarcastic, irritable, happy, excited, and so on. Writing tone corresponds to tone of voice. The tone most common in academic and professional writing is one that is serious and objective.

See Exercise 1-2.

1e Developing your topic

When you have a specific topic that interests you and a purpose for writing about that topic, begin thinking of the particular information that will convey your interest convincingly to your readers. Write down the ideas that occur to you. Some writers explore ideas while listening to music, while bouncing a ball off the wall, or by "talking out" the topic in their minds with an imaginary audience. Some writers find that ideas come more easily if they explore the topic while taking a walk, running, riding the bus, or driving on the open road. Following are some other strategies that might work if your ideas are slow in coming.

 Techniques for developing a topic

- Keep a journal (1e-1).
- Observe your surroundings (1e-2).
- Freewrite with a focus (1e-3).
- Make a list, or brainstorm (1e-4).

23

- Cluster (1e-5).
- Ask the journalist's questions (1e-6).
- Use the patterns of development (1e-7).
- Read with a focus (1e-8).
- Think critically (1e-9).

Keeping a journal

Most of us writers have more good ideas than we use. But, all too often, when we're ready to write we don't remember them. We forget our interesting experiences or how we felt about them. Specific details—sight, sound, smell, touch, taste—are gone. The way some writers save these thoughts and experiences is to write them down while they're fresh. These writers keep **journals.** A journal is an account of thoughts and experiences, recorded daily or when the writer has something to write about.

Try keeping a journal for a set period of time—say a month—and see what effect it has on your writing. Write every day at a specific time. Use pen and a notebook or write at the keyboard. Write about thoughts or questions you've had, something you've read or seen, experiences you'd like to remember. Rewrite your class notes or summarize a textbook assignment. Write whatever you want, but write. At the end of the month, assess your writing. You may find that you're more confident about writing, that ideas flow from your mind once you start putting them into words. You may have a store of ideas that can form the basis of essays. You may find many things. But you won't know unless you try.

Observing your surroundings

Can you describe what a penny looks like—without getting one out and observing it? How much can you say about it? "It's round." "It's copper colored." "It has a picture of Lincoln on one side." Is that about it? What's written in front of Lincoln's face? behind his head? over his head? And then there's the other side of the coin. What does it look like? Why can't you say more? Have you thought about how many everyday things surround us that we don't really look at?

Try writing about something in detail—a penny, for instance, or your mother's dresser. Or look at the people around you—what are they doing? how are they dressed? how do they walk? how do they laugh? Start writing about things you see every day but don't see. We overlook a wealth of information.

Freewriting

Sometimes just pushing the pencil across the page generates ideas. Perhaps you have decided to write about the social interactions at interstate highway rest areas. The idea interests you, but you can't really think of enough to write about. Freewriting sometimes helps writers explore a subject. Begin by writing on a particular topic. Write fast, without pausing to make corrections or revisions; without worrying about spelling, punctuation, or grammar; and without planning yet for a thesis or an orderly arrangement of ideas. Don't stop until you run out of something to say. Even at that point, you might be able to keep going by asking some of the questions suggested throughout this section. When you have finished writing, you won't have an essay, but you will have some ideas that you can turn into an essay.

 Making a list

Another way to explore ideas is to jot them down in list form. Most subjects will require only one list. "Christmas dinners," for example, would lead you to compose a long list of details about the traditional meal as you know it. If you were making a comparison, on the other hand, you would need two lists. In comparing tradition and habit, you would make two columns, one for tradition and the other for habit. Then you would brainstorm, jotting down everything that occurs to you. Here's an example:

TRADITION	HABIT
Family gatherings at Christmas	Brushing teeth before retiring
White wedding dress	Reading bedtime story to a child
Funerals	Dinner at 6:00 PM
Fourth of July parades	Bacon and eggs for Saturday breakfast
Has significance	Grocery shopping on Monday evenings
Connected with special times	Mindless repetition
Usually involves family	May involve self alone or other
Often highly charged with emotion	

This is just the start of a list, which took about ten minutes to write. Given more time and thought, it could yield the subject matter for an essay. The writer might become interested in the contrast between "often highly charged with emotion" in the tradition list and "mindless repetition" in the habit list. Deciding to explore this contrast further, the writer might begin new lists on those subjects and eventually come up with the development for an essay showing how traditions and habits differ in the way people get involved in them.

 Clustering

Another technique for developing a topic, called **clustering** or **mapping,** is something like freewriting and list making in that it draws on free association and rapid writing down of ideas. To use clustering for the topic "social interactions at interstate highway rest areas," you would write the topic in the center of a page and either underline or circle it. Then you would proceed to jot down everything that occurs to you on that topic, such as the variety of things you see people doing—getting soft drinks, checking maps, stretching, waiting in restroom lines, and so on—until you run out of ideas. Draw connecting lines as you go. If you're working at a computer that does not have the capability for drawing lines easily, key in all your ideas at random, print the page, and then draw lines as you contemplate relationships.

When your ideas begin to dry up, pick one of the ideas you've jotted down and pursue that idea until it stops, then pursue something else, and so on. Pretty soon you have a lot of connected thoughts, some of them usable, but many for throwing away. Those that have potential can be restructured and developed further, possibly becoming ideas for an essay.

6 Using the journalist's questions

Asking a series of journalist's questions—starting with *who, what, when, where, why,* and *how*—may lead you to useful information for developing ideas.

Who is involved? Who cares? Who said it? Who knows?

What happened? What are the results? What was said? What is important?

When did it happen? When will it happen?

Where did it happen? Where are the effects felt?

Why did it happen? Why does it matter? Why do I care?

How did it happen? How did I react? How did others react?

Keep asking questions until you get enough answers. Just start with the interrogatory word—*who, what,* and so on—and change the subjects and verbs:

How does it happen?

How does it work?

How do I feel about it?

How do others feel about it?

How does it look?

7 Using the patterns of development

Other questions take advantage of how our minds work. When we file information in our heads, we generally relate it to something that is already there. We categorize information, thinking in terms of how it's like or different from something we already know, how things are caused and by what, what the effects of particular events are, and so on. By trying to find out how things relate to one another, we not only are able to explore what we know but may also have a way of developing our ideas. These patterns of development are familiarly known as **illustration** or **support, definition, division** and **classifi-**

cation, comparison and contrast, analogy, cause-and-effect analysis, and **process analysis.**

Who or what is it? (*Definition.*)

What are some examples of it? (*Illustration.*)

What other things are like it? (*Comparison, analogy.*)

How is it like other things? (*Comparison, analogy.*)

How does it differ from similar things? (*Contrast.*)

What are its component parts? (*Division.*)

How do those parts function? (*Process.*)

What categories can it be sorted into? (*Classification.*)

Is it changing? (*Process, cause and effect.*)

If so, how? (*Process, cause and effect.*)

How much can it change and still be itself? (*Contrast, process.*)

What does it mean? (*Definition.*)

What is its history? (*Process, cause and effect.*)

What are its causes? (*Cause and effect.*)

What effects does it have on other things? (*Cause and effect.*)

Asking these and other questions will help you generate ideas for writing. Even after you've started writing, you can go back to asking questions any time you get stumped.

 Reading

With most writing assignments, it is not necessary for you to rely solely on your own knowledge. You can find out what others think about the subject by **reading** newspapers, magazine articles, books, and so forth. In fact, something you have read may be what started your ideas on the subject; in that case, try to go back to the same piece of writing and read it more carefully. Whenever you read for increased knowledge of a subject, take notes, jotting down main ideas and facts that you might forget. Note also the author's name and the title and location of a piece of writing you're using so that you can give proper credit in your essay.

Reading is not a passive act. When we read, we don't pour ideas into our heads like water into an empty bottle. Instead, we bring our own experiences and thoughts to meet and mix with the writer's thoughts, and the consequence is that we come up with something new—something that we can write about. Pick up a newspaper or magazine and read something—perhaps a commentary or an editorial. Notice what happens: not only do you gain a certain knowledge, but you also get some ideas about that information that were not contained in the article. Neither was what you gained from reading the article

27

the same as what a friend might gain from reading it. You may now have something to write about. (For more on reading, see Chapter 4.)

Note: Do remember when you write about someone else's idea to give appropriate credit to that person, at the very least naming the writer and the title and location of the piece of writing, quoting all the phrases you borrow. (See Chapter 35.)

9 Thinking critically

The various strategies for developing your topic will be most effective if, at the same time, you think critically, as explained in the Introduction to this book. While observing your surroundings, writing in a journal, reading, and so on, you can also analyze, interpret, synthesize, and evaluate.

- **Analysis:** What are the subject's elements or characteristics?
- **Interpretation:** What is the meaning or significance of the elements?
- **Synthesis:** How do the elements relate to each other, or how does this subject relate to another one?
- **Evaluation:** What is the value or significance of the subject?

See Exercises 1-3, 1-4.

See Related Exercises I-3, I-4.

1f Developing your thesis

The **thesis** is the main idea, the controlling idea, the point, the significance of an essay. A **thesis sentence** is a statement of that idea. Not all essays have an explicit statement of the thesis, but in academic expository writing—essays written to inform or explain for an instructor or for other students—readers generally expect to find a clear expression of the main idea. In academic writing, the thesis generally appears near the beginning of the essay, frequently at the end of the introduction, and may be restated in the conclusion. It is the most important sentence in an essay because it tells the reader what your subject is and how you view that subject. It focuses the essay and thus serves as a unifying device for everything that follows. All your paragraphs will be related in some way to the thesis.

1 Conceiving your thesis sentence

To arrive at your statement of the thesis, you must first know what your subject is, what point you want to make about it, and how you can support that point. Sometimes, through using techniques for developing a topic (see

1e), you may know your thesis before you begin writing a first draft. At other times, you may not fully understand your thesis until you have completed a draft, let it set for a while, and then gone back to read it objectively. But thoughts about your thesis can be in your mind throughout your writing, once you have a specific topic to write about.

A thesis sentence does not begin "The purpose of this essay is" or "This essay is about"; such sentences state only the subject. A thesis sentence also makes an *assertion:*

> The design of our library invites students to come in and study. [*Not* "In this paper I will describe the design of our library."]

> Successfully repotting a plant is a simple procedure with the appropriate materials and equipment. [*Not* "This essay is about how to repot a plant."]

> Social interactions at interstate highway rest areas seem limited to people who know one another. [*Not* "I have observed social interactions at interstate highway rest areas."]

Each of these sentences includes not only the subject but also an assertion about the subject. As illustrated below, the subject of the essay usually comes first in the thesis sentence, and the assertion—the point of the essay—follows it.

SUBJECT	ASSERTION
Social interactions at highway rest areas	seem limited to people who know one another

Notice also that these thesis sentences are *restricted* in subject matter: *not* "our library" but "the design of our library"; *not* "caring for plants" but "repotting a plant"; *not* "social interactions" but "social interactions at interstate highway rest areas." A thesis sentence that is too general leads to an impossibly broad essay that is very difficult for anyone to write well.

 Functions of the thesis sentence

- It narrows the topic to a single central idea that you want readers to gain from your essay.
- It names the topic and asserts something specific and significant about it.
- It often provides a concise preview of how you will arrange your ideas in the essay.

The following thesis sentence fulfills all three functions:

SUBJECT	ASSERTION	ARRANGEMENT
Concerned citizens	oppose drug trafficking	on three grounds: social, political, and religious.

When the arrangement of ideas is previewed in the thesis sentence, both writer and reader have an understanding that the essay will deal with the first subtopic: "concerned citizens oppose drug trafficking on social grounds," and then will take up the second and third subtopics—political and religious grounds.

 ### 2 Drafting and revising your thesis sentence

Developing an effective thesis sentence that conveys your purpose completely and concisely may require several attempts. It is a necessary step in writing an essay because until you know—and can express in writing—specifically what you want to say, your essay is likely to wander. If you do see that your writing is wandering, consider the writing you've done so far as preliminary—*prewriting*—something you've done to help you discover what you can say. Then ask yourself, with all your written ideas in front of you, what your perspective on your subject is:

What does this subject have to do with me?

Who am I in relation to the subject?

What purpose might I serve by writing about this subject?

Why do I want to write about it?

What is interesting about it?

Who might be interested in reading about it?

Whom do I want to read about it?

Mull the subject over in your mind until you have a *perspective,* an angle, an insight into your subject that is different from what anybody else has said about it—something that might surprise your reader a little. That's your thesis, and now you're ready to put it in a sentence. Make your thesis sentence *specific, limited,* and *unified.*

 ### Checklist for revising the thesis sentence

- Does the sentence make an *assertion* about your topic?
- Is the assertion *limited* to only one idea?
- Is the assertion *specific* and *significant?*
- Does the sentence convey your *purpose?*
- Is the sentence *unified* so that the parts relate to each other?

The following thesis sentence provides no insight into the subject and because of its generality would lead to a general, unfocused essay.

Volkswagen "beetles" had differences.

This thesis makes an assertion, but the statement is not specific, limited, and unified. If you tried to write an essay with such a general thesis, you would not have any idea where to start and you would not know when you were finished. To write an effective thesis sentence you first would have to ask yourself such questions as the following:

> What does the word *differences* mean?
>
> Are the Volkswagens being compared to one another or to some other make of car?
>
> If compared to one another, what is the basis for comparison?
>
> What is the significance of the differences?

The following sentence answers these questions, making clear to a reader not only the subject of the essay—Volkswagen automobiles—but also the assertion that they only *seem* to be the same, year in and year out. This thesis implies a comparison of several factors.

> Although Volkswagen beetles seemed exactly alike from year to year, a close examination of the differences in two models, for the years 1951 and 1957, shows that the models differed in several ways.

See Exercises 1-5, 1-6.

1g Organizing your ideas

Once you know what you're writing about, who you think might read what you write, what point you want to make, and how you intend to support that point, you may also have some idea of how you're going to organize your ideas. One characteristic of essays is **organization,** a logical, coherent arrangement through which readers can follow the progression of the writer's thoughts.

With some essay topics, especially those of an exploratory or expressive nature, the form of the essay emerges with the writing. Through numerous drafts and revisions, the essay begins to take shape. With most college writing, however, students who understand the basic patterns for shaping ideas can adopt the ones most appropriate for their subjects and purposes.

Sometimes writers find that it is enough to have just a thesis sentence as a guide for writing, especially when the essay is short. This sentence, for example, might for some writers be an adequate plan:

> Concerned citizens oppose drug trafficking on three grounds: social, political, and religious.

To help organize their essays some writers need a few notes in addition to the thesis sentence, a few ideas jotted down and numbered in order of intended use. Still other writers are more comfortable with a formal outline.

Distinguishing the general and the specific

Once you have some ideas, you can try grouping them in different ways to see how they relate to and complement one another. Some of your ideas are more general and some more specific. *Dog,* for example, is more general than *border collie,* because it includes more items in the class. There is room in an essay for both the general and the specific. Specifics usually support generalities. To group your ideas according to general and specific, first pick out your more general ideas and then select specifics that support them.

 Choosing an organizing tool

The organizing plan you select will depend on your topic and on what you want to say about it. The amount of detail will depend on the complexity of your topic and your requirements as a writer. Remember that the only reason for having an outline as a plan is to aid *you,* the writer. Usually your readers won't see your outline, but they *will* benefit from the orderly presentation of your ideas. Two useful work plans are informal and formal outlines. They can be used to organize ideas that started out as freewriting, a brainstorming list, or even scattered thoughts in your head.

An **informal outline** arranges the general and specific points of the essay in the order in which they will appear. It may be little more than your preliminary list of ideas with numbers added to indicate order. If you want to get a little more elaborate, you can rewrite the list in the order you prefer, indicating by indentions the ideas that are subordinate to others. Less important ideas will be subordinate to main ideas, specific facts subordinate to general statements. This extra work will make a neater pattern for you to follow so that, when you're writing, each major point with its subpoints will become a paragraph.

A **formal outline** takes the informal outline one step further. Its more rigid form can help you place elements in careful relation to one another, with levels of subordination (perhaps three or more) clearly indicated. It can also help you fill in gaps, eliminate redundancies, and make wording more precise. For student writers, a formal outline is particularly useful for research papers and other long papers.

The formal outline follows a typical pattern: main points, often corresponding to the topic of an entire paragraph, are preceded by capital Roman numerals (I, II, and so on); chief subpoints, the support for the main points, are preceded by capital letters (A, B, and so on); and specific supporting details, examples, and reasons are preceded by Arabic numerals (1, 2, and so on). (A fourth level of subordination may be indicated by small letters—a, b, and so on.)

You may write the outline in complete sentences or in phrases, but whichever manner of expression you choose, use it consistently throughout the outline. Ideas at the same numbered or lettered level should be parallel in both content and form of expression, and those at sublevels should be logically subordinate to those at the superior level. Be sure that all headings are matched by at least one other heading at the same level, because subheadings in an outline imply that the preceding topic has been divided. An **A** without a **B**, in other words, illogically implies that the preceding level is divided into only one part.

The following detailed topic outline, for a paper on opposition to drug trafficking, illustrates a formal outline.

THESIS SENTENCE

Concerned citizens oppose drug trafficking on three grounds: social, political, and religious.

FORMAL OUTLINE

  I. Introduction
      A. Statistics on drug trafficking
      B. Need for action
      C. Reasons concerned citizens oppose drug trafficking (thesis)
 II. Social grounds for opposition
      A. Associated criminal behavior
          1. Theft
          2. Violence
      B. Medical effects—AIDS
III. Political grounds for opposition—needed legislation
      A. Interdiction of drugs from other countries
      B. Tough laws for drug pushers
      C. Education about dangers of drugs
      D. Rehabilitation
 IV. Religious grounds for opposition
      A. Respect for self and one another
      B. Opposition to self-destruction
  V. Conclusion
      A. Summary
      B. Restatement of thesis

A common use for the formal outline is to check the unity and coherence of an essay. Once you have completed a rough draft, make an outline of its major parts and supporting points. If you find irrelevant ideas or lack of supporting evidence, you can make adjustments in your revision (see 1g-4).

Principles of the formal outline

- Labels and indentions indicate order and relative importance.
- Sections and subsections reflect logical relationships.
- Topics of equal generality appear in parallel headings.

- Each subdivision has at least two parts.
- Headings are expressed in parallel grammatical form.
- The introduction and conclusion may be omitted (though not, of course, from the essay).

---

3 Choosing a structure

There are several common ways to organize an essay that correspond to readers' habitual ways of thinking. One pattern is **spatial,** examining a topic (such as a place or a person) by moving in space from one location to another, as when we survey a scene from the farthest point to the nearest or vice versa. Essays and paragraphs arranged in such a way are largely descriptive. If you were describing your school newspaper spatially, you might start with the first page and move through the paper by sections; if you were describing a painting, you would start with the area of the painting that strikes you first and then move around within the painting, assisting your reader to see it the way you do.

Another common organizing scheme is **chronological,** reporting events as they occur over time, earliest first. Such essays are narrative (telling the history of an event) or process analysis (telling how something is done or how it happens). If you were recounting your drive home over snow-slick highways, you would start with the beginning of your trip, when the roads and weather were deceptively clear, and proceed through worsening conditions, ending with your arrival home and the final frustrating need to shovel out your driveway to get the car in. Or, if you were telling your audience how to make a pot of chili, you'd start again with first things first—getting out the ingredients, browning the meat—and proceed to the end, when the chili was completed and ready to be served.

A third organizing scheme, **emphasis** has several subpatterns. In **general to specific,** the main ideas come before the details that support them, as in an essay that makes initial strong claims about, say, gun control and then presents the evidence for the claims. In the **specific-to-general** pattern the details come first and build to the more general ideas, as in an essay that describes the styles of specific big bands before generalizing about the sound they have in common. A similar pattern is **climactic,** which is the arrangement of material in order of increasing importance. You may also arrange items by the principles of **problem to solution, most familiar to least familiar,** or **simple to complex.**

The patterns of development discussed in 1e-7 suggest additional patterns. Also see 3c for paragraph-length examples of patterns.

Schemes for organizing ideas in an essay

- Space
- Time
- Emphasis
  General to specific   Climactic (increasing importance)
  Specific to general   Decreasing familiarity
  Problem to solution   Increasing complexity

 Checking for unity and coherence

When your informal or formal outline is completed, examine it for unity and coherence. These are two essential qualities of effective writing that will be dealt with in more detail in Chapter 3, but you can anticipate problems by checking your outline for unity and coherence. **Unity** means that the parts of the essay are related to the thesis and to one another. Each paragraph, with its general statements and specific supporting evidence, supports the thesis. Disunity occurs when irrelevant ideas creep in or when the writer moves away from the thesis sentence in mid-essay.

Coherence means that the relations between ideas are clear and that each point leads easily to the one following it. The essay "hangs together," with each part clearly linked to all other parts. The writer leaves clues along the way so that the reader has no trouble following the progression of ideas.

In the preceding formal outline, notice how all the parts under II support the idea of social grounds for opposition to drug trafficking and how all the parts under III and IV relate to the second and third points. Paragraphs developed from these parts would be unified, each paragraph dealing with one idea. They would relate to one another and to the thesis. In the outline, they are coherent because they repeat key ideas expressed in the thesis.

See Exercises 1-7, 1-8, 1-9.

EXERCISE 1-1

Discovering a Subject (1b)

Use these questions for discovering a subject for an essay when you are not assigned one. Answer the questions as completely as you can, using separate paper, or discuss them with groupmates in class.

I. Entertainment

    A. What books, stories, or magazine articles have I read recently?

    B. What programs have I seen recently on television that interested me?

    C. What movies have I seen recently and liked?

    D. What have I encountered on the World Wide Web that informed or surprised me?

II. Choose one of your answers in Part I.

    A. What made that story, program, movie, or Web document good?

    B. Why do I remember it so well?

    C. What did I like best about it? Why?

    D. Which part seemed most realistic to me? Why?

III. Issues

    A. What local or national issues interest me?

    B. Why am I interested in any one of those issues?

    C. What features of that issue are most controversial?

    D. What is the most challenging idea I've heard in the past two weeks?

    E. Why does that idea seem challenging to me?

    F. What interesting discussions have I had lately?

IV. Goals

    A. What is the most important goal in my life?

    B. What am I willing to do to achieve that goal?

    C. How did I decide that it is a worthy goal for me?

V. Persons

    A. What person do I most admire?

    B. What do I admire about that person?

EXERCISE 1-2

Analyzing Tone (1d-3)

Read the following passages and, with a classmate, discuss (1) their tone and the features of the writing that contribute toward the tone, and (2) what assumptions the writer has made about the audience (see Questions about audience on page 22).

1   I bristled every time someone called me Rusty or Red or Ronald McDonald, but I played the part well. I clowned for my elementary-school peers, then cursed my hair color at home. My parents told me I was lucky to have red hair. They said it was special. I didn't see anything lucky or special about it. I hated it. The only thing that infuriated me more than the taunting I received was the pandering. Elderly relatives and passersby patted the top of my amber head and called me cute. They said I looked just like little Jody on TV's "Family Affair," then they would chuckle to themselves. I didn't want to be cute and funny like Jody. I wanted to be dashing and rugged like Johnny Quest. (John S. Pitt, "Don't Call Me Red," *Newsweek* 14 Oct. 1996: 16)

2   She wanted a house with air conditioning. I wanted a house with more than one bathroom. The house we bought has an air conditioner big enough to cool Saudi Arabia. And one bathroom. She wanted a house with hardwood floors. I wanted one with a Jacuzzi big enough for two persons. The house we bought has floors hard enough to shatter a wood-pecker's beak. And a bathtub big enough to hold two minor body parts. She wanted an older house with "character." I wanted a house in which the builders still were pounding the nails three weeks after we moved in. The house we bought has bullet holes in it from the Civil War (*St. Cloud Times* 13 Oct. 1990: 5).

3   Boomers as customers are accustomed to eclecticism, which is the em-bodiment of choice. In spontaneous imitation of that other late-century cathedral, the mall, the megachurch offers a panoply of choices under one roof—from worship styles to boutique ministries, plus plenty of parking, clean bathrooms, and the likelihood that you'll find something you want and come back again. This is what the customer considers value. I saw written up in the local paper a smallish Episcopal church in Orange County that every Sunday morning offers a traditional service, a contemporary ser-vice, and a charismatic service. Another minister I met, Stanley Copeland,

of Pollard United Methodist Church, in Tyler, Texas, referred to his own worship menu as "chocolate, vanilla, and strawberry." He told me, "We do not want to be a church just for people who are already Christian. We are not a church of the Way. We are a church of options." (Charles Trueheart, "Welcome to the Next Church," *The Atlantic Monthly* Aug. 1996: 47.)

EXERCISE 1-3

Developing a Subject Through Freewriting (1e-3)

Choose *one* of the broad subjects in Exercise 1-1, for example "a person I admire" or "my goals in life," and, on separate paper, write about it for fifteen minutes without stopping, without correcting spelling or other errors, and without concern for organization or thesis. Just write. If you're at the computer, try darkening the screen so you're not tempted to stop and make corrections. When you have finished, read what you have written to see whether a central idea is emerging.

EXERCISE 1-4

Generating Ideas (1e)

Choose a specific topic, perhaps one of those you identified in Exercise 1-1. On paper or your computer, develop ideas for a brief essay, using two of the methods discussed on pages 23–28, such as freewriting, list making, clustering, asking the journalist's questions, asking questions based on patterns of development, or reading with a focus. For example, if you'd like to write on a personal goal, you might start by freewriting and then ask questions based on patterns of development.

Name _____ Date _____

EXERCISE 1-5

Thesis Sentence: Revising (1f)

Individually or in a group, rewrite the following thesis sentences to make them specific, limited, and unified.

Example: Legislators do not communicate enough with their constituents.

State legislators should improve communication with voters by scheduling local meetings regularly and by mailing newsletters before and after assembly sessions.

1. Many people believe that baseball players have no right to strike.

2. Religious cults serve a valid purpose.

3. The government owes a college education to every citizen who wants one.

4. The hunting of wild animals, as long as they are not in danger of extinction, can actually help nature.

5. Travel to foreign countries is educational.

6. Silence is often the best response to anger.

EXERCISE 1-6

Thesis Sentence: Developing (1f)

Select one of the subjects you discovered in Exercise 1-1 or 1-3, perhaps the same one you worked with in Exercise 1-4, or use an assigned subject. After answering the following questions about that subject, write a thesis sentence at the bottom of the page.

1. How am I related to the subject (expert, angry citizen, informed student, mature youth, and so on)?

2. What interests me about the subject?

3. Why do I want to write about the subject?

4. How do I want my audience to react to my essay?

5. Who might want to read about my subject?

6. Why do I want to read about it? (Is the answer different from your answer to 5?)

7. What do I want to say? (*Not* "What do I want to write about?"—your subject—but "What do I want to *say* about it?"—your assertion.)

Thesis sentence

Name _____ Date _____

EXERCISE 1-7

The Formal Outline (1g)

With your groupmates, rewrite the following informal outline (which has no indications of subordinate ideas) into a formal outline, using as many subdivisions as necessary to put parallel ideas into parallel format. Refer to the outline on page 33 as a guide, remembering that you will have different divisions and subdivisions.

THESIS SENTENCE

Because flying terrifies me, I have developed several techniques to help me cope with that fear both before and during a flight.

Informal outline

1. Introduction
2. Narrative of last plane trip
3. Recounting fear of flying
4. Statement of thesis
5. Relaxation methods before a flight
6. Trying to sleep the night before
7. Reading an architecture book before sleeping
8. Contemplating pictures before sleeping
9. Riding to the airport
10. Talking to the cab driver
11. Looking out the cab window
12. Reading in the airport lounge
13. Relaxation methods during a flight
14. Taking a seat
15. Choosing a seat location
16. Choosing a travel companion
17. Eating
18. Reading
19. Listening to music
20. Staying in my seat
21. Refraining from looking out the window
22. Conclusion
23. Restatement of thesis

EXERCISE 1-8

Outlining an Essay (1g)

One use for outlines is to check the organization of a piece you've already written. Read the following essay and, on separate paper, write an outline of it, following the guidelines for formal outlines on page 33. Start by stating the thesis.

UNDERSTANDING ENDOMETRIOSIS

Patricia Mahon (Student Writer)

1   Endometriosis—the presence of endometrial tissue outside its normal location lining the uterus—remains a word unfamiliar to many, but its symptoms and complications have baffled doctors for more than a century. Although endometriosis has been wrongly nicknamed "the career women's disease" because it often affects women in their twenties and thirties who postponed having children, experts now know that this disease strikes women of every lifestyle and occupation, from their teens until menopause.

2   The term was coined in 1922 from the word *endometrium*, the tissue lining the uterus which builds up and then sheds each month during a woman's menstrual cycle. *Endo* is a Greek word meaning "within," and *metri* refers to the Greek *metra*, or uterus. *Osis* is a suffix that means an abnormal or diseased condition. Together you have "an abnormal condition within the uterus." Like the lining of the uterus, endometrial growths usually respond to the woman's hormones: they build up tissue, break down, and cause bleeding. However, unlike the lining of the uterus, endometrial tissue outside the uterus has no way of leaving the body. The result is internal bleeding, inflammation of the surrounding areas, and formation of scar tissue.

3   Endometriosis is commonly found in the abdomen—on the ovaries, fallopian tubes, ligaments supporting the uterus, outer surface of the uterus, and lining of the pelvic cavity. Occasionally, the growths are found in abdominal surgery scars, but there have been rare instances of growths outside the abdomen—in the lung, arm, and thigh.

4   The most common symptoms of endometriosis are pain, infertility, and heavy or irregular bleeding. Other symptoms may include fatigue and intestinal upset. Yet, curiously, some of the women with endometriosis have no symptoms at all. Medical research shows that the amount of pain is not always related to the extent of visible growths. Some women with extensive visible endometrial growths have no pain; others with a few small growths have incapacitating pain. This is one of the many puzzles of

endometriosis and an indication of the lack of understanding of the actual disease process. Not all women with endometriosis are infertile, though infertility is a common result with the progression of the condition.

5   Treatment for endometriosis has varied over the years, but no cure other than a hysterectomy and removal of the ovaries has yet been found, and even that treatment may be in question. Recent research has shown that even after such drastic measures, women may see a continuation or recurrence of the disease.

6   Although painkillers are usually prescribed for the pain of endometriosis, hormonal treatments attempt to stop ovulation and put the disease into remission. Because pregnancy often causes a temporary remission of symptoms and because it is believed that infertility is more likely the longer the disease is present, women with endometriosis are often advised not to postpone pregnancy. Conservative surgery, involving removal and cauterization of the growths, is also done and can relieve symptoms and allow pregnancy to occur in some cases.

7   Early information and knowledge will help women to recognize endometriosis. For the first time, the facts about the disease have become available. Endometriosis is now open for discussion, questioning, and exploration, not only by the medical profession, but by all women. [Thanks to the Endometriosis Association, Milwaukee, WI, for reviewing the essay.—P.M.]

EXERCISE 1-9

Writing an Outline for an Essay (1g)

Prepare an outline for an essay, using the ideas you generated in Exercise 1-4. First, repeat the thesis sentence composed in Exercise 1-6. Then outline the ideas, using the form (informal or formal) specified by your instructor. Be sure the outline is unified (all its parts relate to one another and to the thesis) and coherent (the relations among ideas are logical and clear). Your instructor may ask you and a classmate to exchange outlines and check unity and coherence.

Chapter 2

Drafting and Revising the Essay

Careful planning (Chapter 1) often makes drafting and revising an essay easier. But, as this chapter shows, writing is usually not just a linear progression of prewriting, drafting, and revising. Instead, it is more often a circular and repetitive process. Drafting is often preceded by some kind of prewriting—whether formally on paper, informally in discussion with others, or even more informally and unsystematically in our thoughts. But rarely do writers work out their ideas in any complete form before they draft. In drafting, they continue to form and develop their ideas. They also revise. Experienced writers usually do a great deal of revising while developing their drafts. Even so, they go back over their completed drafts as thoroughly and frequently as necessary to make them say what they want them to say, clearly and completely.

2a Writing the first draft

When you begin your first draft, you may have already settled on a purpose and decided on at least part of what you will need to say to achieve that purpose. But the writing of your essay still requires much thought, for it is often only in the writing that you can discover what you really want to say. If you see that the original plan is not conforming to what you now want to say, change the outline and adjust your thesis sentence as well. In most cases it's not necessary to start over from scratch, as if no planning had occurred. If you

47

do not have an outline and a thesis beforehand, you need to give special attention to form and focus when you revise your draft.

In writing your first draft, you are primarily concerned with your ideas, to get them down on paper while you're thinking about them. If you have trouble getting started, try one or more of these techniques.

 Ways to start drafting

- Read over what you've already written—notes, outlines, and so on—and immediately start your draft with whatever comes to mind.
- Freewrite. (See 1e-3.)
- Write scribbles or type nonsense until usable words start coming.
- Pretend you're writing to a friend about your topic.
- Conjure up an image that represents your topic—a physical object, a facial expression, two people arguing over something, a giant machine gouging the earth for a mine, whatever. Describe that image.
- Skip the opening and start in the middle. Or write the conclusion.
- Write a paragraph on what you think your essay will be about when you finish it.
- Using your outline, divide your essay into chunks—say, one for the introduction, another for the first point and so on. Start writing the chunk that seems most eager to be written, the one you understand best or feel most strongly about.

Once you get started, write quickly, not stopping to check punctuation or spelling. You might mark words that you want to look up later or leave blank spaces where you can't think of the right word. You may have long paragraphs that need to be divided or unwieldy sentences that require some tinkering later. You may even find strange things happening to your ideas—they change as you write them down, becoming clearer and better focused. Here are some techniques to *keep* you drafting.

 Ways to *keep* drafting

- Set aside enough time for yourself. (For a brief essay, a first draft is likely to take at least an hour or two.)
- Work in a place where you won't be interrupted.
- Make yourself comfortable.
- If you must stop working, jot a note before leaving the draft about what you expect to do next. Then you can pick up where you left off.
- Be as fluid as possible and don't worry about mistakes. Spontaneity will allow your attitudes toward your subject to surface naturally in your sentences. It will also make you receptive to ideas and relations you haven't seen before.

- Keep going. Skip over sticky spots; leave a blank if you can't find the right word. If an idea pops out of nowhere but doesn't seem to fit in, quickly jot it down on a separate sheet, or write it into the draft and bracket it for later attention.
- Resist self-criticism. Don't worry about your style, grammar, spelling, and the like. Don't worry what your readers will think. These are very important matters, but save them for revision.
- Use your thesis sentence and outline to remind you of your planned purpose, organization, and content.
- But don't feel constrained by these materials. If your writing leads you in a more interesting direction, follow.

While you're writing (and revising), remember who will be reading what you write and then use vocabulary appropriate to that audience (avoiding technical words, for example, with a general audience or slang for an instructor); include details that your audience requires in order to see your subject as you do. (See Chapters 3 and 4 for further discussions of ways to reach your audience.)

Also keep your purpose in mind as you write. By writing this essay, what do you hope to achieve? Do you want to persuade your audience? entertain? complain about something that's gone wrong? explain something? inform or report? summarize, criticize, or spiritually uplift? If you were writing about a trip home on snow-slick roads, what details and language would you use to achieve a purpose of entertaining as opposed to, say, a purpose of criticizing the lack of highway maintenance? Whether you're writing by hand or keyboard, leave space for revisions by double-spacing and allowing wide margins.

2b Revising the first draft

Once you put down the last period of your rough draft, you still have the tough job of shaping and disciplining this creation of yours. If you're word processing, print a copy of your completed draft so you can work with both paper and screen. Here are five ways to help you gain distance from your work, so you can take a fresh, new look at it.

Ways to gain distance from your work

- Take a break after finishing the draft to pursue some other activity. A few hours may be enough; a whole night or day is preferable. The break will clear your mind, relax you, and give you some objectivity.
- Ask someone to read and react to your draft. Many writing instructors ask their students to submit their first drafts so that the instructors and, often, the other members of the class can serve as an actual audience to help guide revision. (See also 2e on receiving and benefiting from criticism.)

- If you handwrite your draft, type a copy on a typewriter or computer before revising it. The act of transcription can reveal gaps in content or problems in structure.
- If you compose on a computer, print out your draft. By working with both paper and screen, you may be able to see weaknesses you would miss on the screen alone.
- Outline your draft by listing all the main points supporting your thesis. (If you're working on a computer, you can copy and paste these sentences.) Then examine this informal outline for logical order, gaps, and digressions. (See 1g-2 for a discussion of outlining.

Except for in-class writing assignments, in which you usually have no time for rewriting, you will probably write several drafts of some sentences, paragraphs, or even the entire essay. Beginning writers often think of revision as proofreading for errors in spelling, grammar, punctuation, and the like. But that is editing, not revision, and it can come fairly late in the writing process. Real revision happens while you are writing and still working with a rough draft. It involves rethinking the arrangement of ideas, their support, and their effectiveness in furthering your purpose. You may decide to add details, statements, or whole paragraphs to sharpen the focus on your purpose; you may decide to strike out details, statements, or entire paragraphs because they detract from your purpose; you may decide to move parts around to achieve greater emphasis or a sense of logical order.

The following checklist may be helpful in guiding your revision. If you need help in any of these areas, read the workbook or handbook section given in parentheses. Note that the checklist is useful also for responding to someone else's writing (see 2e).

 Checklist for revision

- **Purpose:** What is the essay's purpose? Does that purpose conform to the assignment? Is it consistent throughout the paper? (See 1c.)
- **Thesis:** What is the thesis of the essay? Where does it become clear? How well do thesis and paper match: does the paper stray from the thesis? Does it fulfill the commitment of the thesis? (See 1f.)
- **Structure:** What are the main points of the paper? (List them.) How well does each support the thesis? How effective is their arrangement for the paper's purpose? (See 3a–c.)
- **Development:** How well do details, examples, and other evidence support each main point? Where, if at all, might readers find support skimpy or have trouble understanding the content? (See 1e.)
- **Tone:** What is the tone of the paper? How do particular words and sentence structures create the tone? How appropriate is it for the purpose, topic, and intended readers? Where is it most or least successful? (See 1d 3.)

- **Unity:** What does each sentence and paragraph contribute to the thesis? Where, if at all, do digressions occur? Should these be cut, or can they be rewritten to support the thesis? (See 1g-4, 3a, and 3e.)
- **Coherence:** How clearly and smoothly does the paper flow? Where does it seem rough or awkward? Can any transitions be improved? (See 1g-4 and 3b.)
- **Title, introduction, conclusion:** How accurately and interestingly does the title reflect the essay's content? (See below.) How well does the introduction engage and focus the readers' attention? (See 3d-1.) How effective is the conclusion in providing a sense of completion? (See 3d-2.)

A note on titling your essay

An essay's title is usually descriptive, such as "Home Away from Home" and "A Comparison of Two Neighborhoods." But a good title also catches the reader's interest. For that reason you might want to avoid titles such as "Comparison Essay Assignment" and "Summary Paper." Try to balance the two aspects of titles: make them interesting, but also make them reflect the main idea of the essay.

If you don't have a title before you begin writing, don't waste time thinking of one then. By the time you have finished drafting and revising, you'll know better what you're saying and what the emphasis of your paper is. Something you've said may give you an idea for a snappy title. Titles are usually sentence fragments: "Blizzard!" "Six Easy Steps to a New You," "Waiting for Ursula."

Titles on essays and other academic papers are centered at the top of the first page, with the first letter of the first and all major words capitalized. (See 26b.) The title on your paper is not underlined or enclosed in quotation marks.

2c   Editing the revised draft

Once you've made a new working draft, use the revision checklist again to see if you want to make more changes. Try to read your fresh draft as some other reader would, remembering that the reader does not know what has been going on in your mind. If you leave out some important details or don't make your points absolutely clear, your reader will miss something. Here are some tips to help you find out what needs editing.

 ### Ways to find what needs editing

- Take a break, even fifteen or twenty minutes, to clear your head.
- If possible, work on a paper copy, even if you compose and revise on computer. Most people find it much harder to spot errors on a computer screen

than on paper. (Type your draft double-spaced so you have room for changes.)

- Read the draft *slowly,* and read what you *actually see.* Otherwise, you're likely to read what you intended to write but didn't.
- Have a friend or relative read your work. Or, if you share your work in class, listen to the responses of your classmates or instructor. (See 2e.)
- As when revising, read the draft aloud, preferably into a tape recorder, listening for awkward rhythms, repetitive sentence patterns, and missing or clumsy transitions.
- Learn from your own experience. Keep a record of the weaknesses that others have pointed out. (See p. 56 for a suggested format.) When editing, check your work against this record.

You may need to read through your paper many times. If you are inclined to misspell words, read once just for spelling. If you write fragments, read once for nothing but fragments. If verb forms are your problem, read for verbs. Here is another checklist for you to use at this point. (The questions are keyed to chapters of the workbook and handbook where you can look for help.) Note that the checklist may also serve as a guide for reviewing another person's writing (see 2e).

 Checklist for editing

- **Clarity:** How well do words and sentences convey their intended meaning? Which, if any, words and sentences are confusing? Check your paper especially for these:

  Exact words (31-b)

  Parallelism (17)

  Clear modifiers (14)

  Clear reference of pronouns (12)

  Complete sentences (10)

  Sentences separated correctly (11)

- **Effectiveness:** How well do words and sentences engage and direct readers' attention? Where, if at all, does the writing seem wordy, choppy, or dull? See Chapters 16–19 and 31. Check the paper especially for these:

  Smooth and informative transitions (3b-6)

  Variety in sentence length and structure (19)

  Appropriate, specific, concrete words (31a, b)

  Consistent, appropriate tone (1d-3)

- **Correctness:** How little or how much do surface errors interfere with clarity and effectiveness? See Chapters 6–9, 20–30, and 34. Check the paper especially for these:

Spelling. Use a spelling checker if you have one, but look for misspelled homonyms (34)

Pronoun forms (6)

Verb forms, especially *-s* and *-ed* endings and correct forms of irregular verbs (7)

Verb tenses, especially consistency (7)

Agreement between subjects and verbs, especially when words come between them or when the subject is *each, everyone,* or a similar word (8a)

Agreement between pronouns and antecedents, especially when the subject contains *or* or when it is *each, everyone,* or a similar word (8b)

Commas, especially with *and* or *but* (21)

2d **Proofreading and submitting the final draft**

After you have edited your essay and followed the guidelines suggested in 2c, copy or print a clean draft. Then *proofread* for copying errors you might have missed earlier. If you are working with a computer printout, remember that even though the draft looks perfect it may still need a close reading for errors. When you proofread, read the essay through once to make sure you haven't skipped lines, omitted words, or repeated words. When you have made revisions, check for related changes that may be necessary. Then read at least once again for other errors.

It may be helpful for you to remember that proofreading is a special kind of reading. Unlike most reading, in which you concentrate on meaning and take in two or three words at once, proofreading focuses on *errors*. In doing this kind of reading you must slow yourself down so that you look at *every word and punctuation mark*. Force yourself to look at the first and last words in every line, because frequently the reading eye skips over them. Here are some things to try while proofreading.

 Techniques for proofreading

- Read printed copy, even if you will eventually submit the paper electronically. Remember that even though the copy looks clean it may still have errors.
- Read the paper aloud and very slowly, distinctly pronouncing exactly what you see.
- Place a ruler under each line as you read it.
- Read "against copy," comparing your final draft one sentence at a time against the edited draft you copied it from.

- To keep the content of your writing from distracting you, read the essay backward, end to beginning, examining each sentence as a separate unit.
- If you've written on a computer, insert a return at each period so your sentences are lined up as separate units. After proofreading, go back and remove the returns except at paragraph breaks and reprint your essay.

2e Giving and receiving comments

To be an effective writer, you must learn to become a good critic of your own writing. You need to know what is good and what is bad about your compositions and how you can make them better. One way to become a good critic is to observe how other writers write—how they phrase their sentences, what words they choose, how they order their paragraphs, and so forth. In class, you may be asked to respond to your classmates' essays. When you read someone else's writing, keep these guidelines in mind.

 Commenting on others' writing

- Be sure you know what the writer is saying. If necessary, summarize the paper to understand its content. (See pp. 4–5.)
- Read closely and critically. (See pp. 2–3.)
- Unless you have other instructions, address only your most significant concerns with the work. If you point out every flaw you detect, the writer may have trouble sorting out the important from the unimportant. Use the revision checklist on pages 50–51 as a guide to what is significant in a piece of writing.
- Be specific. If something confuses you, say *why*. If you disagree with a conclusion, say *why*.
- While reading, make your comments in writing, even if you'll be discussing the paper with its writer later on. If you are reading the paper on a computer screen, be sure to make clear which part of the paper you are commenting on.
- Remember that you are the reader, not the writer. Resist the temptation to edit sentences, add details, or otherwise assume responsibility for the paper.
- Word your comments supportively. Question the writer in a way that emphasizes the effect of the work on *you* the reader ("I find this paragraph confusing"), and avoid measuring the work against a set of external standards ("This essay is poorly organized"; "Your thesis sentence is inadequate").
- Be positive. Instead of saying "This paragraph doesn't interest me," say "You have a really interesting detail here that seems buried in the rest of the paragraph." And tell the writer what you like about the paper.

Another way to become a good critic of your own writing is to learn from people who give you comments. When a teacher or classmate returns a paper with suggestions for improvements, try observing these guidelines.

● Benefiting from comments on your writing

- Think of your readers as counselors or coaches who will help you see the virtues and flaws in your work and sharpen your awareness of readers' needs.
- Read or listen to comments closely.
- Make sure you know what the critic is saying. If you need more information, ask for it or consult the appropriate section of the workbook or handbook.
- Don't become defensive. Letting comments offend you will only erect a barrier to improvement in your writing. As one writing teacher advises, "Leave your ego at the door."
- When comments seem appropriate, revise your work in response to them, whether or not you are required to do so. You will learn more from the act of revision than from just thinking about changes.
- Keep track of the strengths and weaknesses others identify so you can work with them in later assignments.

In responding to your papers, your instructor may refer you to sections of the workbook or handbook where you can find related discussions. The first paragraph below illustrates how the correction symbols can direct a writer to related sections of the book, the second how the writing looks after it has been edited. You'll find the symbols listed inside the front cover and the plan of the book inside the back cover.

Rough Draft of Paragraph

¶ un
3A

agr
8b

      The trouble with bank credit cards is that they prey on
people where they are most vulnerable. The (banks) take a percentage of purchases made with the card, but that is not how (it)
makes its profit. Instead, the profit comes from the high interest rate on the balances people maintain over thirty days.   shift
                                                                  13a
Thus, the higher (your) balance over time, the more money you owe
to the bank in interest. Though banks usually set a low limit   shift
                                                                  13a
at first on the amount (one) can charge, they just as often raise

frag 10c

that limit as soon as the balance approaches it. Without the

case 6h

sp 34a

(customer) even requesting an increase. In this way the banks encourage (there) customers to incur large debts.

Edited Paragraph

A bank credit card can be dangerous for its holder. The bank takes a percentage of purchases made with the card, but that is not how it makes its profit. Instead, the profit comes from the high interest rate on the balance a customer maintains over thirty days. Thus, the higher a person's balance over time, the more money he or she owes the bank in interest. Though a bank usually sets a low limit at first on the amount a customer can charge, the bank just as often raises that limit as soon as the balance approaches it, without the customer's even requesting an increase. In this way the bank encourages the customer to incur a large debt.

For tracking your errors, you may find it helpful to use a chart like the one below. List the problems that occurred on each assignment, identify the sections of your workbook or handbook where the problem is covered, and make a check mark for each occurrence.

Weaknesses	*Assignment*		
	1	**2**	**3**
not enough details for readers (1d)	✓	✓	
unity—wanders away from thesis (1f)	✓		
parallelism (17)	✓	✓	✓
agreement (8a)	✓		✓
comma splice (11)	✓✓	✓	✓
misspellings (34)	among deceive	rebel seize	omission cruelty

2f Preparing a writing portfolio

The writing portfolio is a collection of your best work to demonstrate your progress and strengths as a writer. Instructors' requirements for portfolios vary on the number and kinds of papers to be included and on whether students may revise those papers before they are placed in the portfolio. Sometimes the portfolios are evaluated by your instructor and sometimes by other readers. Be sure you understand the purpose of your portfolio and the guidelines for assembling it and then follow them closely. If the purpose of the portfolio is to show the progress you've made, you might select papers that demonstrate improvement. But, if the purpose is to show a committee of teachers that you are a competent writer, you would use only your very best work.

Unless the guidelines specify otherwise, provide error-free copies of your final drafts, label all samples with your name, and assemble them in a folder or envelope. Add a cover letter that lists the samples and explains why you've included each one. You may also be asked to include a self-evaluation in which you assess your own progress as a writer.

EXERCISE 2-1

Revising the First Draft (2b)

Individually or with a group, read this rough draft of a student essay and apply the checklist for revision on pages 50–51. Together or each on your own, write a response to a classmate, using the guidelines for commenting on others work on page 54. Make notes in the draft wherever you want to call something to the writer's attention. If you and your groupmates respond individually, compare comments and notes when you finish.

SOCIOLOGY—MORE THAN A CLASS

1   Sociology is a class we take at school. Because it is a required course or we need the extra credits. It is taken so we may become more knowledgeable and intelligent. This in turn helps us to obtain a good passing grade. Therefore, we are able to graduate, from there we go out into society and get a job. When we hear the term sociology we feel it is only a course taken at school, it could not have any essential meaning or value to us. It is often confused with anthropology and psychology. Sociology is not only a class, its a vital force of life.

2   At some point in life we all wonder how a particular event may effect our lives. There is a feeling of bewilderment. If we are ignorant on a certain issue, it's value may be overlooked. We will try to rationalize to ourselves and to others how this is of no significance to us. We are effected by sociology everyday of our lives.

3   Society is made up of people who share the same enviroment. The enviorment in which we live effects the way we act and react to other people and situations. For example, the way we speak to our children may vary, depending on where we are and if their's anyone else nearby. In turn our behavior is being affected, or controlled, by the enviroment. Sociology is what people are doing and how they interact with others. It can also be defined more accurately as the study of social life, and the social consequences of human behavior.

4   Some sociologists believe that people interact with others on three levels; individual interaction, group interaction, and structural interaction. Individual interaction is how we deal with people on a one to one basis. Group interaction is how three or more people interact as a whole. Structural interaction is how people react to a situation that is controlled by the enviroment.

5   Sociology helps us to better understand ourselves, other people, and the framework of society. If we, the society as a whole, could gain a new

perspective on sociology, and the affects it has on humanity, we could understand how and why things happen in this world. If we acknowledge the misconception that sociology is just a class, we are denying ourselves the opportunity to become more enlightened, and perceptive to the ways of life.

EXERCISE 2-2

Using the Correction Symbols (2d)

The errors in the following paragraphs are marked with the correction symbols shown inside the front cover and the related workbook sections shown inside the back cover. Revise the paragraphs according to the markings.

TOUGH TRIP ⁊ 2b

no cap
26f
In the Northern states, traveling in the winter can be   sp 34
sp 34 hazerdous and frusturating. The roads and whether conditions
may be perfectly clear when the travler leaves home but after a   P ⸱ 21a
few days of visiting relatives or taking care of business, the   agr 8a
conditions may have changed drastically. My family and I has
cs 11 experienced such problems often, possibly the worse occurance   ad 9e
was last year after Chirstmas when we were returning from vis-
cap 26 iting our grandparents in Chicago.   sp 34

The trip was particularly bad for the last fifty miles or
so between the Illinois border and Milwaukee. While the highway
going around Chicago was wet and messy; the road as we entered   P 22e
Wisconsin became snow-covered and slick. And the farther we
no cap 26f drove into our home State, the worse the roads become. From the
65-mile-per-hour speed that was common on I-294 and I-94 in   sp 34
Illinois, the traffic slowed to 60, then to 55. Continuing to
drop to about 30 and 35. Even at 30 miles per hour, stoping was   frag 10
cs 11 impossible, we just drove along slowly, hoping that there would
be no need to stop. All along the way the shoulders were punctuated by cars and trucks that had tried to do something dif-   sp 34
frag 10 ferent. Then to plod along at a regular though agonizingly slow
rate of speed. The closer we got to Milwaukee, the worse it   ref 12
became.
sp 34 The absolute worst occured after we entered the city.   frag 10
Choosing to drive through downtown, thinking that those streets

61

frag 10

would most likely be cleared (and going that way was the most
direct route to our house). We drove into a huge traffic snarl
made up of cars, trucks, and buses stuck in and grinding away

p 21f

at the entire eight inches of damp, slushy, slippery no-longer-

cap 26

ab 28

white stuff occupying Jackson St. and Wisconsin avenue. The
plowing crews were waiting for people to go home so they can

7f

clear the streets, but the only way people could go home were

agr 8a

to push their cars around the stuck ones and out of the slush.

After we got home and turned on the radio, we heard what we
already knew: the storm had dumped eight inches of snow on
Milwaukee in just a few hours, whereas areas to the south had

sp 34

recieved a mere two or three inches, and farther to the south

sp 34

their was rain. After shoveling out the driveway, and puting
away the car, we were glad to be home.

p 21j

Chapter 3

Writing and Revising Paragraphs

A paragraph is a group of related sentences marked with beginning indention. While paragraphs have no specific length and no required number of sentences, they do conventionally have three characteristics: they are unified, coherent, and adequately developed. That is, a paragraph presents a single thought, all its parts are clearly related to one another, and its point is sufficiently supported by details, examples, or explanations.

Very seldom do paragraphs stand by themselves; more often they are part of a larger work, which in academic writing is likely to be an essay. In a well-written essay each paragraph supports the thesis sentence; each is directly linked to the thesis and is clearly related to other paragraphs in the essay. The introductory paragraph presents the main point, and the concluding paragraph reinforces it. Body paragraphs develop the idea in such a way as to make the essay interesting, informative, and convincing. Careful linking of paragraphs provides **coherence** to an essay, and if each paragraph in the body supports and develops the single main idea of the entire paper, the essay has **unity.** In a coherent and unified essay paragraphs may be and often are developed by different patterns, selected according to need.

● Checklist for revising paragraphs

- Is the paragraph **unified?** Does it adhere to one general idea that is either stated in a **topic sentence** or otherwise apparent? (See 3a.)

63

- Is the paragraph **coherent?** Do the sentences follow a clear sequence (3b-1)? Are the sentences linked as needed by parallelism (3b-2), repetition or restatement (3b-3), pronouns (3b-4), consistency (3b-5), and transitional expressions (3b-6)?
- Is the paragraph **developed?** Is the general idea of the paragraph well supported with specific evidence such as details, facts, examples, and reasons? (See 3c.)

3a Maintaining paragraph unity

A paragraph is **unified** when all its parts relate clearly to its central, controlling idea. This idea is often expressed in a **topic sentence.**

 Focusing on the central idea

Examine each paragraph you write to be sure all its parts support one central idea. In each paragraph, you should be able either to point to a given sentence that expresses your controlling idea, called the **topic sentence,** or to summarize the idea of each paragraph in a single sentence. Read the following paragraph and see how your expectations as a reader are frustrated when it slips off the topic. (The irrelevant sentences are in italics.)

People who suffer from "winter blues" may be suffering from S.A.D.—seasonal affective disorder. The classic symptoms include depression, mild anxiety, fatigue, withdrawal from social situations, overeating, a craving for sweets and carbohydrates, oversleeping, and a lack of energy, enthusiasm, and concentration. *The craving for sweets, of course, is likely to lead to weight gain, which can be another problem.* The symptoms of S.A.D. peak in the winter months, when the days are shorter and provide less sunshine. *Winter days are colder, too, especially in the northern climates, and a person has to wear extra clothing.* People who suffer from the disorder should try to get as much exposure to light as possible, especially outside, though bright indoor lighting and a sunny vacation can help too.

This paragraph lacks unity because the writer shifts from the topic "seasonal affective disorder" to related topics. The paragraph would be more unified if the italicized sentences were omitted.

 Placing the topic sentence

A paragraph's topic sentence and supporting details may be arranged in different ways. In the most common paragraph shape, the topic sentence falls *first*, sometimes followed by a **clarifying or limiting sentence** that narrows

64

the topic and makes it more specific. In the paragraph below, the first sentence expresses the topic, and the second sentence restricts the broader topic to a specific news program. The remainder of the paragraph develops the topic by naming specific commercials.

> *Most of the evening news programs consist of commercials, and most of the commercials are for products to treat the infirmities of old age.* On "The CBS Evening News" last night I watched a commercial for an iron and vitamin tonic from 6:33 to 6:34. From 6:34 to 6:35 appeared a commercial for arthritis remedies. And that was followed by a thirty-second commercial for sleeping pills. At 6:40 appeared three more commercials: One showed an elderly man eating bran cereal; a second showed a hemorrhoid salve; a third showed a salve for aching muscles. A few minutes later another barrage of commercials came on, and two more series of them appeared still later. These ads dealt with such products as laxatives, life and health insurance, and pain relievers for head and stomach.
>
> —A STUDENT

The central idea may also appear at *the end* of a paragraph, as in the following example.

> Write; don't phone. Use appropriate grammar and correct spelling. Type or word process, allowing yourself absolutely no errors. Use good quality paper that is clean and unwrinkled. Limit yourself to a single page if possible. Strike a tone that is positive, confident, and professional, but avoid being aggressive and self-aggrandizing. Tell why you are the suitable candidate, drawing on your background of experience and education. State your career objective. If you observe these features identified by personnel officers as critical to job application letters, you will be in a better position to have your application given serious consideration.

Or the central idea may appear in *the middle* of a paragraph.

> Measure your waist and hips at their widest points, and divide the waist measurement by the hip measurement. For example, if your waist is 32 inches and your hips 40 inches, your score is .8. If you are a man with a ratio higher than 1 or a woman with a ratio over .85, you may have to lose weight. This is a guideline for weight loss reported by the National Academy of Sciences. It is based on the idea that people who have excess fat around their middles are at a higher risk of heart attack than those who have their excess on their hips and thighs.

The central idea may appear at *the beginning* of the paragraph and then be *restated* or added to at the end. The sample paragraph above about television commercials would have such a shape if it ended with the sentence *I have quit watching television news programs because their commercials make me feel old.*

Also, the central idea may appear at the beginning of the paragraph and be amplified in the middle. This shape would characterize the paragraph about losing weight if the paragraph began with a sentence like this:

> New information about the need for weight loss has become available.

Finally, the central idea may be *unstated.* Use this technique with caution and only if the main idea of the paragraph is obvious from the context. Even if you don't state the topic sentence, you should be able to sum it up in writing. If you cannot summarize it, the paragraph probably needs revision.

In the following description of the revival of Latin in an elementary school class, the central idea, though not explicitly stated, is clearly that the children are enjoying the study of the once-dead language.

> "We're going to play the 'come-up' game," says Leonard, holding aloft a picture. "Quid est [What's this]?" he asks. Hands fly up. "Caseus est [It's cheese]," pipes a nine-year-old named Cheryl. "Optime [Super]!" praises Leonard, and calls the proud pupil up front to play teacher with a new picture. After a relay of come-ups, Leonardus leads a Latin sing-along of *Rome Is Burning* to the tune of *Are You Sleeping, Brother John?* climaxed by a fire dance with everyone shouting *"Flammae, flammae, flammae!"*
>
> —*Time*

See Exercises 3-1 and 3-2.

3b Achieving paragraph coherence

An effective paragraph is not only unified but also **coherent.** All its parts clearly relate to one another. You may have been told at times that your paragraphs are "choppy," that they don't "flow," or you may have noticed this feature in the writing of others. The reading is difficult, the meaning hard to follow, and each sentence seeming to stand alone. There are ways to revise writing to make it smoother and more coherent: organizing the paragraph, using parallel structures, repeating or restating words and word groups, using pronouns, being consistent, and using transitional expressions. You will find these methods effective for gaining coherence *within* paragraphs and *between* paragraphs.

⬤ **Ways to achieve paragraph coherence**

- Organize effectively (3b-1).
- Use parallel structures (3b-2).
- Repeat or restate words and word groups (3b-3).
- Use pronouns (3b-4).
- Be consistent in nouns, pronouns, and verbs (3b-5).
- Use transitional expressions (3b-6).

---

1 Organizing the paragraph

The principal coherence device in an **essay** is a **thesis sentence** that is specific, limited, and unified and that clearly states your purpose. With such a thesis sentence, you are more likely to achieve the second aspect of a coherent essay: organization that flows naturally and reaches a conclusion logically. In a similar way, clearly stated **topic sentences** tie related parts of **paragraphs** together. For paragraphs, patterns of organization are like those for organizing essays. (See also 1e-7.)

One common pattern of paragraph organization, useful in description, is **spatial.** The paragraph begins at one point in space and moves from there to other points, following a logical sequence corresponding to the way you scan a scene or an object: inward to outward, up to down, or side to side. The following paragraph describes a small-town shop.

> Princeton was never a wealthy community, and this was evident in the cracked linoleum and rundown appearance of Reiman's. The shop was quite small with one counter and two tables. Red, cracked stools with scratched, silver bottoms ran the length of the counter, and behind that counter was a large black grill and two deep-fat fryers. Pans, potholders, and utensils hung conveniently around on old nails and pegs. Mrs. Reiman did all the cooking, and she specialized in greasy hamburgers and fried chicken. The french fries came from a nearby freezer covered with tacky green magnetic birds. In the middle of the counter stood an old-fashioned cash register with worn keys and a bent cash drawer.
>
> —A STUDENT

Another common paragraph pattern is **chronological,** in which events are related as they occur over time. The paragraph on page 65 that describes a sequence of television commercials illustrates this pattern.

The **specific-to-general** pattern is well illustrated by the paragraph on page 65 about job application letters, because it moves from specific examples of do's and don'ts to a general statement about such letters. The **general-to-specific** pattern is illustrated below; here the discussion moves from generalities about euphemisms and becomes progressively more specific.

> Many words that started out as euphemisms are now considered standard language. *Cemetery* is one such word, derived from a Greek word meaning "sleeping place"; it replaced *graveyard.* Animals, too, have been given euphemisms. The ass is now *donkey;* the studhorse is now *sire;* and the cock is now *rooster.* Over the years, we have made unusual efforts to avoid the word *cock*—for example, *haystack* for *haycock,* and *weather vane* for *weathercock.* Louisa May Alcott's name is a result of these efforts. Her father changed the family name to Alcott from Alcox, which was formerly Alcock.
>
> —A STUDENT

The **problem-solution** order introduces a problem and then suggests a solution:

© 1998 Addison-Wesley Educational Publishers Inc.

A problem increasingly being seen at airport metal detectors involves a team of thieves who take off with other people's laptop computers and other valuable carry-ons. What happens is that one of the pair passes through the detector without any trouble and then waits at the other end of the conveyor belt. The partner intentionally carries metal items that require the emptying of pockets and repeated trips through the detector. If you put your luggage on the conveyor and then get trapped behind the second thief, the first one has a chance to grab your bag and run. To avoid this problem, put your luggage on the conveyor just as you enter the metal detector, and then keep your eye on it.

Finally, a paragraph may be organized in **climactic** order, from least to most important or dramatic, as in the following paragraph.

Minority students, often feeling overwhelmed on predominantly white campuses, do face special problems. They worry that assimilating into the mainstream might mean surrendering their cultural identity. And if they try, they sometimes face ridicule from outspoken leaders of their own race: at the University of Massachusetts, blacks who socialize with whites are known as "skiers," since skiing is considered a white sport. In the classroom, they lack role models because of the dearth of minority faculty, and they are frequently closed out of informal networks of communication that speed academic and vocational progress. Most of all, they must constantly allay suspicion that they are somehow unworthy of being in the academic community. "It's assumed that a white student deserves to be here," says Georgetown senior Kim Keenan. "But if you're black, you have to prove it."

—*Newsweek*

Using parallel structures

Another way to achieve paragraph coherence is occasionally to use **parallelism** (see also 17a). By representing related ideas in equivalent grammatical form, parallel structures provide a tight link between those ideas. In the following paragraph, the parallel structures are italicized. The participles *standing, weighing,* and *wielding,* for example, are parallel forms linking descriptions of the pronoun *she,* referring to Carry Nation. Similarly, the two parallel verbs *terrorized* and *inspired,* linked with the conjunction *but,* provide a smooth, natural flow of action.

After her first husband died of alcoholism, Carry Nation devoted herself to eliminating consumption of alcohol in the United States. *Standing* nearly six feet tall and *weighing* nearly two hundred pounds, *she intimidated* any drinker. *Wielding* rocks and hatchets, *she destroyed* dozens of saloons. In the course of a ten-year rampage, she *terrorized* thousands of Americans but *inspired* thousands more. Though her campaign ultimately failed, she lives on as a symbol of powerful conviction and unequaled zeal.

—A STUDENT

3 Repeating or restating words and word groups

Repetition can link sentences in a paragraph. While thoughtless repetition can weaken a piece of writing, intentional repetition of key words and phrases and their **synonyms** can hold a paragraph together. The key words in a paragraph are generally found in the topic sentence (and those of an essay in the thesis sentence). Notice in the following paragraph how the key word of the topic sentence, *cemetery,* is repeated, as are the words referring to the supporting ideas, the *yew* tree and the *quiet.* The concluding sentence draws all three ideas together.

> The country *cemetery* today looks, I suspect, much as it did a hundred and fifty years ago, except that there are now more graves. A huge old *yew* tree dominates the grounds, shading the tombstones of the farmers and merchants. As the sprawling branches of the *yew* attract the visitor's eye, intense *quiet* attracts the ear. The intermittent buzzing of insects, whose sounds would go unnoticed in a busier atmosphere, accents the *absence of the noises* of human activity. Cattle graze silently and placidly beyond the barbed wire that fences the *cemetery* off from the surrounding grasslands. The scent of newly mown alfalfa from nearby fields permeates the *cemetery,* but the slightly bitter aroma of the *yew* dominates, cutting through the *quiet* and overriding, with the threat of death, the impression of shelter given by the *tree's* sprawling branches.
>
> —A STUDENT

4 Using pronouns

Pronouns function as nouns (see 5a-2) and can therefore link sentences in the same way that nouns do. Instead of repeating key words, writers can sometimes achieve the same effect by substituting pronouns for those nouns. Such substitutions should be made, however, only when the reference of a pronoun is absolutely clear—that is, when there is no doubt about what the pronoun refers to (see Chapter 12). Reread the paragraph about Carry Nation and see how each time the pronoun *she* occurs it relates back to Nation's name. Then read the following paragraph and see how Maya Angelou uses pronouns to link ideas.

> My education and that of my Black associates were quite different from the education of our white schoolmates. In the classroom *we* all learned past participles, but in the streets and in our homes the *Blacks* learned to drop *s*'s from plurals and suffixes from past-tense verbs. *We* were alert to the gap separating the written word from the colloquial. *We* learned to slide out of one language and into another without being conscious of the effort. At school, in a given situation, *we* might respond with "That's not unusual." But in the street, meeting the same situation, *we* easily said, "It be's like that sometimes."
>
> —MAYA ANGELOU, *I Know Why the Caged Bird Sings*

5 **Being consistent**

Consistency in the person and number of nouns and pronouns and in the tense of verbs (see Chapter 13) is crucial to paragraph coherence, because a paragraph that shifts unnecessarily is hard to read. The following paragraphs illustrate inconsistencies and their revisions.

Shift in person

FAULTY If *a person* wants to buy a computer, the first thing *you* do is decide what *your* needs are. When *the person* is primarily interested in word processing, *you* may not be looking at computers that feature graphic capabilities. And if what *one* wants is video games, *you* probably won't want to look at the most powerful word-processing programs on the market.

REVISED If *you* want to buy a computer, the first thing *you* do is decide what *your* needs are. When *you* are primarily interested in word processing, *you* may not be looking at computers that feature graphic capabilities. And if what *you* want is video games, *you* probably won't want to look at the most powerful word-processing programs on the market.

Shift in number

FAULTY Another thing *a computer shopper* has to look for is cost. If *they* have only $2000 to spend, *they* can't be looking at top-of-the-line machines. On the other hand, *a careful shopper* can get some very good equipment for that amount of money; *they* just need to look around a bit.

REVISED Another thing *computer shoppers* have to look for is cost. If *they* have only $2000 to spend, *they* can't be looking at top-of-the-line machines. On the other hand, *careful shoppers* can get some very good equipment for that amount of money; *they* just need to look around a bit.

Verb shifts (tense and mood)

FAULTY One of the best ways to start looking around at what *is* available in the computer market *would be* to go to the local library and read the latest computer magazines. These publications *will contain* reviews of some of the most recent equipment and software. They also *have provided* price ranges and recommendations about how to use both the machines and the programs to run them.

REVISED One of the best ways to start looking around at what *is* available in the computer market *is* to go to the local library and read the latest computer magazines. These publications *contain* reviews of some of the most recent equipment and software. They also *provide* price ranges and recommendations about how to use both the machines and the programs to run them.

Using transitional expressions

Transitional expressions are words or word groups that connect ideas, both within sentences and between them. Some common transitional expressions are listed below by the connecting function they perform. To become expert in using them, observe carefully how they are used by other writers.

You can see these transitional expressions at work in many of the examples of paragraphs in this chapter.

● **Transitional expressions**

TO ADD OR SHOW SEQUENCE

again, also, and, and then, besides, equally important, finally, first, further, furthermore, in addition, in the first place, last, moreover, next, second, still, too

TO COMPARE

in the same way, likewise, similarly

TO CONTRAST

although, and yet, but, but at the same time, despite, even so, even though, for all that, however, in contrast, in spite of, nevertheless, notwithstanding, on the contrary, on the other hand, regardless, still, though, yet

TO GIVE EXAMPLES OR INTENSIFY

after all, an illustration of, even, for example, for instance, indeed, in fact, it is true, of course, specifically, that is, to illustrate, truly

TO INDICATE PLACE

above, adjacent to, below, elsewhere, farther on, here, near, nearby, on the other side, opposite to, there, to the east, to the left

TO INDICATE TIME

after a while, afterward, as long as, as soon as, at last, at length, at that time, before, earlier, formerly, immediately, in the meantime, in the past, lately, later, meanwhile, now, presently, shortly, simultaneously, since, so far, soon, subsequently, then, thereafter, until, until now, when

TO REPEAT, SUMMARIZE, OR CONCLUDE

all in all, altogether, as has been said, in brief, in conclusion, in other words, in particular, in short, in simpler terms, in summary, on the whole, that is, therefore, to put it differently, to summarize

<small>**To show cause or effect**</small>

accordingly, as a result, because, consequently, for this purpose, hence, otherwise, since, then, therefore, thereupon, thus, to this end, with this object

---

Punctuating transitional expressions

Transitional expressions are usually, but not always, set off by commas from the rest of the sentence:

> The average hot dog supplies 5 to 7 grams of protein for 150 calories. However, a glass of nonfat milk supplies 8 grams of protein for only 90 calories.

Combining devices to achieve coherence

Coherence in writing is commonly achieved through a combination of devices. In the following paragraph, transitional expressions are italicized, parallel structures are underlined, and key words plus their synonyms and pronouns are in boldface.

> People who wear <u>**seat belts**</u> *while* traveling in **automobiles** are much more likely to <u>**survive accidents**</u> than <u>those who do not</u>. *When* an **automobile** strikes another heavy object, the reaction can be described in terms of two **collisions,** according to the National Highway Traffic Safety Administration. The *first* **collision** is the **car** striking the other object. At this **collision,** the **car,** *once* driving at, say, 30 miles per hour, suddenly comes to a complete stop. *Inside,* **unbelted** occupants are still moving at 30 miles per hour. The *second* **collision** occurs within 0.02 seconds, *when* the **unbelted** occupants strike something inside the **car**—<u>the steering wheel, dashboard, or windshield</u>—at a force of 30 miles per hour. The force of this **collision** of person and object is comparable to his or her falling off a three-story building—head first. <u>Serious injuries and fatalities</u> resulting from the force of the second **collision** are greatly reduced by **seat belts** worn properly.

See Exercises 3-3, 3-4, 3-5, 3-6, 3-7, 3-8, 3-9.

Developing the paragraph

An effective paragraph has **development;** that is, the central idea of the paragraph (usually expressed in a topic sentence) is well supported with enough details, examples, or reasons to convince the reader of the point being made. As a writer, you have a variety of patterns available to assist you in developing your ideas.

paragraph, though much briefer, is equally effective in leading the reader into the subject of the essay.

Some strategies for opening paragraphs

- Ask a question.
- Relate an incident.
- Use a vivid quotation.
- Create a visual image that represents your subject.
- Offer a surprising statistic or other fact.
- State an opinion related to your thesis.
- Outline the argument your thesis refutes.

- Provide background.
- Make a historical comparison or contrast.
- Outline a problem of dilemma.
- Define a word central to your subject.
- In some business or technical writing, summarize your paper.

An effective opening paragraph is concise, direct, sincere, and interesting. It often states a viewpoint on the subject, perhaps in the thesis sentence (see 1f). In the thesis sentence of the first example paragraph above, the viewpoint is expressed in the word *far-reaching*. In the second paragraph, the verb *helped* states the perspective the writer is taking toward daydreaming. Make your writing easier for you and its reading easier for your reader by avoiding a simple announcement of your intentions (*not* "In this paper I will describe how to change a toner cartridge"), and don't wander vaguely over subjects broader than or unrelated to your own.

Openings to avoid

- Don't reach back too far with vague generalities or truths, such as those beginning "Throughout human history . . ." or "In today's world. . . ."
- Don't simply mark time with vague generalities or repetition and then rely entirely on your thesis sentence to get moving. You may have needed a warm-up paragraph to start drafting, but your readers can do without it.
- Don't start with "The purpose of this essay is . . . ," "In this essay I will . . . ," or any similar flat announcement of your intention or topic.
- Don't refer to the title of the essay in the first sentence—for example, "This is my favorite activity" or "This is an interesting problem."
- Don't start with "According to Webster . . ." or a similar phrase leading to a dictionary definition. A definition can be an effective springboard to an essay, but this kind of lead-in has become dull with overuse.

79

- Don't apologize for your opinion or for inadequate knowledge of your subject with "I'm not sure if I'm right, but I think . . . ," "I don't know much about this, but . . . ," or similar lines.

 Closing an essay

A proper close to an essay indicates that you have not just stopped writing but have completed what you wanted to say. Whether in a single sentence or in several sentences, a conclusion is usually set off in its own paragraph. The first paragraph below relies on a quotation, while the second makes a recommendation and echoes the introduction.

I'll leave the last word on the subject of vices and virtues to the ancient Taoist wisdom of Chuang Tzu, who counsels: "Rest in the position of doing nothing, and things will take care of themselves. Relax your body, spit out your intelligence, forget about principles and things. Cast yourself into the ocean of existence, unshackle your mind, free your spirit." In other words, the only person who makes the rules is you.

—*Utne Reader*

But even as we bow to the Dow, remember not to worship it. Venerating a relic is one thing. Letting it run your life—or shape your investment strategy—is quite another.

—*Newsweek*

 Some strategies for closing paragraphs

- Strike a note of hope or despair.
- Give a symbolic or powerful fact or other detail.
- Give an especially compelling example.
- Create a visual image that represents your subject.
- Use a quotation.

- Recommend a course of action.
- Summarize the paper.
- Echo the introduction.
- Restate your thesis and reflect on its implications.

In writing a conclusion, avoid several common pitfalls.

Closings to avoid

- Don't simply restate your introduction—statement of subject, thesis sentence, and all. Presumably the paragraphs in the body of your essay have contributed something to the opening statements, and it's that something you want to capture in your conclusion.
- Don't start off in a new direction, with a subject different from or broader than the one your essay has been about. If you arrive at a new idea, this may be a signal to start fresh with that idea as your thesis.
- Don't conclude more than you reasonably can from the evidence you have presented. If your essay is about your frustrating experience trying to clear a parking ticket, you cannot reasonably conclude that *all* local police forces are too tied up in red tape to be of service to the people.
- Don't apologize for your essay or otherwise cast doubt on it. Don't say, "Even though I'm no expert," or "This may not be convincing, but I believe it's true," or anything similar. Rather, to win your readers' confidence, display confidence.

 Using short emphatic or transitional paragraphs

You may use a brief, one- or two-sentence paragraph to make a transition from one part of an essay to another.

> The causes of child abuse are familiar to all of us, but what can we do about them? The experts have several suggestions.

Avoid using transitional paragraphs simply to mark time while you think of what to say next.

Short emphatic paragraphs are sometimes used to draw attention to a particular idea.

> The significance of the governor's actions may not be fully known until long after he has left office.

 Writing dialogue

In recording a conversation between two or more people, begin a new paragraph for the speech of each person so that the reader can tell when one person stops talking and another begins.

> "Why should I be the one to tell him you wrecked his car?" she asked. "I wasn't even there."
>
> "That's why we want you to do it. The rest of us are too frightened."

© 1998 Addison-Wesley Educational Publishers Inc.

81

3e   Linking paragraphs in the essay

Well-written paragraphs contribute to a well-written essay. But an essay made up of paragraphs that are each unified, coherent, and well developed will itself be unified, coherent, and well developed only if all the paragraphs are linked to one another and to the thesis. To accomplish this linking, or coherence, you can use the same devices you use for linking sentences within a paragraph: organization, parallelism, repetition of key words, transitional expressions, and the like.

The most important factor in achieving coherence in an essay is for it to be **unified.** That is, all of your paragraphs must be related in meaning to one another and to the thesis; they must all develop the central idea expressed in the thesis sentence. You can check this unity by making an outline of the thesis sentence and all the topic sentences and then looking for repetition of key words that link your topic sentences to the thesis sentence. As an example of how this process works, consider the essay in Exercise 1-8. The key words in the thesis sentence (the first sentence of the first paragraph) are *endometriosis, uterus, a word, symptoms,* and *complications.* Each time one of these words (or a synonym) is repeated throughout the essay, the tie to the thesis is reinforced. Paragraphs linked to the thesis are likely to be related to one another.

A logical and consistent pattern of organization contributes to overall coherence as well. Notice in Exercise 1-8 how the writer first defines the term *endometriosis,* then deals with exceptional locations of the condition, proceeds to symptoms and next to treatment, and concludes with an echo of the introductory theme.

Since paragraphs rarely stand alone, writers must be able to link them to one another in order to have an essay that is a unified, coherent, well-developed whole.

See Exercises 3-11, 3-12, 3-13.

EXERCISE 3-1

Identifying Irrelevant Details (3a)

The topic sentence is italicized in each of the two paragraphs below. Each paragraph contains sentences that are not directly related to the central idea. Identify these irrelevant sentences by drawing a line through them. Then reread each paragraph to check for improved unity; if all sentences still are not supporting the topic sentence, make further deletions until you are satisfied that all sentences support the central idea.

1.   We tend to view mosquitoes as insects with identical traits and with the primary goal of sucking human juices. *But there is quite a bit of variety among mosquitoes, as their biting behavior illustrates.* The female mosquito tries to lay her eggs where there is water or is certain to be water. It was once thought that only female mosquitoes bite, but in at least one group males also feed and both sexes feed only on flowers, not on animals. In another group, females feed by sticking a tube into an ant's mouth for a secretion the ant has collected from aphids. Mating habits also vary widely among mosquitoes. Feeding on animals, including humans, may occur after mating, when the female needs food for her eggs. But some groups of mosquitoes never do bother humans at all, getting their food instead exclusively from birds or other animals.

2.   *English pubs illustrate English character.* Every neighborhood has a pub that serves as its social center. The local residents congregate in the sedate and home-like atmosphere of soft talk, warm lights, and comfortable furniture, drinking mostly pints of beer or ale. In the United States, by contrast, bars are loud with music, dark and shadowy, and furnished with hard chairs and benches. One can go to an American bar and expect to remain anonymous, hidden from view and free of the annoyances of human interaction. The pubs close their doors promptly at ten on weeknights and eleven on weekends, at which point everyone returns home. Thus the pubs almost dictate English leisure life, whose principle seems to be pleasure under control.

Name _____ Date _____

EXERCISE 3-2

Identifying the Topic Sentence (3a)

The topic sentences in the following paragraphs occur at different points—at the beginning, at the end, or somewhere in between. Working alone or with classmates, identify the topic sentence in each paragraph and underline it.

1   Diamonds are the hardest naturally occurring substance known. They are so hard that they can cut and grind very hard metal. To accomplish such tasks, they are sometimes set in the ends of drills and other tools. At other times they are crushed into dust and baked into industrial tools. Because of their extreme hardness and indestructibility, they are also used as needles in all record players.

2   Diamonds can be broken with a severe blow. If they are put in acid, they will dissolve. If they are heated in the presence of oxygen, they will burn and form carbon dioxide. If they are heated without oxygen, they turn to graphite, a very soft mineral. So, even though diamonds are the hardest natural substance known, there are ways of destroying them.

3   Diamonds are made up of many sides, or facets, each of which must be the right size and shape and be placed at exactly the right angle. Each must be polished. Because of these facets, diamonds are sparklingly brilliant. Each facet reflects light, bends rays of light, and breaks light up into the colors of the rainbow.

4   There are only four major sources of diamonds: Africa, India, Siberia, and South America. Africa is by far the largest producer, mining about 80 percent of the world's supply. Most of the remainder come from Siberia, which produces about 16 percent. India, although once an important source, mines very few of the gems today, and South America also accounts for only a small number.

EXERCISE 3-3

Organizing Paragraphs: Spatial Order (3b-1)

Below is the topic sentence for a paragraph organized spatially. Following the topic sentence, in random order, are the sentences that develop it. Working alone or with classmates, reorder the sentences into spatial order by numbering them in the spaces to their left. The topic sentence is numbered already. Your instructor may ask you to write the paragraph on separate paper, putting the sentences in logical order.

Spatial order:

_____1_____   **Topic sentence:** From head to foot he was clearly dressed for a Minnesota winter.

_____   His chin was somewhere beneath a plaid scarf that encircled his neck and lower face.

_____   His legs were protected from the elements too, encased in lined and quilted pants of a vague greenish color.

_____   The coat was of the type that has an industrial-strength zipper hidden beneath a fly that fastens down with toggles.

_____   His thick coat sleeves ended in sheepskin mittens, the soft leather exposed to the outside, the furry interior wrapping and warming his hands.

_____   A fur-lined parka covered his head and enveloped his wind-burned face, seeming to put his eyes at the end of a dark tunnel.

_____   Under the scarf, his bulky coat—quilted, down-filled, an indistinct grayish brown—attached to the base of the parka.

_____   Finally, on his feet were heavy leather boots, laced up above his ankles, topped with the red-striped cuffs of his wool socks.

_____   One of the toggle buttons was missing, leaving a creased gap that revealed the heavy zipper underneath.

Name _____ Date _____

EXERCISE 3-4

Organizing Paragraphs: Chronological Order (3b-1)

Below is the topic sentence for a paragraph organized chronologically. Following the topic sentence, in random order, are the sentences that develop it. Working alone or with classmates, reorder the sentences chronologically by numbering them in the spaces to their left. The topic sentence is numbered already. Your instructor may ask you to write the paragraph on separate paper, putting the sentences in logical order.

Chronological order:

_____1_____ **Topic sentence:** This is how I make my high-caloric, high-cholesterol, irresistible caramels.

_____ Into a heavy saucepan I put the sugar, the corn syrup, one cup of the cream, and a dash of salt.

_____ Then I remove it from the pan and, with a large sharp knife, cut it into those melt-in-your-mouth, irresistible little cubes.

_____ Once it has begun to boil, I attach a candy thermometer to the side of the pan, turn the heat down, and let the mixture cook to the soft-ball stage, about 235 degrees.

_____ When the soft-ball stage has been reached for the second time, I add the stick of butter and continue cooking until the mixture reaches almost 246 degrees.

_____ First, I get out all the ingredients: a pint of cream, a stick of butter, two cups of sugar, one cup of white corn syrup, a bit of salt, and the bottle of vanilla.

_____ By now it has become a medium brown.

_____ At each soft-ball stage the mixture is a light brown color.

_____ I set the saucepan on medium heat and stir the mixture while it comes to a boil.

_____ I remove the saucepan from the heat, take out the thermometer, and stir in one teaspoon of vanilla.

_____ Then I add the remaining cream, bringing the mixture to a boil again, and I cook it again to the soft-ball stage.

_____ Quickly I pour the hot caramel mixture into a nine-by-nine-inch buttered pan and let it set to cool and become firm.

EXERCISE 3-5

Organizing Paragraphs: Specific to General (3b-1)

Below is the topic sentence for a paragraph organized from specific to general. Following the topic sentence, in random order, are the sentences that develop it. Working alone or with classmates, reorder the sentences into specific-to-general order by numbering them in the spaces to their left. The topic sentence is numbered already. Your instructor may ask you to write the paragraph on separate paper, putting the sentences in logical order.

Specific to general:

___7___ **Topic sentence:** The result is a warehouse stock in the US Department of the Interior of more than 100 million maps.

_____ This entire area must be mapped in detail.

_____ The United States and its territories and possessions measure more than 3.6 million square miles.

_____ Because of the large area to be covered and the various purposes people have for maps, the US Geological Survey issues about 65,000 different geological survey maps.

_____ In addition to maps covering different areas, maps are needed for many official purposes, both scientific and administrative.

_____ Furthermore, there is a great demand for maps for recreational purposes.

_____ Add to this number the multiple copies of the many kinds of maps that are needed to meet public demand.

EXERCISE 3-6

Organizing Paragraphs: Problem and Solution (3b-1)

Below is the topic sentence for a paragraph organized from problem to solution. Following the topic sentence, in random order, are the sentences that develop it. Working alone or with classmates, reorder the sentences into problem-to-solution order by numbering them in the spaces to their left. The topic sentence is numbered already. Your instructor may ask you to write the paragraph on separate paper with the sentences in logical order.

Problem to solution:

_____1_____ **Topic sentence:** Students often wonder how they can gain the experience necessary for a job when they haven't yet worked at that job.

_____ It pays nothing at all, but it's an opportunity for students to develop career-related skills.

_____ Although internships may not pay much—and sometimes pay nothing at all—the experience and connections are like money in the bank.

_____ Fortunately, there is some good news.

_____ It's also a fact that students occupied with getting their education are not employed in their career field.

_____ But what if you can't get an internship?

_____ One way that students can gain valuable experience is through internships offered through their colleges.

_____ Volunteer work is the answer.

_____ In addition to the skills gained, volunteers can develop a network of people who are familiar with the volunteers and who are acquainted with the employers looking for qualified applicants.

_____ The fact is that the best-paying jobs do require experience.

EXERCISE 3-7

Organizing Paragraphs: Climactic Order (3b-1)

Below is the topic sentence for a paragraph organized in climactic order. Following it, in random order, are the sentences that develop it. Working alone or with classmates, reorder the sentences into dramatic order by numbering them in the spaces to their left. The topic sentence is numbered already. Your instructor may ask you to write the paragraph, putting the sentences in logical order.

Climactic order:

_____1_____ **Topic sentence:** I could tell as I saw Dusty step onto the stack of papers that something terrible was about to happen.

_____ As the books quivered under her, the flowerpot with three little seedlings, sitting atop the books to catch the afternoon sun, lost its footing.

_____ First the papers started to slide, exposing beneath them the magazines and computer disks.

_____ When they crashed, it was in a pile of dirt—all except Dusty (she was nowhere to be found) and the seedlings (they were no more).

_____ They too began to move.

_____ The entire stack was immediately in motion, and Dusty began shifting her weight to the books.

_____ When she stepped up to the pile of books, leaving her back paws still on the papers, it began.

_____ Suddenly everything was in the air: papers, magazines, computer disks, books, flowerpot, and cat.

EXERCISE 3-8

Being Consistent (3b-5)

The following paragraphs contain inappropriate shifts in person, number, and tense. Underline each shift and write the correct word in the space above it.

1   One year I went to Dubuque, Iowa, from my home in Oconomowoc, Wisconsin, to count the bald eagles in its migration down the Mississippi. As we traveled between Madison and the river in early January, you could see several flocks of geese flying south—five or six thousand at one time. They probably have spent the early winter at Horicon Marsh and are not ready to move on until their food supply there was exhausted.

2   At Ponderosa the menu is displayed on the wall before the entrance to the area where you order a meal. The selections included mostly steaks or hamburgers and coffee or soda. The price of the meals ranged from five to eight dollars. After ordering, the customers wait in line for their food to be cooked, as you would in a cafeteria. After a few minutes, you are handed your food on trays and we serve as our own waitress. The customer sits down with other customers at a long wooden table in a western-style room.

3   Plants serve two purposes in an aquarium. First, a plant is ornamental, making an otherwise plain aquarium attractive. But more important,

plants help to maintain healthy conditions in aquariums. A plant does this by removing nitrogenous wastes from the water and from the aquarium gravel. Plants do not, as commonly believed, add a significant amount of oxygen to the water. While they do produce oxygen during the day, at night they would take oxygen out of the water.

EXERCISE 3-9

Arranging and Linking Sentences (3b-6,7)

The following list provides all the details for a unified and coherent paragraph about a volcanic eruption on the island of Krakatoa. Through combining sentences, rearranging details, and using some of the coherence devices discussed in this chapter, you can write a paragraph that describes the explosion and its effects. Begin with the topic sentence and combine it with the clarifying sentence, reducing unnecessary words by using only the *when* clause of the clarifying sentence. Select details in chronological order, and finish with the concluding sentence. Use parallelism, repetition of key words, pronouns with clear references, and transitional expressions. When you have finished, compare your paragraph with those of others in your class.

TOPIC SENTENCE

The greatest volcanic eruption of modern times occurred on August 27, 1883.

CLARIFYING SENTENCE

The great eruption occurred when the island of Krakatoa, in what is now Indonesia, blew up.

CONCLUDING SENTENCE

In the aftermath nearly forty thousand people were discovered to have died.

1. The mountains exploded.
2. The island sank into the ocean.
3. At first the island's mountains spewed rocks and ash into the air for a day, blackening the sky.
4. The earth calmed down again.
5. The explosion roared.
6. The collapse of the island caused gigantic tidal waves.
7. Almost nothing remained of the island when things were calm again.
8. The sound could be heard three thousand miles away.
9. The tidal waves swallowed up coastal cities and inland towns.
10. The explosion created winds that circled the earth several times.
11. The waves appeared finally as unusually large waves on the English coast, half a world away.

Name _____   Date _____

EXERCISE 3-10

Using Paragraph Patterns of Development (3c)

Drawing on the topics suggested below or on topics of your own, and selecting appropriate readers and purposes, develop a paragraph for each pattern of development. Underline your topic sentence.

1. Topics for **narration:** an accident; a frightening experience; your first morning at college.

2. Topics for **description:** a new friend; a recent purchase; the car you want to drive.

3. Topics for **examples:** how television commercials mislead; the ideal shopping center; what stage fright is like.

4. Topics for **reasons:** why not to buy sweetened cereals; why to read newspapers; why a particular person makes you feel important.

5. Topics for **definition:** loyalty; authority; education; worrying.

6. Topics for **division:** (parts of) a football team; a concert; a newspaper.

7. Topics for **classification:** (types of) diets; students; comic strips; music.

8. Topics for **comparison, contrast, or both:** two persons' ways of laughing; news reports on radio and television; two diet plans.

9. Topics for **analogy:** In some ways a classroom is like a church or a synagogue; writing is like a bus trip; jealousy is like hunger.

10. Topics for **cause-and-effect analysis:** the physical effects of anger; the effects of a rainstorm (or some other natural event); why you're taking a particular class; why you never (or always) travel by bus or train.

11. Topics for **process analysis:** how to argue with a traffic officer; how dogs (or cats or some other pet) let you know it's time for them to eat; how to clean a room.

EXERCISE 3-11

Parallelism, Repetition, Pronouns, and Transitional Expressions: Identifying (3e)

Read the following paragraph, looking for the ways in which parallelism, repetition, pronouns, and transitional expressions link sentences. Then answer the questions that follow. After completing the exercise, apply the same type of analysis to one of your paragraphs.

The most notable house in Plainville has always been a large and   1
distinguished Victorian on Grant Avenue. The house was built in the   2
1890s by a wealthy industrialist who claimed to see great promise in
the backwater town. The promise was never fulfilled, however, and the   3
town settled instead into permanent shabbiness and obscurity.
Despite his disappointments, the industrialist and three succeeding   4
generations of his family stayed on in the mansion, preserving it for
themselves and thus for their neighbors. Standing a full story above   5
anything else in Plainville, the house remained a source of pleasure
and pride for the community. Painted royal blue with red trim, it pro-   6
vided a bright island in an otherwise colorless setting. Even when the   7
house was finally abandoned in the 1980s, it still recalled Plainville's
optimistic past. Last week that past was demolished along with the old   8
house. Now all that remains in Plainville is the drab present.   9

1. List at least five transitional expressions in the paragraph.

   a. _____   c. _____   e. _____

   b. _____   d. _____

2. Two key words in the first sentence are *house* and *Plainville*. List five repetitions or restatements (pronouns and synonyms) of each one in the order in which they appear in the paragraph.

a. Key word: *house*

Repetitions or restatements: _____ ; _____ ;

_____ ; _____ ; _____

b. Key word: *Plainville*

Repetitions or restatements: _____ ; _____ ;

_____ ; _____ ; _____

3. The paragraph also contains three other words that are repeated in at least two sentences each. List them.

a. _____ b. _____ c. _____

4. Pronouns substitute for three different nouns in the paragraph. Identify each noun and list the pronoun or pronouns substituting for each one.

a. Noun: _____ Pronoun(s): _____

b. Noun: _____ Pronoun(s): _____

c. Noun: _____ Pronoun(s): _____

5. Two descriptive sentences in the paragraph are closely linked by parallelism. Identify the sentences by number.

a. _____ b. _____

EXERCISE 3-12

Opening and Closing an Essay (3d)

Here are the introductions and conclusions for three essays. On the lines below each introduction, tell whether the paragraph uses statement of subject, background information, anecdote, opinion, historical fact or event, question, or something else. On the lines below each conclusion, tell whether the paragraph uses summary, question, facts, quotation, suggestion of a course of action, or something else. For both introductions and conclusions, name as many devices as you find.

1. *Introduction:* Men die about seven years sooner than women. Whether they want to admit it or not, the males of the species are more fragile than the females. Men have a biologic makeup that causes them to over-react to stress, thus putting undue strain on the cardiovascular system and causing it to wear out sooner. But there is good news: men can im-prove their chances for a longer life by making a few changes in their lifestyle.

   _____

   _____

   _____

   Conclusion: As a result of making these few changes—increasing exercise, stopping smoking, adopting a low-cholesterol diet, and possibly changing professions—most men can look forward to enjoying old age with their sweethearts. Now isn't that worth a few lifestyle changes?

   _____

   _____

   _____

2. *Introduction:* In 1956 a group of Africanized killer bees escaped from a re-searcher in Brazil and have been spreading throughout the North and South American continents ever since. They have been moving northward steadily, and perhaps already have reached the southern United States.

Unlike their tamer cousins—the honeybees, well known in this hemisphere—the killer bees are a particularly vicious, aggressive variety, attacking with little provocation.

_____

_____

_____

Conclusion: As these documented instances illustrate, the immigration of the bees is a formidable problem, one for which scientists still have no solution. Let's hope that in the near future researchers will find ways to stop the killer bees or alter their behavior.

_____

_____

_____

3. *Introduction:* An increasing problem on America's waterways is DWI—boaters operating their vessels while under the influence of alcohol or drugs. While there are many reasons to account for boating accidents, at least half of all accidents on the water can be blamed on alcohol and drugs. Fortunately, most states and finally the federal government have laws prohibiting boaters from operating their vessels while under the influence of intoxicants.

_____

_____

_____

Conclusion: With these new laws on the books, perhaps we will see a decrease in the senseless accidents that have frequented our waterways. As one boater has said, "I'm in favor of anything that cleans up the sport." Let's clean it up.

_____

_____

_____

EXERCISE 3-13

Analyzing an Essay's Coherence

Working individually or in a group, analyze the following essay for coherence both within and between paragraphs. Circle all repetitions of key words (and related synonyms and pronouns), drawing lines to connect them. Underline all instances of parallelism, connecting them with dotted lines. Enclose transitional expressions in boxes.

ASSISTANCE

Jane Hill (Student Writer)

1 Most people have a vague idea of what it means to provide assistance to others. In the grocery store, assistance means finding a requested food item or carrying out heavy sacks for an elderly customer; for a parent, assistance means tying shoes or buttoning shirts. In the office, assistance may be providing technical expertise in a specific area. In school, assistance may take the form of tutoring at the writing or reading center. The word *assistance* implies helpfulness and aid. In the world of human services, however, assistance means welfare.

2 For a single parent, assistance provides financial support based on the loss of the absent parent's income. This assistance, or welfare, is provided in the form of cash to meet the maintenance needs of the family. The dollar amounts increase proportionately according to household size. They are set by the legislature and, in this state, have not increased in several years. Can a young mother of two really be expected to shelter, clothe, and

feed her family on the same welfare amount paid out several years ago? Is this assistance?

3   Additional assistance is provided in the form of medical coverage. Families who are found to be eligible for cash benefits are automatically eligible for medical assistance. Medical assistance requires that those found eligible utilize medical assistance providers. However, not all medical care providers accept medical assistance as payment for their services, because the amount paid through this program is less than the amount private insurance allows or self-pay patients are billed. What is this assistance for medical care providing if no physician will see the patient?

4   The problem of medical assistance is intensified for the elderly and disabled, who are allowed to keep only a limited amount of their income and still remain eligible for medical assistance. Should an elderly widow be forced to spend most of her meager income on medicine for the ravages of aging? What type of standard of living have we given to society's parents and grandparents in return for their years of contributions to its well-being?

5   Some people see problems in making assistance readily available to the poor. In this state, a single adult who is destitute may qualify for cash assistance. Because this assistance is not available in all states, it has been cited as a contributing factor in the increased transient and migrant population in the summer months. I have seen little objective evidence to support this contention, however. I am at a loss to understand why a person would relocate from a distance so great as that between states for a mea-

ger $203 per month. Further, I have some difficulty understanding how a person even survives on this amount of money.

6   For many in our society today, assistance, or welfare, has a negative connotation. The word *assistance* in general describes positive events and helpful actions. Has its definition changed, or, perhaps, is our society giving mere lip service to its intended application in the case of welfare assistance? Has the assistance provided by the welfare system really carried out the groceries for its recipients in the same spirit as the grocery store clerk? If not, then it's clear that the word *assistance* in this case is a misnomer.

Reading and Writing Arguments

Chapter 4

Every day of your life, both in and out of school, people try to change your mind—to buy a particular product, to vote for a given candidate, to support a cause, to agree with a particular view. In trying to persuade you, they often use **arguments.** This chapter will help you recognize good arguments when you are reading and writing.

4a Reading arguments critically

Arguments have essentially three parts:

Assertions—statements to be supported; the **thesis** (see 1f) is the central assertion.

Evidence—the facts, examples, expert opinions, and other information that support the assertions.

Assumptions—underlying opinions or beliefs that connect the evidence and the assertions.

 ● **Questions for critically reading an argument**

- What kind of **assertions** does the writer make? (4a-1)
- What kind and quality of **evidence** does the writer use? (4a-2)

- What **assumptions** is the writer making? (4a-3)
- What is the writer's **tone?** How does the writer use **language?** (4a-4)
- Is the writer **reasonable?** (4a-5)
- Is the argument logical? Has the writer committed any logical **fallacies?** (4b)
- Are you convinced? Why or why not?

Testing assertions

A believable assertion distinguishes among fact, opinion, belief, and prejudice and defines terms clearly.

Fact, opinion, belief, and prejudice

A **fact** is a verifiable statement: *Shakespeare was born in 1564.* A reader can check a fact and determine if it is true.

An **opinion** is a judgment based on fact: *Shakespeare was a great writer.* Opinions are essential to an argument—indeed, statements of thesis are opinions—but they must be based firmly on facts. Because opinions can be contested, writers don't convince readers by simply stating their opinions. Writers must present the facts and show how those facts led to their opinions.

An opinion is not the same as a **belief.** An expression like "Nonstriking employees ought to respect picket lines" cannot be called an opinion because it cannot be contested on the basis of fact. It therefore cannot serve as a thesis sentence. But you can at times use statements of belief to support arguments, especially if the audience is likely to agree with you. The preceding statement of belief, for example, might be used in support of a thesis advocating striking to improve working conditions.

A **prejudice** is like an opinion in that it expresses a viewpoint, but a prejudice is based on little or no examination of the evidence. It is a biased view, one that results from prejudging people or issues. A statement such as "women don't know anything about sports" oversimplifies; *some* women don't know anything about sports, but neither do some men, and some women know a great deal about sports. Critical readers will not accept prejudice as support for an argument. Responsible writers will examine the evidence before expressing their views; if the evidence doesn't support their views, they will refrain from stating them and will perhaps change their views to suit the facts.

An effective argument is based on facts or on opinions backed up with facts, not on prejudice.

Defined terms

For assertions to be believable, writers must define terms clearly and use them consistently. When writers fail to define terms, readers may fail to understand and accept the argument. The first sentence in the following example leaves the term *arts* undefined, making the statement vague and unconvincing; the revision, by being more specific, clarifies what the writer means.

104

VAGUE	The city arts council is supposed to be supporting the arts, but the arts in our town have not improved since the council was set up.
CLEARER	The city arts council was created to give financial support to local performing groups, but the number of theater, music, and dance programs in our town has declined since the council was set up.

See Exercise 4-1.

Weighing evidence

Arguable assertions may be supported with several kinds of evidence. Without evidence, writers have no argument. Specific information as discussed in 3c gives weight to general or abstract assertions. In addition, as a critical writer and reader you should consider the following kinds of evidence.

 Evidence for argument

- **Facts:** verifiable statements.
- **Statistics:** facts expressed in numbers.
- **Examples:** specific cases covered by an assertion.
- **Expert opinions:** the judgments of authorities.
- **Appeals to readers' beliefs or needs.**

Kinds of evidence

One common form of support is **facts,** statements that can be verified by checking the right sources.

Richard Caswell was the first governor of North Carolina.

Nuclear reactors used in the United States consist of three main parts: the reactor, the core, and the control rods.

Facts that use numbers are **statistics.**

One of every 25 Americans carries a recessive cystic fibrosis gene. Any child of two carriers has a 25 percent chance of inheriting two CF genes and having the disorder, a 50 percent chance of carrying a recessive gene, and a 25 percent chance of inheriting no CF gene.

Another kind of evidence is **examples**—specific instances that illustrate a point. The paragraph under "expert opinion" (below) has an instance of example.

Expert opinions are statements by recognized authorities in a given field who can speak knowledgeably on the subject. The following paragraph illustrates opinion and example.

As a professional writer for twenty-five years, Dorothy Canfield Fisher has earned her right to be an authority on theme writing. She targets beginning

105

writers by assuring them that almost all authors are at first stymied. One should just start to write. Continue to write as much as one can is her advice. When I am at a loss for ideas, I also write everything I can and then I go back and use bits and pieces. —A STUDENT

Appeals to beliefs or needs ask readers to accept assertions because they coincide with something the readers know to be true. They are generally used in combination with other types of evidence. Here is an example of such an appeal, counting on the reader's desire to do the socially correct thing:

It is sometimes necessary or desirable to use euphemisms. The term "correctional institution" avoids the negative connotations of "prison," and speaking of the "passing on" of someone's dear departed relative is kinder than talking about her death.

The reliability of evidence

To work effectively, evidence must meet four criteria.

Criteria for weighing evidence

- Is it **accurate:** trustworthy, exact, undistorted?
- Is it **relevant:** authoritative, pertinent, current?
- Is it **representative:** true to context?
- Is it **adequate:** plentiful, specific?

Evidence that is *accurate* is correctly reported, drawn from a reliable source, quoted exactly, and undistorted in meaning. *Relevant* evidence relates directly to the point, is current, and is drawn from a source with authority on the topic. *Representative* evidence accurately reflects the sample from which it is said to be drawn, neither underrepresenting nor overrepresenting any segment. And evidence is *adequate* when it is sufficient and specific enough to justify the writer's conclusions. In the following paragraph, the evidence from the American Bar Association could be checked for accuracy, and it is directly relevant to the assertion about laws regulating AIDS transmittal. Readers, however, could question whether the single expert opinion is representative and adequate for supporting the assertion.

Additional laws to regulate transmittal of the AIDS virus are not needed. The criminal justice system already has sufficient power to deal with those who might recklessly endanger others through their actions. This position is supported by a report of the American Bar Association, which has concluded that existing legislation is adequate for combating the AIDS epidemic and that additional measures to criminalize HIV transmission would be redundant.

See Exercise 4-3.

 Discovering assumptions

Assumptions connect *evidence* and *assertions*. Assumptions are beliefs or opinions that the writer supposes to be true. Sometimes the reader shares the assumptions, sometimes not. If the reader does not see them the way the writer does, the writer must use evidence to convince the reader of their truth. Examine the following assertion for its unstated assumptions:

More medical research should include women in its population samples.

The development of this argument would depend on evidence that shows the value of including women in medical research. The assertion is based on the assumption that women subjects are not usually included in medical research. The assumption would require support for most audiences.

Here are three guidelines to help you analyze assumptions:

 Guidelines for analyzing assumptions

- What are the assumptions underlying the argument? How does the writer connect assertions with evidence?
- Are the assumptions believable? Do they express your values? Do they seem true in your experience?
- Are the assumptions consistent with each other? Is the argument's foundation solid, not slippery?

 Watching language, hearing tone

Writing, like spoken language, expresses attitudes through **tone.** You can tell when a speaker is sarcastic or angry just by sound of voice. You can listen for attitudes in writing, too, by paying attention to the words the writer uses. Compare the following sentences for tone:

Millions of animals are victims of cruel experiments each year.

Laboratory animals provide medical research with information not available any other way.

In the first sentence, the words *victims* and *cruel experiments* convey a negative, angry tone, whereas the words in the second sentence convey a conciliatory, defensive tone. By the words they choose, writers express their intentions, biases, and trustworthiness. If the language a writer is using seems to run counter to the expressed purpose, you might question what the true purpose is.

The language of the first sentence, for example, would run counter to an expressed intention of informing a reader about the use of animals for laboratory research; you could expect it in an argument against the misuse of animals.

The language that writers use may express other biases, such as sexism, racism, ageism, and so on. See 31b for a further discussion of language use.

 Judging reasonableness

The **reasonableness** of an argument depends on how fair and sincere a writer is. Reasonable writers treat their subjects with honesty and their readers with respect. They admit their biases, acknowledge another side of the argument, avoid fallacies (covered in the next section), and don't twist their facts.

See Exercise 4-2.

 Recognizing fallacies

Because argument is part of our daily lives, it is important that you understand errors in reasoning so that as both a reader and a writer you can recognize **fallacies.** The fallacies described in this section fall into two groups: those that evade the issue and those that oversimplify the issue.

Checklist of fallacies

EVASIONS
- **Begging the question:** treating an opinion that is open to question as if it were already proved or disproved.
- **Non sequitur** ("it does not follow"): drawing a conclusion from irrelevant evidence.
- **Red herring:** introducing an irrelevant issue to distract readers.
- **Inappropriate appeals:**
  Appealing to readers' fear or pity.
  Bandwagon: appealing to readers' wish to be part of the group.
  Flattery: appealing to readers' intelligence, taste, and so on.
  Argument ad populum ("to the people"): appealing to readers' general values such as patriotism or love of family.
  Argument ad hominem ("to the man"): attacking the opponent rather than the opponent's argument.

OVERSIMPLIFICATIONS
- **Hasty generalization** (or jumping to a conclusion): asserting an opinion based on too little evidence. *Absolute statements* and *stereotypes* are variations.

- **Reductive fallacy:** generally, oversimplifying causes and effects.
- **Post hoc fallacy:** assuming that A caused B because A preceded B.
- **Either/or fallacy** (false dilemma): reducing a complicated question to two alternatives.
- **False analogy:** exaggerating the similarities in an analogy, or ignoring key differences.

Recognizing evasions

Writers may evade the real issues because they have only a weak argument with little evidence or because they don't recognize the real issues. As a reader, watch for arguments that do not face the issues squarely and are not adequately supported with facts and relevant opinions.

Begging the question treats an unproven assumption as if it were a fact.

> Police shows should be removed from television because of their violent nature.

This assertion is based on the unproven assumption that all police shows have violent scenes. To avoid fallacious reasoning, the writer would need evidence of the violent nature of many, if not all, shows depicting the work of the police.

A **non sequitur** is a connection of two unrelated ideas that implies a logical relation between them. One does not follow the other logically.

> School board candidate Louise Smith understands our children's educational needs because she is a devoted mother.

Being a devoted mother means only that Louise Smith loves her children; it does not logically follow that she understands children's educational needs.

A **red herring** is a smoked fish sometimes used to distract hunting dogs from following a trail. In argument, it draws attention from the issue under discussion, generally when the speaker or writer has a weak case.

> We really don't need to consider constructing new areas for student parking; look at the beautiful new library we have. [Instead of arguing about the need for student parking, the writer points to unrelated construction.]

Other inappropriate appeals replace reason with emotion. Be wary of arguments that **appeal to fear or pity,** that appeal to a reader's desire to do something because everyone else does it (**bandwagon**), that **flatter** the reader, that appeal to general values such as patriotism (**ad populum**), and that attack an opponent in an argument rather than the argument itself (**ad hominem**).

> For $12 a month you can give little Marni a more nourishing diet, water that is not contaminated, and a chance to go to school. [Appeal to fear or pity.]
>
> Ninety-five percent of this car's owners are so satisfied that they said they would recommend the automobile to a friend. [Bandwagon.]
>
> This new mid-sized coupe is for adults who love to drive. [Flattery.]

These automobiles are entirely US made. [Ad populum.]

How can you accept the commission's conclusion that marijuana should be legalized when one of the members has admitted she once smoked pot? [Ad hominem.]

 ### Recognizing oversimplifications

Oversimplified arguments make an issue seem simpler than it is by concealing or ignoring underlying assumptions. Several forms are illustrated here.

A **hasty generalization** is a fallacious assertion based on too little evidence.

Vegetarian diets are unhealthful.

A variation of the hasty generalization is the *absolute statement,* a use of words like *all* or *never* when the evidence supports only words like *some* or *sometimes.* The example sentence above implies *all* vegetarian diets even though *all* is not explicitly stated; a more supportable statement is "Some vegetarian diets are unhealthful." Another variation of the hasty generalization is the *stereotype,* which is an oversimplified characterization of a group of people.

Vegetarians are pale and sickly looking.

The **reductive fallacy** (sometimes called oversimplification) is an attempt to explain causes and effects by making them seem simpler than they are. In this type of logical fallacy, a writer interprets two events that are related in a complex way, perhaps with multiple causes and effects, as if one were the only cause of the other.

If eighteen-year-olds are old enough to vote and do military service, they are old enough to drink alcohol.

This assertion borders on question begging because of the assumption that eighteen-year-olds are old enough to vote and serve in the military. A more serious fallacy is the assumption that the first two rights are logically related to the third, the legal consumption of alcohol. The connection would be a difficult one to make.

The **post hoc fallacy** is the assumption that because one event follows another, the first is the cause of the second.

Giving up smoking causes people to gain weight.

People who give up smoking may indeed gain weight, and abstinence from smoking may be one of the causes; but there are other reasons for weight gain, and abstinence may not be one of them for all quitters.

The **either/or fallacy** is the assumption that a complicated question has only two answers.

Either we control the sale of handguns or crime will continue to run rampant.

110

There are other means for reducing crime than controlling the sale of hand-guns, and controlling their sale does not guarantee a reduction in crime.

An analogy compares two unlike things on the basis of their shared features, such as "Capital punishment, like war, is legalized murder." (See also 3c-2.) In **false analogy,** a writer extends the comparison beyond the shared features:

> The perpetrators of capital punishment are as vindictive as those who start wars.

While analogy can be useful for illustration by showing how two things are alike (see 3c-2), it cannot prove a point. And even for purposes of illustration, the similarity between the two things must be valid.

See Exercise 4-4.

 4c Developing an argument

As with reading arguments, writing them depends on the ability to think critically. You use critical-thinking skills to compose your assertions, to find supportive evidence, to analyze readers' beliefs and knowledge, and to evaluate your own argument. You make an effort to find common ground between you and your readers so that you can identify with one another. When you write an argument, refer again to the first three chapters on the writing process and apply that review to the following criteria for an effective argument:

- It presents a thesis, which may be contained in a thesis sentence (see 1f).
- It backs up that thesis with specific assertions, which may be expressed in topic sentences (see 3e).
- It supports each assertion with specific evidence.

 1 Finding a topic and conceiving a thesis

An argument topic must be arguable. Facts are not arguable, nor are personal beliefs and prejudices. Opinions supportable by evidence are appropriate topics for argument.

 Tests for an argument topic

A GOOD TOPIC:

- Concerns a matter of opinion—a conclusion drawn from evidence (see 4a-1).
- Can be disputed: others might take a different position.
- *Will* be disputed: it is controversial.

111

- Is something you care about and know about.
- Is narrow enough to argue in the space and time available (see 1b-3).

A BAD TOPIC:

- Cannot be disputed because it concerns a fact, such as the distance from Saturn or the functions of the human liver.
- Cannot be disputed because it concerns personal preference or belief, such as a liking for the color red or a moral commitment to vegetarianism.
- *Will not* be disputed because few if any disagree over it—the virtues of a secure home, for instance.

Your arguable topic leads to your **thesis,** or the main idea of your paper (see 1f). In your **thesis sentence,** you state your topic plus your assertion about your topic. An example of an arguable topic is "legalizing marijuana." Developed into a thesis, the topic may be stated as the following assertion:

> Because it's no more addictive and hazardous to health than tobacco, marijuana should be legalized.

 2 Analyzing your purpose and your audience

Any time you argue, it's for a **purpose:** to convince someone to see an issue as you do or to persuade others to act. Closely related to your purpose is your **audience**—the people you want to persuade. To make a convincing argument, you need to be consciously aware of both your purpose and the knowledge, beliefs, and interests of your audience. For example, you would use different arguments to convince smokers and nonsmokers of the value of a smoke-free environment. (The questions about audience in 1d-2 can help you analyze your audience.)

Your arguments will usually be intended for audiences that disagree with you or are undecided on the issue, not for audiences that agree with you. You therefore need to build a case strong enough to convince a contrary audience.

 Using reason and evidence

 1 Reasoning inductively and deductively

Inductive reasoning involves beginning with one piece of information and adding others until enough evidence has been accumulated to justify making a general conclusion, or **generalization.** Each piece of evidence implies the conclusion, but no one piece is sufficient for it. When a detective gathers clues and infers from them who may have committed a crime, he or she is reasoning inductively. Induction is based on **inference,** a conclusion drawn from available evidence. You use induction in reading when you infer conclusions from statements the writer has made. In writing, you use induction when you present a succession of relevant facts that together lead to a logical conclusion. Here is an example.

> In April, Representative Smith told a religious coalition that he favored a total cutoff of government funds for abortions. In May, the representative told a medical convention that he favored liberal government funding for abortions. In July, a newsletter from Smith's office stated that "abortions should be legal, but not one cent of government money should go toward paying for one." I refuse to vote for Smith because he appears unwilling to take a consistent stand on this important issue.
>
> —A STUDENT

Deductive reasoning involves beginning with two or more related generalizations and drawing a conclusion from them. No one generalization alone implies the conclusion; information from each one is needed. If a detective knows a crime was committed in the drawing room, and the drawing room was locked until 9:00 PM, the detective can deduce that the crime must have been committed after 9:00 PM or by someone with a key. In writing, you use deduction when you combine two or more generalizations to reach a conclusion.

> Because heavy traffic is hazardous and because the traffic on I-394 is heavy, I-394 is a hazardous highway.

Often one of the generalizations, or **premises,** is unstated. Therefore you might write either of the following.

> Because heavy traffic is hazardous, I-394 is a hazardous highway.
>
> Because of its heavy traffic, I-394 is a hazardous highway.

Premises, whether stated or not, must be backed up with evidence. To support the assertion that I-394 is a hazardous highway, the writer of any of the preceding statements must show (1) that heavy traffic is hazardous and (2) that the traffic on I-394 is heavy. Sometimes writers are unaware that their statements have unstated premises and consequently do not support them; the result is that they beg the question. (See 4b-1.)

Tests for inductive and deductive reasoning

INDUCTION
- Have you stated your evidence clearly?
- Is your evidence complete enough and good enough to justify your assertion? What is the assumption that connects evidence and assertion? Is it believable?
- Have you avoided fallacies? (See 4b.)

DEDUCTION

- What are the premises leading to your conclusion? Look especially for unstated premises.
- What does the first premise assume? Is the assumption believable?
- Does the first premise necessarily apply to the second premise?
- Is the second premise believable?
- Have you avoided logical fallacies? (See 4b.)

 Using evidence

To convince your readers, your argument must be supported with evidence: facts, examples, and expert opinions. (See 4a-2.) The kind of evidence you use will depend on your thesis, your purpose, and your audience. If you want to convince people to donate to world hunger relief, you might use examples of hungry children and facts concerning how the money would be used. If your purpose is to argue for reduction of automobile emissions, you might rely on statistics and expert opinions.

As you use your evidence, be careful to avoid the following traps.

 Responsible use of evidence

- *Don't distort.* You mislead readers when you twist evidence to suit your argument—for instance, when you claim that crime in your city occurs five times more often than it did in 1925, without mentioning that the population is also seven times larger.
- *Don't stack the deck.* Ignoring damning evidence is like cheating at cards. You must deal forthrightly with the opposition. (See 4e-2.)
- *Don't exaggerate.* Watch your language. Don't try to manipulate readers by characterizing your own evidence as pure and rock-solid and the opposition's as ridiculous and half-baked. Make the evidence speak for itself.
- *Don't oversimplify.* Avoid forcing the evidence to support more than it can. (See also 4b-2.)
- *Don't misquote.* When you cite experts, quote them accurately and fairly.

 Reaching your readers

 Appealing to readers

The most convincing argument is one that appeals to both *reason* and *emotion.* It avoids absolute words like *all* and *never,* and it shows that the

114

writer has recognized and weighed all the alternatives before reaching his or her conclusions. Uncontrolled anger or dislike makes readers skeptical about the writer's opinions. For this reason, avoid "shouting" with exclamation marks and loaded words. In the following example the loaded words of the first, emotional sentence overshadow the reason of the point the writer is making.

EMOTIONAL APPEAL	It is ridiculous for elderly people, who usually do not have school-age children, to have to pay high property taxes, since most of that outrageous, legal rip-off goes to pay for schools to educate others' children.
BALANCED APPEAL	Since most of the elderly have paid taxes all their lives, are now living on reduced incomes, and do not have school-age children, they should pay lower public education taxes.

The second sentence appeals to readers' sense of fair play by stating rationally why the elderly should pay lower school taxes; at the same time it relies on compassion for older citizens in their economic plight. It avoids loaded words such as *ridiculous, high, outrageous,* and *rip-off* that contribute no clear meaning to the sentence. The angry tone of the first sentence is moderated in the second, which expresses the same opinion though in a way more acceptable to a skeptical reader.

In addition to the appeals to reason and emotion, a third approach to readers is the *ethical appeal.* This is the sense you give of being informed, fair-minded, honest, and competent—someone worth believing. To convey these characteristics, you must of course possess them. Whatever your topic—say you are arguing against capital punishment—you first make certain you are fully informed about the issues. Whatever your argument, you acknowledge other opinions, you are honest about your own qualifications and biases, and you study arguments critically, your own and others', so that you can understand how to construct them and how they affect readers.

You convey a sense of sincerity and competence by the way you use language, avoiding language that labels you as unfair:

- Insulting words such as *idiotic* and *fascist.*
- Biased language such as *fags* and *broads.* (See 31a-8.)
- Sarcasm—for instance, using the sentence "What a brilliant idea" to indicate contempt for the idea and its originator.
- Exclamation points! They'll make you sound shrill! (See 20f.)

See also 1d-2 and 4a-4 on tone.

 2 Answering opposing views

Writers of arguments must assume that all readers are skeptical and must be convinced. For, if there were no contrary views, there would be no need for arguments. Writers who disregard differing opinions give the impression of not having full knowledge of the subject, and they risk losing credibility with their audience.

Writers of effective arguments acknowledge their opposition, grant whatever truth they see in opposing views, and then show how their own positions are better. You can acknowledge your opposition briefly in the introduction of your essay, or you can give it a full paragraph somewhere in the body. If you think the opposition is strong, you should probably deal with it early in your essay, shortly after the introduction, and be done with it. If, however, you think the opposing view is weak, you may want to present your argument first, showing up the weakness of the opposition by contrast.

Organizing your argument

Arguments are often organized inductively, deductively, or by a combination of both ways. Which methods you use will depend greatly on your audience and purpose. An **inductive organization** moves from specific evidence to a generalization about the evidence. A **deductive organization** begins with a commonly held opinion or belief, applies it to a new case, and draws a conclusion. (See also 4d-1.) In practice, you might begin with a narrative example (induction), and then, after stating your thesis, organize your argument according to the subpoints of your thesis (deduction). To illustrate with a thesis like the one expressed earlier on legalization of marijuana, "Because it's no more addictive and hazardous to health than tobacco, marijuana should be legalized," you might begin inductively with examples of healthy people using marijuana and then a statement of your thesis. But you would organize your argument deductively with evidence showing, first, that marijuana is no more addictive than tobacco and, second, that it is no more hazardous to the health than tobacco. Finally, you would build your case that marijuana should be legalized, the conclusion of your argument.

Shown below is a common scheme for organizing arguments.

● Organization of an argument

INTRODUCTION

Statement of the significance of the argument; background on the issue; statement of thesis. (See 3d-1 on introductions, 1f and 4c-1 on the thesis sentence.) The introduction may be one or more paragraphs, depending on the complexity of the issue and the length of the whole paper.

BODY

Assertions relating to the thesis, each developed in one or more paragraphs (3a) with the evidence for the assertion. If the argument consists of a string of supporting assertions, they are usually best arranged in order of increasing importance or persuasiveness. Sometimes the body of the argument will break into distinct sections, such as description of a problem, proposal for solving the problem, and advantages of the proposal. However arranged, the body is the meat of the argument and will run as long as needed.

ACKNOWLEDGMENT OF THE OPPOSITION

Refutation of opposing views, with evidence; concession to views more valid than your own; demonstration of your argument's greater strength (see 4e-2). This material may come elsewhere in the argument, after the introduction or throughout the body. The choice depends mainly on whether you think readers need the opposition to be dealt with right away or can wait.

CONCLUSION

Restatement of the thesis; summary of the argument; last appeal to readers. (See 3d-2 on conclusions.) The conclusion may be one or more paragraphs, depending on the complexity and the length of your argument.

 ## 4f Revising your argument

Arguments rarely come out finished in the first draft. When you write arguments, allow plenty of time for revision, and then go over your drafts several times, revising first for meaning and structure and then checking for errors. Refer to the checklist in 2b and the one below.

 ## Checklist for revising an argument

- What is your thesis? In what ways is it an arguable assertion? (4c-1)
- Where have you provided the information readers need? Where have you considered their probable beliefs and values? (4c-2)
- Does your thesis derive from induction, deduction, or both? (4d-1) Have you avoided fallacies in reasoning? (4b)
- Where, if at all, is your evidence not accurate, relevant, representative, and adequate? (4a-2)
- How have you combined rational, emotional, and ethical appeals? (4e-1)
- Where have you considered opposing arguments? (4e-2)
- How clear and effective is your organization? (4e-3)

 ## 4g Examining a sample argument

The best way to learn how to write effective arguments is to study how other people construct their arguments. Analyze the components of arguments: their organization, the types of evidence, how other writers use emotional and ethical appeals, whether their arguments contain any logical fallacies, and so on. Put yourself in the other writer's shoes and try to determine why the writer made particular choices of evidence and language.

Exercise 4-5 gives you a sample argument. Analyze it critically on the basis of the instruction in this chapter.

See Exercise 4-5.

EXERCISE 4-1

Testing Assertions (4a-1)

Alone or with classmates, read the following assertions and identify them as
(1) fact, (2) opinion, (3) belief, or (4) prejudice.

> *Example:* ___*1*___ Michael Conrad, sergeant on TV's *Hill Street Blues*, died
> November 22, 1983.

_____ 1. George Washington was the most honorable chief executive the
United States has ever had.

_____ 2. George Washington was inaugurated on April 30, 1789.

_____ 3. The Babylon built by Nebuchadnezzar II was a magnificent city.

_____ 4. Captain William Kidd was hanged in 1701 for piracy.

_____ 5. Indira Gandhi, the prime minister of India, was assassinated on
October 31, 1984, in New Delhi.

_____ 6. Truth comes out of heated discussion.

_____ 7. Every college student should take at least one history course in
order to have a better understanding of world events.

_____ 8. Pro-abortionists have little regard for human life.

_____ 9. These economic policies are designed to encourage local entre-
preneurial activity.

_____ 10. Working mothers neglect their children.

_____ 11. People with AIDS ask only what other people ask—not to be dis-
criminated against.

_____ 12. Parents and guardians who abuse their children should be shot.

_____ 13. Animal experimentation can be beneficial to people.

_____ 14. In 1989, a Texas court sentenced Curtis Weeks to life in prison
because he spit at a prison guard.

_____ 15. Of thirty-two senators who sought reelection, thirty-one won.

Name _____ Date _____

EXERCISE 4-2

Analyzing Assumptions (4a-3)

Alone or with classmates, analyze the following assertions to determine their underlying assumptions. Then decide whether those assumptions need the support of evidence.

1. Murderers should pay for their crimes with their lives.

2. To vote for capital punishment is to vote for killing people.

3. Capital punishment is murder; it is the taking of human life.

4. Spanking is not an appropriate way for parents to discipline their children.

5. Spanking as a means of discipline gives children the message that hitting is okay.

6. There are better ways of disciplining children than spanking.

7. By donating to the Open Your Heart fund, you will ease the plight of hungry and homeless people in your locality.

8. Helping the hungry and homeless is a serious business.

9. We must act quickly to end the slaughter of dolphins.

10. No one knows how many dolphin kills have gone unreported.

EXERCISE 4-3

Examining Evidence (4a-2)

Examine the following essay for the types of evidence supporting its assertions: facts, statistics, examples, expert opinions, and appeals to readers' beliefs or needs. Be prepared to point to at least one example of each and to evaluate it as accurate, relevant, representative, and adequate.

SORRY, SISTERS, THIS IS NOT THE REVOLUTION

Barbara Ehrenreich, *Time*

1   American feminism late 1980s style could be defined, cynically, as women's rush to do the same foolish and benighted things that have traditionally occupied men. And why not? The good and honest things that have traditionally occupied women—like rearing children and keeping husbands in clean shirts—are valued in the open market at somewhere near the minimum wage. And whatever one thinks of investment banking or corporate law, the perks and the pay are way ahead of those for waitressing and data entry. So, every time a woman breaks a new barrier the rest of us tend to cheer—even if she's running a pollution-producing company or toting a gun in some ill-considered war.

2   Two cheers, anyway. Because this is not the revolution that I, at least, signed on for. When the feminist movement burst forth a couple of decades ago, the goal was not just to join 'em—and certainly not just to beat 'em—but to improve an imperfect world. Gloria Steinem sketched out the vision in a 1970 TIME Essay titled "What It Would Be Like If Women Win." What it would be like was a whole lot better, for men as well as women, because, as she said right up front, "Women don't want to exchange places with men." We wanted *better* places, in a kinder, gentler, less rigidly gendered world.

3   We didn't claim that women were morally superior. But they had been at the receiving end of prejudice long enough, we thought, to empathize with the underdog of either sex. Then too, the values implicit in motherhood were bound to clash with the "male values" of competitiveness and devil-may-care profiteering. We imagined women storming male strongholds and, once inside, becoming change agents, role models, whistleblowers. The hand that rocks the cradle was sure to rock the boat.

4   To a certain extent, women have "won." In medicine, law and management, they have increased their participation by 300% to 400% since the early '70s, and no one can argue that they haven't made *some* difference. Women lawyers have spearheaded reforms in the treatment of female vic-

tims of rape and battering. Women executives have created supportive networks to help other women up the ladder and are striving to sensitize corporations to the need for flexible hours, child care and parental leave. Women journalists have fought to get women's concerns out of the "style section" and onto the front page. Women doctors, according to physician-writer Perri Klass, are less paternalistic than their male counterparts and "better at listening."

5   But, I'm sorry, sisters, this is not the revolution. What's striking, from an old-fashioned (ca. 1970) feminist perspective, is just how *little* has changed. The fact that law is no longer classified as a "nontraditional" occupation for women has not made our culture any less graspingly litigious or any more concerned with the rights of the underdog. Women doctors haven't made a dent in the high-tech, bottom-line fixation of the medical profession, and no one would claim that the influx of executive women has ushered in a new era of high-toned business ethics.

6   It's not that we were wrong back in the salad days of feminism about the existence of nurturant "feminine values." If anything, women have more distinctive views as a sex than they did 20 years ago. The gender gap first appeared in the presidential election of 1980, with women voting on the more liberal side. Recent polls show that women are more likely to favor social spending for the poor and to believe it's "very important" to work "for the betterment of American society."

7   So why haven't our women pioneers made more of a mark? Charitably speaking, it may be too soon to expect vast transformations. For one thing, women in élite, fast-track positions are still pathetically scarce. FORTUNE magazine found this past July that in the highest echelons of corporate managers, fewer than one-half of 1% are female. Then there's the exhaustion factor. Women are far more likely to work a "double day" of career plus homemaking. The hand that rocks the cradle—and cradles the phone, and sweeps the floor, and writes the memo and meets the deadline—doesn't have time to reach out and save the world.

8   But I fear, too, that women may be losing the idealistic vision that helped inspire feminism in the first place. Granted, every Out group—whether defined by race, ethnicity or sexual preference—seeks assimilation as a first priority. But every Out group carries with it a critical perspective, forged in the painful experiences of rejection and marginalization. When that perspective is lost or forgotten, a movement stands in danger of degenerating into a scramble for personal advancement. We applaud the winners and pray that their numbers increase, but the majority will still be found far outside the gates of privilege, waiting for the movement to start up again.

9   And for all the pioneering that brave and ambitious women have done, the female majority remains outside, earning 70¢ to the man's $1 in stereotypically female jobs. That female majority must still find a way to

survive the uncaring institutions, the exploitative employers and the deep social inequities the successful few have not yet got around to challenging.

10   Maybe, now that women have got a foot in the door, it's time to pause and figure out what we intend to do when we get inside. Equality with men is a fine ambition, and I'll fight for any woman's right to do any foolish or benighted thing that men are paid and honored for. But ultimately, assimilation is just not good enough. As one vintage feminist T shirt used to say, IF YOU THINK EQUALITY IS THE GOAL . . . YOUR STANDARDS ARE TOO LOW.

EXERCISE 4-4

Identifying Logical Fallacies (4b)

Alone or with classmates, identify the logical fallacies in the following sentences. Each sentence represents one or more of the evasion fallacies (begging the question, non sequitur, appealing to readers' fear or pity, bandwagon, flattery, argument ad populum, and argument ad hominem) or of the oversimplifications (hasty generalization, reductive fallacy, post hoc fallacy, either/or fallacy, and false analogy).

> *Example:* If El Salvador's government is overthrown, Costa Rica's will be next.
>
> *non sequitur*

1. Seat belts are unnecessary; I do not need the government's conscience in my car to make me a safe driver.

2. If young people just set their goals high and work hard, they'll have successful careers.

3. Bureaucrats are concerned only with putting in their time, not with serving the public.

4. How can anyone believe that a car made by dedicated American workers in an American factory is unsafe?

5. People who really know automobiles usually prefer British cars.

6. He must have been drinking, because he is always happy when he has been drinking, and he is happy now.

7. Jane is a lovely, gracious woman, but she has a very sharp business sense.

8. Cars wouldn't be so outrageously expensive if it weren't for all the unnecessary extras like pollution control devices, ignition locks, air bags, and padded dashboards.

9. If anything can go wrong, it will.

10. People's right to adequate medical care will be guaranteed only if Congress passes Senator Schmidt's health insurance bill.

11. Be careful of your grammar when you talk to an English teacher, or you will be criticized.

12. If you want four more years of graft-free city government, reelect Charles Brown as mayor.

13. How can I vote for Charles Brown for mayor when he just divorced his wife last year?

14. Most of the people I know on the fashionable East Side will be voting for him.

15. The game will be exciting because it is for the championship.

16. If scientists can send a spaceship to Mars, they should be able to cure the common cold.

17. Sky diving is just like roller skating—as long as you are careful, you will not get hurt.

18. So many workers belong to unions that high-quality work is rare.

19. If we don't build nuclear power plants, we will be forever dependent on imported oil.

20. Adults need discipline just as much as children do.

EXERCISE 4-5

Analyzing an Argument (4g)

Analyze the following argument, answering these questions:

1. What is the thesis?
2. How is the argument organized?
3. What kinds of evidence does the writer use? As far as you can tell, is the evidence accurate, relevant, representative, and adequate?
4. In what ways does the writer accommodate reader needs?
5. What fallacies do you find?
6. What emotional appeals do you find?
7. How does the writer establish her ethical appeal?
8. How has the writer acknowledged the opposition?

After your initial analysis, your instructor may ask you to compare your findings with those of your classmates.

CAPITAL PUNISHMENT IS A CRIME

Natalie Crowns (Student Writer)

1   Capital punishment is a fancy phrase for legally killing people. It is a great evil—surely the greatest evil except for war. Capital punishment is murder; it is the taking of human life, done without any consideration for mothers, fathers, children, husbands, or wives. And the ones who make the decision to use the death penalty are the very people we look to for protection. Of course, there must be some measure of social revenge for a crime that has been done. However, the killing of one human being as punishment for the killing of another is every bit as violent and immoral as the original act and does not serve as a deterrent to future crimes.

2   A person's most profound emotional response to a murder is to want the criminal to suffer as the victim did. Some argue that retribution requires criminals to pay for their crimes with their lives. An execution is positive proof that the bad guy is not getting away with the crime and that justice is served. A criminal who has violated the trust of a moral community has thereby injured it and must be punished for the sake of justice. However, the taking of life because a wrongdoer deserves it is the total denial of the wrongdoer's dignity and worth.

3   What seems to be peculiarly cruel and horrible about capital punishment is that the condemned person has a period of waiting, knowing how and when she or he is to be killed, which itself is a source of moral suffer-

ing more terrible than death. Criminals usually do not warn their victims of the date when they will inflict a horrible death and from that moment onward confine these victims for months, even years. Such a monstrous act is not encountered in private life.

4   When a man is accused of throwing a child from a high rise terrace, society's emotional, hysterical response is that he should be given an opportunity to see how endless the seconds are from the thirty-first story to the ground. In a civilized society, however, that will never happen. And so people against capital punishment take the position that the death penalty is wrong not only because it consists of stooping to the level of the killers but because it is impossible for something as horrifying as what happened to the victims to happen to the killer; what people want in the death penalty, they will never get.

5   The death penalty is supposedly there to promote deterrence and bring retribution, but when the Supreme Court reviewed all the evidence for deterrence in 1976, it described that evidence as inconclusive. Studies in criminology have presented ample statistical and psychiatric evidence to show that most capital offenses are not committed by the criminally minded, but as a result of a mental illness, an uncontrolled temper under some great provocation, and by sheer accident (Heline 37).

6   The only reason for a death penalty is to exact retribution. Is there anyone who really thinks that it is a deterrent, that there are considerable numbers of criminals who think twice about committing crimes because of the sentence involved? Most criminals believe that it is the other guy who will get caught or they'll bargain for a lesser sentence. In fact, the death penalty not only fails as a deterrent, but it actually increases the amount of violence in society. Statistical evidence proves that widely publicized executions result in more murders rather than fewer (Heline 35).

7   And the death penalty has wider effects on society at large. When there is capital punishment, we are all involved in the horrible business of a long, premeditated killing, and most of us will to some degree share in the emotional response. The advocates of capital punishment do not take into consideration the effects of the execution on the family of the convicted person. They also forget about how the participants in an execution are turned into agents, not people. A priest stands by and certifies that it's a moral event. Witnesses make it a certified happening. A doctor swears death occurred humanely, on schedule, and completely. Yet the priest is dedicated to love, the warden is there to restrain people who have hurt other people, and the doctor is trained to save lives (Jackson and Christian 292).

8   Yet another problem with the death penalty is the possibility of mistakenly executing an innocent person, such as in the case of Timothy Evans. In 1950, Evans, who was of "limited intelligence and confessed to slaying his wife," later retracted his admission of guilt. He was executed anyway, and four years later another man confessed to the murder (Gettinger 184). The death penalty may also be used to discriminate against minorities and the mentally retarded.

9   The advocates of capital punishment can and do accentuate their arguments with descriptions of the awful physical details of such horrendous murders as that of Sharon Tate. All of us naturally respond to those atrocities with shock and horror, and rightly so. But executions are also too horrendous, and there are two important points to remember. First, the murders being described are not being done by us, or in our name, or with our approval; and our power to stop them is very limited. Every execution, on the other hand, is done by our paid servants, in our collective name, and we can stop them all. Secondly, the descriptions of murders are relevant to the subject of capital punishment only on the theory that two wrongs make a right, or that killing murderers can lessen their victims' sufferings or bring them back to life, or that capital punishment is the best deterrent to murder.

10   Is it morally legitimate for us to do in a state of calm reason what someone whose actions we have scorned and condemned did in a state of passion or in a condition of amorality or stupidity? So far as moral reinforcement goes, the difference between life imprisonment and capital punishment is that imprisonment continues to respect the value of human life. The plain message of capital punishment, on the other hand, is that life ceases to be sacred whenever someone with the power to take it away decides to exercise that right.

11   For many people, capital punishment is a sanitized and symbolic issue: an eye for an eye, a tooth for a tooth. To vote for capital punishment is to vote to kill real, live people. "We have learned," said the Minister of Justice in Belgium, a country that abandoned capital punishment almost a century ago, "that the best means to teach respect for human life consists of refusing to take life in the name of the law" (Heline 37). The death penalty does no one in our society any good. It doesn't prevent death, and it does not make society better or nicer or satisfy any moral need. In fact, it perpetuates a faith in the effectiveness of violence as a solution to grim human problems.

Works Cited

Gettinger, Stephen H. *Sentenced to Die*. New York: Macmillan, 1979.

Heline, Theodore. *Capital Punishment: Historical Trends Toward Its Abolishment*. LaCanada, CA: New Age Press, 1965.

Jackson, Bruce, and Diane Christian. *Death Row*. Boston: Beacon, 1980.

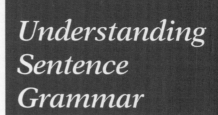

*Understanding
Sentence
Grammar*

Chapter 5

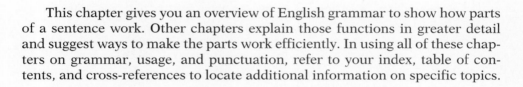

This chapter gives you an overview of English grammar to show how parts of a sentence work. Other chapters explain those functions in greater detail and suggest ways to make the parts work efficiently. In using all of these chapters on grammar, usage, and punctuation, refer to your index, table of contents, and cross-references to locate additional information on specific topics.

5a   Understanding the basic sentence

1   Identifying subjects and predicates

The sentence is the basic unit of writing. It makes a statement—an assertion—about something. The part that names that something is the **subject,** and the part that makes the assertion is the **predicate.**

SUBJECT	PREDICATE
Alfred	lives in New York.
My uncle who works in São Paulo	calls Brazil a country of mystery.
The chemical	damaged the fabric.
The doctors at the convention	were mainly women.
They	attended many meetings.

Observe that these sentences have simple subjects (*Alfred, uncle, chemical, doctors, they*), and that the complete subjects include all the words that modify each simple subject. A subject may be a noun (*Alfred, uncle, chemical, doctors*) or a pronoun (*they*) but not both (not *The doctors they attended meetings*).

gr
5a

2 Identifying the basic words: nouns and verbs

Within the subject and the predicate are two basic words: a noun and a verb. In the sentences above, nouns serve as the subjects (*Alfred, uncle, chemical, doctors*), and verbs make the assertions (*lives, calls, damaged, were*). Nouns and verbs are the basic **parts of speech,** or classes of words.

The parts of speech

(For more information, consult the sections in parentheses.)

Nouns name persons, places, things, or qualities: *Roosevelt, girl, Schuylkill River, coastline, Koran, table, happiness.* (See 5a-2.)

Pronouns usually substitute for nouns and function as nouns: *I, you, he, she, it, we, they, this, that, who, which.* (See 5a-2.)

Verbs express actions, occurrences, or states of being: *run, bunt, inflate, become, be, appear.* (See 5a-2.)

Adjectives describe or modify nouns or pronouns: *gentle, small, helpful.* (See 5b-1.)

Adverbs describe or modify verbs, adjectives, other adverbs, or whole groups of words: *gently, helpfully, almost, someday.* (See 5b-1.)

Prepositions relate nouns or pronouns to other words in a sentence: *about, at, down, for, of, with.* (See 5c-1.)

Conjunctions link words, phrases, and clauses. Coordinating conjunctions and correlative conjunctions link words, phrases, or clauses of equal importance: *and, but, or, nor; both . . . and, not only . . . but also, either . . . or, neither . . . nor.* (See 5d-1.) Subordinating conjunctions introduce subordinate clauses and link them with independent clauses: *although, because, if, whenever.* (See 5c-4.)

Interjections express feeling or command attention, either alone or in a sentence: *hey, oh, darn, wow.* (See 20e, 21c-4.)

NOUNS

Nouns name. They may name people, places, things, and qualities or ideas.

PEOPLE	PLACES	THINGS	QUALITIES
Alfred	New York	chemical	mystery
uncle	country	baseball	justice
doctors	Mount Rainier	Carroll College	beginning
women	home	fabric	permission

132

Nouns take different forms. Most nouns name things that can be counted and have a plural form usually denoted by an *-s* ending: *book, books; coat, coats; pencil, pencils.* Some **count nouns,** rather than taking an *-s* ending to indicate the plural, take an irregular plural form: *woman, women; child, children; sheep, sheep.* Other nouns name things that cannot be counted; they are called **mass nouns,** and they ordinarily do not take an *-s* ending: *music, sugar, literature, anger.* **Collective nouns** such as *committee* or *team* name groups of people or things.

Another way of classifying nouns is as **common nouns,** such as *doctor* and *chemical,* which name general classes of people, places, or things, and as **proper nouns,** such as *Alfred* and *Brazil,* which name specific people, places, or things. Proper nouns are capitalized.

Nouns are often preceded by the **articles** *a, an,* and *the*—sometimes called noun markers or determiners because they indicate that a noun will soon follow.

VERBS

Verbs describe action or occurrence (*hear, mind, listen, build*) or a state of being (*be, seem*). One characteristic of verbs is that, through changes in their form, they tell time, called **tense.** *Opens* indicates action in present time, while *opened* means action in past time, *have opened* means action begun in the past and continuing to the present, and *will open* indicates future action. In present time, all verbs end in *-s* or *-es* when their subjects are singular nouns, indefinite pronouns, or the singular pronouns *he, she,* and *it.*

Carla *writes.*	He *whistles.*
The dog *stretches.*	She *is* here.
Everyone here *knows* Ted.	The wind *blows.*

Verbs used with plural subjects (plural nouns or the pronouns *I, you, we,* and *they*) do not take an ending in present time.

Carla and Jim *write.*	They *whistle.*
Dogs *stretch.*	I *am* here.
The people here *know* Emilio.	Winds *blow.*

Most English verbs indicate tense by a regular change. To show past time they add *-d* or *-ed* to the plain, or dictionary, form: *open, opened; call, called; require, required; type, typed; wash, washed.* Some of the most common verbs have irregular ways of showing past tense: *make, made; see, saw; is, was; read, read; begin, began; have, had; do, did.*

Verbs often combine with **helping,** or **auxiliary, verbs** to form verb phrases that express complex time relations and other attributes: *is living, has lived, will go, should call, may survive, can run.* (See pp. 141–143 and Chapter 7 for further discussion of verbs and verb forms.)

A note on form and function

A word may serve different functions in different sentences. *Support,* for instance, is a noun in *I need your support* but a verb in *I support the represen-*

tative. Work is a noun in *She looked for work* but a verb in *I work on Sundays. Like* is a verb in *I like that picture* but a preposition in *a picture like that is worth keeping.* Thus, determining a word's part of speech often requires examining its function in a sentence.

PRONOUNS

Pronouns function in sentences as nouns do. But unlike nouns, pronouns have no meaning in and of themselves. The noun *truck* calls up a certain image, but the pronoun *it* does not. A pronoun has meaning only through its connection to a noun—to its **antecedent.** When the meaning is clear, a pronoun can take the place of a noun. That is, we can say *It ran over the embankment* if in the preceding sentence we have established that we are writing about a truck.

Personal pronouns refer to specific individuals (*I, you, he, she, it, we,* and *they*).

Demonstrative pronouns (such as *this, that,* and *such*) identify or point to nouns (*This is the right place*).

Relative pronouns (*who, which,* and *that*) relate to a word or group of words and introduce subordinate clauses (*Sheila is the person who saw it happen*).

Indefinite pronouns (such as *everyone, somebody, each,* and *other*) function as nouns but do not substitute for any specific nouns (*Everybody should be here by now*).

Intensive pronouns (such as *himself, themselves*) emphasize a noun or pronoun (*We did it ourselves*).

Reflexive pronouns (the same forms as intensive pronouns—*myself,* for example) indicate that the subject not only performs the action but receives it as well (*She pictured herself as an actress*).

Interrogative pronouns (such as *who, what*) introduce questions.

Sometimes pronouns function as adjectives, modifying the noun that follows them: *her pencil, their story, these people, whose newspaper, that computer.* For a discussion of these and other form changes in pronouns, see Chapter 6.

See Exercises 5-1, 5-2, 5-3.

Related Exercises 8-1, 8-2, 8-3, 8-4, 8-5.

 Forming sentence patterns with nouns and verbs

The English language is capable of an infinite number of sentences, each different from the rest. However, most sentences are built on just five basic patterns that begin with a subject that is followed by a verb. In the following sentences, notice how the subjects remain similar—a noun with perhaps an article—but how the predicates differ.

1. **N** **V**
   A storm approached.

2. **N** **V** **N**
   Citizens opposed the landfill.

3. **N** **V** **N**
   Garbage is a problem.

4. **N** **V** **N** **N**
   The observer told his supervisor the story.

5. **N** **V** **N** **N**
   The tornado left the city a disaster area.

Because their predicates differ, each of these sentences represents a different sentence pattern. The difference is in the nature of the verbs and in the relations between the verbs and the nouns that follow them. The five patterns are diagrammed below.

The five basic sentence patterns

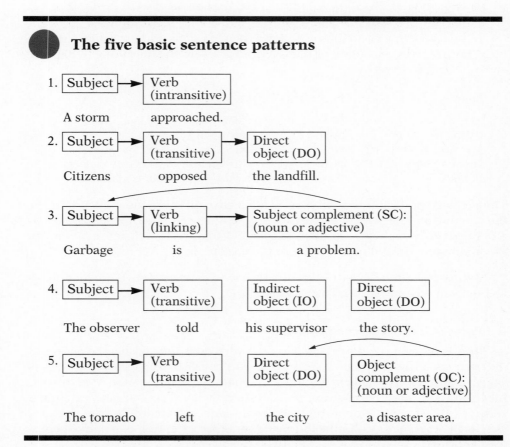

1. Subject → Verb (intransitive)

   A storm   approached.

2. Subject → Verb (transitive) → Direct object (DO)

   Citizens   opposed   the landfill.

3. Subject → Verb (linking) → Subject complement (SC): (noun or adjective)

   Garbage   is   a problem.

4. Subject → Verb (transitive)   Indirect object (IO)   Direct object (DO)

   The observer   told   his supervisor   the story.

5. Subject → Verb (transitive)   Direct object (DO)   Object complement (OC): (noun or adjective)

   The tornado   left   the city   a disaster area.

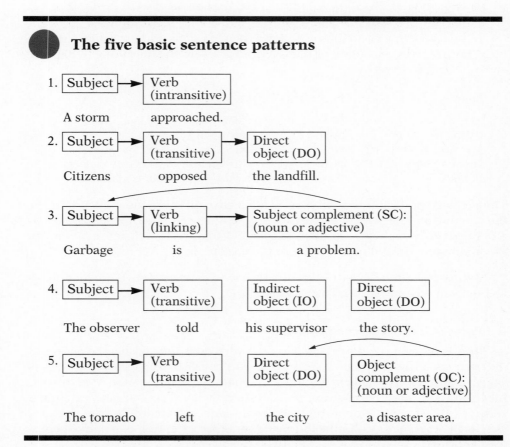

gr
5a

Pattern 1: A storm approached.

The simplest form of this pattern consists of just the subject and verb. With the addition of modifiers, the pattern has many variations, as illustrated in the following sentences.

SUBJECT	PREDICATE
A violent *storm*	*approached* from the west.
Your *friend* who lives in California	*called.*
Your *friend*	*was* here but *has left* again.
Your *friend* and his *roommate*	*called* about the movie tonight.

The verbs in these sentences are called **intransitive;** when used in sentences of this type, they don't take an object, as verbs in pattern 2 do. All these sentences fit pattern 1, even though the second sentence has a *who* clause modifier, the third sentence has two verbs (*was* and *has left*), and the fourth has two subjects (*friend* and *roommate*).

Pattern 2: Citizens opposed the landfill.

In this pattern a noun always follows the verb. This noun is called a **direct object;** it receives the action of the verb and answers the questions "what?" or "whom?" after the verb.

SUBJECT	PREDICATE	
	Verb	*Direct object*
Citizens	opposed	the *landfill.*
My mother	typed	the *letter.*
Detroit, Michigan,	has	thirteen *universities* and *colleges.*
Forests	cover	a *third* of the nation's land.

The verbs in pattern 2 sentences are called **transitive,** because they transfer the action from the subject to the object. The third sentence above has two direct objects (thirteen *universities* and *colleges*), and the fourth has an *of* phrase modifying the direct object (a *third* of the nation's land).

ESL NOTE   Only transitive verbs can have passive voice. Your dictionary will tell you whether a verb has transitive uses. ▪

Pattern 3: Garbage is a problem.

In this pattern the noun following the verb does not receive the action of the verb, as a direct object does, but instead refers back to the subject. It is called a *subject complement* because it renames, or completes, the subject. Like a direct object, it answers the question "what?" or "whom?" after the verb. A subject complement may also be an adjective that describes the subject, as in "I was angry." In the following sentences, the first two subject complements are nouns and the second two are adjectives.

SUBJECT	PREDICATE	
	Verb	*Subject complement*
Garbage	is	a *problem*.
Robert	became	the first college *graduate* in his family.
The pediatrician	seemed	well *qualified*.
My brother	has been	*late* every day this week.

These verbs are called **linking** because they connect the subject complement with the subject.

Pattern 4: *The observer told his supervisor the story.*

Like the verbs in pattern 2 sentences, the verbs in sentences that fit pattern 4 are transitive and have direct objects that receive the action. In addition, they have **indirect objects,** which come before the direct objects and indicate to or for whom the action of the verb is directed. Examples of such verbs are *allow, bring, buy, deny, find, get, leave, make, pay, read, sell, share, teach,* and *write.*

SUBJECT	PREDICATE		
	Verb	*Indirect object*	*Direct object*
The observer	told	his *supervisor*	the *story*.
The tour guide	showed	*me*	the *place*.
Charles	gave	*himself*	a *haircut*.

ESL **NOTE**   Some verbs expressing this kind of action must be followed by *to* or *for* instead of an indirect object. They include *admit, announce, demonstrate, explain, introduce, mention, prove, recommend, say,* and *suggest.*

Theodore introduced the speaker *to the committee.* ▪

Pattern 5: *The tornado left the city a disaster area.*

This is another pattern that takes a transitive verb and a direct object. Following the direct object is a noun or an adjective that renames or describes the direct object. It is called an **object complement** because it completes the direct object. In the following sentences, the first two object complements are nouns and the second two are adjectives.

SUBJECT	PREDICATE		
	Verb	*Direct object*	*Object complement*
The tornado	left	the *city*	a disaster *area*.
The members	elected	*Jill*	*chairperson*.
She	made	*me*	*angry*.
Charles	considered	his *haircut*	*masterful*.

Most English sentences fit into some variation or combination of these five basic patterns.

See Exercises 5-4, 5-5.

5b **Expanding the basic sentence with single words**

Most sentences are longer and more complex than the simple subject-predicate pattern made up of nouns, pronouns, and verbs. We regularly expand this basic pattern with single words and groups of words.

1 Using adjectives and adverbs

The simplest way to expand sentences is to add details with single modifying words. Adjectives and adverbs describe or limit the words they modify.

ADJECTIVES	ADVERBS
quick trip	walked *slowly*
strawberry yogurt	spoke *very carefully*
this person	*never* swore
her coat	*not* known

Adjectives modify nouns, making noun phrases, and sometimes pronouns; **adverbs** primarily modify verbs but may also describe or limit other modifiers. Adverbs usually explain how (drove *recklessly*), where (ran *home*), when (buy *now*, pay *later*), or to what extent (*slightly* overdrawn).

Although adverbs often end in *-ly* (*slowly, carefully*), the ending does not always signal an adverb. Some adjectives also end in *-ly* (*friendly*), and some adverbs do not (*never, very*). To determine whether a word is an adjective or an adverb, you must look at how it functions in its sentence.

Adjectives usually precede the words they modify (*strawberry* yogurt), but sometimes they follow: the equipment *necessary* for the trip. Adjectives may also serve as subject complements after linking verbs and as object complements.

The house was *huge.* [Subject complement.]

The critic declared the movie *pornographic.* [Object complement.]

Adverbs that modify verbs are usually movable: walked *slowly* or *slowly* walked, spoke *very carefully* or *very carefully* spoke. Those that modify adjectives or adverbs generally precede the words they modify: *very carefully.*

Adjectives and adverbs have three different forms, or degrees. The **positive** form is the one listed in the dictionary: *red, bad, serious; well, stupidly.* The **comparative** form indicates a greater degree of the quality named by the word: *redder, worse, more serious; better, more stupidly.* The **superlative** form indicates the greatest degree of the quality named by the word: *reddest, worst, most serious; best, most stupidly.* (See also 9e.)

2 Using other words as modifiers

Words that normally function as nouns can serve as adjectives: *ticket booth, government intervention,* and *taste test.* (See also 9g.)

138

Some pronouns (*this, that, which*) can also serve as adjectives (*this person, that book, which address*). Special forms of verbs also function as modifiers: *the banging door, curled hair*. (See 5c-2 and Chapter 7.)

See Exercises 5-5, 5-6.

Related Exercises 9-1, 9-2.

5c   Expanding the basic sentence with word groups

Groups of words can fulfill the functions of single words. A **phrase** is a group of related words that lacks a subject or a predicate or both. A **clause** is a group of related words that contains both a subject and a predicate. Phrases and clauses often function as single parts of speech: as nouns, adjectives, and adverbs.

1   Using prepositional phrases

A **preposition** links a word or word group to another: He dropped the plate *of* spaghetti. Unlike nouns and verbs, prepositions never change form. Prepositions connect their objects to another element in the sentence by showing how they are related: by time (such as *after*), space (such as *in*), addition (*in addition to*), comparison or contrast (*unlike*), cause or effect (*because of*), concession (*although*), condition (*if*), opposition (*despite*), possession (*of*), and source (*according to*).

Common prepositions

about	before	except for	off
above	behind	excepting	on
according to	below	for	onto
across	beneath	from	out
after	beside	in	outside
against	between	in addition to	over
along	beyond	inside	past
along with	by	in spite of	regarding
among	concerning	instead of	round
around	despite	into	since
as	down	like	through
at	during	near	throughout
because of	except	of	till

to	underneath	up	with
toward	unlike	upon	within
under	until	up to	without

A preposition always takes an object, called the **object of the preposition.** The object answers "what?" or "whom?" after the preposition. (For example, in the sentence "The doll is a souvenir of Cyprus," *Cyprus* answers the question "of what?") Together the preposition, its object, and any modifiers make up a **prepositional phrase.** The preposition connects its object to another word in the sentence, usually the one immediately preceding the preposition, and the phrase functions in the sentence as an adjective, an adverb, or sometimes as a noun. In the sentences below, the prepositional phrases are italicized.

The doll is a souvenir *of Cyprus.* [Adjective phrase modifying *souvenir.*]

A woman *in a brown shirt* stole my car. [Adjective phrase modifying *woman.*]

The neighbor's dog ran *into my garden.* [Adverb phrase modifying *ran.*]

Out of sight is *out of mind.* [Noun phrases serving as sentence subject and subject complement.]

The bus will leave *in an hour.* [Adverb phrase modifying *leave.*]

He stared *at the plate of spaghetti.* [Adverb phrase modifying *stared* and adjective phrase modifying *plate.*]

Punctuating prepositional phrases

Prepositional phrases are ordinarily not set off from the rest of the sentence with commas or other punctuation.

The economics *of the United States and Mexico* are linked *by massive imports and exports.*

Introductory prepositional phrases are sometimes set off with commas.

At a time of international relationships revolving around economics, a Mexican collapse could affect both countries.

But often they are not set off with commas.

In good economic years both countries prosper.

Do not punctuate prepositional phrases as if they were sentences; if you do, you'll have a sentence fragment.

FRAGMENT   In good economic years.

(Fragments are discussed in Chapter 10. For idiomatic use of prepositions, see 31b-3.)

See Exercise 5-8.

Related Exercise 31-5.

Using verbals and verbal phrases

Verbals (such as *falling, written,* and *to go*) are forms of verbs that function as nouns, adjectives, or adverbs. They are a useful stylistic option to writers:

WORDY   In the 1870s, the federal government signed several treaties with American Indians who lived in the Dakota Territory. The government granted the Indians land on reservations.

REVISED   In the 1870s, the federal government signed several treaties with American Indians *living in the Dakota Territory, granting them land on reservations.*

Verbals, sometimes called nonfinite verbs, cannot stand alone as verbs in sentences. The word groups *The rocks falling* and *The paper written* do not have complete verbs and therefore are not sentences. If we add helping verbs (such as *are, has been*), we have sentences: *The rocks* are *falling; The paper* has been *written.*

 Tests for finite and nonfinite verbs (verbals)

TEST 1:   Does the word require a change in form when a third-person subject changes from singular to plural?

YES   Finite verb: It <u>sings</u>. They *sing.*

No   Nonfinite verb (verbal): bird <u>singing</u>, birds <u>singing</u>

TEST 2:   Does the word require a change in form to show the difference in present, past, and future?

YES   Finite verb: It <u>sings</u>. It <u>sang</u>. *It* <u>will sing</u>.

No   Nonfinite verb (verbal): The bird <u>singing</u> is/was/will be a robin.

There are three kinds of verbals: participles, gerunds, and infinitives. **Participles** function as adjectives modifying nouns and pronouns. The present participle is the *-ing* form of the verb (*smoking, ringing*). The past participle usually ends in *-d* or *-ed* (*smoked*), but many irregular verbs form their participles in other ways (*rung, understood*). (See 7a.)

The *burning* question was never answered. [Present participle modifies *question.*]

Stunned, he stared at the open door. [Past participle modifies *he.*]

141

Gerunds function as nouns. Like present participles, gerunds are the *-ing* form of the verb. They are distinguished from participles only by their function in a sentence.

> *Flying* terrifies me. [Gerund as sentence subject.]

> *Flying* gravel struck the headlight. [Participle as adjective.]

> **ESL** **NOTE**   Gerunds can serve as objects of prepositions: *Put your request in* writing. ▨

Infinitives function as nouns, adjectives, and adverbs. They consist of the plain form of the verb—the form listed in the dictionary—usually preceded by *to* (*to smoke, to ring*). They never take an *-s* or *-ing* ending.

> I do not plan *to work*. [Infinitive as noun, direct object of the verb *plan*.]

> That old station wagon is the car *to buy*. [Infinitive as adjective modifying *car*.]

> That lesson was hard *to learn*. [Infinitive as adverb modifying the adjective *hard*.]

> The baby did nothing except *cry*. [Infinitive as noun, object of preposition *except; to* is understood.]

> **ESL** **NOTE**   Infinitives and gerunds of the same verb may differ in meaning: *The teacher wanted* to think. (The teacher is thinking.) *The teacher wanted* thinking. (The teacher wanted the students to think.) ▨

VERBAL PHRASES

Participles, gerunds, and infinitives may take objects, complements, and modifiers to make up **verbal phrases.** Infinitives sometimes also take subjects.

Participial phrases function as adjectives:

> *Sailing against the wind,* we made little headway. [Participial phrase as adjective modifying *we*. The present participle *sailing* is modified by the prepositional phrase *against the wind*.]

> *Backed into a corner by his own argument,* Quentin couldn't think of a thing to say. [Participial phrase as adjective modifying *Quentin*. The past participle *backed* is modified by two prepositional phrases.]

Gerund phrases function as nouns:

> *Watching skydivers* makes me anxious. [Gerund phrase as sentence subject. *Skydivers* is the object of the gerund.]

> After *getting on the bus,* I discovered that I had left my English textbook at home. [Gerund phrase as object of the preposition *after*. The prepositional phrase *on the bus* modifies *getting*.]

Infinitive phrases function as nouns, adjectives, and adverbs:

> I wanted *to win the prize*. [Infinitive phrase as noun, direct object of the verb *wanted*. The infinitive *to win* has an object, *prize*.]

> The team lost its will *to finish the season*. [Infinitive phrase as adjective modifying *will*. The infinitive *to finish* has an object, *season*.]

Andy worked *to overcome his handicap*. [Infinitive phrase as adverb modifying *worked*. The infinitive *to overcome* has an object, *handicap*.]

We urged *him to run for office*. [Infinitive phrase as noun, direct object of *urged*. The infinitive *to run* has a subject, *him*, in the objective case (see 6f) and is modified by the prepositional phrase *for office*.]

Will you just let *me be myself*? [Infinitive phrase as noun, direct object of *let*. The infinitive *be*, with *to* understood, has a subject, *me*, and a subject complement, *myself*.]

(To avoid faulty use of verbal phrases, see 14h.)

Punctuating verbals and verbal phrases

Verbal phrases that appear at the beginning of sentences are usually set off with commas.

Circulating about 350,000 copies a day, De Telegraaf is Amsterdam's largest newspaper.

Verbals and verbal phrases elsewhere in sentences are set off if they do not restrict, or limit, the meaning of the words they modify (see 21c).

Optometrists prescribe about two-thirds of the glasses and contact lenses *worn by people in the United States and Canada*. [A restrictive participial phrase, essential to the meaning of the sentence.]

Optometrists, *prescribing about two-thirds of the glasses and contact lenses in the United States and Canada*, are skilled professionals *devoted to the care of vision*. [Two participial phrases: the first is nonrestrictive; the second is essential to the meaning of the sentence.]

Do not punctuate verbals and verbal phrases as sentences; doing so will make sentence fragments.

> **FRAGMENT**   Prescribing about two-thirds of the glasses and contact lenses worn by people in the United States and Canada.

(For more fragments, see Chapter 10.)

 Using absolute phrases

An **absolute phrase** usually consists of a noun or pronoun and a participle. Unlike participial phrases, absolute phrases contain a subject and do not relate grammatically to any word in the rest of the sentence.

> **ABSOLUTE PHRASE**   *The warning forgotten,* we plunged into the woods. [The participle *forgotten* with its subject, *warning*, does not relate to any other word in the sentence.]
>
> **PARTICIPIAL PHRASE**   *Forgetting the warning,* we plunged into the woods. [The participle *forgetting* modifies the subject of the sentence, *we*.]

143

The participle of *be* is often omitted from an absolute phrase.

My hands *(being)* black with toner, I finally gave up trying to change the cartridge.

Punctuating absolute phrases

Absolute phrases are always set off from the rest of the sentence (see 21d).

I used fifteen references in my paper, *five of them being interviews.*

See Exercises 5-9, 5-10, 5-11.

Related Exercise 14-3.

 Using subordinate clauses

A **clause** is a group of related words with both a subject and a predicate. A **main, or independent, clause** forms a sentence and makes a complete statement by itself. A **subordinate, or dependent, clause,** like a phrase, functions as a single part of speech and cannot stand alone as a sentence.

TWO MAIN CLAUSES	*The waves washed over their houses.* The people fled.
FIRST CLAUSE SUBORDINATED	*When the waves washed over their houses,* the people fled.

Subordinate clauses are connected to main clauses by subordinating conjunctions or relative pronouns. **Subordinating conjunctions** appear at the beginning of their clauses and never change form.

 Common subordinating conjunctions

CAUSE OR EFFECT	**CONDITION**	**COMPARISON OR CONTRAST**	**SPACE OR TIME**
as	even if	as	after
because	if	as if	as long as
in order that	if only	as though	before
since	provided	rather than	now that
so that	since	than	once
	unless	whereas	since
CONCESSION	when	whether	till
although	whenever	while	until
as if	whether		when
even if		**PURPOSE**	whenever
even though		in order that	where
though		so that	wherever
		that	while

144

The following sentences illustrate how subordinating conjunctions link their clauses to the main clause.

> *Unless it stops raining soon,* we won't be able to play the game. [*Unless* shows a conditional relationship between the subordinate clause and the main clause.]

> We can have lunch *while we study for the exam.* [*While* shows a time relationship between the subordinate clause and the main clause.]

> *Before you turn in your paper,* proofread it one more time. [*Before* indicates a time relationship between the subordinate clause and the main clause.]

Relative pronouns not only link two clauses but also serve as pronouns, adjectives, or adverbs within their own clauses. The following sentences illustrate how relative pronouns, adjectives, and adverbs function within their clauses.

> Jeff is rooming with Chuck Janssen, with *whom* he went to high school. [*Whom* functions as the object of the preposition *with.*]

> They are both staying in Kirkland Hall, *which* is the tallest building on campus. [*Which* serves as the subject of the verb *is.*]

> Can you show me a place *where* I can leave my coat? [*Where* is an adverb, modifying the verb *can leave.*]

> Here is a picture of my older brother, *whose* degree is in English. [*Whose* is an adjective modifying *degree.*]

> I don't know *what* you're talking about. [*What* is the object of the preposition *about.* In subordinate clauses, prepositions and their objects are often separated.]

Relative pronouns, adjectives, and adverbs

which	what	who (whose, whom)
whichever	whatever	whoever (whomever)
that	where	why
what		

(See 6g for how to use the alternative forms of *who* and *whoever.*)

Subordinate clauses function as parts of speech—as adjectives, adverbs, or nouns.

ADJECTIVE CLAUSES

She longed to return to the house *where she had grown up.* [Adjective clause modifying *house.*]

People *who can remain calm in emergencies* are well suited for medical careers. [Adjective clause modifying *people.*]

ADVERB CLAUSES

Children should start reading *whenever they are ready.* [Adverb clause modifying *start.*]

As he was bowing to the audience, the conductor fell forward. [Adverb clause modifying *fell.* Because adverbs are often movable, the sentence could also read *The conductor fell forward as he was bowing to the audience.*]

NOUN CLAUSES

We all guessed *how the movie would end.* [Noun clause, object of *guessed.* Compare *We all guessed <u>the outcome.</u>*]

Whoever destroyed the car will be punished. [Noun clause as subject of sentence. Compare *<u>Jack</u> will be punished.*]

ELLIPTICAL CLAUSES

Some subordinate clauses, called **elliptical clauses,** omit the relative pronoun, the second half of a comparison, or other elements.

I knew *(that) she meant me.*

Monkeys are not as intelligent *as apes (are).*

When (I am) in Paris, I will visit Andrew.

Punctuating subordinate clauses

Adjective clauses are set off from the rest of the sentence by commas if they do not restrict the meaning of the word they modify. Adverb clauses are usually set off when they come at the beginning of the sentence and are usually not set off when they follow a main clause. (See 21b and 21c.) Noun clauses, except some appositives (see 5c-5), are not set off from other parts of the sentence.

ADJECTIVE CLAUSES

Greenland, *which lies along North America's coast,* is actually a province of Denmark. [Adjective clause does not restrict the meaning of *Greenland.*]

Cuba and the West Indies are other islands *that lie off the North American coast.* [The adjective clause restricts the meaning of *islands;* the meaning would be altered if the clause were omitted.]

ADVERB CLAUSES

Because newspapers in the United States earn most of their income from the sale of advertising space, they have a large staff of personnel to prepare these ads. [Adverb clause begins the sentence.]

The United States had its first major news service *when the Associated Press established an office in New York in 1848.* [Adverb clause follows the main clause.]

NOUN CLAUSES

The librarian showed us *how to find the periodical.* [Noun clause as direct object.]

Is that *what you want to do?* [Noun clause as subject complement.]

Subordinate clauses must be connected to main clauses. When punctuated as complete sentences, they are sentence fragments. If you want them to function as separate sentences, make them main clauses by omitting the subordinating word.

FRAGMENT	Because the house was left unlocked.
REVISED	The house was left unlocked. [Omission of the subordinating word *because* makes the clause complete in itself.]
REVISED	The thieves were able to enter easily because the house was left unlocked. [The subordinate clause is connected to a main clause.]

See Chapter 10 on sentence fragments.

 Using appositives

An **appositive** is a word or word group that renames a nearby word or word group. Appositives are usually nouns.

The Edsel, *Ford's biggest commercial failure,* is now a classic car.

The Chevrolet Cavalier and Geo Metro, *two gas-efficient cars,* are popular with buyers.

Appositives can be seen as reduced forms of *who* or *which* clauses that have linking verbs and subject complements.

The Edsel, *which is Ford's biggest commercial failure,* is now a classic car.

The Chevrolet Cavalier and Geo Metro, *which are two gas-efficient cars,* are popular with buyers.

Appositives are therefore economical alternatives to such clauses.

Some appositives are noun clauses.

The announcement *that you were leaving the company* surprised all of us. [The appositive renames *announcement*.]

William's excuse, *that his grandmother had died,* was at least tried, if not true. [The appositive renames *excuse*.]

Punctuating appositives

A nonrestrictive appositive should be separated from the word it refers to by a comma, a dash, or a colon. When the appositive restricts the meaning of the word it refers to, it follows or precedes that word with no punctuation.

The largest lake in South America, *Lake Maracaibo,* covers 5000 square miles. [Nonrestrictive appositive.]

Lake Titicaca—*the highest body of water in the world on which steamships operate*—is 12,507 feet above sea level. [Nonrestrictive appositive, set off with dashes because of its length.]

South America's animal population includes many unusual creatures: *armadillos, giant anteaters, capybaras, and sloths.* [Nonrestrictive appositive, set off with a colon because it is a list coming at the end of the sentence.]

The island group *Tierra del Fuego* is separated from the South American mainland by the Strait of Magellan. [Restrictive appositive, essential to the meaning of *The island group,* not set off with punctuation.]

Tierra del Fuego, *"land of fire" in English,* is an odd name considering the heavy rainfall of the country. [Nonrestrictive appositive renaming *Tierra del Fuego.*]

An appositive punctuated as a sentence is a sentence fragment. (See Chapter 10 on fragments.)

Exercises 5-12, 5-13, 5-14.

Related Exercises 16-2, 16-3.

5d Compounding words, phrases, and clauses

Single words and groups of words may be linked to show that they are related; such linking—called **compounding**—has the effect of reducing repetition. You can compound any element of the sentence—clauses, phrases, and any part of speech—but the elements must be equivalent in both grammar and meaning.

Scientific research and common sense declare the *value* and *necessity* of hugging children. [Compound noun phrases as subject and compound object.]

After exercising, I feel *healthy, strong,* and *confident.* [Compound adjectives as subject complements.]

The critic called the movie *thoughtless* and *dull.* [Compound adjectives as object complements.]

The firecracker *sizzled* and then *exploded.* [Compound predicate.]

I hoped for a good grade, and *I got what I wanted.* [Compound sentence.]

Using coordinating conjunctions and correlative conjunctions

Coordinating conjunctions create compound constructions.

● Coordinating conjunctions

and (*addition*)   nor (*alternative*)   for (*cause*)   yet (*contrast*)
but (*contrast*)   or (*alternative*)   so (*effect*)

These conjunctions connect words or word groups of the same kind: nouns, verbs, adjectives, adverbs, phrases, clauses, or whole sentences.

> With a new piece of computer hardware, you *can sit* at a computer screen and *watch* yourself think. [Two verbs.]
>
> *Math* and *science* classes are usually avoided when they are electives. [Two adjectives.]
>
> Many schools in inner *cities* and rural *areas* have outdated *equipment* and *textbooks*. [Two sets of paired nouns.]
>
> *Our infant mortality rate is higher than Singapore's,* and *our life expectancy is lower than that of the Cubans.* [Two main clauses.]

Some compounding conjunctions, called **correlative conjunctions,** come in pairs:

 ### Common correlative conjunctions

both . . . and (*addition*)   neither . . . nor (*negation*)
not only . . . but also (*addition*)   whether . . . or (*alternative*)
not . . . but (*substitution*)   as . . . as (*comparison*)
either . . . or (*alternative*)

> *Both* John *and* the student from Taiwan were defeated in wrestling.
>
> After exercising, I feel *not only* healthy and strong *but also* confident.
>
> *Either* you *or* I will have to go.
>
> *Neither* sizzling *nor* exploding, the firecracker seemed to be a dud.

Punctuating compounded words, phrases, and clauses

Two main clauses in a single sentence are separated in one of two ways: with a comma and a coordinating conjunction (21a) or with a semicolon (22a).

> Space has neither air nor the sensation of gravity, *and* it is subject to extremes of temperature. [Two main clauses separated with a coordinating conjunction and a comma.]

149

Overcoming gravity is the biggest problem for getting into space; gravity pulls everything back to Earth. [Two main clauses separated with a semicolon.]

Separating two main clauses with only a comma results in a comma splice. (See Chapter 11.)

Compounded words, phrases, and clauses in a series of three or more are separated by commas.

A space launch vehicle is used to launch satellites, space probes, *and* other spacecraft. [Three nouns plus their modifiers; note the comma before the coordinating conjunction.]

A comma is used before the coordinating conjunction in only two cases: with a series of three or more sentence elements and between two main clauses. (See 21j-2.) Do not use it with other paired elements.

 2 Using conjunctive adverbs

When identifying **conjunctive adverbs,** remember that (1) they are *not* conjunctions and (2) they *are* adverbs. As we have seen, conjunctions join sentence elements—either equal elements (coordinating conjunctions) or unequal elements (subordinating conjunctions). Adverbs, on the other hand, serve a modifying function; they describe or limit verbs, other modifiers, or groups of words. Conjunctive adverbs modify groups of words and show how their clauses relate to other clauses.

 Common conjunctive adverbs

ADDITION	COMPARISON OR CONTRAST	CAUSE OR EFFECT
also	however	accordingly
besides	in comparison	as a result
further	in contrast	consequently
furthermore	instead	hence
in addition	likewise	therefore
incidentally	nevertheless	thus
moreover	nonetheless	
	otherwise	TIME
EMPHASIS	similarly	finally
certainly		meanwhile
indeed		next
in fact		now
still		then
undoubtedly		thereafter

Like other adverbs that modify verbs or clauses, these connectors are usually movable; conjunctions, in contrast, are not. Compare the following sentences, the first using a conjunctive adverb, the second a coordinating conjunction.

> Mr. Androni talks of nothing except himself; *however,* he is one of the most interesting people I know. [The conjunctive adverb *however* could appear at the end of the clause.]

> Mr. Androni talks of nothing except himself, *but* he is one of the most interesting people I know. [The coordinating conjunction *but* can be used only at the beginning of its clause.]

Punctuating sentences containing conjunctive adverbs

Conjunctive adverbs relate equal clauses. Between the two clauses the punctuation mark must be either a semicolon or a period.

> The season's last game was canceled; *nonetheless,* we won the championship.

Separating two main clauses with only a comma—even though the second one has a conjunctive adverb—results in a comma splice (Chapter 11).

Writers usually, but not always, follow the conjunctive adverb with a comma. Note the two examples above and then the one following.

> Read the directions for the test carefully; *then* follow them exactly.

See Exercises 5-15, 5-16.

Related Exercises 11-1, 11-2, 11-3, 11-4, 16-1, 16-2, 16-3, 17-1, 17-2, 17-3, 22-1, 22-2.

 5e   Changing the usual order of the sentence

Most English sentences follow the basic word order of subject, verb, and object or complement. This basic order also has some common variations.

 Forming questions

Questions are formed mainly in two ways: by inverting normal subject-verb order (sometimes by adding *do*) and by using a question word such as *who, what, when, where, which.*

>   V   S   S   V
> Was the movie interesting? [Normal order: *The movie was interesting.*]

>   V   S   V   S   V   V
> Were you impressed with its music? [Normal order: *You were impressed with its music.*]

   V   S   V
Do you want to see the movie again? [*Do* introduces the question.]

   V S   V
Can we afford to see it again? [*Can* introduces the question.]

    S   V
Who plays in the movie?

        V   S V
With whom did you see the movie? [Or *Whom did you see the movie with?*]

     V S   V
How did you get to the theater?

     V S   V
Why do you want to see the movie again?

Forming commands

To form commands, omit the sentence subject *you.*

Turn to the diagram on the next page. [The subject, *you,* is implied.]
Don't expect much from that course.

Writing passive sentences

The normal **voice** of a verb is **active.** The subject performs the action of the verb and the direct object receives the action.

    S   V   DO
The cat killed the rat.

In the **passive voice,** this order is reversed

The rat was killed by the cat.

In this sentence, the subject receives the action, and the performer of the action is the object of the preposition *by.*
The passive verb consists of some form of *be* plus a past participle.

ACTIVE VERB	PASSIVE VERB
gives	is given
gave	was given
is giving	is being given
has given	has been given

Sometimes writers omit naming the performer of an action:

The rat was killed.

The writer may not know who performed the action, or it may not be important who did it. Careful readers mistrust passive voice and careful writers use it sparingly. (See 7g, 7h, and 18d for additional discussions of passive sentences.)

Writing sentences with postponed subjects

In some sentences the normal subject-predicate order is inverted for emphasis.

        V   S
High in the tree sat an eagle.

Other sentences, called **expletive constructions,** begin with *it* or *there* followed by the verb, a form of *be.* In such sentences the subject follows the verb.

      V   S
There are fifty-seven varieties.

It is unclear how they got there. [*How they got there,* a noun clause, is the subject of *is.*]

Expletive constructions can provide variety in sentences but should be used sparingly because they are often wordy. (See 18e.)

    ESL NOTE   Be careful not to omit *there* or *it* from an expletive construction. (Not *Was nobody home.*)

See Exercise 5-17.

Related Exercises 7-7, 18-1, 19-1.

Classifying sentences

We have already seen how sentences can be described by their subject-predicate patterns (5a). Another way to classify sentences is according to their clause patterns: by how many main clauses they contain and whether they have any subordinate clauses. There are four basic structures: simple, compound, complex, and compound-complex.

Writing simple sentences

A **simple sentence** consists of one main clause. The clause may contain more than one modifying phrase, more than one subject, verb, or object, but as long as it has just one subject-verb pattern, it is a simple sentence. These are all simple sentences:

  S   V
He cleaned the copy machine.

          S   V
Last June Mr. Snapp cleaned Mr. Rollo's copy machine for a small fee.

       S   V   V
Mr. Snapp cleaned and repaired Mr. Rollo's copy machine.

       S   S   V   V
Mr. Snapp and his assistant cleaned and repaired Mr. Rollo's copy machine.

Writing compound sentences

A **compound sentence** contains two or more main clauses separated by a comma and a coordinating conjunction or by a semicolon. The sentence may have modifers, but it has no subordinate clauses.

S   V   S   V
Mr. Snapp cleaned Mr. Rollo's copy machine, but it still left black marks on the paper.

S   V   S   V
Mr. Snapp cleaned Mr. Rollo's copy machine; however, it still left black marks on the paper.

 Writing complex sentences

A **complex sentence** contains one main clause and one or more subordinate clauses.

S   V   S   V
After Mr. Snapp cleaned Mr. Rollo's copy machine, it still left black marks on the paper. [The first half of the sentence is the subordinate clause; the second half is the main clause.]

 Writing compound-complex sentences

A **compound-complex sentence** contains two or more main clauses and one or more subordinate clauses.

S   V   S   V
Mr. Snapp cleaned Mr. Rollo's copy machine, but it still left black marks on the

S   V
paper after he had finished. [Main clause, main clause, subordinate clause.]

See Exercise 5-18.

Related Exercises 5-12, 5-13, 5-14, 5-15, 5-17, 16-1, 16-2, 16-3.

EXERCISE 5-1

Subjects and Predicates: Identifying and Comparing (5a-1)

Divide each of the following sentences into subjects and predicates with vertical lines. All the words that help identify the subject are part of the subject. Then on separate paper compose sentences that follow the patterns of these sentences. Separate your subjects and predicates with vertical lines.

Example: Dairy cows and beef cattle/graze along our highways.

White oaks and red oaks/grow side by side in our forests.

1. The most common dairy cow in the United States is the Holstein.

2. About 70 percent of the dairy cattle in this country are Holsteins.

3. You have probably seen these large black-and-white cows grazing beside the highway.

4. The origin of this breed of cattle is Northern Europe, specifically Friesland.

5. They were later raised also in Holstein, an area of Germany.

6. Dutch settlers probably brought the first Holstein cattle to the United States in the early 1600s.

7. Somewhat smaller than Holsteins, Guernseys are a light brown, almost golden, with white markings.

8. These dairy cattle were developed on the Isle of Guernsey in the English Channel and did not arrive in the United States until the early 1800s.

9. Jersey, another island in the English Channel, is the namesake of the Jersey cow.

10. The Jerseys probably migrated to that island across a land bridge from Europe.

11. Jersey cows are fawn-colored and have an interesting muzzle: black encircled by a light ring.

12. These three breeds—Holsteins, Guernseys, and Jerseys—make up most of the milk-producing cattle in the United States.

13. Their ability to produce large quantities of milk makes them popular with dairy producers.

EXERCISE 5-2

Nouns, Verbs, and Pronouns: Identifying Functions (5a-2)

In the following passages, identify all words functioning as nouns by writing **N** above them, all words functioning as verbs with **V,** and all pronouns functioning as nouns with **P.** Sentences will often have more than one of each.

                  N   V   P V   V   N

Example: Herb decided he had seen enough violence.

1   Most people in the United States remember carnivals from their child-hood and youthful years. These traveling shows included rides, sideshows, and games. They were sometimes set up in parking lots at malls as ways to attract customers and sometimes in fairgrounds as part of county or state fairs. People would attend them for amusement and diversion, occasion-ally winning prizes for their games of skill.

2   Historically, carnivals are periods of feasting that precede the begin-ning of Lent. They sometimes begin early in the new year and continue until Shrove Tuesday, the day before Ash Wednesday. These celebratory carnivals may have originated in ancient Egypt, and they were common in ancient Rome. In the Middle Ages they were assimilated by the Roman Catholic church and took on religious overtones. Carnivals are still com-mon in parts of Europe, and in this country they exist at the Mardi Gras in New Orleans.

Common to amusement carnivals are rides, those mechanical devices that give pleasure through speed, height, or unaccustomed motion. The Ferris wheel is one of these rides. It is a large upright wheel that rotates and transports people from the ground to an elevation high above the carnival and then down again. Occasionally riders are suspended at the top or in midair on the downward slope while passengers exit and enter at the ground level. This popular wheel takes its name from G. W. Ferris, its inventor, who built the first one for the 1893 World's Fair in Chicago. It was a double wheel with a capacity of 2000 riders.

EXERCISE 5-3

Nouns and Verbs: Writing Sentences (5a)

The words shown below can be used as both nouns and verbs. For each word, first write a sentence using it as a noun and then write a sentence using it as a verb.

Example: whistle   *Ruth carried a dog whistle on a chain around her neck.*

Ruth whistled for her dog.

1. experiment

2. number

3. model

4. use

5. supply

6. form

7. surface

8. burn

9. note

10. count

EXERCISE 5-4

Parts of the Sentence: Identifying (5a-3)

The following sentences are grouped by pattern. Within each group, identify subjects, verbs, objects, and complements by writing the appropriate abbreviation above the word. Disregard modifiers.

Pattern 1: S, V

1. Bats live a long time.

2. Bamboo plants grow for many years without flowering.

3. Some fishes cluck, croak, or grunt.

4. Sound waves must travel through a medium.

5. Some unanswered questions about quark matter still remain.

Pattern 2: S, V, DO

6. Some foods may increase chances of getting cancer.

7. However, other foods may provide an effective means of preventing the disease.

8. Pandas eat almost nothing except bamboo.

9. Computer camps offer computer training in a camplike setting.

10. Scientists group butterflies into families according to their physical features.

Pattern 3: S, V, SC

11. Bats are intriguing creatures because of their unusual characteristics.

12. Freon is a common cooling agent.

13. The Doppler effect is an apparent change in pitch.

14. Infrasound means sound with frequencies below the range of human hearing.

15. The sun's rays are strongest between 10:00 AM and 2:00 PM.

Pattern 4: S, V, IO, DO

16. A male frog sends a female frog a hoarse mating call.

17. Zoo officials sometimes must feed baby animals milk from a bottle.

18. Medical technologists very seldom give people high doses of ionizing radiation.

19. Trilobites have given paleontologists evidence of continent formation.

20. According to some botanists, trees sometimes send other trees chemical messages when under attack by insects.

Pattern 5: S, V, DO, OC

21. Scientists call butterflies and moths Lepidoptera.

22. They sometimes call computers "artificial intelligence."

23. Some botanists consider the Cretaceous period the time of the first flowers.

24. Environmentalists have declared the spread of airborne pollutants a major environmental concern.

25. Physicians have named some birth defects "fetal alcohol syndrome."

EXERCISE 5-5

Sentence Patterns: Combining Sentences (5a-3)

Combine each group of sentences according to the designated sentence pattern. Omit all unnecessary repetitions, and do not alter meaning.

Example: **subject**   **verb**

El Salvador is in Central America.

El Salvador is next to Guatemala.

El Salvador is next to Honduras.

> *El Salvador is in Central America, next to Guatemala and Honduras.*

1. **subject**   **verb**

Pyramids still stand today.

The pyramids are Mayan.

The pyramids are enormous.

2. **subject**   **verb**   **direct object**

Mayan Indians settled El Salvador.

Other Indian tribes settled El Salvador.

They settled as early as 3000 BC.

3. **subject   verb   subject complement**

El Salvador's climate is agreeable.

The average temperature ranges from 73 to 80 degrees Fahrenheit.

That is the year-round temperature.

4. **subject   verb   indirect object   direct object**

The climate gives an opportunity.

The opportunity is for El Salvadorans.

They can play soccer.

They play on soccer fields throughout the country.

5. **subject   verb   direct object   object complement**

Spain made a Spanish colony.

El Salvador was the colony.

It happened in 1524.

EXERCISE 5-6

Adjectives and Adverbs: Identifying Function (5b-1)

In the following sentences underline each word functioning as an adjective (modifying a noun). Underline twice each word functioning as an adverb (modifying a verb, an adjective, or an adverb). Then draw an arrow from the modifier to the word it modifies.

Example:　Most people ordinarily assume that drinkable water will always be available to them.

1. Water conservation is becoming an urgent issue.

2. Some areas of the United States have severe water shortages, while others have abundant sources of drinkable water.

3. California, Arizona, and other parts of the Southwest are particularly affected by severe shortages.

4. As people continually move to areas where there is less water, the situation becomes increasingly dire.

5. There are numerous reasons for population growth in areas where water is scarce.

6. People want to live in a warm, sunny climate where they don't have to be inconvenienced occasionally by rain and snow.

7. The Sunbelt is attractive to industry too.

8. But the Southwest commonly has low precipitation and, because of the heat, high evaporation.

9. To make matters worse, the lengthy growing seasons encourage farmers to plant more crops and irrigate them copiously.

10. Scientists estimate that the average person uses approximately 140 gallons of water every day.

11. They further estimate that, for each person in the country, an additional 740 gallons are used every day for agriculture and another 700 gallons for industry.

12. One solution is to use snow melt from nearby mountains to irrigate fields.

13. Another solution is removal of saline from ocean water.

14. Still another answer has been to dam rivers and divert the flow to needy areas.

15. Unfortunately, there is only so much water, and even mighty rivers like the Colorado cannot meet the demand of the Southwest.

16. Even aquifers, those underground rock formations that yield fresh, clean water to deep wells, are fast being depleted by overuse.

17. Some parts of the country have abundant sources of water such as the Great Lakes, the Mississippi, and other rivers.

18. But getting potable water from places where it is plentiful to areas where it is scarce is a problem that has not been satisfactorily solved.

19. Neither have we discovered a practical and inexpensive way of desalinating seawater in amounts adequate to serve the need.

EXERCISE 5-7

Prepositions: Writing Sentences (5c-1)

These sentences use the nine most common prepositions in English: *of, in, to, for, at, on, from, with,* and *by*. Underline the prepositional phrases in each sentence, and then write original sentences that use the same prepositions. Underline your prepositional phrases.

> *Example:*   Babe Ruth is probably the most famous player <u>in baseball history</u>.

> *My brother is the smartest computer pro-grammer <u>in</u> Calhoun County.*

1. In a book by Mary Karr called *The Liars' Club,* the life in an East Texas refinery town in the 1960s looks distinctly unattractive.

2. The future for space stations is uncertain, especially in today's economic climate.

3. People should view solar eclipses only with proper eye protection.

4. In one school of thought, life on earth began somewhere else in the universe.

5. Contrary to other liquids, water freezes from the top.

6. At the surface of the hottest star, the temperature might be 200,000 degrees Fahrenheit.

7. Passover is a Jewish holiday celebrated from the fourteenth to the twenty-second of Nisan in the Jewish calendar, or sometime in March or April.

8. Quartz clocks use the vibrations of quartz crystals driving a motor at a precise rate.

9. With the increase of pollution after World War II, unrestrained waste and use of chemicals were seen by many people as a threat to the planet.

10. The CDC (Centers for Disease Control) based in Atlanta, Georgia, provides consultation on an international basis for the control of preventable diseases.

EXERCISE 5-8

Prepositional Phrases: Identifying Function (5c-1)

In the following paragraph, enclose all the prepositional phrases in parentheses and draw an arrow from each preposition to the word the phrase modifies.

Example: The fence post was embedded (in a block)(of cement).

   As you drive along the highway in the country, you often see beef cattle grazing in pastures. In contrast to dairy cows, which are raised for milk production, beef cattle are raised for their meat and are much larger. Three major breeds of beef cattle in the United States are Black Angus, Charolais, and Hereford. The Black Angus, or Aberdeen Angus, originated in eastern Scotland in the county of Angus. The Black Angus is readily identifiable by its smooth, black coat. It was first imported to the United States in the late 1800s. The Charolais is a fairly recent import, having come to this country by way of Mexico in 1936. The breed originated in France. Charolais cattle are white, and they grow quite large, an adult bull being almost twice the size of a Jersey milk cow, for example. Herefords were developed in Herefordshire, England, and were brought to the United States in the early 1800s. These beef cattle have white faces, reddish coats, and white markings. In addition to these major breeds of beef cattle, two other types are common: the Redpoll and the Shorthorn. These two are used for both dairy and beef production.

169

EXERCISE 5-9

Participles: Using *-ing* and *-ed* (5c-2)

Underline the appropriate participle in each sentence.

> *Example:* An (*amazed*, *amazing*) number of US political parties has come and gone.

1. The Know-Nothings were an (*interested*, *interesting*) political movement of the nineteenth century.

2. When outsiders inquired about (*supposed*, *supposing*) members, the members of the secret groups said they knew nothing.

3. A (*surprised*, *surprising*) fact is that the Know-Nothing party almost won New York in the 1854 election.

4. In fact, this (*unknown*, *unknowing*) party did take Massachusetts and Delaware in that election.

5. The (*guided*, *guiding*) principle of the party was to keep recent immigrants out of political office.

6. Their goal was to combat (*deteriorated*, *deteriorating*) "foreign" influences.

7. But members of the party could not agree on the (*burned*, *burning*) issue of slavery.

8. Many Know-Nothings wanted to reconcile the (*distinguished*, *distinguishing*) differences between North and South.

9. Among these (*dedicated*, *dedicating*) party members was Millard Fillmore.

10. Fillmore joined the (*declined*, *declining*) party following his presidency.

11. The power of this (*intrigued*, *intriguing*) party was broken in the election of 1856.

12. Fillmore and his party, under the newly (*acquired*, *acquiring*) name of "the American party," won only Maryland.

EXERCISE 5-10

Verbal Phrases: Identifying Function (5c-2)

Each of these sentences contains an italicized verbal phrase. On the line at the left, identify the type of phrase—participial (p), gerund (g), or infinitive (i). If the phrase functions as an adjective or an adverb, draw an arrow to the word it modifies. If it functions as a noun, indicate on the line whether it is subject (S), direct object (DO), subject complement (SC), or object of a preposition (OP).

   Example: <u>i DO</u> Reading before writing helps *me focus on an idea.*

_____ 1. Students asked *to write about how they write* say a variety of things.

_____ 2. Most agree that they must first have *something to write about.*

_____ 3. *Finding a subject of interest* is often the most difficult part.

_____ 4. Besides *being interested in the subject,* the writer must know something about it.

_____ 5. When *composing a personal experience essay,* writers often find that the words flow easily.

_____ 6. *Writing a research paper* is much more difficult.

_____ 7. Some students say that the hardest papers for *them to write* are reactions or responses to journal articles.

_____ 8. They are uncertain about the angle *to take in their response.*

_____ 9. When *writing research papers,* some students are more organized than others.

_____ 10. The organized students make note cards to *organize the informa-tion they have gathered* and use the cards as a guide for their writing.

_____ 11. Students differ on the usefulness of *writing an outline.*

_____ 12. Some students report that they make outlines *to organize their thoughts for any of their papers.*

_____ 13. They find it exciting *to write once without an outline.*

_____ 14. They begin by *putting down whatever they are thinking on the subject.*

_____ 15. Rereading what they've written lets *them see if the paper follows along logically.*

_____ 16. They make necessary changes, *adding needed details.*

_____ 17. Sometimes, *seeing irrelevancies,* they delete material.

_____ 18. Since errors are *to be expected when we write,* most writers make corrections at some point.

_____ 19. Some writers edit as they write, others *preferring to wait until they have stopped writing.*

_____ 20. The way students write is often determined by the subject and the amount of time they have for *writing the paper.*

EXERCISE 5-11

Verbal Phrases: Revising Sentences (5c-2, 3)

Rewrite the following sentences by reducing the italicized words to verbal phrases as indicated. Be careful not to alter the meaning when you make your changes.

Example: Grandfather planted seeds indoors in February *so that he could have an early start on his garden in May.* (*Infinitive.*)

> Grandfather planted seeds indoors in February to have an early start on his garden in May.

1. Oceans are the home of many of earth's creatures, *and the oceans cover 70 percent of the earth's surface.* (*Participle.*)

2. The oceans, *which are all interconnected,* are named Pacific, Indian, Atlantic, and Arctic. (*Participle.*)

3. The continental shelves are the parts of the oceans *that are best known.* (*Participle.*)

4. Most commercial fishing is done here, *because the waters are relatively shallow.* (*Absolute.*)

5. Although *it makes up a major part of the earth,* the ocean is still largely unknown. (*Gerund.*)

6. For most people, the very edge of the ocean is the part *that they know the best.* (*Participle.*)

7. They like going to the beach *so they can absorb the sights and sounds of the ocean.* (*Infinitive.*)

8. Oceanographers spend their lives studying the oceans *so that they can know its riches and its perils.* (*Infinitive.*)

9. *So they can get a comprehensive view of the ocean environment,* they study geography, ecology, physics, chemistry, marine biology, and meteorology. (*Infinitive.*)

10. *When you go to the beach next time,* think of the ocean as the habitat for creatures *that share the planet with you.* (*Gerund, then participle.*)

EXERCISE 5-12

Subordinate Clauses: Identifying Function (5c-4)

Each of these sentences has one subordinate clause, italicized. On the line at the left, tell the function of the clause—adjective (adj), adverb (adv), or noun (n). If the clause functions as an adjective or an adverb, draw an arrow to the word it modifies. If it functions as a noun, indicate on the line whether it is subject (S), direct object (DO), subject complement (SC), or object of a preposition (OP).

Example: __adv__ Acquaintance rapes will not end *unless "no" really comes to mean "no."*

_____ 1. Colleges and universities have become concerned about *how to prevent date and gang rapes.*

_____ 2. Rape occurs *whenever a person is intimidated into submitting to sexual intercourse.*

_____ 3. Some surveys show *that 25 percent of women on campuses report having had sex against their wills.*

_____ 4. Other surveys show rates *that are much higher.*

_____ 5. Perhaps women *who are attending college today* are more willing to report such abuse than in the past, or the incidence may actually be increasing.

_____ 6. The attitude of some males is *that a date "owes" them a sexual encounter.*

_____ 7. Colleges have begun campaigns *that combat such an attitude.*

_____ 8. Some of these moves come from campus administrators *who institute educational programs.*

_____ 9. Sometimes fraternities are the ones *that make the first move.*

_____ 10. Rape prevention workshops are one means *that has been adopted.*

_____ 11. Another is educational brochures *that have been prepared and circulated by fraternities, sororities, and college administrators.*

_____ 12. These methods are aimed at changing attitudes, but, *even though these efforts may make some difference,* attitudes change slowly.

_____ 13. California made an attempt to hasten change *when the legislature adopted a resolution suggesting college suspension or expulsion of perpetrators.*

_____ 14. New York also has taken a stand against campus rape by appointing a governor's task force on rape and sexual assault, *which recommended adoption of prevention programs at the state and city of New York universities.*

_____ 15. The real test of these measures is *whether they are effective in deterring campus rapes.*

EXERCISE 5-13

Subordinate Clauses: Combining Sentences (5c-4)

Combine each of the following pairs of sentences by making one of the sentences in each pair into a subordinate clause. Use the connector shown in parentheses and omit any words that are unnecessary in the combined sentence. Use correct punctuation as described in 5c-4.

Example: One magazine is the *National Geographic*.
            Its older editions remain popular on family bookshelves. (*Whose.*)

One magazine whose older editions remain popular on family bookshelves is the National Geographic.

1. It first came out in 1888. (*When.*)
   The *National Geographic* had no pictures.

2. It was rather plain in its beginnings. (*Though.*)
   It is now one of the most colorful of magazines.

3. Gilbert H. Grosvenor founded the National Geographic Society. (*Who.*)
   He was its president for fifty-five years.

4. Subscribers are called "members." (*Who.*)
   They number 10.5 million.

5. The *National Geographic* has published reports from adventurers.
   They have traveled all over the world. (*Who.*)

6. The written reports are often interesting and exciting. (*Although.*)
   It is the pictures that attract many readers.

7. The *Geographic* has published colorful pictures from distant lands.
   (*Because.*)
   Its readers know a little about the culture of many peoples.

8. Its readers have firsthand accounts from explorers.
   They have traveled to exotic places. (*Who.*)

9. A familiar explorer was Jacques Cousteau.
   He recorded his underwater travels. (*Who.*)

10. Reinhold Messner was another *National Geographic* explorer who made
    history.
    He climbed to the top of Mt. Everest. (*When.*)

11. Many explorers have received research support from the Society.
    It has an annual budget of more than $5 million. (*Which.*)

Name _____ Date _____

EXERCISE 5-14

Subordinate Clauses: Writing Sentences (5c-4)

In the following sentences underline each subordinate clause and circle each subordinating word (subordinating conjunction or relative pronoun). Then compose new sentences that use the same subordinating words. Underline your subordinate clauses and circle the subordinating words.

Example: Elephants never forget <u>how a trainer treats them.</u>

Charlene doesn't remember how <u>she made</u>
<u>the cookies.</u>

1. Some people wonder whether vitamin supplements are good for their health.

2. In fact, vitamins might be more important than people once thought.

3. It has been surmised that some vitamins might ward off cancer and heart disease.

4. Vitamin C, which was once suggested for fighting colds, may instead re-duce risk of cancer and heart disease.

5. Vitamin A, or beta carotene, may reduce the risk of many kinds of cancer that are common to either men or women.

6. Because all vitamins are found in foods, the best source of these nutrients is naturally in the food we eat.

7. Vitamin C is best found in citrus fruits and beta carotene, which converts to Vitamin A in the body, is available in dark green leafy vegetables.

8. People who do not regularly eat a balanced diet might be better off taking a comprehensive vitamin supplement.

9. At the same time, they should be aware that vitamin pills do not provide all the nutrients of food.

10. Proteins, carbohydrates, and fiber are three examples of essential nutrients that are not available in vitamin pills.

11. Even though scientists do not fully understand the additional, lesser known nutrients, they recognize their value.

12. The answer seems to be that vitamin pills have value mainly as supplements to a regular balanced diet.

EXERCISE 5-15

Compound Constructions: Revising Clauses (5d)

Make two kinds of compound sentences by joining the following pairs of sentences *twice,* first with coordinating conjunctions and then with conjunctive adverbs. Try to use the most appropriate connectors. Remember that coordinating conjunctions should be preceded by commas; conjunctive adverbs that begin their clauses should be preceded by semicolons.

Example: People experiencing the heat of summer often yearn for relaxation in the cool north woods. They begin packing their bags for Wisconsin.

> People experiencing the heat of summer often yearn for relaxation in the cool north woods, so they begin packing their bags for Wisconsin.
>
> People experiencing the heat of summer often yearn for relaxation in the cool north woods; then they begin packing their bags for Wisconsin.

1. Madison is the capital of Wisconsin. Milwaukee is the largest city.

2. In summer Wisconsin's lakes attract swimmers and boaters. In winter they attract iceboaters and snowmobilers.

3. Wisconsin is the nation's leading milk producer. It is called "America's Dairyland."

4. Wisconsin's cities are mainly Democratic. Its rural areas are largely Republican.

exer
5

5. Milwaukee was once a fur-trading center. Now it is known for its manufacturing.

6. Milwaukee is known also for its variety of ethnic cultures. Most of its residents were born in the United States.

7. The Wisconsin climate is characterized by warm summers and severely cold winters. Along the lake shorelines the temperatures are somewhat modified.

8. The Lake Michigan shoreline is a flypath for migrating birds. Bird watchers flock to eastern Wisconsin every spring and fall.

9. Jean Nicolet, a French explorer, landed on the shore of Green Bay in 1634. He is said to be the first white person to set foot in Wisconsin.

10. The Ringling Brothers started their first circus in Baraboo, Wisconsin, in 1884. The Circus World Museum there commemorates this event with circus memorabilia.

EXERCISE 5-16

Compound Constructions: Combining Words and Phrases (5d)

The following pairs of sentences are wordy and repetitious. Rewrite each of them into a single main clause by compounding words and phrases. Since the coordinating conjunction will not be joining main clauses, it should *not* be preceded by a comma.

> *Example:* Meteorologists use barometers for measuring air pressure. They use hygrometers for measuring relative humidity.
>
> *Meteorologists use barometers for measuring air pressure and hygrometers for measuring relative humidity.*

1. The sun's rays strike the earth at a 90-degree angle at the equator. They strike the earth at acute angles at the poles.

2. Hurricane Andrew uprooted trees. Hurricane Andrew destroyed houses.

3. Forecasters analyze reports from hurricane hunters. They learn where the hurricane's center is located.

4. Hurricane hunters are US Air Force pilots. Hurricane hunters are US Navy pilots.

5. Methods of weather forecasting differ in the kinds of maps used. They differ in the details given.

6. To forecast weather, meteorologists must know present conditions. They must know past conditions.

7. High-pressure winds blow clockwise in the Northern Hemisphere. They blow counterclockwise in the Southern Hemisphere.

8. Precipitation is water droplets that fall to earth. Precipitation is ice crystals that fall to earth.

9. Clouds precede the arrival of a warm front. Steady rain or snow precedes the arrival of a warm front.

10. Much of the sun's energy is absorbed by the earth. This energy is changed into heat.

EXERCISE 5-17

Order of Sentences: Rewriting Sentences (5e)

Rewrite the passive sentences to active voice and the inverted sentences to normal order. Be careful to keep meaning and verb time the same.

Examples: Some people are intimidated by computer technology.

> *Computer technology intimidates some people.*

There are some people who are afraid to use computers.

> *Some people are afraid to use computers.*

Change from passive to active.

1. Computers have been accepted as a part of everyday life by almost everyone.

2. Computer specialists are called on to assist decision makers.

3. The speed of computer transactions has come to be expected by most people.

4. Long-distance telephone calls are completed by computers in a matter of seconds.

5. Airline and other reservations are made almost immediately by computers.

Change from inverted to normal order.

6. It is easy to forget what life was like before computers.

7. There are inexpensive computer programs being marketed.

8. There are some programs that are still costly.

9. It is programs like these that are newer and more specialized.

10. There are many people who depend on computers for survival on the job.

EXERCISE 5-18

Compound, Complex, and Compound-Complex Sentences: Writing (5f)

The sentences below have structures that are compound, complex, or compound-complex. Observe the structure of each one; then write a sentence of your own that uses the same clause pattern. Use the same conjunctions or different ones.

> *Example:*   Some of the most familiar stories are fables that originated many centuries ago. (*Complex.*)
>
> *The limerick is a humorous verse that is often ribald and erotic.*

1. The fable is an ancient mode of instruction that takes the form of a story narrative. (*Complex.*)

2. It is somewhat like a tale because it tells a story and somewhat like a parable because it conveys a hidden meaning. (*Complex.*)

3. But the fable is unlike both tale and parable in that its primary purpose is moral instruction. (*Complex.*)

4. The fable seeks improvement in human conduct, but it conceals this purpose within the tale. (*Compound.*)

5. A fable anthropomorphizes animals and plants when it endows them with personalities and motivations, and in so doing it indirectly instructs the audience about its morals. (*Compound-complex.*)

6. A fabulist, or a person who writes fables, advises audiences about their behavior; at the same time, the fabulist avoids directly telling audiences that their behavior needs improving. (*Compound-complex.*)

7. Besides instructing an audience on moral improvement, the fabulist sometimes draws attention to praiseworthy behavior that others might seek to emulate. (*Complex.*)

8. The fabulist uses anthropomorphism effectively; another tool for creating a fable is humor. (*Compound.*)

9. One of the most famous fabulists was Aesop, an ancient Greek who wrote his fables in the sixth century BC. (*Complex.*)

10. One of Aesop's most famous fables is "The Fox and the Grapes"; another is "The Tortoise and the Hare." (*Compound.*)

Chapter 6

Case of Nouns and Pronouns

Case is the form of a noun or a pronoun that shows how it functions in a sentence: *subjective* for subjects and words referring to subjects, *objective* for objects, and *possessive* to show ownership. The following chart shows the case forms of nouns and pronouns.

● Case forms of nouns and pronouns

		SUBJECTIVE	OBJECTIVE	POSSESSIVE
NOUNS				
	Singular	boy	boy	boy's
		Buick	Buick	Buick's
	Plural	boys	boys	boys'
		Buicks	Buicks	Buicks'
PERSONAL PRONOUNS				
	Singular	I	me	my, mine
		you	you	your, yours
		he	him	his, his
		she	her	her, hers
		it	it	its, its
	Plural	we	us	our, ours
		you	you	your, yours
		they	them	their, theirs

	SUBJECTIVE	OBJECTIVE	POSSESSIVE
RELATIVE AND INTERROGATIVE PRONOUNS	who whoever which, that, what	whom whomever which, that, what	whose, whose
INDEFINITE PRONOUNS	everybody	everybody	everybody's

6a Use the subjective case for all parts of compound subjects and for subject complements.

Use the subjective form when a pronoun is a subject or a subject complement (see 5a and 5b) and for all compounds of these functions.

SUBJECT

I came late.

Carlos and *I* came late.

SUBJECT COMPLEMENT

It was *she* who rang the bell.

The co-chairpersons were *he* and *Emily.*

In speech and other informal usage, it is common to say *It's me* or *It's him*, but these forms are not generally acceptable in formal, written English. If as a writer you're uncomfortable using the correct forms, such as *The guiltiest one was he* (and you're right—that sentence does sound awkward), you have the option of revising your sentence to some other grammatically correct phrasing, such as *He was the guiltiest one.*

6b Use the objective case for compound objects.

Use the objective form when the pronoun is the direct or indirect object of a verb or verbal or the object of a preposition (see 5a and 5c) and for all compounds of these functions.

OBJECT OF VERB

We provided *him* with dry clothes.

We provided *Jodie* and *him* with dry clothes.

INDIRECT OBJECT

We gave *him* dry clothes.

We gave *him* and *Jodie* dry clothes.

OBJECT OF A PREPOSITION

The party was for *me*.

The party was for *Stavros* and *me*.

OBJECT OF A VERBAL

After taking *him* home, she went shopping. [Object of gerund.]

Having nominated *Lin Wong* and *me*, the committee adjourned. [Object of participle.]

We tried to find *him* and his *roommate* in the crowd. [Object of infinitive.]

 A test for case forms in compound constructions

1. Identify a compound construction (one connected by *and, but, or, nor*).

   (*He, Him*) and (*I, me*) won the prize.

   The prize went to (*he, him*) and (*I, me*).

2. Write a separate sentence for each part of the compound.

   (*He, Him*) won the prize. (*I, Me*) won the prize.

   The prize went to (*he, him*). The prize went to (*I, me*).

3. Choose the pronoun that sounds correct.

   He won the prize. *I* won the prize. [Subjective.]

   The prize went to *him*. The prize went to *me*. [Objective.]

4. Put the separate sentences back together.

   He and *I* won the prize.

   The prize went to *him* and *me*.

6c **Use the appropriate case when the plural pronouns *we* and *us* occur with a noun.**

In the following sentences, the pronouns—*we* and *us*—are in the same case as their appositive nouns. To determine which pronoun to use, read each sentence without the appositive; your acquired sense of grammar will tell you which pronoun is correct. See 5c-5.

The coach threw a party for *us* players. [Read: *The coach threw a party for us. Us* is the object of the preposition *for,* and *players* is its appositive.]

We players also held a party of our own. [Read: *We also held a party of our own. We* is the subject of the sentence and *players* is its appositive.]

6d In appositives the case of a pronoun depends on the function of the word it describes or identifies.

In the following sentences (in contrast to the sentences above), the pronoun is the *appositive*, renaming its preceding noun. The case of the pronoun is the same as that of the noun it renames. To determine which pronoun to use, read the sentence without the word the appositive identifies. See 5c-5.

Two victims, Homer and *I*, sued the company. [Read: *Homer and I sued the company.* The appositive pronoun, *I*, with *Homer*, renames *victims*, the subject of the sentence.]

The company was sued by two victims, Homer and *me*. [Read: *The company was sued by Homer and me.* The appositive pronoun, *me*, with *Homer*, renames *victims*, the object of a preposition.]

6e The case of a pronoun after *than* or *as* in a comparison depends on the meaning.

The case of a pronoun after *than* or *as* in a comparison is what it would be if the clause were completed.

Axel likes pizza more than *I* [*like pizza*].
Axel likes pizza more than [*he likes*] *me*.
Axel likes pizza as much as *I* [*like pizza*].
Axel likes pizza as much as [*he likes*] *me*.

If you don't like the sound of sentences such as *Axel likes pizza more than I*, add the verb form at the end: *Axel likes pizza more than I do.*

6f Use the objective case for pronouns that are subjects or objects of infinitives.

Infinitives, being verbals, can take subjects and objects even though they cannot function as verbs. Subjects and objects of infinitives are in the objective case. (See 5c-2.)

We want *him* to learn. [*Him* is the subject of the infinitive *to learn.*]

To win *her* over requires patience. [*Her* is the object of the infinitive *to win.*]

6g The case of the pronoun *who* depends on its function in its clause.

1 At the beginning of questions use *who* if the question is about a subject, *whom* if it is about an object.

Who ate the macaroni? [Question about a subject. Compare: *They ate the macaroni.*]

Whom are you kidding? [Question about an object. Compare: *You are kidding them.*]

In speech and informal writing, *who* is commonly used whenever it begins a question. Formal writing, however, requires *whom* for objects.

SPOKEN

Who did you appoint to the position?   *Who* did you write the letter to?

WRITTEN

Whom did you appoint to the position?   To *whom* did you write the letter?

 Tests for *who* versus *whom*

QUESTIONS

1. Pose the question.

   (Who, Whom) makes that decision?   *(Who, Whom)* does one ask?

2. Answer the question, using a personal pronoun. Choose the pronoun that sounds correct.

   (She, Her) makes that decision. *She* makes that decision.
   One asks *(she, her)*. One asks *her*.

3. Use the same case *(who* or *whom)* in the question.

   Who makes that decision? [Subjective.]
   Whom does one ask? [Objective.]

SUBORDINATE CLAUSES

1. Locate the subordinate clause.

   Few people know *(who, whom) they should ask.*
   They are unsure *(who, whom) makes the decision.*

2. Rewrite the subordinate clause as a separate sentence, substituting a personal pronoun for the *who* form. Choose the pronoun that sounds correct.

> They should ask *(she, her)*. They should ask *her*.
>
> *(She, her)* makes the decision. *She* makes the decision.

3. Use the same case *(who* or *whom)* in the subordinate clause.

> Few people know *whom* they should ask. [Objective.]
>
> They are unsure *who* makes the decision. [Subjective.]

ca
6h

▲**2** In subordinate clauses use *who* and *whoever* for all subjects, *whom* and *whomever* for all objects.

The case of the relative pronoun is determined by its function *in its own clause,* not by the function of the clause in the sentence.

> I do not know *who* can help me. [*Who* is the subject of the subordinate clause *who can help me.* Compare: *She can help me.* The entire subordinate clause is the direct object of the verb *know.*]
>
> *Whoever* wants the dog can have it. [*Whoever* is the subject of the subordinate clause *Whoever wants the dog.* Compare: *He wants the dog.*]
>
> I know *whom* he was writing about. [*Whom* is the object of the preposition *about.* Compare: *He was writing about her.*]
>
> I do not know *whom* to criticize. [*Whom* is the object of the infinitive to *criticize.* Compare: *to criticize him.*]
>
> She will hire *whomever* she chooses. [*Whomever* is the object of the verb *chooses.* Compare: *She chooses him.*]

6h Ordinarily, use a possessive pronoun or noun immediately before a gerund.

A *gerund* is the *-ing* form of a verb used as a noun (see 5c-2).

> We couldn't listen to *his* singing.
>
> *Oxnard College's* running ruined our game plan.

While these sentences are grammatically correct, the use of the possessive might at times sound awkward to the ears of both writers and readers. If you are in doubt about the sound of your sentences, revise them. The second sentence above could be recast as follows:

> The running of *Oxnard College* ruined our game plan.

See 23b on the misuse of apostrophes in possessive personal pronouns.

See Exercises 6-1 and 6-2.

Related Exercises: 5-2, 23-1, and 23-2.

EXERCISE 6-1

Pronoun Case: Revising Sentences

A. Change the following statements to questions that begin with *who* or *whom* as replacements for the underlined words.

Example: <u>Professor Rogers</u> will be teaching this class.

Who will be teaching this class?

1. The new dean will be <u>Dr. Brown</u>.

2. This car belongs to <u>Mr. Jackson</u>.

3. <u>Kathryn</u> plans to drive to Indiana.

4. We can count on <u>Jacob and Sarah</u> to work at the hospital.

5. I can ask <u>Mr. Schwartz</u> about organic gardening.

6. <u>Brad</u> was the last person to leave the room.

7. I should call <u>Mrs. Shipman</u> if I'm delayed.

8. Applicants should send their checks to <u>John Iverson</u>.

9. We can ask <u>George</u> to make the sign.

10. <u>Everyone</u> has read the assigned chapter.

B. In the sentences below, cross out each underlined noun (or phrase) and substitute an appropriate pronoun.

Example: The committee should have appointed <u>Kevin</u> and me.
               him

1. The handmade ornament is one donated by <u>Diane</u> and me.

2. I am not as smart as <u>Peter</u>, but my grades are just as good.

3. <u>Elizabeth</u> and Karen were born on the same day.

4. It must have been <u>the students in Mrs. Linden's class</u> who left the books.

5. The dispute was between <u>Jim</u> and the clerk.

6. <u>My sister</u> and my brother bought a tape deck.

7. Hardly any love remains between <u>Beth</u> and me.

8. After practice, the batboy brought <u>Janet</u> and me cold drinks.

9. <u>Julie</u> and the teacher disagreed over the grade.

10. We expected <u>Michael</u> to win, not Delgado.

11. The winning chess players—<u>André</u> and you—will get free tickets to the concert.

12. No one is more deserving than you and <u>André</u>.

13. I've selected the other members of the group—you and <u>Pablo</u>.

14. Ingrid cannot play chess as well as <u>André</u> and you.

15. The game was well played by <u>Luis</u> as well as by Ines.

C. Circle the correct pronoun in each pair below.

   Example: (*We,* *Us*) math majors are required to take the class.

1. I explained to the policeman, "I'd appreciate (*you, your*) giving me just a warning."

2. The bank would not grant (*we, us*) fraternity members a loan.

3. Show the map to (*whoever, whomever*) plans to drive.

4. (*We, Us*) students all get discounts.

5. John is stronger than either Larry or (*I, me*).

6. Chris tells old jokes to (*whoever, whomever*) will listen.

7. The two latecomers, Judith and (*I, me*), agreed on who would do the work.

8. (*We, Us*) freshmen no longer are subject to hazing from sophomores.

9. Between you and (*I, me*), I think the play was a flop.

10. (*Who, Whom*) did you meet in the library?

11. The members of the chorus knew (*who, whom*) was singing off key.

12. And they were wondering about (*who, whom*) would talk with that person.

13. (*Who, Whom*) will we ask to give the keynote address?

14. Senator Jackson was apologetic about (*him, his*) missing the keynote address.

15. Most of the voters expected that the election would be won by the candidate (*who, whom*) the governor openly favored.

16. (*Who, Whom*) do you think will win the election?

17. Patricia was asking herself (*who, whom*) she should ask to write letters of recommendation for her.

18. She decided to ask people (*who, whom*) she had worked for and people (*who, whom*) were acquainted with her character.

EXERCISE 6-2

Pronoun Case: Rewriting a Text

Rewrite this short narrative, changing first-person references to third-person pronouns. Begin the first sentence as follows:

Sherlynn decided to drive out to Laramie, Wyoming, . . .

When you finish, the narrative will be written from the perspective of an observer.

I decided to drive out to Laramie, Wyoming, by myself last June to visit my sister Laura and her family. No one could have been more surprised at the turn of events than I! From my departure in Minnesota to my arrival in Wyoming, there was one incident after another.

Like any careful car owner, I had my car serviced before I left—oil changed and the whole deal. I even had it washed—the super duper deluxe treatment. Then, because there was a good chance of rain over the next couple of days, I and my next-door neighbor decided to apply Rain-X to my windshield so I'd have less trouble seeing the road during downpours.

As we anticipated, there was rain. In fact, it rained the entire first day. But at least the Rain-X worked: the raindrops beaded off the windshield with little help from the wipers. And at least it wasn't hot. I was comfortable in a tee shirt and lightweight jeans. I stopped overnight at a small town in South Dakota, where I found a little restaurant that served locally grown beef—plus something that kept me and my stomach awake all night. Before turning in, I spent some time walking along the dusty streets to remind my legs that they still had a function other than taking over from the cruise control whenever called upon.

The next day I drove through the Badlands—VERY impressive as dirt piles go! Then of course it was important for me and my car to visit the Black Hills. The landscape there is lovely, but I skipped a close-up of Mount Rushmore because the parking lot was too full. Driving away from the area, I was sorry to leave the dark green hills behind but had no regrets about getting away from all the people. I think I get claustrophic when I'm too closed in.

Did I tell you that the air-conditioning in my car had quit working the day I left? Now the weather was turning hot as I struck out into western South Dakota, and I was getting quite uncomfortable, even in shorts and tee shirt. So my attitude was not good when I entered a construction zone and freshly applied blacktop. My attitude did not improve when a passing truck kicked up a rock onto my windshield and cracked it—a jagged, six-inch gash near the wipers. My mental totaling of the repair bill—air conditioner and now windshield—was damaging my confidence in myself as an intrepid traveler.

Well, I made it to Laramie, and I did enjoy myself. One day, Laura and I drove up into the mountains, and the air was cold. In fact, we noticed that most of the hiking trails were still snow-covered. Was the trip worth the trouble? It was, but I wish it hadn't been necessary for me to take the car directly to the shop when I returned.

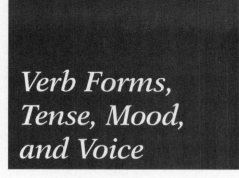

Chapter 7

Verb Forms, Tense, Mood, and Voice

The verb is the central core of the sentence, changing forms to meet a variety of language needs. In this chapter, verbs are explained in terms of form, tense, mood, voice, person, and number.

 Terms used to describe verbs

FORM

The spelling of the verb that conveys time, mood, and other information. *Kick, kicked, kicking,* and *kicks* are forms of *kick.* (See p. 202.)

TENSE

The time of the verb's action—for instance, present (*kick*), past (*kick<u>ed</u>*), future (<u>*will*</u> *kick*). (See p. 209.)

MOOD

The attitude of the verb's speaker or writer—the difference, for example, in *I kick the ball,* <u>*Kick*</u> *the ball,* and *I* <u>*suggest that you*</u> *kick the ball.* (See p. 215.)

VOICE

The distinction between the **active,** in which the subject performs the verb's action (*I kick the ball*), and the **passive,** in which the subject is acted upon (*The* <u>*ball is kicked*</u> *by me*). (See p. 216.)

PERSON

The verb form that reflects whether the subject is speaking (*I/we kick the ball*), spoken to (*You kick the ball*), or spoken about (*She kicks the ball*). (See 8a.)

NUMBER

The verb form that reflects whether the subject is singular (*The girl kicks the ball*) or plural (*Girls kick the ball*). (See 7c, 8a.)

VERB FORMS

All verbs except *be* have five forms. The first three forms are the verb's **principal parts:** the infinitive (or plain form), the past tense, and the past participle. The fourth form is the present participle, and the fifth is the *-s* form.

Forms of common verbs

PLAIN FORM	PAST TENSE	PAST PARTICIPLE	PRESENT PARTICIPLE	-S FORM
Regular verbs				
ask	asked	asked	asking	asks
close	closed	closed	closing	closes
open	opened	opened	opening	opens
pass	passed	passed	passing	passes
scratch	scratched	scratched	scratching	scratches
talk	talked	talked	talking	talks
Irregular verbs				
be (am, are)	was, were	been	being	is
come	came	come	coming	comes
do	did	done	doing	does
go	went	gone	going	goes
have	had	had	having	has
swim	swam	swum	swimming	swims
write	wrote	written	writing	writes

The **infinitive**—or **plain**—form of the verb has no endings. It expresses present time when the subject is *I, we, you, they,* or any plural noun:

I *go.*   You *come.*   Dogs *scratch.*

The **past-tense** form indicates completed action. Verbs have only one past-tense form, used with all subjects:

I *went.* You *went.* They *went.* The car *went.* Cars *went.*

You *swam.* We *swam.* The frog *swam.* The frog and his brothers *swam.*

Dogs *scratched.* Fido *scratched.* The sweater *scratched.* I *scratched.*

I *passed.* The truck *passed.* The students *passed.*

As the chart above shows, the past tense of regular verbs is usually formed by adding -*d* or -*ed* to the plain form, although some of our most common verbs are formed irregularly. (See also 7a.)

The **past participle,** which for regular verbs has the same form as the past tense, combines with *have, has,* or *had:*

I *have gone.*   Joshua *has swum.*   Dogs *have scratched.*   I *had passed.*

It also combines with a form of *be* in the passive voice:

The windows *were washed.*   The floors *are being scrubbed.*

The past participle may be used as an adjective to modify nouns and pronouns:

The freshly *scrubbed* floors look shiny.

The *closed* door is *unlocked.*

All verbs form their **present participle** by the addition of -*ing* to their plain form: *going, passing, scratching, being, having.* This form may combine with a helping verb to form a verb phrase, called the **progressive form,** used to indicate a continuing activity. (See 7d.)

I *am going.*   The dog *has been scratching.*   Joshua *was swimming.*

The -*ing* form may also serve as a modifier or as a noun:

Scratching dogs don't bite. [Adjective modifying *dogs.*]

Joshua cools off after work by *swimming.* [Noun functioning as object of the preposition *by.*]

Without a helping verb, the -*ing* form cannot function as the verb in a sentence. (See 10c.)

The **-s form** of all verbs except *be* and *have* is made by adding -*s* or -*es* to the plain form of the verb: *opens, closes, brings, touches.* The *be* and *have* forms also end in -*s: be* changes to *is,* and *have* to *has.* The -*s* form of all verbs shows present-time or habitual action when the subject is *he, she, it,* or any singular noun or pronoun. (See 7e-1.)

She *goes.*   Joshua *swims.*   The dog *scratches.*   Everybody *passes.*

Helping, or **auxiliary, verbs** combine with other verbs in verb phrases to indicate time and other meanings. (See Tense, p. 209.) These are the most common helping verbs:

be able to	had better	must	used to
be supposed to	have to	ought to	will
can	may	shall	would
could	might	should	

Forms of *be:* am, is, are, was, were, been, being

Forms of *have:* have, has, had, having

Forms of *do:* do, does, did

See 7d for more on helping verbs.

7a Use the correct form of regular and irregular verbs.

Most verbs are **regular,** forming their past tense and past participles with -*d* or -*ed* added to the plain form: *expect, expected, expected; wash, washed, washed.* Regular forms do not often cause problems in writing. Some verbs, however, do not have predictable past tense and past participle forms. The following list contains the principal parts of some of the nearly two hundred **irregular verbs** in English, arranged in the order dictionaries use.

Principal parts of common irregular verbs

PLAIN FORM	PAST TENSE	PAST PARTICIPLE
arise	arose	arisen
become	became	become
begin	began	begun
bid	bid	bid
bite	bit	bitten, bit
bleed	bled	bled
blow	blew	blown
break	broke	broken
bring	brought	brought
burst	burst	burst
buy	bought	bought
catch	caught	caught
choose	chose	chosen
come	came	come
cut	cut	cut
dive	dived, dove	dived
do	did	done
draw	drew	drawn
dream	dreamed, dreamt	dreamed, dreamt
drink	drank	drunk
drive	drove	driven

PLAIN FORM	PAST TENSE	PAST PARTICIPLE
eat	ate	eaten
fall	fell	fallen
find	found	found
flee	fled	fled
fly	flew	flown
forget	forgot	forgotten, forgot
freeze	froze	frozen
get	got	got, gotten
give	gave	given
go	went	gone
grow	grew	grown
hang	hung (suspend)	hung
hang	hanged (executed)	hanged
hear	heard	heard
hide	hid	hidden
hold	held	held
keep	kept	kept
know	knew	known
lay	laid	laid
lead	led	led
leave	left	left
let	let	let
lie	lay	lain
light	lighted, lit	lighted, lit
lose	lost	lost
pay	paid	paid
plead	pleaded (pled)	pleaded (pled)
prove	proved	proved, proven
ride	rode	ridden
ring	rang	rung
rise	rose	risen
run	ran	run
say	said	said
see	saw	seen
set	set	set
shake	shook	shaken
sing	sang, sung	sung
sink	sank, sunk	sunk
sit	sat	sat
slide	slid	slid
speak	spoke	spoken
spring	sprang, sprung	sprung
stand	stood	stood
steal	stole	stolen
swim	swam	swum
swing	swung	swung
take	took	taken
tear	tore	torn
throw	threw	thrown

vb
7a

PLAIN FORM	PAST TENSE	PAST PARTICIPLE
wear	wore	worn
wind	wound	wound
write	wrote	written

7b Distinguish between *sit* and *set,* *lie* and *lay,* and *rise* and *raise.*

The principal parts of *sit* and *set,* *lie* and *lay,* and *rise* and *raise* are often confused because of their similarities of form.

sit	sat	sat
set	set	set
lie	lay	lain
lay	laid	laid
rise	rose	risen
raise	raised	raised

Sit, *lie,* and *rise* are **intransitive verbs;** *set,* *lay,* and *raise* are **transitive verbs,** meaning they take objects.

Intransitive (no objects)
They *sit (sat, have sat)* in class like zombies.
The books *are sitting* on the table. [Present progressive of *sit.*]
I often *lie* awake at night. [Present of *lie.*]
Last night I *lay* awake half the night. [Past of *lie.*]
I *have lain* awake every night this week. [Present perfect of *lie.*]
The bread dough *rises* faster with active yeast. [Present of *rise.*]

Transitive (with objects)
We *set* the pole against the wall yesterday. [Past of *set;* object is *pole.*]
She has *set* the baby in the chair. [Present perfect of *set;* object is *baby.*]
Lay the books on the desk. [Present of *lay;* object is *books.*]
I *laid* the books on the desk this morning. [Past of *lay;* object is *books.*]
I *haven't laid* the books down yet. [Present perfect of *lay;* object is *books.*]
The crane easily *raised* the heavy timbers. [Past of *raise;* object is *timbers.*]

7c Use the *-s* and *-ed* forms of the verb when they are required.

The present-tense verb form *-s (asks)* and the past-tense and past-participle form *-ed (asked)* often are not pronounced in speech and might therefore mistakenly be omitted in writing. Be especially careful not to omit the ending when the verb's plain form ends in sounds like *s, sk,* or *g* and when the ending does not add another syllable.

> When Bobby *asked* [not *ask*] to leave the room, his teacher *excused* [not *excuse*] him.
>
> Ramon was *supposed* [not *suppose*] to be here at five o'clock.
>
> I *used* [not *use*] to read more than I do now.

In some familiar dialects, the *-s* form of some verbs is replaced by other forms.

> He *don't* want to go home.
>
> Elaine *ain't* ready to take the test yet.
>
> *Don't* nobody *have* books.

While such forms are appropriate in everyday speech in some communities, they should be avoided in writing.

> He *doesn't* want to go home yet.
>
> Elaine *isn't* ready to take the test yet.
>
> Nobody *has* books.

7d Use helping verbs with main verbs appropriately.

 Use helping verbs when they are required.

Some familiar dialects omit helping verbs required by standard English. In the sentences below, the verbs shown in parentheses are necessary for completeness.

> Felicia (*has*) *been* at school all day.
>
> You told your mother you (*would*) *be* home early tonight.

 Combine helping verbs and main verbs appropriately for your meaning. ESL

Helping verbs combine with main verbs in specific ways.

Form of *be* + present participle

The **progressive tenses** indicate action in progress (see p. 212). Use *be, am, is, are, was, were,* or *been* with the main verb's present participle.

> Miguel *is taking* singing lessons.

With *be* and *been,* use additional helping verbs to form progressive tenses.

can	might	should			have		
could	must	will	}	*be* taking	has	}	*been* taking
may	shall	would			had		

Be sure to use the *-ing* form of the verb for progressive tenses.

FAULTY   She is *consider* returning home.

REVISED   She is *considering* returning home.

Form of be + past participle

Use the **passive voice** (see pp. 216–219) to indicate that a subject receives the action of the verb. Use *be, am, is, are, was, were, being,* or *been* followed by the main verb's past participle.

Her letter *was published* in the school newspaper.

With *be, being,* and *been,* use additional helping verbs to form passive voice.

have				am	was		
has	}	*been* published		is	were	}	*being* published
had				are			

will *be* completed

Be sure to use the past participle of the main verb when you use passive voice.

FAULTY   The letter was *wrote* in her English class.

REVISED   The letter was *written* in her English class.

Use only transitive verbs for passive voice.

FAULTY   Marco's painting *will be appeared* in the art gallery next week. [*Appear* is not a transitive verb.]

REVISED   Marco's painting *will appear* in the art gallery next week.

Forms of have

Have and its forms *has, had,* and *having* form the perfect tenses when used with the main verb's past participle.

The class *has passed.*
The dogs *have scratched.*
The bus *had gone* before I arrived.

Will and other helping verbs are sometimes used with *have* in the perfect tenses.

The plane *will have arrived* before we get to the airport.

Forms of do

Use *do* with the infinitive (or plain) form of the verb to ask questions and to show negation and emphasis:

*Do*n't you *want* your ticket? [Question.]

We *did*n't *see* the plane arriving. [Negation.]

We *did expect* the package yesterday. [Emphasis.]

Be sure to use the infinitive when you use *do* as a helping verb.

FAULTY   We did *expecting* the package yesterday.

Modals

The modals combine with the plain form to alter the meaning of the verb.

You *can* work. [Ability or permission.]

You *may* work. [Possibility or permission.]

You *must* work. [Necessity or obligation.]

You *will* work. [Intention or necessity.]

You *should* work. [Advisability.]

You *could* work. [Condition.]

See Exercises 7-1, 7-2, 7-3, 7-4, 7-8.

Related Exercises 5-1, 5-2, 5-3, 5-4, 5-9, 5-10, 5-11

TENSE

Tense shows the time of a verb's action. The **simple tenses** indicate present, past, and future. The **perfect tenses** indicate action that was or will be completed before another action or time.

 7e **Use the appropriate tense to express your meaning.**

Forms that indicate tense in verbs can sometimes be troublesome for both native speakers of English and those using English as a second language. It is good practice when editing a piece of writing to read it for appropriate tense.

 Tenses of a regular and an irregular verb (active voice)

	SINGULAR	PLURAL
SIMPLE TENSES		
Present		
First person	I work/write	we work/write
Second person	you work/write	you work/write
Third person	he/she/it works/writes	they work/write

	SINGULAR	PLURAL

Past
First person — I worked/wrote — we worked/wrote
Second person — you worked/wrote — you worked/wrote
Third person — he/she/it worked/wrote — they worked/wrote

Future
First person — I will work/write — we will work/write
Second person — you will work/write — you will work/write
Third person — he/she/it will work/write — they will work/write

PERFECT TENSES

Present perfect
First person — I have worked/written — we have worked/written
Second person — you have worked/written — you have worked/written
Third person — he/she/it has worked/written — they have worked/written

Past perfect
First person — I had worked/written — we had worked/written
Second person — you had worked/written — you had worked/written
Third person — he/she/it had worked/written — they had worked/written

Future perfect
First person — I will have worked/written — we will have worked/written
Second person — you will have worked/written — you will have worked/written
Third person — he/she/it had worked/written — they will have worked/written

PROGRESSIVE TENSES

Present progressive
First person — I am working/writing — we are working/writing
Second person — you are working/writing — you are working/writing
Third person — he/she/it is working/writing — they are working/writing

Past progressive
First person — I was working/writing — we were working/writing
Second person — you were working/writing — you were working/writing
Third person — he/she/it was working/writing — they were working/writing

Future progressive
First person — I will be working/writing — we will be working/writing
Second person — you will be working/writing — you will be working/writing
Third person — he/she/it will be working/writing — they will be working/writing

	SINGULAR	PLURAL
Present perfect progressive		
First person	I have been working/ writing	we have been working/ writing
Second person	you have been working/ writing	you have been working/ writing
Third person	he/she/it has been working/writing	they have been working/ writing
Past perfect progressive		
First person	I had been working writing/	we had been working/ writing
Second person	you had been working/ writing	you had been working/ writing
Third person	he/she/it had been working/writing	they had been working/ writing
Future perfect progressive		
First person	I will have been working/ writing	we will have been working/ writing
Second person	you will have been working/writing	you will have been working/writing
Third person	he/she/it will have been working/writing	they will have been working/writing

 Observe the special uses of the present tense.

The present tense, besides indicating action occurring in the present, can be used in several other situations.

TO DESCRIBE HABITUAL OR RECURRING ACTION
I *vote* for Democrats.

TO STATE A GENERAL TRUTH
Oak *is* a hardwood.

TO DISCUSS THE CONTENT OF A BOOK, MOVIE, OR OTHER CREATIVE WORK
Michael Corleone *is* the Godfather's favorite son.

TO INDICATE FUTURE TIME
We *leave* for Europe next Monday.

 Observe the uses of the perfect tenses.

The perfect tenses indicate action completed before another action or time. The present perfect tense also indicates action begun in the past and continued into the present. The perfect tenses are formed from a verb's past participle plus *have, has,* or *had.*

PRESENT PERFECT

Hosea *has written* a letter of thanks to his grandmother. [Action is completed at the time of the statement.]

The sun *has shone* every day this week. [Action began in the past and is still continuing.]

PAST PERFECT

The bus *had* already *left* by the time our cab arrived. [Action of the verb *had left* is completed before the action of the verb *arrived.*]

My grandmother *had written* a living will before she was hospitalized. [Action of the verb *had written* is completed before the action of the verb *was hospitalized.*]

FUTURE PERFECT

If the sun shines again tomorrow, it *will have shone* eight days straight. [The future perfect *will have shone* indicates action that began in the past and will be continuing at a future time.]

 Observe the uses of the progressive tenses. ESL

The progressive tenses use a form of *be* plus the *-ing* verb to indicate continuing action. The present progressive is often used to show present action.

What *are* you *doing?* I *am writing.* [Present progressive.]

Joshua *was swimming.* [Past progressive.]

Our brother *has been cooking* dinner. [Present perfect progressive.]

Mental states or activities rather than physical actions are usually not expressed in progressive verbs—verbs such as *adore, appear, believe, belong, care, hate, have, hear, hope, know, like, love, need, prefer, remember, see, taste, think, understand,* and *want.*

FAULTY   Li *was hating* to leave his family.

REVISED   Li *hated* to leave his family.

7f Use the appropriate sequence of verb tenses.

The **sequence of tenses** is the relation between the verb in a main clause and the verbs or verbals in a subordinate clause or phrase. Sometimes the correct sequence calls for the same tense, but, as the following sentence indicates, the verbs in the different constructions need not always have identical tenses to be in sequence.

Glenna *will explain* why she *is* so unhappy. [Action of the future verb *will explain* occurs after that of the present verb *is.*]

1 Use the appropriate tense sequence with infinitives.

The tense of an infinitive is determined by the tense of the verb in the predicate. The **present infinitive** is the infinitive preceded by *to: to kick, to write.* It shows action occurring at the same time as or later than that of the verb.

> I *prefer to stay* right here. [The action of the present infinitive *to stay* occurs at the same time as that of the present verb *prefer.*]

> She *would have liked to join* you. [The action of the present infinitive *to join* occurs at the same time as that of the present perfect verb *would have liked.*]

The **perfect infinitive** combines *to have* with a past participle: *to have kicked, to have written.* It shows action that occurred earlier than that of the verb.

> We now *know* what *to have studied* for the test. [The action of the perfect infinitive *to have studied* occurs before that of the present verb *know.*]

> My father *would like to have been* an actor. [The action of the perfect infinitive *to have been* occurs before that of the verb *would like.*]

 2 Use the appropriate tense sequence with participles.

The tense of a participle is determined by the tense of the verb in the predicate. The present participle shows action occurring at the same time as that of the verb.

> *Walking* into the house, I *greeted* each of my relatives in turn. [Action of the present participle *walking* occurs at the same time as that of the verb *greeted.*]

The past participle and the present perfect participle show action occurring earlier than that of the verb.

> *Injured* in his fall from the tree, my brother *rode* to the hospital in an ambulance. [Action of the past participle *injured* occurs earlier than that of the verb *rode.*]

> *Having seeped* through the walls, the water *left* large orange stains in the wallpaper. [Action of the present perfect participle *having seeped* occurs earlier than that of the verb *left.*]

 3 Use the appropriate tense sequence with the past or past perfect tense.

When the verb in the main clause is in the past or past perfect tense, the verb in the subordinate clause must also be past or past perfect.

vb
7f

She *thought* the dog *had spoken*. [The past perfect verb in the subordinate clause, *had spoken*, indicates action before that of the past main verb, *thought*.]

Judith *had* already *called* when I *arrived*. [The past verb in the subordinate clause, *arrived*, indicates action occurring after that of the past perfect main verb, *had called*.]

While we *filled* the feeders, the birds *watched* in the trees. [The action of both verbs takes place in the past.]

EXCEPTION: A subordinate clause that expresses a general truth, such as *people are funny*, can be stated in the present tense even though the verb in the main clause is past tense.

She *said* that people *are* funny. [Past and present.]
She *thought* that dogs *can speak*. [Past and present.]

 Use the appropriate tense sequence in conditional sentences.

A conditional sentence usually begins with *if*, *when*, or *unless* and relates cause and effect, makes a prediction, or speculates about something that might happen.

When the time *changes* twice a year, people *adjust* their diurnal rhythms. [Causal relation; two present tense verbs.]

When the time *changed* last year, many people *failed* to adjust their diurnal rhythms. [Causal relation; two past tense verbs.]

When the time *changes* again, some people *will forget* to reset their clocks. [Prediction; verbs in present and future tense.]

If the time *remained* the same throughout the year, people *would* not *need* to make adjustments. [Speculation; past tense and the modal *would*.]

But if we had not changed to daylight time in the spring, we *would* not *have enjoyed* the long summer evenings. [Speculation; past perfect tense and the modal *would* with the present perfect verb.]

 Use the appropriate tense sequence with indirect quotations.

Indirect quotations report what someone said but not in the exact words and not in quotation marks. They appear in subordinate clauses (usually beginning with *that*) and make certain changes in wording. Besides using different pronouns, indirect quotations often change the verb tense of the original.

George *says* that he *hopes* his boss will give him a raise. [Main clause in present tense, indirect quotation in the same tense as the original: "I *hope* my boss will give me a raise."

George *said* that he *hoped* his boss would give him a raise. [Main clause in past tense, indirect quotation changes to past tense.]

George *said* that he *had* always *hoped* his boss would give him a raise. [Main clause in past tense, indirect quotation changes past perfect tense to present perfect: "I *have* always *hoped* my boss will give me a raise."]

When the direct quotation states a general truth or reports a situation that is still true, the verb does not change.

George *said* that his boss *is* a fair man. [Quotation: "My boss *is* a fair man."]

See Exercises 7-5, 7-6, 7-8.

Related Exercises 13-1, 13-2.

MOOD

The **mood** of a verb indicates the writer's or speaker's attitude toward what he or she is saying. The **indicative mood** states a fact or opinion or asks a question. It is the mood used most often in speech and writing:

The trees *are changing* color.
What *makes* the colors *change?*
They *changed* almost overnight.

The **imperative mood** expresses a command or direction and omits the understood subject *you:*

Turn left at the light.
Simmer the mixture for half an hour.

The **subjunctive mood** expresses a requirement, a desire, a suggestion, or a condition contrary to fact:

We insisted that she *come.* [Suggestion; in the indicative mood, *come* would have an -*s* ending.]

If she *were* present, we could finish the job faster. [Condition contrary to fact; in the indicative mood, the verb would be *was.*]

Because the indicative and imperative moods are used so commonly, they cause few problems for most writers. The subjunctive, however, is used less commonly in speech and consequently is sometimes troublesome in writing.

7g Use the subjunctive verb forms appropriately.

The subjunctive mood uses distinctive verb forms in only a few kinds of constructions.

 1 Use the subjunctive in contrary-to-fact clauses beginning with *if* or expressing desire.

If you *were* well, you would not have a fever.

I wish I *were* somewhere else.

 2 Use *would* or *could* only in the main clause of a conditional statement.

NOT I wouldn't have voted for Senator Smith if I *would have known* about his views on abortion.

BUT I wouldn't have voted for Senator Smith if I *had known* about his views on abortion.

 3 Use the subjunctive in *that* clauses following verbs that demand, request, or recommend.

The rules required that she *start* over. [Demand.]

They suggested that he *step* outside. [Request.]

The counselor suggested that I *be* more self-confident. [Recommendation.]

4 Use the subjunctive in some set phrases and idioms.

Far *be* it from me to interfere.

If that's the way you want it, then so *be* it.

I move that the meeting *be* adjourned.

VOICE

Verbs indicate whether their subjects are acting or are acted upon. When the subject is the actor, or doer, of the action, the verb is in the **active voice:** *John opened three presents.* When the subject receives the action, the verb is in the **passive voice:** *Three presents were opened by John.* A verb in the passive voice consists of the verb's past participle and a form of *be.* Only transitive verbs—verbs that take objects—can form the passive voice.

Active and passive voice

ACTIVE VOICE: THE SUBJECT ACTS.

The city   controls   rents.

PASSIVE VOICE: THE SUBJECT IS ACTED UPON.

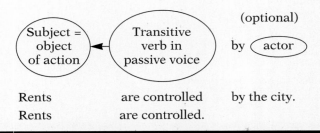

Rents   are controlled   by the city.
Rents   are controlled.

Converting active to passive

To change a sentence from *active to passive voice,* move the direct object or indirect object to the subject position; if you want to say who performed the action, use a *by* prepositional phrase, making its object the doer of the action. Change an active verb to passive by using the past participle and the form of *be* that is appropriate for the tense of the sentence.

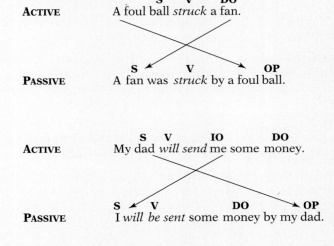

ACTIVE

PASSIVE

ACTIVE

PASSIVE

Converting passive to active

To change a sentence from *passive to active voice,* find out who or what is performing the action (expressed in a *by* phrase or omitted) and make that noun or pronoun the subject of the sentence; the subject of the passive sentence becomes the direct object or indirect object in the active sentence. In changing the verb, omit *be* and change the past participle to the appropriate tense form. (See also 5e-3.)

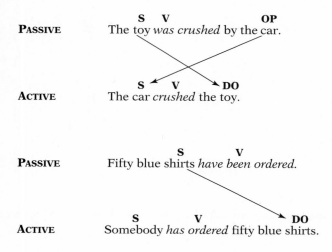

| | S V | | OP |
| PASSIVE | The toy *was crushed* by the car. | | |

| | S | V | DO |
| ACTIVE | The car *crushed* the toy. | | |

| | S | V |
| PASSIVE | Fifty blue shirts *have been ordered.* | |

| | S | V | DO |
| ACTIVE | Somebody *has ordered* fifty blue shirts. | | |

7h Generally, prefer the active voice. Use the passive voice when the actor is unknown or unimportant.

Use the passive voice with caution. It is wordier and less direct than the active voice, and it often omits the important information of who or what is performing the action, as illustrated in the following sentences.

WEAK PASSIVE   If budget allocations for this fund are *to be generated* solely by federal income tax, a sixfold increase *would be required.* [The passive infinitive *to be generated* puts the doer of the action in the by phrase; the passive verb *would be required* avoids saying who must increase taxes.]

STRONG ACTIVE   If federal income tax alone is *to generate* budget allocations for this fund, Congress *will have to increase* taxes sixfold.

There are times, however, when the passive is appropriate, most commonly when the reader does not need to know who performed the action or when the actor is not known. Here are examples:

The back window *was broken* during the night. [Nobody knows who broke the window.]

The pamphlets *will be printed* in color. [It is not important to know who will print the pamphlets.]

See Exercises 7-7, 7-8, 7-9.

Related Exercises 5-1, 5-2, 5-3, 5-4, 5-15, 13-1, 18-1.

OTHER COMPLICATIONS

 ### Use a gerund or an infinitive after a verb as appropriate. ESL

Gerunds and infinitives may follow some verbs and not others. Sometimes the meaning depends on whether the verb is followed by a gerund or an infinitive.

Either gerund or infinitive

These verbs do not change meaning when they are followed by either a gerund or an infinitive: *begin, can't bear, can't stand, continue, hate, hesitate, intend, like, love, prefer, pretend,* and *start.*

I hate *leaving* home. I hate *to leave* home.

Meaning change with gerund or infinitive

With the verbs *forget, remember, stop,* and *try,* gerunds contribute different meanings than infinitives.

Getting no laughs, the clown tried *singing.* [The clown attempts to entertain.]

Getting no laughs, the clown tried to *sing.* [Implies that the clown cannot sing.]

Gerund, not infinitive

Use a gerund, not an infinitive, after these verbs:

adore	dislike	postpone	resist
admit	enjoy	practice	risk
appreciate	escape	put off	suggest
avoid	finish	quit	understand
deny	imagine	recall	
detest	keep	recollect	
discuss	mind	resent	

The clown finally quit trying.

Infinitive, not gerund

Use an infinitive, not a gerund, after these verbs:

agree	decide	mean	refuse
ask	expect	offer	say
assent	have	plan	wait
beg	hope	pretend	want
claim	manage	promise	wish

The clown pretended to be happy.

Noun or pronoun + infinitive

The verbs *ask, expect, need, want,* and *would like* may be followed by an infinitive alone or by a noun or pronoun and an infinitive. With the noun or pronoun the meaning is changed.

She wanted *to leave*. She wanted *him to leave*.

With some verbs, the infinitive must be preceded by a noun or pronoun:

advise	encourage	oblige	require
admonish	forbid	order	teach
allow	force	permit	tell
cause	hire	persuade	train
challenge	instruct	remind	warn
command	invite	request	urge
convince			

She requested *him to leave*.

Do not use *to* before the infinitive when it follows a noun or pronoun and one of these verbs: *feel, have, hear, let, make ("force"), see,* and *watch.*

She watched him *walk* out the door.

7j   Use the appropriate particles with two-word verbs. ESL

Some verbs are followed by a particle (a preposition or an adverb) to change their meaning from that of the verb itself, for example *catch* as opposed to *catch on* or *catch up.* Many of these combinations cannot be separated in a sentence.

Inseparable two-word verbs

catch on	go out	look into	speak up
come across	go over	play around	stay away
get along	grow up	run on	stay up
give in	keep on	run out of	take care of

FAULTY		You should *go* quickly *over* the paper.
REVISED		You should *go over* the paper quickly.

Separable two-word verbs

Most transitive two-word verbs may be separated by their direct objects.

vb
7j

bring up	give back	make up	take out
call off	hand in	pick up	take over
call up	hand out	point out	try on
drop off	help out	put away	try out
fill out	leave out	put back	turn down
fill up	look over	put off	turn on
give away	look up	see off	wrap up

FAULTY		When you finish writing your papers, *hand in* them.
REVISED		When you finish writing your papers, *hand* them *in*.

NOTE: Because many of these two-word verbs are more common in speech than in academic and professional writing, consider replacing them with synonyms of a more formal nature: *complete* rather than *fill out,* or *investigate* instead of *look into*. Rely on your ESL dictionary whenever you are uncertain of the meaning and usage of two-word verbs.

See Exercises 7-10, 7-11.

Related Exercises 5-1, 5-2, 5-3, 5-8, 5-15, 13-1, 18-1.

EXERCISE 7-1

Principal Parts of Irregular Verbs—Comparing Forms (7a–b)

Circle the correct form of the verb from each pair in parentheses. If necessary, consult a dictionary or the list of irregular verbs on pages 204–206.

Example: I had to (*lie*, *lay*) down.

1. We had (*swum*, *swam*) only an hour before the storm struck.

2. The problem of boarding the dog had not (*came*, *come*) up before.

3. We had (*wrote*, *written*) a letter of complaint to the company.

4. We should have (*drunk*, *drank*) some water before the race.

5. Anthony (*saw*, *seen*) everything that happened.

6. Pat could have (*ran*, *run*) the mile in record time.

7. The book had (*laid*, *lain*) on the shelf all week in plain sight.

8. We should have (*begun*, *began*) our explanation with the facts.

9. We must have (*chose*, *chosen*) the wrong path.

10. You should not have (*driven*, *drove*) while drunk.

11. The tires were (*wore*, *worn*) so thin that there was no tread left.

12. Karen should not have (*went*, *gone*) home without thanking you.

13. Michael (*throwed, threw*) the ball faster than anyone else on the team.

14. Your briefcase has (*sat, set*) on the chair since this morning.

15. Maybe you shouldn't have (*ate, eaten*) just before running.

16. Elizabeth and Carl couldn't have (*saw, seen*) us through that window.

17. I wish I had (*ridden, rode*) my bike to town.

18. We were afraid that the child might have (*fell, fallen*) into the water.

19. We should have (*knew, known*) it would rain.

20. My grandfather (*grew, growed*) the best tomatoes I've ever had.

21. Rhonda might have (*laid, lain*) the paper on the desk.

22. We (*cut, cutted*) the melon in half, then in quarters.

23. The envelope was (*tore, torn*) beyond recognition.

24. We should have (*taken, took*) a later train.

25. I have already (*gave, given*) as much as I can afford.

26. My feet were almost (*froze, frozen*) after skiing home.

27. The bell (*rung, rang*) for the start of class.

28. We couldn't have (*done, did*) anything about it.

29. The window might have been (*broke, broken*) in the storm.

30. The conventioneers should have (*sung, sang*) the national anthem.

EXERCISE 7-2

The *-s* Forms of Verbs: Rewriting a Text (7c)

Rewrite the following paragraphs, changing all verbs as necessary to describe present circumstances. Begin with the following sentence:

It is still thought necessary for people to drink eight glasses of water a day.

It was once thought necessary for people to drink eight glasses of water a day. Water, it was said, kept the body functioning, nourished, and cool. Water made up about 60 percent of the human body, and that level had to be maintained for good health. The water that left the body through the normal processes of perspiration and urination needed to be replenished.

About 7 percent of the body's water content circulated in the bloodstream. If the volume of water in the body dropped, so did the volume of blood that circulated throughout the body. This decrease was accompanied by a corresponding increase in the chemical substances in the blood. The brain began to get the message that water was necessary and sent a message of thirstiness to the mouth. By this time the body had already begun dehydrating.

What did dehydration mean? If the person ignored the call for water, it possibly meant headaches, fatigue, muscle cramps, and mental dullness.

In hot weather, the body temperature rose, because the natural cooling process of perspiration was stymied. In the long term, the person risked kidney damage.

These problems could be avoided if people drank lots of water. Because alcohol and caffeinated cola, tea, and coffee flushed water out of the body, they counteracted the benefits of the liquid they introduced. But water excelled. It was almost free and had no calories.

EXERCISE 7-3

The *-ed* Forms of Verbs: Rewriting a Text (7c)

Rewrite the following short essay to read as if the writer were recounting experiences in the past. Your first sentence will read:

> When I learned to write, my dictionary was a close companion.

As you rewrite the essay, you will need to change all verbs to the past tense, in many cases using *-ed* forms. Avoid using *would* or *used to* with the verbs.

When I write, my dictionary is a close companion. I refer to it throughout the writing process for several purposes. Before I start writing, I often look up the meaning of a key word so that I clearly understand my subject. At that time I also locate related words and check their meanings.

I probably refer to the dictionary least while I carry out the actual writing. At that time my writing so absorbs my thoughts that I overlook spelling and, when I can't think of the right word, I use any word that comes close in meaning. I place a mark in the margin as a reminder to myself that I need to find a different word later.

After I affix my last period, I prepare to dig into my dictionary. Then I ask myself if each word I use is appropriate for my meaning. If I have any doubt, I look up the word and check its meaning. At that point, I also investigate other words given as synonyms; if they seem better than the ones

I have, I use them instead. As I revise, I also check the spellings of words I'm not sure about.

My final use for the dictionary occurs when I am writing the final draft. I need to know how to divide words at the ends of lines. My dictionary has little dots between syllables to tell me where the syllables divide.

Because my dictionary is so useful to me while I write, I keep it handy all the time.

EXERCISE 7-4

Helping Verbs and Main Verbs:
Comparing Forms (7d)

exer
7

Underline the correct words in parentheses.

Example: A clown might (*making, make*) people laugh.

1. Have you ever (*considering, considered*) being a clown?

2. I mean a clown whose face has been (*paint, painted*) all funny.

3. Clowns can (*entertained, entertain*) children in schools and hospitals.

4. They might also (*work, working*) in circuses.

5. To have a clown face, you must (*start, started*) with white makeup.

6. After you (*had covered, have covered*) your face with white makeup, you go
    to the next step.

7. You should (*applied, apply*) white talcum powder over the white makeup.

8. To finish your face, you should (*use, used*) red and black makeup.

9. A good professional clown will (*color, colors*) only the mouth and nose and
    will (*make, makes*) only one or two other marks.

10. Children are sometimes (*scare, scared*) when clowns make up their faces
    too much.

11. Clowns who (*been, have been*) working as clowns for years have other advice too.

12. They (*be recommending, recommend*) that you not make up your upper lip.

13. Mouth expressions (*made, are made*) by the lower lip.

14. Making up the lower lip (*exaggerates, has exaggerating*) the expressions.

15. After you have (*painting, painted*) your face, you are ready to be a clown.

EXERCISE 7-6

Verb Tenses: Writing Sentences (7e)

Underline the verbs in the following sentences. Then rewrite each sentence twice, changing the verb to the tenses indicated in parentheses.

Example: Sometimes an element of truth <u>evolves</u> into a gross untruth.

(*Past.*)   Sometimes an element of truth evolved into a gross untruth.

(*Future.*)   Sometimes an element of truth will evolve into a gross untruth.

1. Scientific truth about the human brain has led to untrue assumptions.

(*Past.*)

(*Present.*)

2. One misinterpretation is that artistic, or visual, ability exists only in the right half of the brain.

(*Past, past.*)

(*Present perfect, present.*)

3. People assumed, falsely, that only the left half of the brain took on analytical, logical tasks and only the right half creative and visual work.

(*Present, present.*)

(*Past perfect, past.*)

4. But further research has shown the left brain to be just as perceptive visually as the right brain.

(*Present.*)

(*Past.*)

5. The primary distinction between the two halves of the brain is that the left brain controls language.

   (Present perfect, present.)

   (Past, past.)

6. In most people, only the left brain has the ability to name objects.

   (Past.)

   (Past perfect.)

7. The right brain recognizes those objects but doesn't have a name for them.

   (Present perfect, present.)

   (Past perfect, past.)

8. The left brain and right brain are connected to one another by the corpus callosum, a thick band of nerve fibers.

   (Future.)

   (Future perfect.)

9. Through this bundle of nerves the two halves of the brain send information to one another.

   (Future.)

   (Present perfect.)

10. Because of this connection, it is a misinterpretation of scientific evidence to call a person "left-brained" or "right-brained."

    (Present perfect.)

    (Future.)

EXERCISE 7-7

Subjunctive Verb Forms: Rewriting Sentences (7g)

Rewrite the following sentences, changing each italicized verb to a subjunctive form.

> *Example:*   If that *was* the case, he would have protested.
>
> *If that were the case, he would have protested.*

1. The assignment sheet requires that each student *writes* a research paper.

2. If she *was* wise, she would take a mathematics course this term.

3. If the storm *was* to cause a blackout, we would be in trouble.

4. The requirement is that he *pays* before entering.

5. If the tax *was* repealed, the city would go bankrupt.

6. His mouth moved as if he *was* speaking.

7. If I *was* certain I could get a job in the space industry, I would major in engineering.

8. If the president *was* elected by popular vote instead of by the electoral college, the country would be more of a democracy.

EXERCISE 7-8

Verb Forms, Tense, and Mood: Editing a Text (7e–g)

In the following paragraphs cross out any errors in verb forms, tense, or mood. Then write the correct verb above the error.

Don't get me wrong. I'm all for a clean environment—recycling, reducing pollution, and all that. But my sister do go overboard—just a bit. My biggest problem is that she's a bird-watcher. Have you ever rode in a car drove by a bird-watcher? It's not something you'd get use to.

First, her car is full of what she call birding gear. She gots binoculars, a book full of bird pictures that she call a field guide, a notebook that she say is her birding journal, and, believe it or not, a vest kind of like those fishing vests with about a million pockets. I look at that vest once. What I see is a pen in a little pocket just the shape of a pen, a tablet in another pocket, a big white handkerchief in another one, and I don't know what else.

The really scary part of riding in the car with my sister come when we going down the road. Wherever we are, whatever the traffic, if she see a bird she stops. She just slammed on the brakes and stops—right in the middle of the road. Yesterday we driving in to school and she see a big bird flying overhead. "A HERON!" she yells, and there we are, stopped in the middle of the street. Cars are honking their horns behind us, and she just calmly pulls out her binoculars to take a close look at that bird. I should of taken over the wheel.

Well, you see what I mean. Anyone that devoted to bird-watching is a menace. I'll keep recycling cans, but caring for every bird in the sky is not my business.

EXERCISE 7-9

Active and Passive Voices: Revising Text (7h)

Some of the sentences in the following passage are ineffective because of their passive constructions. Draw a line through those sentences and rewrite them in the active voice. The sentences with active verbs can remain as they are.

Example: ~~Eating disorders are experienced by many people, especially young women.~~

Many people, especially young women, experience eating disorders.

1   Bulimia is an eating disorder common to an estimated 18 percent of females in high school and college. People with this binge-and-purge disorder consume large amounts of junk food and then force themselves to vomit it up. Sometimes laxatives or diuretics are taken as a means of purging the body. Usually the bingeing is done in secret because the bulimics are ashamed of their habit. Yet the bingeing and purging are usually repeated as a result of the young woman's conviction that she is fat.

2   Only in recent years has bulimia been described in medical journals separately from another eating disorder, anorexia nervosa. Since 1980, bulimia has been considered a psychiatric illness. However, even though the causes of the bingeing and then purging are psychiatric, the effects of the purging are largely physical.

3   The amount of an essential chemical in the body, potassium, is reduced by frequent purging of the body with vomiting, laxatives, or diuret-

ics. Muscle weakness, even paralysis and kidney disease, may be caused by insufficient potassium. Other possible effects are damage to the esophagus and stomach, resulting in ulcers, stomach and throat pain, and difficulty in breathing. Even the teeth may be affected because of the acidity of the stomach fluids.

4   Treatment of bulimia usually involves both medical doctors and psychiatrists. Hospitalization is sometimes recommended, and treatment may last for months and years. The disorder can often be prevented with early medical consultation.

EXERCISE 7-10

Gerunds and Infinitives: Using as Appropriate (7i)

Fill each blank with an infinitive or a gerund as appropriate.

Example: Tomás promised <u>to return</u> (*return*) the book.

1. Miguel enjoyed _____ (*attend*) the art show.

2. He liked it so much he wanted _____ (*go*) back again.

3. But Anna persuaded him _____ (*wait*) a few days.

4. She reminded him that he risked _____ (*fail*) his history exam.

5. Miguel reluctantly agreed _____ (*wait*) until after the exam.

6. Mrs. Wang instructed five-year-old Angela _____ (*leave*) the table.

7. Angela had not yet finished _____ (*eat*).

8. But she was having a temper tantrum and refused _____ (*eat*) her vegetables.

9. Her father ordered her _____ (*go*) to her room until she was ready to eat.

10. He hoped she would appreciate _____ (*have*) good food to eat.

11. Patrick decided _____ (*buy*) a computer.

12. He wanted _____ (*use*) it mainly for word processing.

13. But he also planned _____ (*practice*) his statistics on it.

14. He hoped _____ (*get*) his equipment for under $2,000.

15. He invited his friend Charlie _____ (*help*) him shop for it.

16. They discussed _____ (*go*) to a computer store or a discount electronics store.

17. They both admitted not _____ (*know*) much about computers.

18. In the end, they delayed _____ (*make*) a decision until they got more information.

EXERCISE 7-11

Two-Word Verbs: Understanding Meaning (7j)

In the blank spaces at the left, substitute synonyms for the italicized two-word verbs. Use your dictionary as necessary.

Example: _Completing_   *Filling out* forms is a necessary part of school registration.

_____ 1. Yung Lam *ran across* something interesting yesterday.

_____ 2. It happened when he was *looking over* his English assignment.

_____ 3. He was checking his spelling before *handing* the paper *in.*

_____ 4. He wanted to *clean up* all his errors.

_____ 5. But he also *found out* something new.

_____ 6. His rereading *brought up* a new idea.

_____ 7. He was surprised when the reading *brought* it *up.*

_____ 8. He decided that he would have to *think* it *over.*

_____ 9. He wondered if he should *write* the paper *over.*

_____ 10. The problem was that he had *left out* an important point.

_____ 11. He finally decided that he would not need to *throw* the paper *away.*

_____ 12. He could *fill in* a new paragraph to cover the omitted point.

_____ 13. Then he could *hand* the paper *in* knowing it was the best he could do.

_____ 14. He *called up* the paper on his word processor and made the changes.

Chapter 8 Agreement

Verbs agree in person and number with their subjects, and pronouns agree in person, number, and gender with the nouns or pronouns they refer to.

 Aspects of agreement

PERSON

First person, the speaker(s): *I, we*

Second person, the person(s) spoken to: *you*

Third person, the person(s) or thing(s) spoken about: *he, she, it, they;* nouns; indefinite and relative pronouns

NUMBER

Singular, one: *I, you, he, she, it;* nouns naming one; indefinite and relative pronouns referring to singular nouns and pronouns

Plural, more than one: *we, you, they;* nouns naming more than one; indefinite and relative pronouns referring to plural nouns and pronouns

GENDER

Masculine: *he,* nouns naming males, indefinite and relative pronouns referring to males

Feminine: *she,* nouns naming females, indefinite and relative pronouns referring to females

8a ▉ Make subjects and verbs agree in number.

Subjects and verbs are singular or plural depending on whether they refer to one of something or more than one. The subject always determines the number of the verb.

1 The -*s* and -*es* endings work differently for nouns and verbs.

Adding -*s* or -*es* to a noun usually makes the noun **plural.** An -*s* or -*es* on a present-tense verb makes the verb **singular.**

SINGULAR	PLURAL
A tree grows.	Trees grow.
A car runs.	Cars run.
The house is green.	The houses are green.

The -*s* or -*es* ending often is not distinctly pronounced in speech and thus is wrongly omitted in writing.

Elroy often asks the teacher for advice. [Singular verb.]

The monkey passes his hat when the organ grinder finishes. [Two singular verbs.]

The tests were more difficult than I thought they would be. [Plural noun.]

2 Subject and verb should agree even when other words come between them.

Subjects and verbs must agree whether they are side by side or separated by other words.

The problem with all of Riley's poems *is* that they are sentimental. [*Problem* is the subject, not *poems.*]

The goals of this construction work *are* not clear. [*Goals* is the subject, not *work.*]

Prepositional expressions such as *as well as, together with, along with,* and *in addition to* add meaning, a second performer of the action, but they have no influence on the number of the verb.

Mrs. Rapjohn, as well as the Zimmers, *goes* to Damascus often. [*Mrs. Rapjohn* is the subject of the sentence; *Zimmers* is the object of the preposition *as well as.*]

To avoid the awkwardness of such a sentence, a good writer would probably use the conjunction *and: Mrs. Rapjohn and the Zimmers go to Damascus often.*

Summary of subject-verb agreement

- Basic subject-verb agreement (8a-1):
  Singular: The kit*e* fli*es*.
  Plural: The kite*s* fly.
- Words between subject and verb (8a-2):
  The kite with two tails *flies* badly. The tails of the kite *compete*.
- Subjects joined by *and* (8a-3):
  The kite and the bird *are* almost indistinguishable.
- Subjects joined by *or* or *nor* (8a-4):
  The kite or the bird *dives*. Kites or birds *fill* the sky.
- Indefinite pronouns as subjects (8a-5):
  No one *knows*. All the spectators *wonder*.
- Collective nouns as subjects (8a-6):
  A flock *appears*. The flock *disperse*.
- Inverted word order (8a-7):
  Is the kite or the bird still blue? *Are* the kite and the bird both blue?
- Linking verbs (8a-8):
  The kite *is* a flier and a dipper.
- *Who, which, that* as subjects (8a-9):
  The kite that *flies* longest wins. Kites that fall *lose*.
- Subjects with plural form and singular meaning (8a-10):
  Aeronautics *plays* a role in kite flying.
- Titles and words named as words (8a-11):
  Kite Dynamics *is* one title. Vectors *is* a key word.

 Subjects joined by *and* usually take plural verbs.

Even when one or more parts of a compound subject are singular, the entire subject takes a plural verb. The *and* that joins two subjects in effect adds things together, resulting in more than one—that is, plural.

Howard and Emma *like* to go deer hunting together.

The Zimmers and Mrs. Rapjohn *go* to Damascus often.

Occasionally a compound subject refers to a single person or thing or is preceded by *each* or *every*. Then the verb is singular.

Our friend and ally *was* happy to help. [*Friend and ally* refers to one person.]

Every log and stick *was* burned. [*Every* is grammatically singular.]

When parts of a subject are joined by *or* or *nor,* the verb agrees with the nearer part.

Unlike compound subjects joined by *and,* compounds joined by *or* or *nor* are not added together; the verb agrees with the nearer subject. In effect, when the parts of a subject joined by *or* or *nor* are singular, the verb is singular. When the parts are plural, the verb is plural.

Jones or Albertson *is* to be arrested on Monday.

Neither the horses nor the cows *have* been sold.

The practice of this rule is most troublesome when one part of the subject is singular and the other plural. However, the rule is still the same: the verb agrees with the closer part.

Either the roadbed or the curbs *are* scheduled for repair next week.

Either the curbs or the roadbed *is* scheduled for repair next week.

Use the construction that seems least awkward.

 With an indefinite pronoun, use a singular or plural verb as appropriate.

Indefinite pronouns function very much like nouns except that they do not refer to specific persons or things.

● Common indefinite pronouns

SINGULAR		PLURAL
anybody	no one	
anyone	nothing	both
anything	one	few
each	somebody	many
either	someone	several
everybody	something	
everyone		
everything	**SINGULAR OR PLURAL**	
much	all	
neither	any	
nobody	more	
none	most	
	some	

Unlike pronouns that take their meaning from their antecedents, indefinite pronouns function on their own to refer to persons or things in general. They

248

do not form plurals and are generally considered singular, taking singular verbs. (See 8b-3 for indefinites as antecedents of other pronouns.)

> *No one* knows the real danger.
>
> *Everyone* has caught the flu.

Many indefinites can function also as adjectives: *some* news, *any* person, *each* one, *either* way, *neither* paper, *one* fence, *every* street. The same agreement rules apply; that is, the nouns they modify usually take singular verbs.

A few of the indefinites—*all, any, none,* and *some*—may be either singular or plural depending on the noun or pronoun they refer to. If they refer to a plural noun (see 5a-2), they are plural; if they refer to a singular noun, they are singular.

> All of the gas *is* held in tanks. [*All* refers to the singular *gas.*]
>
> All of the people *are* eager to have some news. [*All* refers to the plural *people.*]
>
> Some of the soap *has* spilled on the floor. [*Some* refers to the singular *soap.*]
>
> Some of the dogs *have* escaped the kennel. [*Some* refers to the plural *dogs.*]
>
> Every dog and cat *has* been recaptured. [*Every* makes the subject singular.]

 Collective nouns take singular or plural verbs depending on meaning.

Collective nouns such as *committee, family,* and *team* have singular form but name groups of individuals or things. Collective nouns take singular verbs when the group is considered as a unit and plural verbs when the group's members are considered individually.

> The committee *has* the power to decide.
>
> The committee *have* argued over every decision.

Collective nouns are rarely used in their plural sense. Instead, sentences are phrased differently:

> The members of the committee have argued over every decision.

A few collective nouns commonly take either plural or singular verbs depending on the phrase that follows them. With words such as *rest, half, part,* and *number,* the meaning varies.

> The rest of the book *was* easy to read. [*Rest* refers to the singular *book.*]
>
> The rest of the newspapers *were* lost. [*Rest* refers to the plural *newspapers.*]
>
> Half of the sugar *is* gone already. [*Half* refers to the singular *sugar.*]
>
> Half of the eggs *are* gone too. [*Half* refers to the plural *eggs.*]

The word *number* takes a singular verb when preceded by *the* and a plural verb when preceded by *a.*

The number of highway deaths *has* decreased.

A number of officials *attribute* the decrease to the new speed limit.

ESL Some collective nouns are always plural: *clergy, military, people, police.* To refer to one person in the group, use a different phrase, such as *police officer* or *member of the clergy.*

The verb agrees with the subject even when the normal word order is inverted.

There *are* many reasons for voting in school elections. [The subject is *reasons*, not *There*.]

Has the cause of Alzheimer's disease been discovered yet? [The subject is *cause*.]

On the shelves *was* a clutter of toys. [The subject is *clutter*.]

A linking verb agrees with its subject, not the subject complement.

Subject complements sometimes differ in number from the subjects they rename, but the verb must still agree with its subject.

The chef's selection *is* pork chops. [The verb agrees with *selection*, the subject of the sentence.]

Pork chops *are* the chef's selection. [The verb agrees with *chops*, the subject of the sentence.]

Who, which, and *that* take verbs that agree with their antecedents.

When a **relative pronoun**—*who, which,* or *that*—serves as a subject, the verb should agree with the noun or pronoun the relative pronoun refers to (its antecedent).

The paintings that *were* on display have been sold. [*That* refers to *paintings*, a plural noun.]

The painting that *was* on display has been sold. [*That* refers to *painting*, a singular noun.]

Mary is the only one of the actors who *knows* her lines. [*Who* refers to *one*, a singular indefinite pronoun.]

Mary is one of the actors who *want* to strike. [*Who* refers to *actors*, a plural noun.]

250

Nouns with plural form but singular meaning take singular verbs.

Some nouns ending in *-s,* such as *news, athletics, politics,* and *United States,* are generally regarded as singular in meaning and thus take singular verbs. Measurements and figures ending in *-s* may also be singular when the quantity they refer to is a unit.

Economics *is* not being offered this spring.

Politics *takes* patience and compromise.

Two quarts *is* the capacity of each jar.

Thirty dollars *is* too much money.

 Titles and words named as words take singular verbs.

Even though words in a title may be plural, the title is a single thing, and it takes a singular verb. The same is true when words are referred to as words.

"Swans" *is* going to win the literature prize.

Ladies *is* misspelled in your essay.

See Exercises 8-1, 8-2, 8-3, 8-5.

Related Exercises 5-1, 5-2, 5-4.

8b Make pronouns and their antecedents agree in person, number, and gender.

An antecedent is the noun or pronoun that a pronoun refers to. Pronouns and their antecedents agree in person—first (*I, we*), second (*you*), or third (*he, she, it, they*). They also agree in number (singular or plural) and gender (masculine, feminine, or neuter). (See the pronoun chart on pp. 189–190 and Aspects of agreement on p. 245.)

 Summary of pronoun-antecedent agreement

- Basic pronoun-antecedent agreement:
  Old Faithful spews *its* columns of water, each of *them* over 115 feet high.
- Antecedents joined by *and* (8b-1):
  Old Faithful and Giant are geysers known for *their* height.

- Antecedents joined by *or* or *nor* (8b-2):

  Either Giant or Giantess ejects *its* column the highest.
- Indefinite pronouns as antecedents (8b-3):

  Each of the geysers has *its* own personality. Anyone who visits has *his or her* memories.
- Collective nouns as antecedents (8b-4):

  A crowd amuses *itself* watching Old Faithful. The crowd *go* their separate ways.

 Antecedents joined by *and* usually take plural pronouns.

Two or more antecedents joined by *and* take a plural pronoun even when each individual antecedent is singular.

Ann and Grace sold *their* textbooks.

Occasionally, a compound antecedent refers to a single person or thing or is preceded by *each* or *every.* Then the pronoun is singular.

The chief cook and bottlewasher wanted *his* name on the menu. [*Cook* and *bottlewasher* refer to one person.]

Every boy and man sang *his* loudest. [*Every* makes the antecedents *boy* and *man* singular.]

 When parts of an antecedent are joined by *or* or *nor,* the pronoun agrees with the nearer part.

When all parts of an antecedent joined by *or* or *nor* are singular, the pronoun is singular; when all parts are plural, the pronoun is plural.

Either Anne or Jane left *her* umbrella behind.

Scientists do not know how either walruses or sea cows get *their* food.

When the antecedents differ in number, the pronoun agrees with the nearer part.

Neither the Smiths nor Ms. Hogan weakened in *her* determination.

The awkwardness of this sentence can be avoided by rephrasing.

Neither Ms. Hogan nor the Smiths weakened in *their* determination.

With an indefinite pronoun as antecedent, use a singular or plural verb as appropriate.

Unlike other pronouns, **indefinite pronouns** do not have antecedents; instead, they function on their own like nouns, to refer to persons or things in general. And like nouns, indefinite pronouns can be antecedents for other pronouns. Since the indefinites are usually singular, the pronouns referring to them are singular too. (See also 8a-5.)

> Neither of those two Boy Scouts paid *his* dues. [*Neither* is the antecedent.]
>
> Each of the women succeeded in *her* chosen career. [*Each* is the antecedent.]

Avoid using the pronouns *he, him,* and *his* to refer to antecedents of unspecified gender.

BIASED	Everyone took *his* seat.
REVISED	Everyone took *his or her* seat.
REVISED	All the students took *their* seats.
REVISED	Everyone took seats.

 ## Ways to avoid the generic *he*

GENERIC *HE*

None of the students had the credits *he* needed.

- Substitute *he or she.*
  None of the students had the credits *he or she* needed.
- To avoid awkwardness, don't use *he or she* more than once in several sentences.
- Recast the sentence using a plural antecedent and pronoun.
  All the students lacked the credits *they* needed.
- Rewrite the sentence to avoid the pronoun.
  None of the students had the *needed credits.*

For more on avoiding bias in writing, see 31a-8.

Four indefinite pronouns are always plural in meaning: *both, few, many, several.* Pronouns referring to them are also plural.

> A *few* were unable to find their way to the stadium.

Five indefinite pronouns are singular or plural antecedents: *all, any, more, most, some.*

> *Most* of the fans found the stadium without any trouble. [Plural.]
>
> However, *most* of the game was over by the time they began to watch it. [Singular.]

Collective noun antecedents take singular or plural pronouns depending on meaning.

Collective nouns such as *team* or *committee* are singular or plural depending on whether they refer to the group as a whole or to the individuals making up the group. They are used most commonly in the singular sense. Pronouns correspond to the intended meaning.

The herd of wildebeests is too cramped in *its* small pasture.

The couple divided *their* belongings evenly.

See Exercises 8-4, 8-5.

Related Exercises 6-1, 6-2, 12-1, 12-2, 12-3.

EXERCISE 8-1

Subjects and Verbs: Editing Sentences (8a)

In these sentences, the subjects are underlined once and the verbs twice. If a verb agrees with its subject, mark the sentence *C* on the line to the left. If a verb does not agree with its subject, cross out the verb and write the correct form on the line.

Example: __are__ There ~~is~~ three <u>problems</u> to work out before we can proceed.

_____ 1. The <u>difference</u> between twins <u>are</u> often surprising.

_____ 2. Both the <u>drinks</u> and the <u>dessert</u> <u>was</u> left off the bill.

_____ 3. <u>Each</u> of the puzzles <u>require</u> thirty minutes to solve.

_____ 4. <u>Neither</u> of us <u>enjoy</u> the outdoors.

_____ 5. There <u>is</u> only three original <u>songs</u> in the band's repertoire.

_____ 6. The <u>price</u> of every one of the houses in our neighborhood <u>is</u> beyond our reach.

_____ 7. The <u>cabinet</u> for the stereo components <u>are</u> made of oiled oak.

_____ 8. The <u>subject</u> I want to write about <u>are</u> the effects of acid rain on the environment.

_____ 9. Delaware's two <u>senators</u> and one <u>representative</u> <u>is</u> the state's only representation in Congress.

_____ 10. Among the crowd <u>was</u> three <u>pickpockets</u>.

_____ 11. Neither the <u>ring</u> nor the <u>watch</u> <u>were stolen</u>.

_____ 12. There <u>are</u> a little <u>group</u> of houses at the curve in the road.

_____ 13. The <u>pieces</u> of the grandfather clock <u>was spread</u> over the floor.

_____ 14. Three <u>kinds</u> of film <u>is</u> sold at the shop.

_____ 15. When <u>are</u> the committee <u>members</u> to meet?

_____ 16. If the <u>audience</u> <u>fails</u> to applaud, the play will close.

_____ 17. Either the <u>motorcycle</u> or the <u>car</u> <u>is</u> to remain uninsured.

_____ 18. The first <u>thing</u> that I saw at the festival <u>were</u> the cheerful faces of the crowd.

_____ 19. <u>One</u> of the students <u>who</u> <u>rides</u> to school with me <u>falls</u> asleep each morning in class.

_____ 20. Neither the <u>books</u> nor the <u>record</u> <u>are</u> his.

_____ 21. The <u>number</u> of students <u>who</u> <u>favor</u> the new dean <u>are</u> not large.

_____ 22. <u>Some</u> of the statistics released by the state <u>shows</u> that <u>New</u>
<u>Browntown</u> <u>has</u> a high rate of murder.

_____ 23. He <u>is</u> one of the many students <u>who</u> <u>plays</u> basketball well.

_____ 24. The <u>style</u> of clothes that my <u>roommates</u> <u>wear are</u> now very popular.

_____ 25. The <u>similarity</u> in their clothes <u>is</u> just one of those things <u>that</u>
<u>make</u> my roommates seem like one person.

_____ 26. <u>All</u> of our exported wheat <u>is</u> not enough for all of the people <u>who</u>
<u>is</u> starving.

_____ 27. The top two <u>teams</u> in each division <u>gets</u> to go to the playoffs.

_____ 28. The <u>family</u> <u>eat</u> together every evening.

_____ 29. Neither the <u>sofa</u> nor the <u>chairs</u> <u>needs</u> recovering.

_____ 30. Only <u>one</u> of the houses <u>that</u> <u>were sold</u> <u>has</u> a garage.

EXERCISE 8-2

Subjects and Verbs: Rewriting Sentences (8a)

Rewrite each of the following sentences, changing the italicized words in the first group from singular to plural and those in the second group from plural to singular. Underline these changes. Make all other necessary changes. Check your work by reading your rewritten sentences aloud.

> *Example:*   A good *grade* was her only goal.
>
> *Good grades were her only goal.*

Singular to plural

1. A *star* is a giant *ball* of glowing gas.

2. A *star* shines both day and night, even though *it* is visible only at night.

3. A *meteor* looks like a falling *star* but is really a *piece* of rock or metal.

4. A *double star* consists of a *pair* of stars.

5. A *quasar* sends out strong radio waves.

6. The *life* of a *star* is billions of years.

7. An *astronomer* gets information about the *life* of a *star* by studying star clusters.

8. After a *star* begins to shine, *it* starts to change slowly.

9. The *speed* of this process depends on the mass of the *star*.

10. A *photometer* measures the brightness of a *star*.

Plural to singular

1. *Sounds* are caused by vibrations traveling through the air.

2. Sound *vibrations* travel in waves.

3. *Animals* hear sounds that *humans* do not hear.

4. *Pitches* affect the loudness of a sound.

5. *Echoes* are produced by sound waves striking reflecting *surfaces*.

6. *Bats* make high-pitched *sounds* as *they* fly in the dark.

7. *Microphones* change sound waves into electric currents.

8. Human *ears* hear sounds with frequencies ranging from 20 to 20,000 vibrations a second.

9. The highest *tones* on a piano have a frequency of about 4000 vibrations a second.

10. *Sounds* travel faster through dense *substances* than through less dense *ones*.

EXERCISE 8-3

Subject-Verb Agreement: Review (8a)

Some of the sentences in the following passage have errors in subject-verb agreement. Draw a line through each faulty verb and write the correct form above it.

Example: A story sometimes ~~have~~ *has* an important lesson.

1   One of the symbols of our nation consist of sticks tied in a bundle. These sticks represent the individual states, and the bundle represent the United States. The symbol, like our flag, makes a statement. The symbol means "United we stand; divided we fall." The symbol and the statement comes from an old story, one of the fables told by an ancient Greek story-teller named Aesop.

2   In this story, a man have several sons who are always quarreling with one another. The father, with frequent admonitions, try to get the sons to stop their arguing and fighting. But nothing works. Finally, the father decide to give his sons a practical lesson in the effects of disunity. He ask them to bring him a bundle of sticks. Handing the bundle to each of his sons, he tells them to break it in two shorter pieces. Each of the sons try to break the bundle, but none of them are able to do so. There is too much strength when the sticks has been tied together. Next the father unties the bundle and hand a single stick to each of his sons and ask each son to break his stick. Of course, all of the sons is able to break the sticks easily.

261

3   The father then tell his sons, "You are like the sticks. If you are united like the bundle of sticks, you are strong enough to withstand any attacks from enemies. But if there is quarreling and fighting among you, your enemies will be able to defeat you easily." The motto of the United States mean the same thing. The individual states become strong when they are united, but if they try to stand alone, they can be picked off one by one.

EXERCISE 8-4

Pronouns and Antecedents: Editing Sentences (8b)

Draw an arrow to the antecedent of each italicized pronoun in the following sentences. If the pronoun agrees with its antecedent, mark the sentence *C* on the line to the left. If the pronoun does not agree with its antecedent, cross out the pronoun and write the correct form on the line.

   Example: ___*his*___   Neither Tom nor Bud enjoyed their vacation.

_____   1. No one can know if *they* will get a job in June.

_____   2. The growing complexity of economics has not lessened *their* appeal to students.

_____   3. The teachers' union lost *their* right to bargain.

_____   4. Anyone who turned in a late paper had *their* grade reduced.

_____   5. Does everybody know where *they're* going now?

_____   6. Neither Herbert nor his brothers could find *their* book bags.

_____   7. An elephant never eats leaves or bark that has fungus growing on *them*.

_____   8. Bettors tend to follow *his or her* own whims at the racetrack.

_____   9. Every dog on the block barked *themselves* hoarse that night.

_____   10. The College of Arts and Sciences changed *their* entrance requirements.

_____   11. Neither of the two cars is known for *their* fuel economy.

_____   12. Every police officer anticipated the danger *they* would encounter.

_____   13. The manager or the employees will get *their* raises, but not both.

_____ 14. No one could see where *they* were going because of the fog.

_____ 15. Each of the employees got a raise on *his or her* anniversary with the company.

_____ 16. Someone had left *his* shoes in my locker.

_____ 17. Either Ms. Orosco or Ms. Olsen will receive an award for *her* teaching.

_____ 18. If a person has no pride in *their* appearance, others can always tell.

_____ 19. None of the engineers bidding on the contract thought *his* bid would be too high.

_____ 20. Families should install at least one smoke alarm in *their* homes.

_____ 21. Young children, it seems, are just as likely to suffer from stress and anxiety as *his or her* parents do.

_____ 22. Imagine the surprise when it was discovered that bacteria have developed antibiotic-resistance in some of *its* strains.

_____ 23. The average American receives about 25 credit-card offers per year in *their* mail.

_____ 24. The National Highway Traffic Safety Administration estimates that 67 percent of motorcyclists in accidents would not have suffered brain damage if *he or she* had been wearing a helmet.

_____ 25. Scientists say that both length and mass change with *their* velocity.

_____ 26. Each of the speakers wanted to deliver *their* speech first.

_____ 27. Neither the motorists nor the cyclist seemed to know what *they* had been thinking when the accident occurred.

_____ 28. Every one of the women was married and had brought *her* children to the seminar.

_____ 29. Neither of the encyclopedias had adequate coverage in *its* entry on data communication.

_____ 30. The basketball team was celebrating *their* victory all the way home.

EXERCISE 8-5

Agreement: Rewriting Text

Rewrite the following passage, changing each occurrence of *person* to *people*. Change corresponding verbs and pronouns, together with other related words as necessary. Underline all changes as you make them.

Example: (*Second sentence.*)

> One side says that terminally ill <u>people</u> should be allowed to die without having <u>their lives</u> extended with special treatments and equipment.

An argument new to our modern age is that of the right to die. One side says that a terminally ill person should be allowed to die without having his or her life extended with special treatments and equipment. The other side says that a dying person should be kept alive by his or her doctor for as long as possible. In earlier days, before the advent of modern technology, a terminally ill person simply died in his or her bed. Now that life can be extended for weeks and months in a period of protracted dying, we have the problem of how much a person should have to say about his or her own death.

In many states, it is legal for a person who believes strongly in his or her right to die to draw up a "living will." With this document, a person can direct physicians not to extend his or her life by artificial means—that is, not to use any treatment whose sole purpose is to put off an inevitable death. A person draws up this living will while he or she is still in good health and of sound mind. And in the states where these documents are legal, physicians will abide by them.

There is still some opposition to such a practice, however. A person should be kept alive, so goes the argument, to leave the way open for a miraculous recovery or a new treatment or cure. The next step after allowing a person to die is to take that person's life in order to shorten his or her pain and suffering. Called *euthanasia* or *mercy killing,* this practice is less widely accepted than that of writing living wills, although there are many who say that a terminally ill, suffering person should be assisted in his or her death.

The problem is a difficult one that has no easy solution.

EXERCISE 8-6

Agreement: Review

Fill in each blank with an appropriate verb or pronoun, as specified.

Example: Both fanatics and the casual viewer _____*like*_____ to watch The Weather Channel.

Verbs

1. World Wide Web sites and an online service _____ access to weather maps and forecasts.

2. Especially when tornadoes or a hurricane _____ approaching, people flock to sources of weather information.

3. There _____ available to people in this electronic age many sources of information about the weather.

4. One of the biggest hindrances to getting to and from work locations _____ the weather.

5. Snow is known to be a common hindrance, as _____ wind, rain, and ice.

6. A person who spends a great deal of time watching weather on television and a computer screen and who reads in the newspapers about the big storms _____ to know if weather is becoming more disastrous.

Pronouns

1. The person who is really hooked on weather forecasting can get the latest satellite images on _____ computer screen.

2. Nearly everyone was watching The Weather Channel on _____ television set during the 1996 blizzard in the eastern United States.

3. Neither most of the major networks nor the Cable News Network could show better ratings on _____ programs.

4. Meteorologists say that severe storms are normal and no worse than a reasonable person can expect _____ to be.

5. Neither way of accounting for the occurrence of weather-related disasters can make any person who has lost _____ home feel any better.

6. Nevertheless, people wanting to make _____ feel in better control of the elements turn on _____ sets or screens.

Adjectives and Adverbs

Chapter 9

Adjectives and adverbs are modifiers that describe, limit, or restrict the words they relate to. An **adjective** modifies a noun or a pronoun. An **adverb** modifies a verb, an adjective, another adverb, or a group of words. (See 5b-1).

 Functions of adjectives and adverbs

Adjectives modify nouns:	*serious* student	
	pronouns:	*ordinary* one
Adverbs modify verbs:	*warmly* greet	
	adjectives:	*only* three people
	adverbs:	*quite* seriously
	phrases:	*nearly* to the edge of the cliff
	clauses:	*just* when we were ready to leave
	sentences:	*Fortunately,* she is now employed.

9a Use adjectives only to modify nouns and pronouns.

Using adjectives to modify verbs, adverbs, or other adjectives is nonstandard.

NONSTANDARD	She speaks Spanish *good*.
STANDARD	She speaks Spanish *well*. [Well modifies the verb *speaks*.]
NONSTANDARD	We played a *real* good game.
STANDARD	We played a *really* good game. [Really modifies the adjective good.]
NONSTANDARD	They watched the children *close*.
STANDARD	They watched the children *closely*. [Closely modifies the verb *watched*.]

ESL   To negate a verb or an adjective, use the adverb *not:* They are *not* smiling. They are *not* happy. To negate a noun, use the adjective *no:* There were *no* smiles. ■

9b Use an adjective after a linking verb to modify the subject. Use an adverb to modify a verb.

A **linking verb** connects a subject and its noun or adjective complement. The linking verbs include *be, seem, become, appear, remain,* and verbs associated with the senses, such as *look, sound, smell, feel,* and *taste*. When a linking verb connects a subject and a modifier, the modifier is an adjective, not an adverb. (See 5a-3.) However, since some of these verbs may also function as nonlinking verbs, they are sometimes modified by adverbs. The only sure way to tell whether you need an adjective or an adverb is to look at how the individual word functions in its sentence.

He felt *strong*. [Adjective modifying *He*.]
He felt *strongly* about the election. [Adverb modifying *felt*.]

Chris appeared *calm*. [Adjective modifying *Chris*.]
Chris appeared *suddenly*. [Adverb modifying *appeared*.]

He felt *bad*. [Adjective modifying *He*, meaning "sorry" or "ill."]
The orchestra performed *badly*. [Adverb modifying *performed*.]
Return to classes when you are *well* again. [Adjective modifying the subject *you*.]

You played the game *well*. [Adverb modifying the verb *played*.]
She felt *good* about her recital. [Adjective modifying the subject *She*.]

9c After a direct object, use an adjective to modify the object and an adverb to modify the verb.

The only sure way to tell whether you need an adjective (object complement) or an adverb following a direct object is to look at how the individual word functions in its sentence. (See 5a-3.)

The mayor considered the proposal *appropriate*. [Adjective; the proposal was appropriate.]

The mayor considered the proposal *appropriately*. [Adverb; the considering was done in an appropriate way.]

9d When an adverb has a short form and an *-ly* form, distinguish carefully between the forms.

Some adverbs have both an *-ly* form and a short form without the *-ly*; these include *high, highly; late, lately; loud, loudly; near, nearly; quick, quickly; sharp, sharply; slow, slowly; wrong, wrongly.* Sometimes the meanings of the two forms are different, but with others the meanings are similar. When there is little difference in meaning, the short form is more often used informally and the *-ly* word is used for writing that is more formal.

DIFFERENCE IN MEANING

The ambulance arrived too *late*. [*Late* modifies *arrived*.]

He has been missing class *lately*. [*Lately* modifies *has been missing*.]

SIMILARITY IN MEANING

Drive *slow* around the corner. [Or *slowly; slow* is informal, modifying *Drive.*]

Slowly the clouds passed across the moon. [Appropriate usage; *Slowly* modifies *passed*.]

9e Use the comparative and superlative forms of adjectives and adverbs appropriately.

Most adjectives and adverbs have three forms. The **positive form** describes without comparing (*small, quickly*). The **comparative form** indicates a difference or similarity between two items (*smaller, more quickly*). The **superlative form** indicates a difference or similarity among three or more items (*smallest, most quickly*). (Negative comparisons are formed with *less* and *least: quickly, less quickly, least quickly.*)

 ### Degrees of irregular adjectives and adverbs

POSITIVE	COMPARATIVE	SUPERLATIVE
Adjectives		
good	better	best
bad	worse	worst
little	littler, less	littlest, least

271

POSITIVE	COMPARATIVE	SUPERLATIVE
many ⎫ some ⎬ most ⎭	more	much
Adverbs		
well	better	best
badly	worse	worst

 Use the correct form of irregular adjectives and adverbs.

Irregular adjectives and adverbs change the spelling of their positive form to show comparative and superlative degrees. Many of the following irregular forms can be used as both adjectives and adverbs.

 Use -er/-est or *more/most,* not both.

The *-er* and *-est* endings are not used in conjunction with the words *more* and *most*.

This is the *sharpest* (not *most sharpest*) knife I have.

 In general, use the comparative form for comparing two things and the superlative form for comparing three or more things.

This is the *longer* of the two plays.
The *longest* play we ever performed was *shorter* than this one.

 Use comparative or superlative forms only for modifiers that can logically be compared.

Modifiers like *unique, dead, perfect,* and *impossible* cannot logically be compared, because their positive forms describe their only state.

NOT   That was the *most impossible* trick I ever tried.

BUT   That trick was *almost impossible*.

9f Avoid double negatives.

Though common in some everyday speech, the **double negative** is avoided by most careful writers. In the example *Jamie didn't do nothing,* the *not (n't)* and *nothing* seem to say that Jamie did something. Examples of words that have this effect are *no, none, neither, never, barely, hardly,* and *scarcely*. Avoid using two of them in the same clause.

DOUBLE NEGATIVE   We couldn't *hardly* see the sun.

REVISED   We could *hardly* see the sun.

REVISED   We could*n't* see the sun.

9g   Use nouns sparingly as modifiers.

Overusing nouns as modifiers causes writing to be wordy or confusing.

NOT   The device is a wind speed measurement instrument. [Three nouns—*wind, speed,* and *measurement*—modify *instrument*.]

BUT   The device measures wind speed. [One noun, *wind,* remains as modifier. *Measurement* is now a verb, and *instrument* is unnecessary.]

NOT   The purpose of the seminar is knowledge reconstruction studies. [*Knowledge* and *reconstruction* modify *studies*.]

BUT   The seminar studies how knowledge is reconstructed. [*Knowledge* is a noun, *reconstruction* and *studies* are now verbs, and *purpose* is unnecessary.]

NOT   The student admission fee policy announcement needs clarification. [*Student, admission, fee,* and *policy* are all nouns modifying *announcement*.]

BUT   We need to announce more clearly what our policy is on student admission fees. [*Policy* is a noun, *announcement* is now an infinitive, and *clarification* is now an adverb modifying *to announce*.]

See Exercises 9-1, 9-2.

Related Exercises 5-5, 5-6.

9h   Distinguish between present and past participles as adjectives. ESL

Present and past participles may serve as adjectives: a *boring* person, a *bored* person. With those derived from verbs expressing feeling, the meaning may be entirely different, as in the preceding examples. Be careful how you use these participles:

amazing/amazed	fascinating/fascinated
amusing/amused	frightening/frightened
annoying/annoyed	frustrating/frustrated
astonishing/astonished	interesting/interested
boring/bored	pleasing/pleased
confusing/confused	satisfying/satisfied
depressing/depressed	shocking/shocked
embarrassing/embarrassed	surprising/surprised
exciting/excited	tiring/tired
exhausting/exhausted	worrying/worried

See Exercise 5-8.

9i Use *a, an, the,* and other determiners appropriately. ESL

Determiners precede nouns and mark them as nouns. Examples are the **articles** *(a, an, the),* and *my, their, whose, this, these, those, one, some,* and *any.* How determiners are used depends on their context and the kind of nouns they precede:

- A **count noun** names something that can be counted; it can form a plural: book/books, computer/computers, woman/women.
- A **noncount noun** names something that usually cannot be counted; it does not form a plural. Here are some noncount nouns:

advice	happiness	mail	silver
baggage	health	meat	supervision
cereal	homework	money	traffic
confidence	information	oil	truth
courage	intelligence	police	underwear
equipment	knowledge	pollution	water
evidence	legislation	research	wealth
furniture	lightning	satisfaction	weather
hair	love	scenery	work

- A **proper noun** names a particular person, place, or thing and begins with a capital letter:

Mississippi, Jell-O, James.

 1 Use *a, an,* and *the* where they are required.

With singular count nouns

A or *an* precedes a singular noun representing something previously not identified.

A minnow is *a* small, usually drab fish, *an* important aspect of aquatic life.

The precedes a singular count noun that has been previously identified or will be identified immediately.

> *The* importance of minnows cannot be overestimated.

The also precedes a singular count noun that is one of a kind or that refers to something shared by a community.

> *The* moon will be full on *the* fifteenth of June.
> *The* essay has become an established part of college composition courses.

Do not use *the* before a singular noun that names a general category.

> *Life* goes on.

With plural count nouns

Do not use *a* or *an* before a plural noun, nor *the* before a plural noun that names a general category.

> *Children* learn to trust their parents.

With noncount nouns

Do not use *a* or *an* before a noncount noun. Use *the* before a noncount noun that names specific representatives of a general category.

> *Research* is needed on women's illnesses.
> *The* furniture in her new apartment is rather worn.

With proper nouns

Do not use *a* or *an*, and in most cases *the*, before a proper noun.

> *Liu* grew up in *Beijing*.

The is common, however, before names of ships (*the Titanic*), oceans (*the Atlantic*), mountain ranges (*the Himalayas*), regions (*the East Coast*), rivers (*the Missouri*), and some countries (*the United States*).

 Use other determiners appropriately.

Use other determiners according to context and the kind of noun.

With singular count nouns

my, our, your, his, her, its, their, possessive nouns (*cat's, cats'*)
whose, which(ever), what(ever)
this, that

275

one, any, some, every, each, either, neither, another, the other
one, the first, the second, etc., *the last*

Their bank account is overdrawn.
Every dollar was spent.

With plural count nouns

my, our, your, his, her, its, their, possessive nouns *(cat's, cats')*
whose, which(ever), what(ever)
these, those
some, any, both, many, enough, more, most, other, the other, such, few, a few,
  fewer, fewest, several, all, all of the, a lot of
no, two, three, etc., *the first, the second* etc., *the last*

Those numbers are incorrect.
Some mistakes were made.

With noncount nouns

my, our, your, his, her, its, their, possessive nouns *(cat's, cats')*
whose, which(ever), what(ever)
this, that
some, any, much, more, most, enough, other, the other, such, little, a little, less,
  least, all, all of the, a lot of
no, the first, the second etc., *the last*

That money should be saved.
Would *more* evidence convince you?

See Exercise 9-3.

EXERCISE 9-1

Adjectives and Adverbs: Comparing Forms

In each sentence, circle the appropriate form from the pairs in parentheses. Identify the circled modifiers as adjectives *(adj)* or adverbs *(adv)* on the lines to the left.

Example: __adv__ Skating has become a *(real,* (really)*)* popular sport.

_____ 1. A sport that has grown *(fast, fastly)* in popularity is in-line skating.

_____ 2. In-line skates *(can't hardly, can hardly)* be compared to traditional roller skates.

_____ 3. They are *(more, most)* like ice skates.

_____ 4. These *(most unique, unique)* new skates have all four wheels in a row.

_____ 5. They were invented to keep hockey players in *(better, more better)* shape off season.

_____ 6. In-line skates are *(faster, more faster)* than traditional roller skates.

_____ 7. They also are *(most, more)* maneuverable.

_____ 8. Skaters like the excitement they get from skating *(rapidly, rapid)* downhill or over the road.

_____ 9. Since their introduction several years ago, in-line skates have become *(less costly, less costlier)* than at the beginning.

_____ 10. In-line roller skates were made *(first, firstly)* in Minnesota.

_____ 11. However, the market is *(bigger, biggest)* in California.

_____ 12. Of the two kinds of roller skates, in-line and traditional, thrill-seekers consider the newer model *(more attractively, more attractive)*.

277

EXERCISE 9-2

Adjectives and Adverbs: Editing Forms

In each sentence below, identify any incorrect form of a modifier by crossing it out and inserting the correct form on the line to the left. If the adjectives and adverbs are correct as given, write *C* on the line.

Example: _worst_ July is the ~~worse~~ time to visit the Southwestern deserts.

_____ 1. They never complained of being real lonely.

_____ 2. A special designed mirror enabled him to drive.

_____ 3. We tourists located the hotel easy.

_____ 4. Doesn't nobody know how to repair this clock?

_____ 5. Greg is surely going to lose his job.

_____ 6. It was so foggy that we couldn't hardly see the road.

_____ 7. Playing bad for one game was no reason to give up.

_____ 8. Keith was one of the most brightest students to graduate from this school.

_____ 9. The bus driver applied the brakes quick to avoid hitting the bicyclist.

_____ 10. Don't never speak bluntly to the dean of students.

_____ 11. Beating the Hartford tennis team is near impossible.

_____ 12. Of the two athletes, Reggie has the highest average.

_____ 13. How sudden did he stop?

_____ 14. Harry always takes arguments serious.

_____ 15. San Francisco's transportation system remains most unique.

_____ 16. Oliver executed the pass play perfectly.

EXERCISE 9-3

Articles: Using them Appropriately

exer
9

Insert *a*, *an*, or *the* as appropriate in the blank spaces, or leave the space blank if an article is not needed.

> *Example:* Many students rent _____ apartments while they are in
>
> _____ school. [No articles.]

1. Renting _____ apartment can be less stressful if you observe

    _____ few tips.

2. First, try to view _____ apartment you have in mind rather than

    _____ similar one.

3. Make sure _____ apartment is big enough for you, your room-

    mates, and all of your belongings.

4. Plan to pay no more for _____ rent than 30 percent of your in-

    come.

5. Request _____ written lease and read it carefully.

6. Do not sign _____ lease until you understand it.

7. Ask for _____ check-in sheet to list damage in _____

    apartment before you move in.

8. Make _____ copy of _____ list for your record.

9. Find out what _____ policy is for vacating _____ apart-

    ment.

10. If _____ policy requires _____ month's notice, you could pay extra for _____ late notice.

11. Invest in _____ renter's insurance; _____ cost is minimal and could be worthwhile.

12. Know _____ person you should contact for _____ repairs.

13. When you move, leave _____ forwarding address with _____ apartment owner.

14. Ask for _____ receipt when you turn in _____ keys.

Chapter 10

Sentence Fragments

A **complete sentence** consists of both a subject and a predicate—a verb that asserts something about the subject. (See 5a.) A phrase or clause that lacks a subject or a predicate or both but is set off like a sentence (with a capital letter and a period) is a **sentence fragment.** A clause that begins with a subordinating word and is set off like a complete sentence is also a sentence fragment. (See 5c.) These incomplete structures are generally avoided by careful writers because in most cases they represent incomplete thoughts.

FRAGMENTS

For example, when I play the piano.

Especially in the rain.

Which is what I meant to say in the first place.

 Complete sentences versus sentence fragments

A complete sentence or main clause
- contains a subject and a verb (*Candy is sweet*);
- and is not a subordinate clause (beginning with words such as *because, whereas,* or *who*).

A sentence fragment
- lacks a verb (*The horse running away*);
- *or* lacks a subject (*And ran away*);
- *or* is a subordinate clause not attached to a complete sentence (*Because it was confused*).

281

10a   Test your sentences for completeness, and revise any fragments.

The best test of sentence completeness is to rely on your own sense of grammar. To do this you must treat the word group between periods as a separate entity, something that makes a complete statement on its own.

FRAGMENT   Because Carla had already registered for the class.

As a separate entity, this subordinate clause is clearly a fragment. To assist you in identifying fragments, try reading your essays or paragraphs backward, period by period. (*Note:* In looking for fragments, don't be distracted by pronouns; a sentence is not incomplete just because it has a pronoun without an antecedent. The following word group is a complete sentence: *He ran five miles before the sun came up.* But see Chapter 12 for pronoun reference.) Here are some tests for sentence completeness that you can apply to your sentences.

 Tests for sentence fragments

A sentence is complete only when it passes *all three* tests.

1. Find the verb.
2. Find the subject.
3. Make sure the clause is not subordinate.

Test 1: Find the verb.

Look for a verb in the group of words. If there is none, the word group is a fragment.

FRAGMENT   Five blocks down this street and to the right. [This word group has no verb. Compare: *The theater is five blocks down this street and to the right.*]

Sentence verbs must be **finite,** meaning they can change form, as illustrated:

	FINITE VERBS IN COMPLETE SENTENCES	**VERBALS IN SENTENCE FRAGMENTS**
SINGULAR	The pizza *bakes*.	The pizza *baking*.
PLURAL	Pizzas *bake*.	Pizzas *baking*.
PRESENT	The pizza *bakes*.	
PAST	The pizza *baked*.	The pizza *baking*.
FUTURE	The pizza *will bake*.	

See Chapter 7 for a further discussion of verb forms.

Test 2: Find the subject.

If you find a verb in your group of words, look for a subject by asking who or what is performing the action of the verb: Who or what *does?* Who or what *is?* If you do not have a subject and if the word group is not a command, you have a fragment.

> **FRAGMENT**   And consequently went six blocks in the wrong direction. [This group of words has a verb, *went,* but it does not state who performed the action. But *Go six blocks past the theater* is not a fragment; it is a command.]

Test 3: Make sure the clause is not subordinate.

If you find a verb and a subject, look for a subordinating word at the beginning of the word group: *because, after, when, if, which, where,* and the like. Turn to the lists of subordinating conjunctions and relative pronouns on pp. 144–145. These words signal subordinate clauses that must be attached to main clauses. Exceptions are words used to introduce questions (such as <u>Which</u> *book did you ask for?*).

> **FRAGMENT**   Which is why the hostages weren't released sooner. [The relative pronoun *which* subordinates the entire clause.]
>
> **FRAGMENT**   When twenty-four people were captured by the rebels. [The subordinating conjunction *when* makes the clause a fragment.]

Revising sentence fragments

You can revise a sentence fragment in one of two ways:

Revision of sentence fragment

- Rewrite the fragment as a complete sentence.
- Combine the fragment with the appropriate main clause.

These two methods are illustrated below.

> **FRAGMENT**   Music videos began to make their appearance in late 1980. *Some of them concert performances and some technological innovations.*
>
> **REVISED**   Music videos began to make their appearance in late 1980, *some of them concert performances and some technological innovations.* [Fragment attached to the sentence, separated by a comma.]
>
> **REVISED**   Music videos began to make their appearance in late 1980. *Some of them were concert performances and some were technological innovations.* [A verb, *were,* is added to the fragment, making it a sentence.]

FRAGMENT	Some people think the best time to have champagne is in the morning. *Or just before a meal.*
REVISED	Some people think the best time to have champagne is in the morning *or just before a meal.* [Fragment attached to the sentence with no separating punctuation.]
REVISED	Some people think the best time to have champagne is in the morning. *Some prefer it just before a meal.* [Fragment expanded to a sentence with the addition of a subject and a verb.]
FRAGMENT	Videocassette recorders are sold in a variety of stores. *Video specialty shops, supermarkets, hardware stores, and other mass-market outlets.*
REVISED	Videocassette recorders are sold in a variety of stores: *video specialty shops, supermarkets, hardware stores, and other mass-market outlets.* [Fragment attached to the sentence, separated by a colon.]
REVISED	Videocassette recorders are sold in a variety of stores—*video specialty shops, supermarkets, hardware stores, and other mass-market outlets.* [Fragment attached to the sentence, separated by a dash. The dash is less formal than the colon.]
REVISED	Videocassette recorders are sold in a variety of stores. *You might find them in video specialty shops, supermarkets, hardware stores, and other mass-market outlets.* [Fragment expanded to a sentence with a subject and a verb.]

10b A subordinate clause is not a complete sentence.

A subordinate clause has both a subject and a predicate and begins with a subordinating conjunction (such as *after, although, because, since*) or a relative pronoun (*who, which, that*). (See 5c-4.) When set off from the main clause on which it depends for its meaning, a subordinate clause is a sentence fragment.

FRAGMENT	The return on the investment was 20 percent. *Which was higher than he expected.*
REVISED	The return on the investment was 20 percent, which was higher than he expected. [Subordinate clause linked to main clause.]
REVISED	The return on the investment was 20 percent. The earnings were higher than he expected. [Subordinate clause rewritten as main clause.]

If the fragment starts with a subordinating conjunction, sometimes the fragment can be corrected by omitting the conjunction.

FRAGMENT	Because the stock market had risen fifteen points.
REVISED	The stock market had risen fifteen points.

10c **A verbal phrase or a prepositional phrase is not a complete sentence.**

A **verbal phrase** consists of an infinitive *(to spend)*, a participle *(spending, spent)*, or a gerund *(spending)*, along with its objects or modifiers. (See 5c-2.)

FRAGMENT	I went to the convocation for one reason. *To hear the architect speak.*
REVISED	I went to the convocation for one reason: to hear the architect speak. [Verbal phrase linked to main clause.]
REVISED	I went to the convocation for one reason. I wanted to hear the architect speak. [Verbal phrase rewritten as main clause.]
FRAGMENT	He has one purpose in life. *Spending money.*
REVISED	He has one purpose in life—spending money. [Verbal phrase linked to main clause.]
REVISED	He has one purpose in life. He wants only to spend money. [Verbal phrase rewritten as main clause.]

A **prepositional phrase** consists of a preposition (such as *by, on, to, with*) plus its object and the object's modifiers. (See 5c-1.) Since it has neither a subject nor a predicate, a prepositional phrase set off as a sentence is a fragment.

FRAGMENT	The accident occurred at the main intersection. *During the evening rush hour.*
REVISED	The accident occurred at the main intersection during the evening rush hour. [Prepositional phrase linked to main clause.]

10d **Any word group lacking a subject or a verb or both is not a complete sentence.**

Fragments are created when a writer punctuates a noun plus its modifiers, an appositive, or the second part of a compound predicate as a sentence. Nouns plus their modifiers are sometimes so long that they seem like sentences, but without verbs they cannot stand alone as sentences.

FRAGMENT	*The flash flood warning that came on the television screen during the Dallas/Green Bay football game.* It caused quite a stir in the family.
REVISED	The flash flood warning that came on the television screen during the Dallas/Green Bay football game caused quite a stir in the family. [Fragment replaces *It* as the subject of the main clause.]

Appositives are nouns, plus any modifiers, that rename other nouns (see 5c 5).

FRAGMENT	The car was a gift from her eccentric uncle. *Hubie Crumbacher.*
REVISED	The car was a gift from her eccentric uncle, Hubie Crumbacher. [Appositive linked to main clause.]
REVISED	The car was a gift from her eccentric uncle. Hubie Crumbacher was his name. [Appositive rewritten as main clause.]

A **compound predicate** consists of two or more verbs and their objects and modifiers (see 5d).

FRAGMENT   The rescuers loaded their backpacks with food and bandages. *And struck out for the woods.*

REVISED   The rescuers loaded their backpacks with food and bandages and struck out for the woods. [Second part of compound predicate linked to main clause.]

FRAGMENT   We accepted their congratulations. *And the reward money.*

REVISED   We accepted their congratulations and the reward money. [Second part of compound object linked to main clause.]

10e Be aware of the acceptable uses of incomplete sentences.

The sentence subject is omitted in commands and some exclamations.

(*You*) Learn these rules.   (*You*) Forget it!

Sometimes incomplete sentences are used for question-and-answer patterns and for transitions from one idea to another.

Got it? Sure.   First a word of explanation.

Titles are usually fragments.

"Reflections on a Summer Pond"
Twenty-Thousand Leagues Under the Sea
ER

Fragments are often seen in advertising—a medium that frequently uses a telegraphic style to save space and the reader's time.

A few of their favorite things. From G.E.

Nissan manufactures and assembles cars and trucks in 21 countries. From America to Australia. From Peru to Portugal.

Finally, experienced writers sometimes use sentence fragments that do not fit any of these patterns and that violate the rules for avoiding fragments discussed in this chapter. These sentence fragments can be effective structures. However, unintentional fragments are usually distractions in the communication of thoughts. In most academic writing, you show control of your sentences by avoiding fragments.

See Exercises 10-1, 10-2, 10-3, 10-4.

Related Exercises 5-1, 5-4, 5-12, 5-13, 5-14.

EXERCISE 10-1

Sentence Fragments I: Revising

Most of the following passages contain a sentence fragment. Underline each fragment and then rewrite the passage to correct each fragment. Add the fragment to a complete sentence in the passage or change the fragment to make it a complete sentence. If there is no fragment in the passage, write *C* in the left margin.

Example: After studying French for three years, I tried to translate a poem. <u>Without much success.</u>

I didn't have much success.

1. The contrast between the two cats is great. One of them being arrogant and the other highly sociable.

2. They moved into a condominium in a quiet neighborhood. Quiet being all they wanted.

3. The National Geographic specials have been very popular. Sponsored in part by an oil company. PBS has shown several.

4. The river was polluted with insecticides. Funds for cleaning it up were not available. The chemical company had gone bankrupt.

5. Chris has one quality that her roommate doesn't have. Patience. Chris is so patient that others take advantage of her.

6. Riding the subway, I always read the advertisements above the windows. Trying to figure out what gimmicks the advertisers use.

7. I tried to be gentle with the old woman. Who had insulted me the day before but now needed my help.

8. Perry can be loudmouthed and overbearing. For example, his saying he should be in a dorm with "better-quality people."

9. The salary starting at $15,000 a year. The job failed to attract qualified applicants. The advertisement ran for three weeks.

10. Mike seems to be a good father. For example, taking his children to ball games or on trips, or just staying around the house teaching his children new games.

EXERCISE 10-2

Sentence Fragments II: Revising

The following passages are of the type you might find in advertising copy. Rewrite any sentence fragments as complete sentences, combining them with main clauses or adding words where necessary. If there is no fragment, write *C* in the left margin.

> *Example:*   He had a dream of earning a college degree. A dream that all but died.
>
> *He had a dream of earning a college degree, a dream that all but died.*

1. The name of the game is knowing the right people. Because they'll help you invest your money in the right bank.

2. There are two reasons why you should buy Wheatgerms Cereal. It's good for you. And it tastes great.

3. It's the last word in computers. And the very best of its kind.

4. The whole system is state of the art. And we've made it even better.

5. Come in today. See the difference.

6. It's the best pen you'll ever buy. Which is why you should try one today.

7. Gold-plated. Roller-ball tip. For men and women.

8. Luxury. Beauty. Performance. See your dealer today.

9. Wholefarm Bacon. Because there is no better bacon.

10. Toughguy Mowers. Dependability and efficiency worth the price.

11. See Alaska. Write now.

12. Free. Latest catalog. Call now.

13. Seeing the best. Buying what you see.

14. Free for the asking. Send today.

15. Looking for good music?

16. One of the most nutritious foods. Raisins. Sweet and good.

17. Think cheese. Made with real milk.

18. Northcountry frozen potatoes. The taste is in the bag.

19. When all you want to do is stop the pain.

20. Announcing the beginning of a new age.

EXERCISE 10-3

Sentence Fragments III: Revising

Some of the following items are sentence fragments. Rewrite each fragment by expanding it to a complete sentence or connecting it to a complete sentence. If the word group is a complete sentence, write *C* to the left of it.

Example: A common cause of death and property loss.

> *Home fires are a common cause of death and property loss.*

1. Many homes do not have fire extinguishers.

2. Devices for putting out small fires, such as those started in wastebaskets or mattresses.

3. A fire extinguisher, in addition to a smoke detector.

4. Both devices can protect a home from the hazards of fire.

5. Because every day fires break out in 2000 homes in the United States.

6. Every home should have at least one fire extinguisher.

7. Preferably several, and the homeowner or renter should know how to operate each extinguisher.

8. Rated by a system of numbers and letters.

9. Higher numbers indicating an extinguisher capable of putting out larger fires.

10. Such as 9B having a greater capacity than 3B.

11. And 2A having a greater capacity than 1A.

12. The A rating refers to fires that burn ordinary materials.

13. B refers to flammable liquid fires.

14. C to fires in electrical equipment.

EXERCISE 10-4

Sentence Fragments: Revising Text

In each passage below, circle the number preceding any word group that is a sentence fragment. Then revise each fragment by linking it to a main clause or by rewriting it as a main clause.

A. [1]The Great Barrier Reef, stretching for 1200 miles along Australia's northeastern coast. [2]Sometimes called the world's largest living thing. [3]The reef is made up of living coral. [4]Purple, green, and pink animals called marine polyps. [5]More than three hundred kinds of coral have been identified. [6]Each having a scientific name as well as a common name describing its shape. [7]For example, mushroom or needle.

[8]In addition to the coral in the Great Barrier Reef, the surrounding sea carries an abundance of other exotic sea life. [9]Parrot fish, butterfly fish, sea anemones, and giant clams. [10]Unfortunately, the snorkeled tourist swimming off the sandy beaches may encounter a deadly jellyfish known as the sea wasp. Of which there are many. [11]Or sharks around the reef. [12]But the sharks, it is said, have never attacked. [13]And with a little care swimmers can avoid the jellyfish. [14]A tour aboard a glass-bottomed cruise boat, including supervised snorkeling in the warm waters around the reef. [15]A safe, exhilarating experience. [16]Even for a stranger to the waters.

[17]People from North America wanting to visit the Great Barrier Reef should travel to Australia during the northern winter months. [18]If they

want to experience Australia's summer. [19]Landing in Sydney, they would need to travel north to Cairns. [20]The nearest city to the Great Barrier Reef.

B.   [1]In the African nation of Dahomey. [2]A man's wives were put to death at his funeral. [3]Their spirits being supposed to keep him company in the afterlife. [4]When a king died, many attendants and wives were put to death. [5]The people believed that a dead person had desires and emotions. [6]Such as anger. [7]The dead person could take revenge on the living if his desires were not satisfied. [8]Thus a king remained very powerful even after death. [9]With as much power as he had had when he was alive. [10]Since the dead were so powerful, the survivors had to prevent the dead from becoming envious. [11]As well as angry. [12]So the survivors often sacrificed possessions. [13]Along with attendants and wives. [14]Appropriate possessions for sacrifice being cattle, food, and jewelry. [15]Such sacrifices guaranteeing continual poverty for the people. [16]War frequently resulted. [17]Because through war the people renewed their wealth. [18]The additional result, however, was the destruction of even more lives. [19]Only in this century did these mourning sacrifices disappear. [20]And now the people seem to live in a state of spiritual uneasiness.

Comma Splices and Fused Sentences

Chapter 11

Two problems commonly occur in linking main clauses in a single sentence. The first, the **comma splice,** occurs when two or more main clauses are separated only by a comma, with no coordinating conjunction between them. *(The car was bright red, its interior was black.)* The second, the **fused sentence** or **run-on sentence,** occurs when two or more main clauses are joined with no punctuation or conjunction between them. *(The car was bright red its interior was black.)*

 ## Situations that may produce comma splices and fused sentences

- First clause is negative, second positive:

  SPLICE   Petric is not a nurse, she is a doctor.

  REVISED   Petric is not a nurse; she is a doctor.

- Second clause amplifies or illustrates the first:

  FUSED   She did well in college her average was 3.9.

  REVISED   She did well in college: her average was 3.9.

- Second clause contains a conjunctive adverb such as *however, therefore,* or *instead* (see 11b):

    SPLICE   She had intended to become a biologist, *however,* medicine seemed more exciting.

    REVISED   She had intended to become a biologist; *however,* medicine seemed more exciting.

- The subject of the second clause repeats or refers to the subject of the first clause.

    FUSED   Petric is an internist *she* practices in Topeka.

    REVISED   Petric is an internist; *she* practices in Topeka.

- Splicing or fusing is an attempt to link related ideas or to smooth choppy sentences:

    SPLICE   She is very committed to her work, she devotes almost all her time to patient care.

    REVISED   *Because* she is very committed to her work, she devotes almost all her time to patient care.

    REVISED   She is *so* committed to her work *that* she devotes almost all her time to patient care.

- Words identifying the speaker divide a quotation between two complete sentences. (See p. 409 for the punctuation to use in this case.)

    SPLICE   "Medicine is a human frontier," Petric says, "The boundaries are unknown."

    REVISED   "Medicine is a human frontier," Petric says. "The boundaries are unknown."

COMMA SPLICES

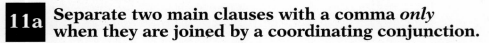

11a   **Separate two main clauses with a comma *only* when they are joined by a coordinating conjunction.**

COMMA SPLICE   The mattress caught fire, the flames spread quickly.

REVISED   The mattress caught fire, *and* the flames spread quickly.

A comma splice can be corrected in various ways, each one establishing a different relation between the clauses.

1. Insert a coordinating conjunction (*and, but, or, nor, for, so, yet*) after the comma that separates the two main clauses (see 5d-1), as in the preceding revised example.

2. Make separate sentences of the two main clauses:

   The mattress caught fire. The flames spread quickly.

3. Insert a semicolon rather than a comma between the main clauses:

   The mattress caught fire; the flames spread quickly.

4. Replace the comma with a semicolon and add a conjunctive adverb (see 11b):

   The mattress caught fire; unfortunately, the flames spread quickly.

5. Make one of the main clauses into a subordinate clause by using a subordinating conjunction such as *although, since,* or *when* or a relative pronoun (*that, which, who*) (see 5c-4):

   After the mattress caught fire, the flames spread quickly.

6. Reduce one of the main clauses to a subordinate phrase (see 5c):

   The mattress having caught fire, the flames spread quickly.

11b Separate main clauses related by *however, thus, for example,* and so on.

Conjunctive adverbs include *also, consequently, however, then, thus,* and *therefore* (see the list in 5d-2). Because these words are modifiers, not conjunctions, the two main clauses that they relate must be separated by a semicolon or a period. The words themselves are often set off by commas.

COMMA SPLICE	The house looked run-down, however the inside was in beautiful shape.
REVISED	The house looked run-down; however, the inside was in beautiful shape.
REVISED	The house looked run-down. However, the inside was in beautiful shape.
REVISED	The house looked run-down. The inside, however, was in beautiful shape. [A conjunctive adverb may often be placed at the beginning, middle, or end of its clause.]

FUSED SENTENCES

11c Combine two main clauses only with an appropriate connector or punctuation mark between them.

A fused, or **run-on, sentence** joins two or more main clauses with no connecting word or punctuation between them. It can be corrected in the same ways as a comma splice.

299

FUSED	Dr. Ling is director of the hospital he also maintains a private practice.
REVISED	Dr. Ling is director of the hospital, *but* he also maintains a private practice. [Comma and coordinating conjunction]
REVISED	Dr. Ling is director of the hospital. He also maintains a private practice. [Separate sentences]
REVISED	Dr. Ling is director of the hospital; he also maintains a private practice. [Semicolon]
REVISED	Dr. Ling is director of the hospital; *however,* he also maintains a private practice. [Semicolon and conjunctive adverb]
REVISED	Dr. Ling is director of the hospital, *although* he also maintains a private practice. [Subordinating conjunction]
REVISED	Dr. Ling is director of the hospital and maintains a private practice. [Coordinating conjunction joining second verb phrase]

See Exercises 11-1, 11-2, 11-3, 11-4.

Related Exercises 5-15, 5-18, 22-1, 22-2.

cs/fs
11c

300

EXERCISE 11-1

Comma Splices and Fused Sentences: Revising

Most of the following items are either comma splices or fused sentences. Correct each error in one of five ways: (1) by inserting a coordinating conjunction or both a comma and a coordinating conjunction; (2) by forming separate sentences; (3) by using a semicolon; (4) by reducing one of the main clauses to a subordinate clause; or (5) by reducing one of the main clauses to a phrase. If an item contains no error, write *C* to the left of it.

Example: Pollution from smoking is a major cause of illness, ~~it affects~~ *affecting* smoker and nonsmoker alike.

1. Evidence continues to mount it shows that passive smoke causes diseases.

2. Nonsmokers can be victims of cancer, heart disease, and respiratory illnesses that are caused by smoke in the air they breathe.

3. Parents who smoke in the home are putting their children at risk, roommates endanger nonsmoking partners.

4. Passive smoke is smoke exhaled by the smoker, it is also the smoke emitted from the end of a cigarette.

5. Most of the smoke in a room has not been exhaled by a smoker, it has come from the end of a burning cigarette.

6. A smoker inhales, his or her lungs remove some of the tar, nicotine, and harmful gases.

7. The smoke from the end of a cigarette is more hazardous, none of the chemicals have been removed.

8. Some of the more dangerous components of smoke are acetylene, benzene, formaldehyde, hydrogen cyanide, nicotine, and propane, they readily enter the bloodstream of smoker and nonsmoker alike.

9. Setting aside a section of a room to separate smokers from nonsmokers is not adequate protection for nonsmokers, the smoke still circulates in the air.

10. The only way to protect nonsmokers from the harmful effects of smoke is to ban all indoor smoking, public buildings and workplaces must have restrictions.

11. Another problem with smoking tobacco is addiction, data shows it begins in the teen years.

12. This early addiction has long been known by tobacco companies, for that reason they target young teenagers in their advertising.

13. There is evidence that nine out of ten people who begun smoking in their midtwenties quit again within the year.

14. It is obvious why tobacco companies target the teens, they need the business.

15. Many addicted smokers wish they had never started they were just kids and didn't think they would become addicted.

EXERCISE 11-2

Comma Splices and Fused Sentences: Combining Sentences

exer
11

The following pairs of sentences are correct as written. Combine each pair into a single sentence, making the change noted in parentheses.

Example: The factory once employed five hundred persons. Now there is a parking lot in its place. (*Comma and coordinating conjunction.*)

> The factory once employed five hundred persons, but now there is a parking lot in its place.

1. Human cells contain two hundred thousand genes. Each controls specific traits. (*Semicolon.*)

2. Mars was named for the Roman god of war. Its reddish color was likened to blood spilled in wars. (Because *clause.*)

3. Most diamonds are thought to be very old. In fact, they are among the oldest minerals on earth. (*Semicolon.*)

4. Most meteors that enter the earth's atmosphere burn up before striking the ground. Some do not. (*Comma and coordinating conjunction.*)

5. Time zones are divided by meridians. Meridians run between the north and south poles. (*Relative clause.*)

6. Mercury was the Roman god of commerce. Curiously, he was also the god of thievery. (*Semicolon.*)

7. Reindeer have been domesticated for centuries in Lapland. They provide meat, milk, clothing, and transportation. (*Adverb clause.*)

8. Mohandas K. Gandhi gave up a Western way of life. He led a life of abstinence and spirituality. (*Compound predicate.*)

9. Gothic romance novels originated with writers such as Mary Shelley and Horace Walpole in the eighteenth and nineteenth centuries. These novels are popular reading today. (*Relative clause.*)

10. According to Saint Thomas Aquinas, theology and science cannot contradict one another. There cannot be any conflict between theology and philosophy. (*Comma and coordinating conjunction.*)

EXERCISE 11-3

Comma Splices and Fused Sentences: Patterning

exer
11

Each of the following sentences is a compound sentence with correct punctuation between two main clauses. Write a sentence patterned after each sentence.

Example: Deficiency diseases result from a diet lacking certain elements; for example, a lack of vitamin A results in night blindness.

> Our library has several features to help the new students; for example, a librarian is always seated at the information desk.

1. The official language of Djibouti, a small country in eastern Africa, is Arabic, but most of the people speak Afar or Somali.

2. The bottle-nosed dolphin has a keen sense of hearing, good eyesight, and an excellent sense of taste; however, it has no sense of smell.

3. A dormouse is about three inches long; its tail is another three inches.

4. Werewolves exist in stories of the supernatural; according to legend, they are people who somehow change into threatening wolves.

5. The ancient Egyptians wrote on a paperlike material called papyrus; in fact, they may have been its inventors.

6. The Monroe Doctrine was intended to protect the Latin American countries from European colonialism; however, it more often these days is seen as US imperialism.

7. One week after the Normandy invasion, Hitler sent the first V-1 rockets over London; the British called them "buzz bombs."

8. Yams look very much like another root vegetable, the sweet potato, and many people mistakenly confuse the two.

9. The large country in Africa's midsection was called Zaire; until its independence in 1971 it was known as the Belgian Congo.

10. Approximately 97 percent of the earth's water is in the oceans, and an additional 2 percent is in glaciers and icecaps.

Name _____ Date _____

EXERCISE 11-4

Comma Splices and Fused Sentences: Review

In the following essay, circle the number preceding any sentence that has a comma splice or is a fused sentence. Then revise each faulty sentence in the most appropriate way.

THE COUNTRY "DOWN UNDER"

[1]The landing of 1000 convicts on the shores of what is now Sydney marks what Australians claim was the beginning of their nation, it had been "discovered" by Captain James Cook in 1770. [2]In 1788 the first ship arrived with criminals from British prisons they were settled as Australia's first citizens. [3]Since its rough beginning as a British penal colony, Australia has become a country of unique contrasts.

[4]With a national population of about sixteen million, about one million Australians boast convict ancestry. [5]About 20 percent of the population today is foreign born. [6]Many are Middle Eastern and Asian settlers, they have come because of the nation's liberal immigration policies. [7]The original settlers, the aborigines, are in the minority, numbering about 160,000, they are virtual outcasts in Australia today. [8]The country's population is a study in contrasts and diversity.

[9]The land itself provides the greatest contrasts. [10]Geologists say that the continent split off from what we now call South America and

Antarctica about sixty million years ago. [11]Its coasts are fertile, but its inland—the outback—is arid, the northeast is tropical rain forest. [12]Off the northeastern coast is the magnificent natural wonder the Great Barrier Reef, to the south the Great Bight provides marvelous surfing. [13]Distances are vast between some of the cities but even more so between settlers in the outback, people may live as much as two hundred miles apart.

[14]Australia has been known for many years for its characteristic animals. [15]Its koalas, kangaroos, wallabies, and platypuses live nowhere else in the world except in captivity. [16]Kangaroos are the national symbol, every year millions are slaughtered as farmers try to prevent them from destroying crops.

[17]Americans know about Australia from the *Crocodile Dundee* movies, from the novel and television miniseries *The Thornbirds,* and from comedian Paul Hogan, these and other entertainment media give us a glimpse of the world "down under," we can learn more if we want to Australia is definitely in the news.

Chapter 12

Pronoun Reference

A **pronoun** is a substitute for a noun and has no meaning by itself. The pronoun takes its meaning from the noun it stands for and refers to, called its **antecedent.** Thus the connection between the pronoun and the antecedent must be clear. (See Chapter 6.)

CONFUSING   When my mother stopped speaking to my aunt, *she* rewrote *her* will. [Antecedent of *she* and *her* unclear.]

CLEAR   My mother rewrote *her* will when *she* stopped speaking to my aunt. [Antecedent of *her* and *she* is clearly *mother.*]

CLEAR   My aunt rewrote *her* will when my mother stopped speaking to *her*. [Antecedent of *her* both times is clearly *aunt.*]

Most pronoun reference problems occur because the pronoun could refer to more than one antecedent (as in the preceding example), because the pronoun is so far from its antecedent that its meaning is unclear, or because the antecedent is not specific or cannot be located at all.

12a   Make a pronoun refer clearly to one antecedent.

A plural pronoun may refer to a compound antecedent.

Smith and *Bean* doubled *their* profits.

But a pronoun will be unclear if it can refer to *either* one of two antecedents.

CONFUSING	Mort told Anna that Hildy lost *her* money.
CLEAR	Mort told Anna that Hildy lost *Anna's* money. [Pronoun replaced with appropriate noun.]
CLEAR	Mort told Anna, "Hildy lost your money." [Sentence rewritten to quote Mort directly.]

Principal causes of unclear pronoun reference

- More than one possible antecedent (12a):

CONFUSING	To keep birds from eating seeds, soak *them* in blue food coloring.
CLEAR	To keep birds from eating seeds, soak *the seeds* in blue food coloring.

- Antecedent too far away (12b):

CONFUSING	Employees should consult with their supervisors *who* require personal time.
CLEAR	Employees *who* require personal time should consult with their supervisors.

- Antecedent only implied (12c):

CONFUSING	Many children begin reading on their own by watching television, but *this* should be discounted in government policy.
CLEAR	Many children begin reading on their own by watching television, but *such self-instruction* should be discounted in government policy.

See also 12d, 12e, and 12f.

12b Place a pronoun close enough to its antecedent to ensure clarity.

Avoid separating a pronoun and its antecedent with other nouns that the pronoun could refer to.

CONFUSING	During a scuffle with a mugger on the subway, Maria almost lost her watch. Fortunately, she only sprained her toe. *It* was a gift from her fiancé.
CLEAR	Maria almost lost her *watch, which* was a gift from her fiancé, during a scuffle with a mugger on the subway. Fortunately, she only sprained her toe.

310

A clause that begins with a relative pronoun (*who, which, that*) is generally placed immediately after the noun it modifies.

> **CONFUSING**   The article pointed out that the spaceships on the surface of Mars, *which* can never be recovered, form the beginning of a garbage dump on the planet.

> **CLEAR**   The article pointed out that the spaceships, *which* can never be recovered, form the beginning of a garbage dump on Mars.

Make a pronoun refer to a specific antecedent, not an implied one.

 Use *this, that, which,* and *it* cautiously.

In **broad reference** a pronoun such as *this, that, which,* or *it* refers to an entire phrase, clause, sentence, or even paragraph instead of to a single noun. Such references are generally unclear. Unless the meaning of the pronoun is unmistakable, avoid making a broad reference. Think of *this* (or *that* or *which*) as an adjective: *this something.* By filling in a noun after *this,* you will clarify your own thinking and make your meaning clear to your readers.

> **CONFUSING**   In an apparently bloodless coup, a group of military officers seized governmental power. *This* happened just eight days after the country's president died.

> **CLEAR**   In an apparently bloodless coup, a group of military officers seized governmental power. *This coup* happened just eight days after the country's president died.

> **CONFUSING**   As we watched, the two men began hitting each other and yelling for help. *This* started the riot.

> **CLEAR**   As we watched, the two men began hitting each other and yelling for help. *This fight* started the riot.

> **CLEAR**   We saw the riot start when the two men began hitting each other and yelling for help.

2 Implied nouns are not clear antecedents.

Modifiers—adjectives, nouns used as adjectives, and the possessives of nouns and pronouns—do not provide specific antecedents for pronouns.

> **WEAK**   In the *teacher's* desk, she kept a paddle and a pint bottle.

> **REVISED**   The *teacher* kept a paddle and a pint bottle in her desk.

> **WEAK**   The *sick* man claimed he caught it from a cow at the 4-H fair.

> **REVISED**   The sick man claimed he caught *his illness* from a cow at the 4-H fair.

3 **Titles of papers are not clear antecedents.**

TITLE	A Shortage of Locksmiths
NOT	*This* explains the increase in burglaries.
BUT	In "A Shortage of Locksmiths," the author explains the increase in burglaries.

12d Use *it* and *they* to refer to definite antecedents. Use *you* only to mean "you, the reader."

The use of *it* and *they* with no clear antecedent, though well established in conversation, is generally unacceptable in writing because such pronouns can be vague and lead to wordiness.

WEAK	*It* says in the directions that the small box should be opened first.
REVISED	The directions say that the small box should be opened first.
WEAK	On the television advertisement *they* said that science had finally conquered the common cold.
REVISED	The television advertisement said that science had finally conquered the common cold.

You is acceptable when it is used to mean "you, the reader": *You can see that I had no choice.* But *you* should not be used indefinitely in other contexts.

WEAK	Citizens of Mudburg know that *you* can have *your* car towed away for illegal parking.
REVISED	Citizens of Mudburg know that *people* can have *their* cars towed away for illegal parking.

12e Use the pronoun *it* only one way in a sentence.

Writers use the pronoun *it* in a number of ways: as a personal pronoun standing for many nouns, in certain set expressions, and as a way to delay the subject or direct object.

It's raining. It's almost two o'clock. [Set expressions.]

It's no secret that John wants to move. [Delayed subject: *that John wants to move,* a noun clause.]

Fred's financial situation made it important that he look for a job. [Delayed direct object: *that he look for a job.*]

While all three uses of *it* are standard, using the pronoun in more than one way in a sentence can confuse the reader.

ref
12e

312

| CONFUSING | *It* was an inaccurate forecast: *it* predicted rain, but *it* is snowing. |
| CLEAR | The forecast was inaccurate: it predicted rain, but instead we have snow. |

12f Use *who, which,* and *that* for appropriate antecedents.

Writers commonly use *who* to refer to persons and to animals that have names:

My dog Carly, *who* ran away last spring, turned up yesterday at the high school.

Which refers to animals and things:

I'd hoped to inherit my grandfather's diamond stickpin, *which* my father wore at my wedding.

That refers to animals and things and occasionally to persons:

The book *that* you recommended was missing seventy pages.

He studies babies *that* are just beginning to see.

(See also 21c-1 for the use of *which* and *that* in nonrestrictive and restrictive clauses.)

See Exercises 12-1, 12-2, 12-3, 12-4.

Related Exercise 5-2.

EXERCISE 12-1

Pronoun Reference: Revising Sentences

Circle each pronoun in the following sentences. Then revise the sentences to make all pronouns refer clearly to their antecedents.

1. Gerardo and Maria checked their bags at the ticket counter, but then they weren't sure if they were safe.

2. The car seemed to be rolling down the road by itself, but when it curved a little to the left I could see a child's hands on the steering wheel.

3. When you lived in the nineteenth century, your feet and your horses were your only private means of transportation.

4. Workers in today's jobs who develop multiple skills find that they function better.

5. Some critics charge that school districts have spent millions of dollars to install computers, yet their potential is not being met.

6. The exam was scheduled for Tuesday, which was not in my plans.

7. In some cities, children encourage friends, neighbors, and relatives in their recycling efforts.

8. After discussing the repair for the car, we knew it was time it was taken care of.

9. On the Internet, students can access data, resources, and experts in their areas of interest.

10. People serving on established committees that want more business could use the results of this survey.

11. They say that trouble comes in threes.

12. Fears are normal in childhood, but how they overcome them differs from child to child.

13. In Marilyn French's groundbreaking novel *The Women's Room,* she questions accepted norms regarding women's roles.

14. Some people get nervous when they hear the word *software.* This makes them reluctant to use computers.

EXERCISE 12-2

Pronoun Reference: Replacing Vague Pronouns

exer
12

Rewrite the following paragraphs, replacing the italicized pronouns with nouns that express their meaning more clearly. In some cases you will need to change other words for careful phrasing.

Harriet likes to anthropomorphize. *That* means she attributes human characteristics to animals. She does *it* with birds, squirrels, deer, raccoons, and any other living thing that happens to pass her way. She especially attributes *them* to cats, of which she has two.

She thinks that squirrels eat her petunias just to upset her, whereas they probably do *it* because they like the way *they* taste. *They* probably also have their squirrel reasons for digging up the lawn and dropping acorn scraps on *her* patio, *which* only faintly resemble human motivations. *That* is probably true of the deer and the raccoons too. They probably enjoy the corn she sets out in the yard, but as they stand there munching *it* they probably don't give the slightest thought to how it got there or who put it there. In fact, if they saw her coming around the corner of the house, they would quickly disappear.

It's different with *her* cats. They don't run away; instead they hang around and expect *her* to care for them. At least she sees *it* that way. Maybe they're not actually grateful, she thinks, but they do expect *it*. And when she talks to them, they respond with reasoned answers, *which* has to be an extreme case of anthropomorphism. When she asks if they're hungry, they of course answer "M-yah." When she left them out in the rain one day they scolded her severely in answer to her question if they were wet. Well, anyone who knows cats would agree that they probably were indeed annoyed about *it*.

But Harriet really does take *it* too far. Animals do think and feel, but *that* does not mean they're like people.

EXERCISE 12-3

Pronoun Reference: Combining Sentences

Rewrite the following sentences, replacing *Lennie* with *Lennie, Annie, and Gus*. Change all other words as necessary. Your first sentence will read:

Lennie, Annie, and Gus were students at Riverland Community College.

Lennie was a student at Riverland Community College. Because he was a nontraditional student, he took some of his courses through the office of continuing studies. As a student who took one of these courses, he would not meet in a classroom; instead, he would do all the work at home. The courses were called "self-paced."

Lennie liked doing a self-paced course, because he could adjust his work schedule more easily and could work around his other courses. But there were things he didn't like about the self-paced course too. One was that he missed the interactions with other students in the classroom. Another was the specter of procrastination. Lennie had never prided himself on his self-discipline. Now that he had no deadlines for getting his assignments done, he seemed to always be falling behind. He could take an "incomplete" at the end of the term, but his problem was still there. The only difference was that now it had carried over into the next term.

He decided he really must do something about disciplining himself.

EXERCISE 12-4

Pronoun Reference: Review

In the following paragraph, circle any pronoun whose antecedent is unclear, remote, implied, or indefinite. Then revise the sentences as necessary so that all pronouns refer clearly and appropriately to a definite and stated antecedent.

Before 1889 the little town of Westin had no lumberyard where their citizens could buy it. Lumber was available only at the sawmills, and they didn't sell them to the general public. This was a problem for a person that wanted to build their own house or to add a room or a porch. But it was an opportunity for an enterprising businessman. William Rand was such a person, who had just migrated from Germany with his family. He was a skilled carpenter, and he knew wood. But William didn't have any money, which was a problem.

He discussed it with the owner of one of the sawmills in the area around Westin, and he agreed that it was a good plan. They decided to go into business together and start one in downtown Westin. So, with the sawmill owner putting up the money and Rand running it, they opened their lumberyard with five loads of unsorted lumber as initial stock that they got from the mill.

Today the business is still owned by the Rand family, but it's his grandsons now who are in charge of it. And you can still buy your lumber there.

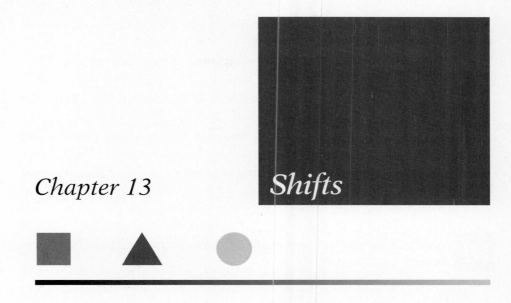

Chapter 13 — *Shifts*

To be clear, a sentence, a paragraph, or an essay should be consistent in such grammatical elements as person, number, and tense unless grammar or meaning requires a shift. The following guidelines address each of these elements.

13a Keep a sentence or related sentences consistent in person and number.

In speaking and writing, we deal with persons (and things) in three ways: (1) we can *be* one, (2) we can talk or write *to* one, and (3) we can talk or write *about* one. In grammar these ways of dealing with people and things are called *person:* first person (*I*), second person (*you*), and third person (*he, she, it, tree* and other nouns). With *number,* we indicate whether we are referring to one or more than one (*I/we; he, she, it/they; tree/trees* and all other nouns).

Writing that shifts unintentionally from one person to another—say from writing *about* someone to writing *to* someone (from third person to second), or that shifts in number, using a singular noun but referring to that antecedent with a plural pronoun—is difficult for readers to follow.

INCONSISTENT   *We* learned before going on the desert tour that *you* should leave *your* itinerary with the park rangers. [Shift from first person to second person.]

REVISED   *We* learned before going on the desert tour that *we* should leave *our* itinerary with the park rangers.

321

| INCONSISTENT | A football *player* should be in good condition even before *they* begin training. [Shift from singular to plural.] |
| REVISED | A football *player* should be in good condition even before *he* begins training. |

Consistency sometimes requires that words other than the pronouns—usually nouns—agree in number.

| INCONSISTENT | All the countries represented at the convention displayed their *flag*. |
| REVISED | All the countries represented at the convention displayed their *flags*. |

The consistency in the nouns in the revised sentence is called **logical agreement.**

13b Keep a sentence or related sentences consistent in tense and mood.

By their forms, verbs tell time of action (tense) and mood (7e and 7g). Unintentional shifts in either tense or mood distract a reader from understanding the writer's meaning.

INCONSISTENT	Doctors *had* no way to prevent polio until Salk *develops* the vaccine. [Shift from past tense to present tense.]
REVISED	Doctors *had* no way to prevent polio until Salk *developed* the vaccine.
INCONSISTENT	The committee moved that Clarice *attend* the conference and that she *should represent* the organization. [Shift from subjunctive to indicative mood.]
REVISED	The committee moved that Clarice *attend* the conference and *represent* the organization.

13c Keep a sentence or related sentences consistent in subject and voice.

Within a sentence, writers sometimes change from active to passive voice, or vice versa, to keep their subjects consistent, and sometimes they change subjects from one part of the sentence to another while keeping their voices consistent (see 7h).

SHIFT IN VOICE	If the *petition had been signed* by all the students, *it would have won* reduced fees. [Shift from passive to active voice; subject is consistent.]
SHIFT IN SUBJECT	If *all the students had signed* the petition, *it would have won* reduced fees. [Shift from *all* to *it*, meaning "petition"; voice is consistently active.]

But inconsistency with both voice and subject in the same sentence can cause confusion.

SHIFT IN VOICE AND SUBJECT	If the *petition had been signed* by all the students, *we would have won* reduced fees. [Shift in subject from *petition* to *we* and in voice from passive to active.]
NO SHIFT	If *all the students had signed* the petition, *we would have won* reduced fees.

shift
13d

13d Keep a quotation or a question consistently indirect or direct.

Direct quotations or **questions** report the exact words of a speaker or writer. **Indirect quotation** also reports what someone said or wrote, but not in the exact words and not in quotation marks.

DIRECT QUOTATION	Jack asked, "Why do the Cubs keep losing? Is there going to be a management change?" [Consistent direct quotation.]
FAULTY SHIFT	Jack asked why the Cubs kept losing and is there going to be a management change? [Shift from indirect quotation to word order of direct quotation.]
INDIRECT QUOTATION	Jack asked why the Cubs kept losing and whether there would be a management change. [Consistent indirect quotation.]

See Exercises 13-1, 13-2.

Related Exercise 7-8.

EXERCISE 13-1

Consistency: Revising Sentences

The sentences below have unnecessary shifts in person, number, tense, mood, subject, voice, or form of quotation, as identified in parentheses. Revise each sentence to achieve consistency.

Example: The meeting was to be attended by representatives from three colleges, but they could not agree on where to meet. (*Subject, voice.*)

Representatives from three colleges were to attend the meeting, but they could not agree on where to meet.

1. He said he bought the recorder without asking would it work. (*Quotation.*)

2. A person should stay clear of credit cards because they encourage you to spend more money than you have. (*Person.*)

3. To have it printed, take it to the shop on Wednesday, and then you should call the next day. (*Mood.*)

4. Although the poet's words are fascinating, I do not know what they meant. (*Tense.*)

5. She wanted to buy flannel, but it was learned that she was allergic to flannel. (*Voice.*)

6. If one wants to get the most from college, you must work hard, ask questions, and keep an open mind. (*Person.*)

7. The two countries had had peaceful relations for a decade when suddenly a border dispute erupts into a war. (*Tense.*)

8. He said my face was red and asked was I embarrassed? (*Quotation.*)

9. When someone receives repeated nuisance phone calls, they have no choice but to change their number. (*Number.*)

10. After a mugger attacked the elderly woman, she was taken to the hospital by police. (*Subject, voice.*)

11. Everyone should be aware that poor night vision can endanger your life. (*Person.*)

12. The characters in the movie are average people, but they had more than average problems. (*Tense.*)

EXERCISE 13-2

Shifts: Review

In the following paragraph, underline any unnecessary or confusing shifts in person, number, tense, mood, subject, voice, or form of quotation. Then revise the paragraph to achieve appropriate consistency both within sentences and from sentence to sentence.

Our trip to the beach got off to a bad start when the car has two flat tires a mile from home. You can always count on some trouble with our car but usually nothing this annoying. We arrived at the motel late, but fortunately our reservations had not been canceled by the manager, who remembers us from the last time we vacationed there. He asked how long would we be staying and did we want the seafood special for dinner. We checked into our room, and our luggage was unpacked. Everything was going smoothly. Then we went to dinner and turned in for the night. One would have expected that the rest of the vacation should be routine if not fun. But that night each one of us gets sick from their seafood dinner. The next morning the rain came, and for three days we just sat in the room playing cards until it was time that our trip home could be made.

Chapter 14

Misplaced and Dangling Modifiers

MISPLACED MODIFIERS

A **misplaced modifier** does not clearly modify the word intended by the writer.

14a Place modifiers where they will clearly modify the words intended.

Modifying phrases and clauses function as adjectives and as adverbs. As adjectives they generally come directly after the nouns or pronouns they modify:

The house *across the street* is being repainted. [The prepositional phrase functions as an adjective, modifying the noun *house.*]

As adverbs they may follow the words they modify, or, like single-word adverbs, they may appear elsewhere in the sentence if their function is clear:

The house is being repainted *despite the weather.*
Despite the weather, the house is being repainted.

Faulty placement of phrases and clauses can lead to confusion or unintended humor at the expense of the writer.

CONFUSING	The first thing you need to do is beat the eggs in a bowl *with a wire whisk.* (The prepositional phrase tends to modify *bowl* instead of *beat.*)
CLEAR	The first thing you need to do is put the eggs in a bowl and beat them with a *wire whisk.*
CONFUSING	The teacher said that she expected us to do well on the exam *during her lecture.* [The prepositional phrase seems to modify *exam* instead of *said,* as intended.]
CLEAR	*During her lecture,* the teacher said that she expected us to do well on the exam.
CONFUSING	I heard that Mayor Miller was accused of slander *on the evening news.* [Does *on the evening news* modify *heard* or *was accused?*]
CLEAR	I heard *on the evening news* that Mayor Miller was accused of slander.
CLEAR	I heard that *on the evening news* Mayor Miller was accused of slander.
CONFUSING	The house was in the woods *that burned last night.*
CLEAR	The house *that burned last night* was in the woods.
CONFUSING	I like the blue shirt with the white egrets *that Jack is wearing.*
CLEAR	I like *Jack's* blue shirt with the white egrets. [If the subordinate clause can't be made clear, you can recast the sentence.]

14b Place limiting modifiers carefully.

Limiting modifiers—such as *almost, even, just, only,* and *simply*—modify the word or word groups that immediately follow them.

Aaron sold *only* one car today. [He sold no more than one.]
Only Aaron sold one car today. [No one else sold one car.]
Aaron *only* sold one car today. [He did nothing else but sell one car.]

14c Make each modifier refer to only one grammatical element.

A modifier can modify only one grammatical element in a sentence—the subject, the verb, the object, or something else. A **squinting modifier** confusingly seems to modify either the word preceding it or the one following it. The reader may not read the modifier the way the writer intended it.

SQUINTING	People who walk *normally* are healthier than those who don't. [Does *normally* modify *walk* or *are healthier?*]
CLEAR	People who walk are *normally* healthier than those who don't.
CLEAR	*Normally,* people who walk are healthier than those who don't.

14d Keep subjects, verbs, and objects together.

Modifiers commonly interrupt a subject and its predicate or a verb and its object or complement.

The people *who take that attitude* deserve to be friendless. [The italicized clause separates the subject, *people,* from the verb, *deserve.*]

However, a long modifier in such a position may make a sentence awkward or confusing, especially if the modifier precedes the word it modifies or relates to the whole sentence.

<table>
<tr><td>AWKWARD</td><td>The old papers were, just as I had suspected when I found them in the attic, valuable.</td></tr>
<tr><td>REVISED</td><td>The old papers were valuable, just as I had suspected when I found them in the attic.</td></tr>
</table>

14e Keep parts of infinitives or verb phrases together.

It is normal practice to separate parts of a **verb phrase** with single-word modifiers, as in *had surely known* or *hasn't entirely seen.* However, dividing these parts with a long modifier can create awkwardness.

<table>
<tr><td>AWKWARD</td><td>Charles has, whether he admits it or not, known about the exam. [Verb phrase has known is split.]</td></tr>
<tr><td>REVISED</td><td>Whether he admits it or not, Charles has known about the exam.</td></tr>
<tr><td>REVISED</td><td>Charles has known about the exam, whether he admits it or not.</td></tr>
</table>

It is sometimes natural and acceptable to split an **infinitive** (see 5c-2) with a single-word modifier when the alternative would be awkward: <u>*To openly shun*</u> *younger students is not only arrogant but also rude.* However, dividing infinitives with a long modifier is usually unacceptable.

<table>
<tr><td>AWKWARD</td><td>The aides are expected to, whether they want to or not, do whatever the head nurse asks. [Infinitive split.]</td></tr>
<tr><td>REVISED</td><td>The aides are expected to do whatever the head nurse asks, whether they want to or not.</td></tr>
</table>

See Exercises 14-1, 14-4.

Related Exercise 5-11.

14f Position adverbs of frequency with care. ESL

Adverbs telling how frequently something happens—such as *always, seldom, rarely, often, sometimes,* and *never*—usually come between helping verbs and main verbs.

331

| AWKWARD | Typewriters *are used seldom* any more. |
| REVISED | Typewriters *are seldom used* any more. |

With the verb *be,* adverbs of frequency follow the verb.

| AWKWARD | Computers *usually are* the writing instrument of choice. |
| REVISED | Computers *are usually* the writing instrument of choice. |

14g Arrange adjectives appropriately. ESL

Adjectives precede nouns in particular orders depending on each adjective's function. The first would be a determiner, the last a noun used as an adjective.

1. Determiners (such as *a, an, the, some, many, this, all*)
2. Opinion (such as *good, funny, lazy, wonderful*)
3. Size or shape (such as *large, round, tiny*)
4. Age (such as *old, recent, fourteen-year-old, twentieth-century*)
5. Color (such as *red, yellow, brown, black*)
6. Origin (such as *Chicano, Taiwanese, Italian*)
7. Material (such as *plastic, woolen, cotton, silk, glass*)
8. Noun used as adjective (such as *company, typewriter, house, apartment*)

Here are a few examples:

a wonderful silk shirt   the large apartment building
some round wooden knobs   good twentieth-century literature
this yellow cotton dress   recent Taiwanese immigrants

Strings longer than three adjectives are rare. For guidelines on punctuating two or more adjectives before a noun, see 21f.

See Exercise 14-2.

Related Exercise 5-6.

DANGLING MODIFIERS

14h Relate dangling modifiers to their sentences.

A **dangling modifier** is a modifier that does not relate sensibly to any word in its sentence.

| DANGLING | To win the marathon, the weather should be cool. [The modifying phrase *To win the marathon* seems, illogically, to describe *weather.*] |

DANGLING	Looking closer, the string was obviously an electrical cord. [Because the person doing the looking is not named, the modifying phrase *Looking closer* seems to modify *string*.]

A dangling modifier usually appears at the beginning of a sentence. It is usually a participial phrase (*screaming for help*), an infinitive phrase (*to arrive on time*), a prepositional phrase in which the object of the preposition is a gerund (*after riding the subway*), or an elliptical phrase in which the subject is understood (*while in school*). (See 5c-2.)

All of these modifiers imply that somebody is performing the action they describe (somebody is screaming, somebody arrives on time, somebody rides the subway, somebody is in school). Readers generally understand that the doer of the action is the person or thing named in the subject of the main clause. In each of the following sentences, the connection is clear; the subject of the main clause is the same as the implied subject of the introductory modifier.

Screaming for help, the woman ran out of the burning house. [The woman was screaming.]

To arrive on time, I'll have to leave soon. [I want to arrive on time.]

After riding the subway, Cleo walks six blocks to school. [Cleo rides the subway.]

While in school, Karen tries to forget her troubles at home. [Karen is in school.]

Usually if the implied subject of the modifier is different from the subject of the main clause, the modifier dangles.

Dangling modifiers can be corrected in two ways: (1) by expanding the modifier into a clause and naming the subject or (2) by revising the main clause so that its subject is the same as the subject implied in the phrase.

DANGLING	*After riding the subway*, Cleo's wallet was missing. [Prepositional phrase appears to modify *wallet*, the subject of the sentence. The possessive noun *Cleo's* functions as an adjective.]
REVISED	*After Cleo had ridden the subway*, his wallet was missing. [The phrase is expanded into a clause to include the subject.]
REVISED	*After riding the subway*, Cleo discovered that his wallet was missing. [The subject of *discovered* is the same as that of *riding*.]
DANGLING	*When cut in half*, you can see the shape in the lines of the onion. [The elliptical phrase *When cut in half* appears to modify *you*.]
REVISED	*When the onion is cut in half*, you can see the shape of its lines. [The phrase is expanded into a clause.]
REVISED	*When you cut the onion in half*, you can see the shape of its lines. [The phrase is expanded into a clause, active voice.]
DANGLING	*Generally considered a childhood disorder*, many adults may be afflicted with Attention Deficit Disorder. [The implied subject of *considered* is *Attention Deficit Disorder*, not *adults*. The passive voice of the main clause contributes to the faulty connection. See 5e-3.]

333

REVISED   *Generally considered a childhood disorder,* Attention Deficit Disorder may afflict many adults. [The problem is corrected by recasting the main clause into active voice.]

See Exercises 14-3, 14-4.

Related Exercises 5-10, 5-11.

EXERCISE 14-1

Misplaced Modifiers: Revising Sentences

In the following sentences, underline each misplaced modifier and then revise
the sentence so that the meaning is clear. Write *C* to the left of sentences that
are correct.

Example: A vegetarian lifestyle is easier to maintain today than it was a
number of years ago <u>with the accessibility of plant products.</u>

*With the accessibility of plant products, a
vegetarian lifestyle is easier to maintain
today than it was a number of years ago.*

1. Many people have, as a lifestyle, chosen vegetarianism.

2. They feel that eating all animal flesh is wrong.

3. People who see immorality in eating meat often become vegetarians.

4. Some vegetarians just eat plant products.

5. They limit their diet to grains, legumes, vegetables, fruits, nuts, and seeds
   for maintaining nutrition and their sense of morality.

6. Others only supplement their diet with dairy products such as cheese and
   milk.

7. Still others eat, as well as plants and milk products, eggs.

8. It is not necessary, in order to have adequate protein in the diet, to eat meat.

9. Many plant products have high levels of protein such as nuts and legumes.

10. A vegetarian feels that carnivores, if they were to consider the source of their meat, would have less of an appetite for it.

11. Consumers see carcasses hanging in the butcher shop or chickens being slaughtered no longer.

12. Meat comes packaged and ready for cooking today.

13. Vegetarians say that a trip to a slaughterhouse might cure carnivores of their taste for meat some day.

14. Vegetarians also remind meat eaters of the risk of raising cattle to the environment.

15. South American rain forests are destroyed so that more cattle can be raised to supply beef for North American fast-food restaurants at an alarming rate.

EXERCISE 14-2

Adjectives and Adverbs: Arranging Appropriately

Place the adjectives and adverbs in their correct positions before their nouns.

    Example: her __*paperback*__ __*history*__ book (*history, paperback*)

1. the _____ _____ _____ tree (*oak, twisted, old*)

2. some _____ _____ _____ laws (*religious, Hindu, modern*)

3. any _____ _____ _____ typewriter (*functional, electric, moderately*)

4. the _____ _____ newspaper (*daily, week-old*)

5. a _____ _____ _____ sandwich (*ham, hot, thick*)

6. one _____ _____, _____ _____ banana (*overripe, forgotten, long, disgustingly*)

7. a pair of _____ _____ _____ _____ shoes (*leather, new, red, patent*)

8. a _____ _____ _____ pen (*felt-tip, black, worn-out*)

9. the _____ _____ _____ car (*fourteen-year-old, yellow, convertible*)

10. some _____ _____ _____ software (*computer, released, recently*)

11. two _____ _____ _____ shirts (*silk, gray, extra-large*)

EXERCISE 14-3

Misplaced and Dangling Modifiers: Revising Text

Underline any misplaced or dangling modifiers in the following paragraph. Then revise the paragraph by moving modifiers, adding words, or rewriting sentences as necessary.

Not wanting to be known for their lack of discrimination, mystery novels are shunned by some serious readers. When viewing mystery novels, it is believed that they are all formulaic and unperceptive. People who read books in this genre avidly will agree that many mystery novels are indeed empty of real substance. As prolific readers, particular authors and particular books that fit the description can be named. These books are quickly written apparently with insufficient editing, so that careful readers find dangling modifiers, subject-verb disagreement, unclear pronoun reference, and so on. Worse yet, the plots and motivations lack credibility, and the characters are flat and one-dimensional. But this description only fits part of the books in this genre. Some authors who specialize in mystery novels diligently care about their craft and view their mystery writing seriously and professionally. To learn which writers are careful and which ones only are in a hurry to get the next blockbuster on the market, it is important to do a lot of reading.

EXERCISE 14-4

Dangling Modifiers: Revising Sentences

exer
14

Most of the following sentences contain dangling modifiers. Revise each incorrect sentence by changing either the phrase or the main clause. When you keep the verbal phrase, make sure that its implied subject (the person or thing performing the action) is the same as the subject of the sentence. If a sentence is already correct, write *C* in the space below it.

Example: To operate a citizen's-band radio, the fee is no longer required.

To operate a citizen's-band radio, one no longer needs to pay a fee.

1. When reading poetry, rhythm often contributes to meaning.

2. After buying a new pair of boots, they should be treated with a protective finish.

3. To recover from the surgery, the vet recommended that we leave our puppy overnight.

4. When painting the walls, care should be taken to protect the floor from dripping brushes.

5. After adding three cups of ground chickpeas, the pot should be heated.

6. Taking a look at the gifts, the smallest box was the one the child selected.

7. Going for a touchdown, the quarterback lofted the ball.

8. Being a nonconformist, a multicolored wig was what she chose to wear.

9. With no concern that the audience was bored, Carson's lecture continued for two hours.

10. To get the employer's attention, your résumé should be attractive and informative.

11. To get the costumes done in time for tonight's taping, help is needed in the costume department.

12. As the best player on the team, we all cheered when Davidson entered the game.

13. Having been told the qualifications for jurors and then shown a videotape, it was time for lunch.

14. When entering the building, your identification card should be in clear view.

15. Having broken my ankle, my brother has been driving me to school.

Chapter 15

Mixed and Incomplete Sentences

MIXED SENTENCES

A **mixed sentence** is a sentence whose parts do not fit together in grammar or in meaning.

15a Untangle sentences that are mixed in grammar.

A sentence mixed in grammar begins with one grammatical structure and ends with another.

1 Make sure subject and verb fit together grammatically.

Do not begin a sentence one way and end it another.

MIXED	During the worst part of the storm frightened all of us. [Prepositional phrase used as a subject.]
REVISED	During the worst part of the storm, all of us were frightened. [Main clause revised to include a subject.]
REVISED	The worst part of the storm frightened all of us. [Preposition omitted; its object, *part*, becomes the subject of the sentence.]

MIXED	By doing these things has made me a better person.
REVISED	By doing these things, I have become a better person. [Main clause revised to include a subject.]
REVISED	Doing these things has made me a better person. [Preposition omitted.]

2 State parts of sentences, such as subjects, only once. ESL

Do not use pronouns to repeat subjects or objects that have already been stated in the same clause.

FAULTY	Some trees *they* have long roots called tap roots. [The subject *trees* is repeated.]
REVISED	Some trees have long roots called tap roots.
FAULTY	The tree that the longest tap root was found on *it* was a South African fig tree. [The pronoun *it* repeats *that* as object of the preposition *on.*]
REVISED	The tree that the longest tap root was found on was a South African fig tree.

15b Match subjects and predicates in meaning.

The mixed constructions in 15a-1 are faulty because they have no element that can function as the grammatical subject. Other mixed constructions result from **faulty predication,** in which the subjects and predicates do not fit together, especially when they are joined by a linking verb. While such constructions are common in speech, they are generally unacceptable in formal writing.

MIXED	A prank that irks me is my brother jumping out from behind corners. [The prank is not the brother.]
REVISED	A prank that irks me is my brother's jumping out from behind corners. [The prank is the jumping.]

Another common mixed construction occurs when the linking verb is followed by a *when, where,* or *because* clause. Such clauses are adverbial, but the linking verb requires a noun—or a phrase or clause that can function as a noun.

MIXED	Happiness is when you know what you want from life. [The *when* clause is an adverb; the construction requires a noun.]
REVISED	Happiness is knowing what you want from life. [The gerund phrase beginning with *knowing* functions as a noun.]
MIXED	The reason for her failure is because she was ill. [The *because* clause is an adverb; the construction requires a noun.]
REVISED	The reason for her failure is that she was ill. [The *that* clause functions as a noun.]

INCOMPLETE SENTENCES

15c Omissions from compound constructions should be consistent with grammar or idiom.

Writers and speakers commonly omit unnecessary or repetitious words from their sentences, and such omissions are entirely acceptable. Here is an example of an acceptable omission:

COMPLETE   My mother graduated from both high school and college, my father only from high school. [The verb *graduated* can be omitted in the second part of the sentence.]

Sometimes, however, we omit words that only seem unnecessary, when in fact they are needed for grammatical completeness.

mixed/inc
15d

INCOMPLETE   My grandparents' generation was indoctrinated in conventional morality and strong-minded as a result.

REVISED   My grandparents' generation was indoctrinated in conventional morality and *was* strong-minded as a result. [The first *was* is part of a passive construction; the second is a linking verb.]

INCOMPLETE   Most of us lack knowledge or comfort with science.

REVISED   Most of us lack knowledge *of* or comfort with science. [Idiom requires different prepositions with *knowledge* and *comfort*. (See also 31b-3.)]

INCOMPLETE   Interest in four-wheel steering on automobiles is positive but opinions mixed.

REVISED   Interest in four-wheel steering on automobiles is positive, but opinions are mixed. [*Interest* takes a singular verb, *is*, but the second subject, *opinions*, requires a plural verb, *are*.]

15d All comparisons should be complete and logical.

1 State a comparison fully enough to ensure clarity.

UNCLEAR   Mars is nearer to us than Pluto.
CLEAR   Mars is nearer to us than *it is to* Pluto.
CLEAR   Mars is nearer to us than Pluto *is*.
UNCLEAR   Your chances of winning are *as great*, if not greater than, mine.
CLEAR   Your chances of winning are *as great as*, if not greater than mine.

The items being compared should in fact be comparable.

UNCLEAR   The chimpanzee's thumb is smaller than a *human*.
CLEAR   The chimpanzee's thumb is smaller than a *human's*.

 Use *any* or *any other* appropriately in comparisons.

ILLOGICAL   The Pacific is larger than *any* ocean in the world.
LOGICAL   The Pacific is larger than *any other* ocean in the world.

ILLOGICAL   Toyotas are more popular than *any other* American car.
LOGICAL   Toyotas are more popular than *any* American car.

 Comparisons should state what is being compared.

NOT   That restaurant is *better*.
BUT   That restaurant is *better than the other one we went to*.

15e Include all needed articles, prepositions, and other words.

Writers sometimes omit necessary words because of dialectal differences or inattentive proofreading.

INCOMPLETE   She sat moodily in front the fireplace.
REVISED   She sat moodily in front *of* the fireplace.

INCOMPLETE   Why you making your presence known?
REVISED   Why *are* you making your presence known?

Do not omit the articles *a, an,* or *the* when they are needed. See 9i for guidelines.

Writers often omit *that* when it introduces a noun clause:

We realized Joe was responsible. [We realized *that* Joe was responsible.]

But sometimes such an omission causes an initial misreading:

UNCLEAR   He suggests the term *league* better represents the ideals of the group. [We first read *term,* rather than the entire clause, as the direct object of *suggests.*]
REVISED   He suggests that the term *league* better represents the ideals of the group.

See Exercises 15-1, 15-2, 15-3, 15-4.

Related Exercises 5-13, 5-15, 5-17.

EXERCISE 15-1

Mixed Sentences: Revising

Revise each mixed sentence below by changing, adding, or deleting words as needed to make its parts fit together in grammar and meaning.

Example: The team that won was the result of bad refereeing.

The team's winning was the result of bad refereeing.

1. While bargaining for a discount was how she made the clerk angry.

2. Just because you took a course in computer programs doesn't mean you're an expert.

3. Hesitation is when you lose your chance.

4. For someone who knows that fighting and sports are not necessarily related could be very disturbed at a hockey game.

5. The hardware store that burned down on First Street was caused by an arsonist.

6. The reason he was lonely was because he had a quick, violent temper.

7. When you have a college education means that you have more skills for the job market and a better knowledge of the world.

8. By revising my résumé has improved my chances of a job interview.

9. Psychology is where people study behavioral characteristics.

10. The use of good oral communication skills can make you a more attractive candidate for the job.

11. If you want to know the time of the meeting, it starts at 6:15.

12. By sending your order now qualifies you for a special gift.

13. Because the bus was late was why I missed class.

14. On the way to the train was when I fell and broke my ankle.

EXERCISE 15-2

Incomplete Sentences: Revising

Adding or changing words as necessary, revise the following sentences to provide any omitted words or to complete the compound constructions and comparisons.

exer
15

Example: The apartment was as roomy as any other house.

The apartment was as roomy as any house.

1. We suspect that Judy is more devoted to music than Andy.

2. The administration claims to believe and plan for the college's future.

3. Some brands of vodka contain more alcohol than any beverage.

4. I was going seventy miles per hour and stopped for speeding.

5. The Hilton's room service is as good as the Astor.

6. They were fond and totally devoted to their grandchild.

7. The second-night audience found the play more impressive than the opening-night audience.

8. This sandwich is as good, if not better than, the ones my mother makes.

9. Thank you if you have supported us in the past and in the future.

10. Faulkner's novels are more complex than any author's.

11. The audience saw the musician on the podium was unable to proceed.

12. Fruit juice stains are harder to remove than grass.

13. I came to realize some points in the article are true.

14. All those opposed or in favor of the resolution raised their hands.

EXERCISE 15-3

Mixed and Incomplete Sentences: Review

Underline any mixed or incomplete sentences in the following paragraphs. Then revise the paragraphs by changing, deleting, or adding words.

During my first day at college was somewhat frightening for me. As a student who is older, I was unsure of my ability to do as well if not better than the younger students, fresh out high school. I knew I had brains, but I felt a little rusty because it had been fifteen years since I graduated high school. Also, I had a family that still expected me to cook most of their meals, see they had clean clothes, and tuck them into bed at night. When I wanted to go back to school was all right with them as long as it didn't inconvenience them too much.

So there I was, on campus my first day. I had already undergone the horrors of registering for classes and now faced with finding the classrooms, enduring the pandemonium of the bookstore, and memorizing the bus schedule to make sure I got to class on time and home before my kids did.

By sitting in class was the easy part. The instructors seemed very open, friendly, and knowledgeable, and the assignments, I thought, were manageable. The biggest surprise was the students. They were less actively involved in the classes, and their questions didn't seem any more intelligent.

I learned that they have outside jobs that take time comparable to my housework and that many of them had, like my situation, been out of high school for a few years.

So I ended that frightening first day feeling confident in my ability to manage college work and my home responsibilities.

EXERCISE 15-4

Omissions and Faulty Repetitions: Revising Text

Add needed subjects, expletives, or verbs, and delete faulty repetitions of subjects, objects, or other words.

Example: Mexico City, the capital of Mexico, ~~it~~ was built on the site of the
Aztec capital city.

Were two major earthquakes in Mexico City 1985. The two quakes they happened on September 19 and 20. They measured 8.1 and 7.3 on the Richter scale. The powerful earthquakes killed more than 7000 people and damaged thousands buildings. Was a bad time for the people of that city. Afterwards, was rubble all over the city.

Some scientists think the reason for the intensity of the quakes it was the underlying geological formations of the region. Mexico City built on an ancient lake bed and bog, making it shake like Jell-O in an earthquake. Another reason, that the city is near the boundary of two tectonic plates. These tectonic plates, which make up the earth's crust, they collided, and one slipped under the other, causing the quake. The center of the quake 224 miles from Mexico City.

Was another serious earthquake in Mexico City only 27 years earlier. Was in 1957 that extensive damage occurred. Many of places that were destroyed they were never rebuilt.

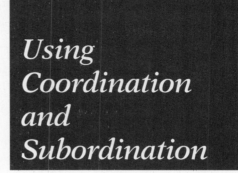

Using Coordination and Subordination

Chapter 16

Use **coordination** to give equal emphasis to the meanings in two or more sentence elements: *The conductor fainted, but the orchestra played on.* Use **subordination** to emphasize the meaning in one element over that in another: *Even though the conductor fainted, the orchestra played on.* The box below and the following sections provide guidelines for using coordination and subordination.

 Ways to coordinate and subordinate information in sentences

Use **coordination** to relate ideas of equal importance (16a).

- Link main clauses with a comma and a coordinating conjunction (*and, but, or, nor, for, so, yet*). (See 5d-1.)

  Independence Hall in Philadelphia is now restored, *but* fifty years ago it was in bad shape.

- Relate main clauses with a semicolon alone or a semicolon and a conjunctive adverb (*however, indeed, thus,* etc.). (See 5d-2.)

  The building was standing; *however,* it suffered from decay and vandalism.

- Within clauses, link words and phrases with a coordinating conjunction (*and, but, or, nor*). (See 5d-1.)

353

The people *and* officials of the nation were indifferent to Independence Hall *or* took it for granted.

- Link main clauses or other structures (words and phrases) with a correlative conjunction: *both . . . and, not only . . . but also,* and so on.

People *not only* took the building for granted *but also* neglected it.

Use **subordination** to deemphasize ideas (16b).

- Use a subordinate clause beginning with a subordinating conjunction (*although, because, if, whereas,* and so on.). (See 5c-4.)

Although some citizens had tried to rescue the building, they had not gained substantial public support.

- Use a subordinate clause beginning with a relative pronoun (*who, whoever, which, that*). (See 5c-4.)

The first strong step was taken by the federal government, *which made the building a national monument in the 1950s.*

- Use a phrase.

Like most national monuments, Independence Hall is protected by the National Park Service. [Prepositional phrase. (See 5c-1.)]

Protecting many popular tourist sites, the service is a highly visible government agency. [Verbal phrase. (See 5c-2.)]

- Use an appositive. (See 5c-5.)

The National Park Service, *a branch of the Department of Interior,* also runs Yosemite and other wilderness parks.

- Use a modifying word.

At the *red brick* Independence Hall, park rangers give *guided* tours and protect the *irreplaceable* building from vandalism.

16a Coordinating to relate equal ideas

Coordination is achieved by linking sentence elements with the coordinating conjunctions *and, but, or, nor,* and sometimes *for, so,* and *yet* (see 5d-1); by relating elements with conjunctive adverbs such as *however* and *therefore* (see 5d-2); or by expressing elements in the same grammatical construction (see Chapter 17 on parallelism). By linking ideas, coordination shows a relation between them that simple sentences alone rarely can.

Men in the Middle Ages granted women few political rights. Men idolized women in literature. [No relation established.]

Men in the Middle Ages granted women few political rights, *but* they idolized women in literature. [Coordinating conjunction.]

Men in the Middle Ages granted women few political rights; *however,* they idolized women in literature. [Conjunctive adverb.]

Men in the Middle Ages *excluded women from politics* but *idolized them in literature.* [Parallelism and coordinating conjunction.]

Punctuating coordinated words, phrases, and clauses

A comma is conventionally used between two main clauses joined by a coordinating conjunction. (See also Chapter 11.) The comma is not used between other sentence elements joined by the conjunction.

Some varieties of sweet alyssum grow about nine inches high, *but* others are much shorter. [Two main clauses joined by *but* are separated by a comma. (See 21a.)]

The alyssum plant has clusters of tiny lavender *or* white flowers. [The two adjectives *lavender* and *white* are joined by the conjunction *or* but are not separated with a comma.]

The alyssum is a hardy plant *and* starts easily from seed. [The two verbs *is* and *starts* are joined by the conjunction *and* but are not separated with a comma. (See 21j-2.)]

Two main clauses that are not joined by a coordinating conjunction are separated with a semicolon, whether or not the second clause contains a conjunctive adverb.

Some varieties of sweet alyssum grow about nine inches high; others are much shorter. [Two main clauses not joined by a conjunction. (See 22a.)]

Some varieties of sweet alyssum grow about nine inches high; however, others are much shorter. [The second main clause begins with a conjunctive adverb. (See 22b.)]

Commas are used for separating two kinds of coordinate elements: (1) coordinate adjectives not joined by a conjunction and (2) items in a series.

Sweet alyssum is a low, spreading plant. [The coordinate adjectives *low* and *spreading* are not joined by a conjunction; they are separated by a comma. (See 21f-2.)]

Sweet alyssum is a popular plant for borders because it *grows low, spreads broadly,* and *flowers profusely.* [The series of three verbs plus modifiers are separated by commas. (See 21f-1.)]

 Using coordination effectively

Though coordination can be used effectively to establish relations between ideas, it can be used excessively. Strings of compounded elements, such as a series of clauses connected with *and* or *so,* may blur relations. You can clarify the way parts relate to one another by a judicious use of both coordination and subordination.

Excessive Coordination	I spent Easter vacation at the beach, and I met my future wife, and three months later we were married.
Revised	During Easter vacation at the beach, I met my future wife. Three months later we were married.

 Coordinating logically

Faulty coordination occurs when two coordinated ideas do not seem related in fact.

Faulty	The crash occurred at night, and all the passengers were rescued.
Revised	Because the crash occurred at night, darkness hampered rescue efforts. However, all the passengers were rescued.

See Exercises 16-1, 16-3.

Related Exercises 5-14, 5-15, 5-17.

16b Subordinating to distinguish main ideas

Subordination allows writers to play down less significant information and to stress important points by placing them in main clauses. Subordinate information may be conveyed in a subordinate clause (introduced by a subordinating conjunction such as *although* or *when* or a relative pronoun—*who, which,* or *that*), in a phrase, or in a single word. (See 5c-4, 5c-3, and 5b.)

> The dog snarled at me, and then it ran toward the fence. [Compound sentence gives equal emphasis to both ideas by placing both in main clauses.]
>
> The dog snarled at me as it ran toward the fence. [Subordinate clause reduces emphasis on the dog's running and shows how the running relates to the snarling.]
>
> Running toward the fence, the dog snarled at me. [Participial phrase subordinates the dog's running.]
>
> Snarling at me, the dog ran toward the fence. [Participial phrase subordinates the dog's snarling and emphasizes its running.]
>
> The snarling dog ran toward the fence. [Adjective gives minimum emphasis to the dog's snarling.]

How can you decide which ideas should be subordinate? Generally, writers know what their main ideas are. If you do at times have some trouble, consider this rule of thumb: details of time, cause, condition, concession, purpose, and identification are usually subordinate; that is, they are details that can serve adjective or adverb functions.

Punctuating subordinate constructions

A modifying word, phrase, or clause that introduces a sentence or clause is usually set off with a comma (21b).

Islamic law influenced Turkish life for nearly a thousand years; *however,* the new republican government outlawed many Islamic practices. [The conjunctive adverb that introduces the second clause is set off with a comma.]

The Turkish Ottoman Empire ended in 1922; *the next year,* Turkey became a republic. [The phrase *the next year* introduces the second clause and is set off with a comma.]

Although in landmass Turkey is little larger than Texas, it has more than three times as many people. [The introductory clause is set off with a comma.]

An interrupting or concluding modifier that restricts the meaning of the word it modifies is not set off with commas (21c).

Leaves *of various species of trees* differ in size and shape. [Essential prepositional phrases.]

The trunks of trees are made up of four layers of plant tissue *wrapped around one another.* [Essential participial phrase.]

Some tree buds contain a shoot *that develops into a leaf-bearing twig.* [Essential clause.]

When interrupting subordinate constructions do not restrict meaning, they are set off with commas (or sometimes with dashes). (See also 21c and 5c-4.)

A tennis ball may be hit either on the fly, *which is called a volley,* or after the first bounce, *which is called a ground stroke.* [Both *which* clauses are not essential to the meaning of the sentence.]

Adverb clauses are usually set off when they come at the beginning of the sentence and are usually not set off when they follow a main clause. (See 21c and 5c-4.)

 Subordinating logically

Faulty subordination occurs when the idea expressed in a subordinate clause or a phrase seems more important than the idea expressed in the main clause.

FAULTY   Elephants have ruled the plains for millions of years, although they are now being squeezed out by humans.

REVISED   Although elephants have ruled the plains for millions of years, they are now being squeezed out by humans.

Using subordination effectively

Excessive subordination occurs when too many subordinate constructions, containing details only loosely related, are strung together in a single sentence. The result is not only awkward but confusing. A common kind of excessive subordination occurs with a succession of modifying *which* clauses. Use other modifying structures to simplify the sentence.

EXCESSIVE SUBORDINATION	The internal structure of minerals was shown by X-ray studies, the first of which occurred in 1912, at which time scientists did not really understand crystals, which is what minerals are.
REVISED	In 1912, before scientists really understood what crystals are, X-ray studies showed that the internal structure of minerals is made up of crystals.

16c Choosing clear connectors

 Using *as* and *while* clearly

Because the subordinating conjunction *as* can indicate a relation of time, cause, or comparison, its meaning in a sentence may be unclear.

UNCLEAR	As I was awaiting a visitor, the telephone's ringing surprised me.
CLEAR	*When* I was awaiting a visitor, the telephone's ringing surprised me.
CLEAR	*Because* I was awaiting a visitor, the telephone's ringing surprised me.

Similarly, the subordinating conjunction *while* can indicate a relation of time or concession. If your meaning of *while* is not unmistakably clear, use a more precise connector.

UNCLEAR	*While* the downtown stores were renovated, customers flocked to the shopping malls.
CLEAR	*Until* the downtown stores were renovated, customers flocked to the shopping malls.
CLEAR	*Although* the downtown stores were being renovated, customers flocked to the shopping malls.

Using *as*, *like*, and *while* correctly

As is a nonstandard substitute for *whether* or *that*.

NONSTANDARD	Jim didn't know *as* he wanted to play his guitar.
REVISED	Jim didn't know *whether* he wanted to play his guitar.

Like used as a subordinating conjunction is common in everyday speech but is avoided in writing and standard speech. Use *as, as if, as though,* or sometimes *that* instead.

INFORMAL	The singer sounded *like* she was getting tired.
REVISED	The singer sounded *as if* she was getting tired.
INFORMAL	It seems *like* every time I want to go out the car dies.
REVISED	It seems *that* every time I want to go out the car dies.
INFORMAL	He looked *like* he was going to turn, but he didn't.
REVISED	He looked *as if* he was going to turn, but he didn't.
INFORMAL	He plays soccer all winter, *like me.*
REVISED	He plays soccer all winter, *as* I do.

Avoid using the subordinating conjunction *while* when you mean *and* or *but.*

FAULTY	Jack wanted to go to the theater, *while* his wife preferred to stay home and watch television.
REVISED	Jack wanted to go to the theater, *but* his wife preferred to stay home and watch television.

coord/sub

16c

See Exercises 16-2, 16-3.

Related Exercises 5-12, 5-13, 5-14, 5-18.

© 1998 Addison-Wesley Educational Publishers Inc.

EXERCISE 16-1

Coordination: Combining Sentences

Combine each pair of simple sentences into one sentence, using the coordinating conjunction that is most appropriate for meaning. Choose *and, but, or, nor, for, so,* or *yet.*

> *Example:* Many animals, including humans, perceive colors. The ways they see colors may differ.
>
> Many animals, including humans, perceive colors, but the ways they see colors may differ.

1. The human eye can distinguish about 10 million colors. We have names for only a few.

2. A friend may tell you that his new car is blue. The blue you imagine may not be the blue of his car.

3. The cells in the eye that distinguish colors function only in light. In dim light we see only tones of gray.

4. The cells that perceive colors are called *cones*. Those that perceive black and white are called *rods*.

5. Rods function better than cones in semidarkness. They are sensitive to movement in dim light.

6. People who are color-blind may have some nonfunctioning cones. They cannot see particular colors.

7. You can call red, blue, and yellow the primary colors. You might also designate them as red, blue, and green.

8. The eye is quite adept at distinguishing fine differences in color. Sometimes the eye makes mistakes.

9. After looking at something dark, you see a light image when you look away. After looking at a color, such as green, you see its opposite, such as red.

10. This type of mistake is called *successive contrast*. It's a normal part of vision.

EXERCISE 16-2

Subordination: Combining Sentences

Combine each pair of simple sentences below into one sentence by placing the less important information in a subordinate clause, a phrase, or a single word, as specified in parentheses. Some subordinate elements will begin sentences, and some will end them.

> *Example:*   Many Americans favor handgun control. Congress has not enacted any laws requiring it. (*Subordinate clause beginning with* although.)
>
> *Although many Americans favor handgun control, Congress has not enacted any laws requiring it.*

1. His shoulders are slightly stooped. He still looks energetic. (*Subordinate clause beginning with* although.)

2. Tonight he played his greatest role. It was Lothario. (*Single word.*)

3. We were nearly at the end of our trip. Then we were stopped by the state police. (*Phrase beginning with* nearly.)

4. The meeting ended. The hall was again deserted. (*Subordinate clause beginning with* after.)

5. Sparrows are unwelcome pests. They may eat as much as 6 percent of a grain crop. (*Phrase beginning with* unwelcome.)

6. She wore jogging shoes. The waiter refused to seat her. (*Subordinate clause beginning with* because.)

7. The patient was recovering. He was depressed and irritable. (*Single word.*)

8. He felt embarrassed. He could not get a word out. (*Phrase beginning with* feeling.)

9. German stereo components are often of high quality. They are usually more expensive than Japanese components. (*Subordinate clause beginning with* although.)

10. I did not know how to interpret the question. It had four possible answers. (*Subordinate clause beginning with* because.)

EXERCISE 16-3

Coordination and Subordination: Revising Text

On separate paper, revise each passage to use both coordination and subordination effectively in establishing relations among ideas and in distinguishing main ideas from less important ones.

1. A good example of corruption occurred in the US Navy. The event occurred recently. A Washington columnist told the story. An officer was demoted. He had reported some of his fellow officers. The officers were responsible for training recruits. The officers had sold the recruits uniforms. The uniforms were supposed to be issued free.

2. A triangle was tattooed on the back of his hand. He got the tattoo when he was sixteen. It was a symbol of the instrument he had played. He had played in a rock band. His instrument had been a brass triangle.

3. The night was black, and the road was slippery, and the car, which ran up an embankment, rolled over twice, an action that caused the occupants to be thrown out, even though no one was injured. The car was a total loss.

4. The first Earth Day is said to have initiated the environmental movement in the United States. It was held on April 22, 1970. About 20 million Americans participated. It was the largest organized demonstration to that date. Local demonstrations involved nature walks. They involved direct action against polluters. An eco-fair was held in New York City. The eco-fair was held in Union Square. The eco-fair was attended by 100,000 people. The US Congress formally adjourned for the day. Its members were able to attend teach-ins in their districts. People have an increased awareness of the need to stop polluting and to begin recycling. This increased awareness was caused by Earth Day. A far-reaching effect was the creation of the Environmental Protection Agency in 1971.

5. Wyatt Berry Stapp Earp was born in 1848. He began his life in Monmouth, Illinois. He was a lawman and gunfighter in the American frontier. He first served as a policeman in Kansas. Later he moved to Tombstone, Arizona. There he participated in the infamous gunfight at the O.K. Corral. The gunfight occurred in 1881. Earp obviously survived the gunfight. He died much later. Records show that he died in 1929.

exer
16

Chapter 17

Using Parallelism

Parallelism is the duplication of grammatical form between two or more coordinate elements.

I was beckoned by   the   broad   blue   horizon
             and   the   straight   open   road.

Parallelism gives the same grammatical form to elements with the same function and importance. It also emphasizes important points and gives a sentence coherence.

 ## Patterns of parallelism

Use parallel structures for all coordinated elements.

- For elements connected by coordinating or correlative conjunctions (17a-1, 17a-2):

In 1988 a Greek cyclist, backed up by ‖ *engineers,*
‖ *physiologists,*
and ‖ *athletes,*

broke the world's record for human flight
with <u>neither</u> ‖ *a boost*
      <u>nor</u> ‖ *a motor.*

- For elements being compared or contrasted (17a-3):

rather than ‖ *Pedal power*
‖ *horse power*
propelled the plane.

- For items arranged in a series or outline (17a-4):

The four-hour flight was successful because

and ‖ (1) the cyclist was very fit;
‖ (2) he flew a straight course over water;
‖ (3) he kept the aircraft near the water surface.

17a Using parallelism for coordinate elements

1 Using parallelism for elements linked by coordinating conjunctions

The coordinating conjunctions *(and, but, or, nor,* and *yet)* link words and word groups with parallel structures. The very term *coordinating* implies equivalence—balanced ideas and balanced grammatical structures. (See 5d and 16a:)

FAULTY	A commercial should be *informative* and *of interest*. [An adjective is paired with a prepositional phrase.]
REVISED	A commercial should be *informative* and *interesting*. [Two adjectives.]
FAULTY	The rookie pitched an uneven game, *allowing only three hits* but *he walked seven batters*. [Participial phrase is paired with a clause.]
REVISED	The rookie pitched an uneven game, *allowing only three hits* but *walking seven batters*. [Two participial phrases.]

The coordinated elements need not be matched word for word.

PARALLEL	Mosquitoes lay their eggs in *marshes, swamps,* and *other pools of quiet water*. [Three nouns coordinated as objects of the preposition *in;* only the third noun is modified by an adjective and another prepositional phrase.]

2 Using parallelism for elements linked by correlative conjunctions

Correlative conjunctions (such as *not only . . . but also, either . . . or, both . . . and*) link parallel elements. Be sure that the element after the second connector matches the element after the first connector.

368

FAULTY	The poet wrote not only *of Greece* but also *Asia Minor*.
REVISED	The poet wrote not only *of Greece* but also *of Asia Minor*.
FAULTY	He said either *to wait* or *go* without him.
REVISED	He said either *to wait* or *to go* without him.
FAULTY	You can either *pay by cash* or *by check*.
REVISED	You can pay either *by cash* or *by check*.

 Using parallelism for elements being compared or contrasted

FAULTY	*To ride* in a parade is better than *watching* one.
REVISED	*Riding* in a parade is better than *watching* one.
FAULTY	I'd rather *ride* in a parade than I *would watch* one.
REVISED	I'd rather *ride* in a parade than *watch* one.

 Using parallelism for lists, outlines, or headings

FAULTY	The most dangerous forms of transportation are *motorcycles, cars,* and *riding a bicycle*.
REVISED	The most dangerous forms of transportation are *motorcycles, cars,* and *bicycles*.

FAULTY	**PARALLEL**
1. Photosynthesis	1. Photosynthesis
2. Can we feed the world?	2. Food for the world
3. Getting fuel from biomass	3. Fuel from biomass

 Using parallelism to increase coherence

Parallelism helps strengthen the relation between elements in a sentence.

WEAK	The brightest object in the night sky is the moon, which gives off no light of its own.
PARALLEL	The moon is the brightest object in the night sky, but it gives off no light of its own. [The contrast is emphasized through parallel grammatical structure—two main clauses joined by the pivotal coordinating conjunction *but*—and with the same subject, *moon* and *it,* for both clauses.]

Parallelism also makes it possible for writers to reduce wordiness and repetition while strengthening the focus of their statements.

WORDY	Some moon craters are located on the tops of small mountains. Craters have also been seen in the centers of low, rounded hills.
PARALLEL	Some moon craters are located on the tops of small mountains or in the centers of low, rounded hills.

See Exercises 17-1, 17-2, 17-3.

Related Exercises 5-15, 5-16, 5-18, 16-1, 21-4.

//
17b

EXERCISE 17-1

Parallelism: Writing Sentences

Each of the sentences below has parallel elements. For each sentence, underline the parallel elements, circle the coordinating conjunction, and then write
a new sentence patterned after the original.

Example: F. Scott Fitzgerald wrote <u>colorful short stories</u> (and) <u>romantic novels.</u>

*Professor Smithson sings tuneful folk songs
and operatic arias.*

1. Brazil is bordered by Venezuela, Guyana, Suriname, and French Guiana.

2. Brazil is a federation of 22 states, four territories, and the federal district
   of Brasilia.

3. The official language is Portuguese, but the population is an amalgam.

4. Brazil's economy depends heavily not only on agriculture but on its mineral resources as well.

5. Occupying nearly half of the continent and having a varied topography,
   Brazil is the largest country in South America.

6. Rio de Janeiro is Brazil's second-largest city and its former capital.

7. Tourists flock to Rio to attend its pre-Lenten carnival and to take in its natural setting.

8. Brasilia, one of the world's newest cities and the capital of Brazil since 1960, is situated in the sparsely settled interior.

9. The largest city in Brazil is São Paulo: Brazil's commercial, financial, and industrial center.

10. The Amazon River traverses through northern Brazil and into the Atlantic Ocean.

EXERCISE 17-2

Parallelism: Combining Sentences

Combine each set of sentences into a single sentence, using parallel structures where appropriate.

Example: English began as a Germanic language. It acquired thousands of words from French. It acquired numerous Latin words. It acquired many words from other languages.

English began as a German language, then acquired thousands of words from French, numerous words from Latin, and many words from other languages.

1. The history of English has been divided into three stages. The first stage is Old English. The second stage is Middle English. The third stage is Modern English.

2. Old English ran from about 600 to about 1100. Middle English ran from about 1100 to about 1500. Modern English ran from about 1500 to the present.

3. These dates mean that *Beowulf* was written in the Old English period. They mean that Chaucer wrote *Canterbury Tales* during the Middle English period. They mean that Shakespeare wrote during the Modern period.

4. The Modern period is sometimes divided. The first Modern period is Early Modern, ending in 1700. The second Modern period is Late Modern. It began in 1700 and continues to the present.

5. English has its roots in the language of three Germanic tribes. One of these tribes was the Angles. The second was the Saxons. The third was the Jutes. These tribes are commonly called Anglo-Saxons.

6. Some of the most common words in use today have their origin in Anglo-Saxon. Old English is Anglo-Saxon. One of these words is *the*. Another is *man*. Another is *mother*. Another is *and*.

7. Middle English dates from the Norman Conquest of England in 1066. Middle English was strongly influenced by the French-speaking Normans.

8. Thousands of French words entered the English vocabulary during this period. Many of them are among our most common. One example is *beef*. Another is *music*. Another is *nice*. Another is *flower*.

9. Modern English is characterized by changes in pronunciation. *Sea,* for example, once rhymed with *hay*. *Moon,* for example, once rhymed with *loan*.

10. These changes in pronunciation contributed toward apparent inconsistencies in spelling today. The invention of the printing press in 1475 contributed toward apparent inconsistencies in spelling today.

EXERCISE 17-3
Parallelism: Editing Text

The following text has sentences weakened by faulty parallelism. Underline each occurrence and, in the space above it, correct the fault.

1   The birthplace of Martin Luther King, Jr., in Atlanta, Georgia, is a national historic site run by the National Park Service. Located at 501 Auburn Avenue in the Atlanta neighborhood known as Sweet Auburn, the King house is a tourist attraction that opens daily and free of charge. It is part of a neighborhood made up both of two- and three-story Victorian houses owned by black professional people and the row houses of the black poor.

2   The house where King grew up is a Queen Anne frame building with two stories and has a large front porch. The historic structure, painted white and with dark shutters at the windows, gives testimony of the civil rights leader's boyhood. The lower floor has a front parlor with a piano and having other original furniture. There the King children would play games like Monopoly and play Old Maid after they had finished their chores—to stoke the furnace or brushing crumbs from the dinner table. In the kitchen is a 1930s-style icebox, a black stove, and a big kitchen cabinet stands there too. Visitors can imagine King's mother, Alberta, preparing the family meals here while the children played on the green

exer
17

linoleum floor. Upstairs are the bedrooms. In the big bedroom that belonged to the parents, all the King children were born.

3   One block to the west is the Center for Non-Violent Social Change, directed by Coretta Scott King, Martin Luther King's widow. The Center houses a museum that informs visitors about King's adult life and which is open to the public. Visitors to this museum can see both personal items and view public mementos. One historical item is a replica of King's Nobel Peace Prize, awarded in 1964. A touching personal memento is the key to the door of the hotel room where he was staying the day he was assassinated, and another being the wallet he had with him on that day.

4   April 4, 1968, the day King was shot in Memphis, Tennessee, is a day of infamy. But King will long be remembered as the foremost champion of civil rights and as being the upholder of peace and brotherhood.

5   Atlanta tourists can either visit one of these buildings or they can visit both of them. Admission to both is free, and visitors can take free guided walking tours of the Sweet Auburn district as well.

Chapter 18

Emphasizing Main Ideas

18a Arranging ideas effectively

When you use sentence construction to emphasize your main ideas, keep two principles in mind:

- Beginnings and endings of sentences are the most emphatic positions.
- In a parallel series, the elements are more emphatic if arranged in increasing order of importance.

1 Using sentence beginnings and endings

The most emphatic positions in a sentence are the beginning and the end. Don't bury an important idea in the middle of a sentence.

UNEMPHATIC	Because its winds sometimes exceed 500 miles per hour and it has more energy than an atomic bomb, *the tornado is one of the most destructive forces on earth,* and it can strike without warning.
REVISED	*The tornado is one of the most destructive forces on earth* because its winds sometimes exceed 500 miles per hour, because it has more energy than an atomic bomb, and because it can strike without warning.
REVISED	Because its winds sometimes exceed 500 miles per hour, because it has more energy than an atomic bomb, and because it can strike without warning, *the tornado is one of the most destructive forces on earth.*

The first revision above is a **cumulative,** or **loose, sentence:** The main point comes first and is followed by explanation. The second revision is a **periodic sentence:** All the explanation comes first, and the main point comes at the end. Since the main clause is withheld until the end of the sentence, the periodic sentence creates suspense.

 Ways to emphasize ideas

- Put important ideas in the beginnings or endings of sentences (18a-1).
- Arrange series items in order of increasing importance (18a-2).
- Use an occasional balanced sentence (18a-2).
- Carefully repeat key words and phrases (18b).
- Set off important ideas with punctuation (18c).
- Use the active voice (18d).
- Write concisely (18e).

 Arranging parallel elements effectively

Elements in parallel constructions (see Chapter 17) should be arranged in order of increasing importance.

UNEMPHATIC   The friends he had, the life he led, the books he read, the sports he played—all brought him satisfaction.

REVISED   The books he read, the sports he played, the friends he had, the life he led—all brought him satisfaction.

A **balanced sentence**—one made up of directly parallel clauses—can be very emphatic.

The screen filled with color, and the hall filled with music.

The climb was painfully difficult; the descent was refreshingly simple.

18b Repeating ideas

Needless repetition will weaken a sentence, but careful repetition of a key word or phrase can effectively emphasize that word or phrase.

Cholera, which kills by dehydration, should be treated *by giving* the victim huge amounts of water, *not by giving* food intravenously and *not by giving* a drug.

18c Separating ideas

Setting a statement off from related ideas emphasizes it. In the following sentences the emphasis increases as the separation becomes stronger, from coordinating conjunction to semicolon to period.

> The bill of the marabou stork is long and wedge-shaped, and its head is nearly bald.
>
> The bill of the marabou stork is long and wedge-shaped; its head is nearly bald.
>
> The bill of the marabou stork is long and wedge-shaped. Its head is nearly bald.

Using dashes to set off a part of a sentence is another way to gain emphasis.

> The bill of the marabou stork is long and wedge-shaped—its head is nearly bald.

18d Preferring the active voice

In the **active voice** the subject acts; in the passive voice the subject is acted upon. (See 7h.) Active constructions are usually more direct and emphatic than passive constructions.

PASSIVE	The game was watched with great interest by the scout.
ACTIVE	The scout watched the game with great interest.

18e Being concise

Unnecessary words weaken sentences. Concise sentences convey the essential meaning in as few words as possible and thus help emphasize ideas. (See also 31c.) Examine your sentences for empty phrases as well as for needless repetition.

WEAK	It is unlikely that a complete resolution of conflicts between the Arabs and Israelis will be achieved.
EMPHATIC	Arab-Israeli conflicts probably will not be resolved.
WEAK	She behaved in such a way as to alienate her friends.
EMPHATIC	She alienated her friends.
WEAK	A problem of communication arose between the roommates, who did not speak to each other.
EMPHATIC	The roommates did not speak to each other.

emph
18e

Ways to achieve conciseness

- Cut or shorten empty words or phrases (31c-1).

  Shorten filler phrases, such as *by virtue of the fact that.*
  Cut all-purpose words, such as *area, factor.*
  Cut unneeded qualifiers, such as *in my opinion, for the most part.*
- Cut unnecessary repetition (31c-2).
- Simplify word groups and sentences (31c-3).
- Make the subject and verb of each sentence identify the actor and action.

  Replace clauses with phrases, phrases with single words.
  Use strong verbs.
  Rewrite passive sentences as active.
  Avoid expletive constructions beginning *there is* or *it is.*
  Combine sentences.
- Cut or rewrite jargon (31c-4).

See Exercises 18-1, 18-2.

Related Exercises 5-5, 5-16, 5-17, 16-3, 17-2, 17-3, 19-1, 19-2, 31-7.

emph
18e

EXERCISE 18-1

Emphasis: Revising Sentences

Rewrite each sentence or group of sentences below to emphasize the main idea, following the instructions in parentheses. Make your sentences as concise as possible.

Example: Sea gulls quarrel frequently over food. They quarrel noisily. But they are graceful in flight. (*Make one sentence, putting the main idea at the end of the sentence.*)

> *Though they quarrel frequently and noisily over food, sea gulls are graceful in flight.*

1. The prize will be awarded by the foundation for the first time in fifty years. (*Use the active voice.*)

2. Legal gambling can increase tax revenues. It can increase tourism. It can also increase crime. (*Make two sentences, putting the main idea in a separate sentence.*)

3. The kitchen contains poisons that can kill instantly. It is a room filled with perils. It also contains appliances that can be heated to 500 degrees. (*Make one sentence, putting the main idea at the end.*)

4. He had only six dollars left for his heart medicine, to buy food for his cat, and for his dinner. (*Use parallelism for series elements and arrange them in order of importance.*)

5. It was the winning point that was scored by Shank. (*Use normal word order and the active voice.*)

6. Carrying its prey in its beak, the hawk swooped upward. The hawk was flapping its wings. (*Make one sentence, putting the main idea at the beginning of the sentence.*)

7. A lock was placed on the warehouse door by the guard, who was afraid of theft. (*Use the active voice and place the main idea at the beginning or end of the sentence.*)

exer
18

8. Because of the steady downpour, the ball could not be held on to by the players, three players tore ligaments, and the uniforms were ruined by the players. (*Use parallelism for series elements and arrange them in order of importance. Change passive voice to active.*)

9. For three hours the speaker discussed nutrition in a monotonous voice. (*Place the main idea at the beginning of the sentence.*)

10. There is some likelihood this year that raises may be withheld by management. (*Use normal word order and the active voice.*)

EXERCISE 18-2

Emphasis: Combining Sentences

Combine each group of sentences below into one or two sentences that emphasize the main idea of the group. Make your sentences effective with an appropriate combination of beginnings and endings, parallelism, arrangement of elements in order of increasing importance, careful repetition, separation, and the active voice. Be concise.

Example: She does not own a crystal ball. She does not understand sports. She won the baseball pool. A four-leaf clover was not found by her.

> *She does not own a crystal ball or a four-leaf clover, and she does not understand sports. Yet she won the baseball pool.*

exer
18

1. The largest bank cut its lending rate. The other large banks followed. The experts thought the rates would keep dropping. The rates held steady.

2. My telephone does not work during rainstorms. I receive calls for wrong numbers. I got twenty-seven calls for an ice-cream shop one rainy afternoon. I was trying to study.

3. Summer jobs were hard to find. There was no construction work in town. The gas stations were going broke. No businesses were hiring.

4. Police officers have to keep their car keys handy. They have to know how to drive at high speed. Police officers need special driving skills and habits. They have to know how to drive with caution. They must always remember to park facing an exit.

5. The old woman had white hair. Her face had many wrinkles. She pulled a revolver and took my wallet. Her blue eyes twinkled. She looked innocent.

6. A visit to a nursing home can be depressing. It does not have to be. Taking time to smile and say hello cheers up the residents. Bringing along a small child cheers up the residents.

7. *Breakout* by Ron LeFlore is an inspiring story. It describes his life in prison. It is my favorite biography. He used his skill at baseball to rejoin society.

8. Twelve head of cattle died in the fire. Gasoline spread across the highway and ignited a field. The tanker truck overturned.

9. The old and tattered magazine described Leon Spinks. He could have been a champion for several years. He seemed to lose faith in himself.

10. Dachshunds shed very little. They are great pets. They are obedient. Dachshunds are gentle with children.

Chapter 19

Achieving Variety

Sentences work together to convey meaning. A string of similar sentences is not only dull but also potentially confusing because important ideas do not stand out. Instead, vary your sentences in length, structure, and arrangement of elements to reflect the importance and complexity of your thoughts.

 Ways to achieve variety among sentences

- Vary the length and structure of sentences so that important ideas stand out (19a).
- Vary the beginnings of sentences with modifiers, transitional words and expressions, and occasional expletive constructions (19b).
- Occasionally, invert the normal order of subject, predicate, and object or complement (19c).
- Use an occasional command, question, or exclamation (19d).

19a Varying sentence length and structure

1 Varying length

A paragraph filled with sentences of the same length lacks variety, especially if the sentences are all very short (say, ten or fifteen words) or very long

385

(thirty or more words). Check your sentences to be sure they are not primarily of similar lengths.

Rewriting strings of brief and simple sentences

A series of brief, simple sentences can be choppy and dull. Use connecting and subordinating words to combine sentences, emphasize important ideas, and de-emphasize lesser ones.

> **WEAK**   The lab is modern and bare. It is almost frightening. It has fluorescent lights. The walls are green. The floors are gray. The equipment is shiny. All these produce a cold atmosphere. They remind the visitor of the work done here.
>
> **REVISED**   The lab is modern, bare, and almost frightening. Its fluorescent lights, green walls, gray floors, and shiny equipment produce a cold atmosphere that reminds the visitor of the work done here.

Rewriting strings of compound sentences

A string of compound sentences can be just as monotonous as a string of simple sentences. Vary the sentences and emphasize important ideas by changing some main clauses into modifiers and varying their positions.

> **WEAK**   I opened the door, and a salesperson stood on the porch. He began his pitch, but he seemed drowsy. His voice was expressionless, and it finally trailed off in midsentence. I was startled, but I did not know what to do. He clearly was not going away, so I just shut the door on him.
>
> **REVISED**   I opened the door to a salesperson on the porch. Though he began his pitch, he seemed drowsy, and his expressionless voice finally trailed off in midsentence. I was startled. Not knowing what to do and seeing that he was not going away, I just shut the door on him.

19b Varying sentence beginnings

Most English sentences begin with their subjects. You can vary the pattern and avoid the dullness of repetition by beginning some sentences with elements other than subjects. An **adverb modifier** postpones the subject.

Mercilessly, the loan shark's agents pursued her. [Adverb.]

Because she had no money, she could not pay the interest on the loan. [Adverb clause.]

386

A **participial phrase** is another way to postpone the subject.

Sitting on the bench, Oscar plucked his guitar.

A **coordinating conjunction** or **transitional expression** (see 3b-6) not only varies a sentence beginning but also links two sentences containing related ideas.

Meteors rarely burn for more than a few seconds. One occasionally leaves a shining trail that lasts several minutes. [No connector.]

Meteors rarely burn for more than a few seconds. But one occasionally leaves a shining trail that lasts several minutes. [Coordinating conjunction as connector.]

Meteors rarely burn for more than a few seconds. However, one occasionally leaves a shining trail that lasts several minutes. [Conjunctive adverb as connector.]

Occasionally, you may want to vary sentence beginnings by using an **expletive construction** such as *there is* or *it is* (see 5e-4), although frequent use of expletives will make your writing wordy and vague. One of the best uses of the expletive *there* is to announce something.

There were nine invitations in the mail.

There are two ways for a student to register for classes in this school.

19c Inverting the normal word order

Normal word order for English sentences is subject, verb, and complement or object. Occasionally reversing this order can provide sentence variety and sometimes emphasize an idea.

Near the center of town stood a large orange sculpture. [Prepositional phrase, verb, subject.]

One question we asked without hesitation. [Direct object, subject, predicate.]

Never in my life have I seen such a snowfall. [Beginning with the modifier *Never in my life* requires inversion of the verb, *have,* and the subject, *I.*]

19d Mixing types of sentences

Since most sentences we use in writing are statements, a sparing use of questions, commands, or exclamations can introduce variety. Questions, especially, can raise the central issue of a discussion or emphasize an important point.

Visitors appreciate the warmth of Homer's hotel. But why, they wonder, is it called the Hairless Raccoon? Legend has it that Homer once demonstrated a hair-growth tonic on the back of a raccoon. The raccoon lost its hair, and Homer lost his business. In his next venture, operating a hotel, Homer immortalized his victim.

See Exercises 19-1, 19-2.

Related Exercises 5-4, 5-5, 5-13, 5-15, 5-17, 16-2, 16-3, 18-1, 18-2.

var
19d

EXERCISE 19-1

Sentence Beginnings: Revising for Variation

Postpone sentence subjects by rewriting each sentence or pair of sentences as specified in parentheses.

> *Example:*   The union remained on strike after the votes were counted. (*Begin with* After.)
>
> *After the votes were counted, the union remained on strike.*

1. Penicillin can cure her disease. She is allergic to penicillin. (*Begin one sentence with a coordinating conjunction or a transitional expression.*)

2. The bamboo basket, which looks frail, is really quite sturdy. (*Begin with Although.*)

3. The speech was priced at one dollar a copy, and not one copy was sold. (*Begin with* Because.)

4. The crane fell five stories to the street and smashed a truck. (*Begin with a participial phrase.*)

5. The party invitations omitted the address. Just a few people came. (*Begin one sentence with a transitional expression.*)

6. He never became a great architect, but he was not obscure. (*Begin with* Even though.)

7. Johnson won the game by sinking a shot from thirty feet. (*Begin with a participial phrase.*)

8. Money for travel is in the budget. (*Begin with* There.)

9. Being a good photographer certainly requires skill. It also requires money. (*Begin one sentence with a transitional expression.*)

10. We were swimming in the pond and we heard a shot from across the meadows. (*Begin with a participial phrase.*)

EXERCISE 19-2

Varying Sentences in Paragraphs

The following paragraphs lack sentence variety. Rewrite each paragraph to stress main ideas by changing some main clauses into modifiers and by varying sentence lengths and beginnings.

1. Almost everyone is afraid of something. Some people are paralyzed by multiple phobias, however. They cannot leave the house for fear of an emotional collapse. Treating such people is a slow process. They have to become comfortable with each feared object or situation. The treatment may occur in a laboratory. It may also occur in natural surroundings. The phobias are eliminated one at a time. The patient can often resume a normal life at the end of treatment.

2. Some business executives are concerned about the quality of education in the public schools. They worry about whether students are learning English, math, science, social studies, and communications. These executives are concerned about the future. They are concerned that they will have to hire illiterate workers. They are concerned that their workers will not be able to keep pace with changes in industry. Workers who cannot read well affect productivity and efficiency. Some businesses offer training classes for their new employees. The businesses teach basic skills, and these skills are grammar, typing, and spelling. The executives are not happy with the present state of affairs. They think that uniform testing may be an answer.

3. Some business leaders recommend uniform testing, and they think it may improve the quality of education. The tests, they say, should be uniform for each state and should be comprehensive and reliable. They would be given to all schoolchildren. The tests would make the schools more accountable to the public, and they would tell taxpayers how well students are learning. Taxpayers support the public schools. Accountability is important. Substantive, informed changes are important too, and many business leaders and educators know this.

exer
19

Chapter 20

End Punctuation

THE PERIOD

20a **Use a period to end a statement, a mild command, or an indirect question.**

STATEMENT   The crisis resolved itself.

MILD COMMAND   Turn to the illustration on the next page.

INDIRECT QUESTION   They asked whether I intended to vote.

20b **Use periods with many abbreviations.**

Mr.   Dr.   i.e.   p.
Mrs.   Rev.   e.g.   George H. Packer

Though *Ms.* is not an abbreviation, it is punctuated like one; however, *Miss* is not followed by a period. Periods are commonly omitted from abbreviations for organizations and agencies (CBS, FDA). They are always omitted from **acronyms,** which are pronounceable words made from the first letters of the words in a name (UNESCO, NATO), and from ZIP code abbreviations.

UNESCO	NATO	IL
NAFTA	NBC	CA
YMCA	NAACP	NY
NFL	AMA	WY

Use only one period when an abbreviation comes at the end of a sentence: *Our speaker was G. Maurice Dunning, MD.*

See also Chapter 28 for a further discussion of abbreviations.

THE QUESTION MARK

 20c **Use a question mark after a direct question.**

Do we know what caused the fire?

After indirect questions, use the period: *He asked whether I knew what caused the fire.* (See 20a.)

CAUTION: Never use a question mark with another question mark, a period, or a comma.

FAULTY	He asked, "Which way to the dance hall?."
REVISED	He asked, "Which way to the dance hall?"

 20d **Use a question mark within parentheses to indicate doubt about the correctness of a number or date.**

At the time of Chaucer's birth in 1340 (?), only a few people could read.

THE EXCLAMATION POINT

 20e **Use an exclamation point after an emphatic statement, an interjection, or a command.**

EMPHATIC STATEMENT	We must not allow it!
EMPHATIC INTERJECTION	Oh! I wish I had my camera.
EMPHATIC COMMAND	Stop talking!

CAUTION: Never use an exclamation point with another exclamation point, a period, or a comma.

FAULTY	"He stole my wallet!," I yelled.
REVISED	"He stole my wallet!" I yelled.

20f Use exclamation points sparingly.

Don't use exclamation points to express amazement or sarcasm or to stress important points. Avoid using multiple exclamation points (!!!).

FAULTY	These facts prove that women office workers are discriminated against in this city!
REVISED	These facts prove that women office workers are discriminated against in this city.

See Exercises 20-1 and 25-2.

.?!
20f

EXERCISE 20-1

End Punctuation: Editing Sentences

Circle the place in each sentence where punctuation should be added or is used incorrectly. Then write the correct punctuation, along with the adjacent words, on the line to the left. If the sentence is already punctuated correctly, write *C* on the line.

Example: ___*address?" he*___ "Why must I have an address(?,") he asked.

_____ 1. She shouted, "Watch out for the dog!!!"

_____ 2. Let's watch the news on CBS tonight.

_____ 3. We discussed the question of where to put the file cabinet?

_____ 4. Carry your dirty dishes to the kitchen!

_____ 5. Did he say "Never?"

_____ 6. The title of the story was "Who Was That Kid."

_____ 7. I wondered whether I should finish the exercise?

_____ 8. Dr Baer allowed a 24-hour extension on the paper.

_____ 9. Whether you like it or not, that's the way it's going to be!

_____ 10. Make sure you have a bright enough light for reading

_____ 11. He asked, "When will the package arrive?".

_____ 12. We wanted to know if Jim was late for work again?

_____ 13. The oak leaves are still falling in January

exer
20

_____ 14. Norbert asked whether the copies were made yet?

_____ 15. The FBI investigation is almost over.

_____ 16. "For the last time, get out!".

_____ 17. We wondered who was going to pick up the video-tape?

_____ 18. "Watch out!," yelled the chimney sweep.

_____ 19. Rev Winters visited Jessica's brother in the hospital.

_____ 20. "Why are you late?," she asked.

_____ 21. David Woo recently moved to Washington, D.C..

_____ 22. For more information you can write C.A.R.E. at its New York office.

_____ 23. I wonder how anyone can live in Greenland!

_____ 24. AMA stands for both American Medical Association and American Marketing Association.

_____ 25. This coat is the best value for your money!

_____ 26. I'm not sure I'll ever get my PhD degree.

_____ 27. "Oh! I wish I had brought my umbrella," exclaimed Clara.

_____ 28. Mrs. Horning is a financial planning consultant.

_____ 29. This class will meet from 7:00 to 10:00 p.m..

_____ 30. St John's University hoped to beat St Olaf College in the football game.

Commas, semicolons, colons, dashes, and parentheses

(For explanations, consult the sections in parentheses.)

Sentences with two main clauses

The bus stopped[,] *but* no one got off. (21a)

The bus stopped[;] no one got off. (22a)

The bus stopped[;] *however,* no one got off. (22b)

The mechanic replaced the battery, the distributor cap, and the starter[;] *but* still the car would not start. (22c)

Her duty was clear[:] she had to locate the problem. (25a-1)

Introductory elements

MODIFIERS (21b)

After the argument was over[,] we laughed at ourselves.

Racing over the plain[,] the gazelle escaped the lion.

To dance in the contest[,] he had to tape his knee.

Suddenly[,] the door flew open.

With 125 passengers aboard[,] the plane was half full.

In 1988[ ]he won the Nobel Prize.

ABSOLUTE PHRASES (21d)

Its wing broken[,] the bird hopped about on the ground.

Interrupting and concluding elements

NONRESTRICTIVE MODIFIERS (21c-1)

Jim's car[,] *which barely runs*[,] has been impounded.

We consulted the dean[,] *who had promised to help us.*

The boy[,] *like his sister*[,] wants to be a pilot.

They moved across the desert[,] *shielding their eyes from the sun.*

The men do not speak to each other[,] *although they share a car.*

NONRESTRICTIVE APPOSITIVES

Bergen's daughter[,] *Candice*[,] became an actress. (21c-2)

The residents of three counties[—]*Suffolk, Springfield, and Morrison*[—]were urged to evacuate. (25b-2)

Our father demanded one promise[:] *that we not lie to him.* (25a-1)

RESTRICTIVE MODIFIERS (21j-3)

The car[ ]*that hit mine*[ ]was uninsured.

We consulted a teacher[ ]*who had promised to help us.*

The boy[ ]*in the black hat*[ ]is my cousin.

They were surprised to find the desert[ ]*teeming with life.*

The men do not speak to each other[ ]*because they are feuding.*

399

RESTRICTIVE APPOSITIVES (21j-3)

Shaw's play *Saint Joan*□was performed last year.
Their sons *Tony, William, and Steve*□all chose military careers, leaving only Joe to run the family business.

PARENTHETICAL EXPRESSIONS

We suspect□, *however*□, that he will not come. (21c-3)
Jan is respected by many people—*including me.* (25b-2)
George Balanchine □(*1904–1983*□) was a brilliant choreographer. (25c-1)

ABSOLUTE PHRASES (21d)

The bird□, *its wing broken*□, hopped about on the ground.
The bird hopped about on the ground□, *its wing broken.*

PHRASES EXPRESSING CONTRAST (21e)

The humidity□, *not just the heat*□, gives me headaches.
My headaches are caused by the humidity□, *not just the heat.*

CONCLUDING SUMMARIES AND EXPLANATIONS

The movie opened to bad notices□: *the characters were judged shallow and unrealistic.* (25a-1)
We dined on gumbo, blackened fish, and jambalaya—*a Cajun feast.* (25b-3)

Items in a series

THREE OR MORE ITEMS

Chimpanzees□, *gorillas*□, *orangutans*□, *and gibbons* are all apes. (21f-1)
The cities singled out for praise were *Birmingham, Alabama*□; *Lincoln, Nebraska*□; *Austin, Texas*□; *and Madison, Wisconsin.* (22d)

TWO OR MORE ADJECTIVES BEFORE A NOUN OR PRONOUN (21f-2)

Dingy□ *smelly* clothes decorated their room.
The luncheon consisted of *one tiny*□*watercress* sandwich.

INTRODUCTORY SERIES (25b-3)

Appropriateness, accuracy, and necessity—these criteria should govern your selection of words.

CONCLUDING SERIES

Every word should be□*appropriate, accurate, and necessary.* (25a-4)
Every word should meet three criteria□: *appropriateness, accuracy, and necessity.* (25a-1)
Pay attention to your words—*to their appropriateness, their accuracy, and their necessity.* (25b-3)

Chapter 21

The Comma

The comma is often essential to separate parts of a sentence and to provide clarity.

COMMA NEEDED	Seventy stories below the basement caught fire.
REVISED	Seventy stories below, the basement caught fire.

However, overused commas can break up sentences unnecessarily.

UNNEEDED COMMA	The question is, whether we should write a letter or call on the telephone.
REVISED	The question is whether we should write a letter or call on the telephone.
UNNEEDED COMMA	My sister and I decided, that we would not go to the game.
REVISED	My sister and I decided that we would not go to the game.

21a Use a comma before *and, but,* or another coordinating conjunction linking main clauses.

The coordinating conjunctions are *and, but, or, nor, for, so,* and *yet.* When one of them links main clauses, it should be preceded by a comma. Do not use a comma before a coordinating conjunction that joins sentence elements other than main clauses. (See 21j-2.)

Principal uses of the comma

- To separate main clauses linked by a coordinating conjunction (21a).

Main Clause ⟩ { and or for / but nor so / yet } main clause .

The steering was stiff, *but* the car rode smoothly.

- To set off most introductory elements (21b).

Introductory element ⟩ main clause .

Fortunately, the ride would be comfortable.

- To set off nonrestrictive elements (21c).

Main clause ⟩ nonrestrictive element. .

We dreaded the trip, *which would take sixteen hours*.

Beginning of main clause ⟩ nonrestrictive element ⟩ end of main clause .

Our destination, *Oklahoma City*, was unfamiliar to us.

- To separate items in a series (21f-1).

. . . item 1 ⟩ item 2 ⟩ { and / or } item 3 . . .

We would need *a new home, new schools, and new friends*.

- To separate coordinate adjectives (21f-2).

. . . first adjective ⟩ second adjective word modified . . .

A *bumpy, cramped* car ride would have been unbearable.

- Other uses of the comma:

   To set off absolute phrases (21d).
   To set off phrases expressing contrast (21e).
   To separate parts of dates, addresses, and long numbers (21g).
   To separate quotations and explanatory words (21h).
   To prevent misreading (21i).

See also 21j for when *not* to use the comma.

I had three accidents, *and* my insurance costs doubled. [Two main clauses.]

The book listed poisonous plants *but* did not mention poison ivy. [One main clause.]

My high school teachers did not help me learn to write, *nor* did they encourage me to read extensively. [Two main clauses.]

The movie went way over budget, *for* the director insisted on shooting most of it in the jungle. [Two main clauses.]

I bought the text secondhand, *yet* it cost over $20. [Two main clauses.]

Many poverty-stricken Americans get inadequate eye care *and* as a result have impaired sight or blindness. [One main clause.]

A semicolon may clarify the division between long main clauses that contain internal punctuation (see 22c).

The trip was sixteen hours long, involving three plane changes, two hours waiting in airports, and two taxi rides; *but* I arrived feeling almost fresh.

A comma is usually omitted before *so* in the sense of *so that*. (In this sense, *so* is a subordinating conjunction. See 5c-4.)

Newspapers sometimes take comics polls *so* they can rank their readers' favorite comic strips.

A comma may be omitted between main clauses when the clauses are short and closely related in meaning, although the comma is always correct.

We give little *and* we expect much.

21b Use a comma to set off most introductory elements.

Grammatical elements that begin sentences—such as modifying verbal phrases, long prepositional phrases, and subordinate clauses—should be set off with commas.

Although the bank offered "free checking," it tripled the charge for printing checks. [Subordinate clause.]

Expecting a green and tree-filled campus, I was shocked to find it surrounded by highways and parking lots. [Verbal phrase.]

Shouting, Max ran down the hall. [Participle.]

Because of insufficient numbers of eye care specialists in rural areas, the rural poor would not get adequate treatment even if they could afford it. [Long prepositional phrase.]

If the introductory element is short, especially if it is a short prepositional phrase, the comma is often omitted.

At times football rivalry gets out of hand.

Remember, however, that clarity may require the comma.

403

COMMA NEEDED	At three thoroughbred horses are eligible to run in the Kentucky Derby.
REVISED	At three, thoroughbred horses are eligible to run in the Kentucky Derby.

Although *modifying* phrases and clauses are often set off with commas, *noun* phrases and clauses are not.

What the reporter said may be wrong. [Noun clause as subject.]

Walking to work gives me needed exercise. [Noun phrase as subject.]

Raymond noticed *that the crack in the sidewalk was widening.* [Noun clause as direct object.]

See Exercises 21-1, 21-6, 22-2, 25-1.

Related Exercises 5-7, 5-14, 11-1, 11-2, 11-3, 11-4, 16-1, 16-2.

21c Use a comma or commas to set off nonrestrictive elements.

Restrictive elements limit the meaning of the word or words they refer to and thus cannot be omitted without changing meaning. They are not set off by commas or other punctuation. **Nonrestrictive elements** add information but do not limit meaning. They are set off by commas or other punctuation.

RESTRICTIVE	All the students *who graduated in June* found jobs. [The *who* clause cannot be omitted without changing meaning.]
NONRESTRICTIVE	The school library, *which now has 500,000 books,* is adequate for most undergraduates. [The *which* clause adds important information, but its omission would not change the meaning of the main clause.]

 Use a comma or commas to set off nonrestrictive clauses and phrases.

RESTRICTIVE	The car *that was stolen* was mine. [The *that* clause identifies which car and is essential to the meaning of the sentence.]
	The police officers *on the case* didn't know me. [The prepositional phrase identifies the police officers, so it cannot be removed without obscuring the meaning of the sentence.]
NONRESTRICTIVE	Farm accidents, *which claim as many as 1,400 lives each year,* are largely preventable. [The *which* clause is useful information but can be omitted without altering the meaning of the main clause.]

404

Moline, Illinois, *located on the Mississippi River,* is known as the farm implement capital of the world. [The participial phrase, though important, can be removed from the sentence without changing the meaning.]

 ### Test for restrictive and nonrestrictive elements

1. Identify the element.

   Hai Nguyen *who emigrated from Vietnam* lives in Denver.
   Those *who emigrated with him* live elsewhere.

2. Remove the element. Does the meaning of the main clause change?
   Hai Nguyen lives in Denver. **No.**
   Those live elsewhere. **Yes.** [Who are *those?*]

3. If **no,** the element is *nonrestrictive* and *should* be set off with punctuation.

   Hai Nguyen⎕ who emigrated from Vietnam⎕ lives in Denver.

   If **yes,** the element is *restrictive* and should *not* be set off with punctuation.
   Those⎕who emigrated with him⎕live elsewhere.

Adjective clauses introduced by *that* or an understood *that* are always restrictive and are not set off with commas. Adjective clauses that follow proper nouns are almost always *nonrestrictive.*

NOTE: Most adverb clauses are restrictive and are set off only when they introduce or interrupt sentences (see 21b). Adverb clauses at the ends of sentences are set off only when they are truly nonrestrictive, adding incidental information.

RESTRICTIVE   I'll buy the rest of my books *when I get enough money. When I get enough money,* I'll buy the rest of my books.

NONRESTRICTIVE   I didn't buy all my books, *since I didn't have enough money.*

 ### Use a comma or commas to set off nonrestrictive appositives.

Appositives and modifiers following a proper noun are almost always nonrestrictive, since the name identifies the person or place.

NONRESTRICTIVE	The concert will be held in Hadley Hall, *the place where most music events are held.* [The meaning of the main clause doesn't change if the appositive is omitted.]
RESTRICTIVE	The jazz pianist *Keith Jarrett* will perform here next year. [Without the appositive the sentence is meaningless.]

 3 **Use a comma or commas to set off transitional or parenthetical expressions.**

Parenthetical expressions interrupt a sentence to explain or make a transition or to add extra information. Brief parenthetical expressions are sometimes set off with commas. (See also Chapter 25 on the uses of dashes and parentheses to set off parenthetical elements and 3b-6 for a list of transitional expressions.)

The cost of living, *believe it or not,* actually declined this month.

The bus, *for example,* has not been on time once in twenty days.

The tail, *almost twenty inches long,* acts as a fly swatter.

 4 **Use a comma or commas to set off *yes* and *no*, tag questions, words of direct address, and mild interjections.**

Yes, we would be willing to perform for the patients.

You went to the interview, *didn't you?* [Tag question.]

Felicia, we appreciate your support. [Direct address.]

Well, I didn't expect to receive an A. [Mild interjection.]

21d Use a comma or commas to set off absolute phrases.

An **absolute phrase** usually consists of a participle and the noun or pronoun performing the action of that verbal. (See 5c-3.) Because it includes the subject of its action, an absolute phrase modifies an entire sentence or main clause rather than a single word and can therefore function at different positions in the sentence. Wherever it appears, however, it is set off with commas.

Remaining healthy is not easy for basketball players, *foot and toe injuries being the leading causes of player pain.*

The meeting (being) over, the reporters called their newsrooms. [The participle *being* is often omitted.]

The decision (having been) made, the committee members finally went home. [The participle *having been,* a form of *be,* is sometimes omitted.]

21e Use a comma or commas to set off phrases expressing contrast.

We saw the play, *not the movie.*

The comma is optional for contrasting phrases that begin with *but.*

The dean invited faculty *but not students* to the reception.
The dean invited faculty, *but not students,* to the reception.

See Exercises 21-2, 21-3, 21-6, 22-1, 22-2, 25-2.

Related Exercises 5-14, 21-5.

21f Use commas between items in a series and between coordinate adjectives.

1 Use commas between words, phrases, or clauses forming a series.

A **series** consists of three or more items of equal importance.

The sauce contained *mustard, ground cloves,* and *sherry.*

The last item in the series is usually preceded by a coordinating conjunction, most commonly *and.* Though usage varies on including the comma before the conjunction, most careful writers use it to prevent confusion over whether the last two items are coordinated separately from the other items.

CONFUSING	The house had missing storm windows, shoddy plumbing and electrical outlets in inconvenient places.
CLEAR	The house had missing storm windows, shoddy plumbing, and electrical outlets in inconvenient places.

21f

 Punctuating two or more adjectives

1. Identify the adjectives.
   She was a *faithful sincere* friend.
   They are *dedicated medical* students.
2. Can the adjectives be reversed without changing meaning?
   She was a *sincere faithful* friend. **Yes.**
   They are *medical dedicated* students. **No.**

3. Can the word *and* be inserted between the adjectives without changing meaning?

   She was a *faithful and sincere* friend. **Yes.**
   They are *dedicated and medical* students. **No.**

4. If **yes** to *both* questions, the adjectives *are* coordinate and *should* be separated by a comma.

   She was a *faithful⬚ sincere* friend.

   If **no** to both questions, the adjectives are *not* coordinate and should *not* be separated by a comma.

   They are *dedicated⬚medical* students.

When the elements in a series are long, grammatically complicated, or internally punctuated, they can be separated by semicolons (see 22d).

> Sylvia had three brothers: Jim, 16; Alfred, 14; and Billy, 2.

▲2 Use commas between two or more coordinate adjectives that equally modify the same word.

Coordinate adjectives are two or more adjectives modifying the same word equally. Such adjectives may be separated either by a coordinating conjunction or by a comma.

> A *kinder, gentler* approach to restricted smoking is not effective.
>
> A *kinder and gentler* approach to restricted smoking is not effective.
>
> A *gentler, kinder* approach to restricted smoking is not effective.

As these examples show, two adjectives are coordinate (1) if they can be reversed without a change in the meaning and (2) if *and* can be inserted between them. If these changes cannot be made, then the adjectives are not coordinate and they should not be separated by a comma.

> **FAULTY**   My father owned a pair of unique, rubber boxing gloves.
>
> **REVISED**   My father owned a pair of unique rubber boxing gloves.

Do not use a comma between the final adjective and the noun the adjectives modify.

> **FAULTY**   A *kinder, gentler, approach* to restricted smoking is not effective.
>
> **REVISED**   A *kinder, gentler approach* to restricted smoking is not effective.

21g Use commas according to convention in dates, addresses, place names, and long numbers.

> August 23, 1943, is the day she was born. [The second comma is required to complete setting off the year.]

She was born on 23 August 1943. [No commas are used when the day precedes the month.]

She was born in August 1943. [No comma separates the month from the year.]

She moved here from Axtel, Kansas, in 1975.

He lived at 1321 Cardinal Drive, Birmingham, Alabama 35223, for only a year. [No comma is used before the ZIP code.]

The comma separates long numbers into groups of three, starting from the right: *83,745,906*. The comma is optional in four-digit numbers: both *4,215* and *4215* are acceptable.

 Use commas with quotations according to standard practice.

 Ordinarily, use a comma with identifying words before or after a quotation.

Ginott tells parents, "Resist the temptation to preach."

"Get out of my life," she said coldly.

Do not use a comma when the quotation ends in a question mark or exclamation point: *"Did they go?" I asked.* (See 20c and 20e.) Do not use a comma when you introduce your quotation with *that* or when your sentence does more than introduce the quotation.

The health food expert observed that "when desserts are outlawed, only outlaws will eat desserts."

There are no "good foods" or "bad foods," only too much food.

Use a colon to introduce a quotation when the quotation is long or weighty (see 25a).

 With an interrupted quotation, precede the identifying words with a comma and follow them with the punctuation required by the quotation.

"Our attitude toward money," Harvey Cox says, "is unrealistic in the extreme." [The explanatory words interrupt a sentence in the quotation.]

"We have been drifting for years," the speaker said. "It is almost too late." [The explanatory words fall at the end of a sentence in the quotation.]

409

3 **Place commas within quotation marks when they follow quotations.**

"No split infinitives," she muttered in her sleep.

For further guidance on punctuating quotations, see 24g.

21i Use commas to prevent misreading.

Even when it is not required by a rule, a comma may be necessary to prevent words from running together in ways that cause confusion.

CONFUSING Always before she had bought her tickets in advance. [The short introductory phrase does not require a comma, but clarity does.]

CLEAR Always before, she had bought her tickets in advance.

See Exercises 21-4, 21-6, 22-2, 25-2.

Related Exercises 14-2, 17-1, 24-1.

21j Use commas only where required.

 Principal misuses of the comma

- Don't separate subject-verb or verb-object (21j-1).

  FAULTY *Anyone* with breathing problems, *should not exercise* during smog alerts.

  REVISED Anyone with breathing problems☐should not exercise during smog alerts.

- Don't separate a pair of words, phrases, or subordinate clauses joined by *and, or,* or *nor.* (21j-2).

  FAULTY Asthmatics are affected by *ozone, and sulfur oxides.*

  REVISED Asthmatics are affected by ozone☐and sulfur oxides.

- Don't use a comma after *and, but, although, because,* or another conjunction (21j-3).

  FAULTY Smog is dangerous and, sometimes even fatal.

  REVISED Smog is dangerous and sometimes even fatal.

410

- Don't set off restrictive elements (21j-3).

FAULTY Even people, *who are healthy*, should be careful.

REVISED Even people who are healthy should be careful.

- Don't set off a series (21j-4).

FAULTY *Cars, factories, and even bakeries*, contribute to smog.

REVISED Cars, factories, and even bakeries contribute to smog.

- Don't set off an indirect quotation or a single word that isn't a nonrestrictive appositive (21j-5).

FAULTY Experts *say, that* the pollutant, *ozone,* is especially damaging.

REVISED Experts say that the pollutant ozone is especially damaging.

 Delete any comma that separates subject and verb or verb and object.

FAULTY The bearded man in the black coat and dirty hat, was arrested by the police. [Subject separated from verb.]

REVISED The bearded man in the black coat and dirty hat was arrested by the police.

FAULTY The local bar association proposed, a 10 percent increase in fees. [Verb separated from direct object.]

REVISED The local bar association proposed a 10 percent increase in fees.

In the following sentence, the nonrestrictive appositive *my uncle* comes between the subject and verb and must be set off with two commas.

  The bearded man, my uncle, was arrested for demonstrating.

(See also 21c for use of commas with nonrestrictive elements.)

2 Delete any comma that separates a pair of words, phrases, or subordinate clauses joined by a coordinating conjunction.

Although a comma is conventionally used between two main clauses joined by a coordinating conjunction, commas are *not* usually used between other sentence elements joined by coordinating conjunctions.

FAULTY The concerts in the chapel, and all other musical events are free. [Two subjects, *concerts,* and *events,* are incorrectly separated.]

REVISED The concerts in the chapel and all other musical events are free.

21j

FAULTY	I found the book on Thursday, and returned it to the library on Friday. [Two verbs, *found* and *returned*, should not be separated.]
REVISED	I found the book on Thursday and returned it to the library on Friday.
FAULTY	Accounts differ as to who fired first, and how many died at Wounded Knee. [Two subordinate clauses should not be separated.]
REVISED	Accounts differ as to who fired first and how many died at Wounded Knee.

 Delete any comma after a conjunction.

Use a comma after a coordinating conjunction (*and, but,* and so on) or a subordinating conjunction (*because, although,* and so on) only when the conjunction is followed by an interrupting clause or phrase that must be enclosed with commas. Do not use *although* as you would *however;* the result would be a sentence fragment.

FAULTY	Money can be anything that people agree to accept in exchange for goods and services, but, most nations today use metal coins, paper bills, and bank checks.
REVISED	Money can be anything that people agree to accept in exchange for goods and services, but most nations today use metal coins, paper bills, and bank checks.
REVISED	Most nations today use metal coins, paper bills, and bank checks, but, if a country wanted to do so, it could use beads or shells for money. [The interrupting *if* clause is set off with commas.]
FAULTY	The US monetary system was based on both gold and silver during most of the nineteenth century. Although, a full gold standard was in effect during the twentieth century. [The clause beginning *although* is a fragment.]
REVISED	The US monetary system was based on both gold and silver during most of the nineteenth century. However, a full gold standard was in effect during the twentieth century. (As a conjunctive adverb rather than a subordinating conjunction, *however* can begin a sentence.]

 Delete any commas that set off restrictive elements.

FAULTY	Any miner, who contracts black lung disease, is eligible for compensation.
REVISED	Any miner who contracts black lung disease is eligible for compensation.

FAULTY	Lillian Jackson Braun's novel, *The Cat Who Saw Red,* is one of a series of mysteries featuring a crime-solving cat. [The commas imply that Braun has written only one novel.]
REVISED	Lillian Jackson Braun's novel *The Cat Who Saw Red* is one of a series of mysteries featuring a crime-solving cat.

Adjective clauses beginning with *that* are always restrictive and should not be set off by commas.

FAULTY	Countries, that have completely socialized medicine, pay for all medical care with public funds.
REVISED	Countries that have completely socialized medicine pay for all medical care with public funds.

See also 21c.

 Delete any comma before or after a series unless a rule requires it.

FAULTY	Tragedies, comedies, and tragicomedies, are represented in the text.
REVISED	Tragedies, comedies, and tragicomedies are represented in the text.
FAULTY	The main ingredients of the stuffing are, bread, celery, and onions.
REVISED	The main ingredients of the stuffing are bread, celery, and onions.

 Delete any comma setting off an indirect quotation or a single word that isn't a nonrestrictive appositive.

FAULTY	He asked, who was responsible.
REVISED	He asked who was responsible.
FAULTY	My roommate pronounces, "Washington," as, "Warshington."
REVISED	My roommate pronounces "Washington" as "Warshington."

See Exercises 21-5, 21-6, 25-2.

Related Exercises 5-13, 5-14, 5-16, 21-2, 21-3, 22-2.

21j

EXERCISE 21-1

Commas Between Main Clauses and After Introductory Elements: Revising Text (21a, b)

Add commas where they are required in the following paragraphs. Some sentences may require more than one comma, and some may require none.

> *Example:*   By studying common features of languages**,** linguists learn about
> the history of the languages.

1   Discovering the origin of English is like a detective story. Applying deductive reasoning to available clues linguists have traced its beginnings to a hypothetical language called Indo-European. This language did actually exist but there is no record of it other than in the languages that derived from it. In addition to English among these languages existing today are German, Swedish, French, Greek, and Russian. To discover languages' similar roots linguists traced common words. For example *night* in English is *nacht* in German, *natt* in Swedish, *nuit* in French, *nuktos* in Greek, and *noch* in Russian. Interestingly some of these languages that derive from Indo-European are classified as Romance, or Latinate and some are Germanic. Still others have other histories.

2   On the basis of the presence or absence of certain words in the related languages linguists speculate that Indo-European existed in Eastern Europe several thousand years before Christ. They found evidence of words for *bear* and *snow* but they discovered no common words for *camel*

exer
21

415

and *ocean*. Using this evidence they supposed that the language was spoken by an inland people that experienced winter climates.

3   At some point Indo-European split into Eastern and Western branches and these branches then divided again. Like English Swedish derived from a branch of Western Indo-European, the Germanic. Greek and French also derived from a branch of Western Indo-European but Russia's origins are in Eastern Indo-European.

exer

21

EXERCISE 21-2

Commas in Sentences with Nonrestrictive Elements, Absolute Phrases, and Phrases of Contrast: Editing (21c, d, e)

Add commas where required in the following sentences. (Some sentences may require more than one comma.) If a sentence is already punctuated correctly, write *C* to the left of it.

Example: The poster **,** a picture of a singer **,** cost $4.98.

1. The trial, which lasted for three days ended with a verdict of guilty.
2. No one who is related to a police officer would say police work is easy or safe.
3. The American director who may be most popular now is Steven Spielberg.
4. All the banks I hear, refuse to lend money to students.
5. Two men one of them wearing a ski mask robbed the small grocery store where I work.
6. The woman who called me claimed to work at the White House.
7. We are after all here to get an education.
8. There are few surprises I thought, in tonight's game.
9. Senator Cuomo who chairs the finance committee voted against tax reform.
10. Her health failing Sarah called her children around her.
11. The audience becoming impatient the theater manager asked for a little more time to get the sound system working.
12. My dog whose name is Jasper eats two rawhide bones a day.
13. The tax forms six pages of figures were mailed yesterday.
14. The delay during which the pitcher's arm tightened up lasted an hour.
15. The famous New York restaurant Four Seasons has many imitators.
16. I replied, "Yes I would like to play music professionally."
17. Every morning I drink grapefruit juice which contains vitamins and eat a brownie which tastes good.
18. Hypnotism still not allowable in court testimony is a fertile method for developing one's memory.
19. The songs of birds for instance, are more complex than they sound.
20. The music blaring next door I was unable to concentrate on my reading.

exer
21

EXERCISE 21-3

Commas with Nonrestrictive Elements, Absolute Phrases, and Phrases of Contrast: Combining Sentences (21c, d, e)

Combine each group of sentences according to the directions for the section. Punctuate appropriately.

A. Combine each pair of sentences into a single sentence that contains a non-restrictive element. Use a variety of nonrestrictive elements.

Example: The Gus S. Wortham Theater Center is lavish and huge.
The Gus S. Wortham Theater Center is Houston's new performing facility.

The Gus S. Wortham Theater Center, Houston's new performing facility, is lavish and huge.

1. The Wortham Theater Center now houses Houston's Grand Opera and the Houston Ballet.
The Wortham Theater Center was built over a six-year period.

2. No public money was used to build the Wortham.
The Wortham cost $72 million.

3. The building was given to the city of Houston.
The city now operates it together with the Opera and the Ballet.

4. Its lobby is huge.
Its lobby is one of the largest in America.

exer
21

5. The Wortham is so big that it makes people feel small.
   It is like other postmodern architecture.

6. The Wortham covers two city blocks.
   The Wortham's exterior is brown Texas brick, rose-colored granite, and glass.

7. Inside the lobby are eight large steel sculptures.
   They seem almost too small for this huge lobby.

8. The Wortham has two theaters and five large rehearsal halls.
   All of them are contained in one of the city blocks.

9. The Brown Theater seats 1176.
   It is the opera house.

10. The Roy Cullen Theater is smaller.
    It seats 1100.

B. Combine each pair of sentences into a single sentence that contains an absolute phrase.

   Example: The Ganges is the world's holiest river.
                  Hindu mythology actually calls it God.

   The Ganges is the world's holiest river, Hindu mythology actually calling it God.

1. The Ganges is named for the goddess Ganga.
   The Indians believe that she frees their souls.

2. The Ganges is heavily polluted.
   Upstream industries and urban sewage have dirtied it.

3. Many people come to the river to die.
   One of its major pollutants is the ashes and bones of cremated bodies.

4. Its waters carry many diseases.
   Thousands of devout Hindus bathe in the Ganges every day.

5. The Indian government's health standards are in conflict with religion.
   The Indian government wants to clean up the river.

6. Part of the plan is to build sewers and treatment facilities.
   Waste water would be processed there.

7. About 75 percent of Ganges pollution comes from waste water.
   The treatment facilities would make a big difference.

8. The government also proposes to build large electric crematories.
   This move is more controversial than that of waste treatment facilities.

9. The old wooden crematories would be replaced by the new ones.
   The old crematories' waste and ash greatly pollute the river.

10. The government also proposes to build public laundries.
Detergents from people doing their laundry in the river would thus be contained and treated.

C. Combine each of the following pairs of sentences to make a single sentence that contains a phrase of contrast.

Example: It was Plato who wrote *Gorgias.*
It was not Aristotle who wrote *Gorgias.*

> It was Plato, not Aristotle, who wrote *Gorgias.*

1. Aristotle wrote *The Art of Rhetoric.*
Plato did not write *The Art of Rhetoric.*

2. Aristotle describes a rhetoric of persuasion.
He does not describe a rhetoric of exposition.

3. Aristotle felt that rhetoric had noble aims.
He was unlike some politicians today.

4. For Aristotle, rhetoric was a means of uplifting an audience.
It was never a means of insulting them.

5. But rhetoric could be used to evoke negative emotions like anger.
It was not used just to evoke positive ones like honor.

EXERCISE 21-4

Commas with Series, Coordinate Adjectives, Dates, Addresses, Long Numbers, and Quotations: Editing (21f, g, h)

Place commas in the following sentences wherever they are required. (Some sentences will require more than one comma.) If the sentence is already punctuated correctly, write *C* to the left of it.

> *Example:* Our team played tournaments last year in Canada, Japan, and Australia and lost only in Canada.

1. A high-priced skimpy meal was all that was available.
2. After testing 33107 subjects, the scientist still thought she needed a bigger sample.
3. "Please, can you help me?" the old woman asked.
4. "I need fifty volunteers, now" the physical education teacher said ominously.
5. The excited angry bull was shot to death after it destroyed the garden.
6. The shop is located at 2110 Greenwood Street Kennett Square Pennsylvania 19348.
7. The open mine attracted children looking for adventure couples needing privacy and old drunks seeking a place to sleep.
8. The area around Riverside California has some of the most polluted air in the country.
9. The records disappeared from the doctor's office in Olean New York yesterday.
10. Seven lonely desperate people come to the neighborhood center for counseling every night.
11. The lantern has a large very heavy base.
12. The town council designated the area's oldest largest house as a landmark.
13. The evil day of 29 October 1929, when the stock market crashed, marked the beginning of the Great Depression.
14. The office is located at 714 W. Lincoln Harlingen Texas.
15. The November 17 1944 issue of the *Times* carried the submarine story.
16. The team lost its final games by scores of 72–66 72–68 and 72–70.
17. Through the wide-open door I could hear them by turns squabbling laughing and crying.

exer
21

EXERCISE 21-5

Misused and Overused Commas: Editing (21j)

Circle each misused or overused comma. If a sentence is punctuated correctly, write *C* to the left of it.

> *Example:* Tourists who want to visit Canada⊙ should acquaint themselves with entry requirements before leaving home.

1. Legal residents of the United States can enter Canada, without a passport.
2. Visitors to Canada, who do not have US citizenship, must have a valid passport.
3. US citizens who want to enter Canada, should carry some identification.
4. This identification might be, a birth certificate, a baptismal certificate, or a voter's certificate.
5. Naturalized US citizens should carry their naturalization papers with them, or some other proof of citizenship.
6. People taking pet dogs and cats across the border, must have a certificate showing that the animals have recently been vaccinated against rabies.
7. However, puppies and kittens under three months of age are not restricted.
8. Seeing-eye dogs also, are not required to have certification.
9. People who want to take other kinds of pets with them, such as, turtles and parrots, should check requirements.
10. Visitors to Canada should also know, that there are restrictions on plants.
11. There are also restrictions regarding one's return to the United States.
12. Merchandise over certain limits, is subject to customs duty.
13. US residents who have been in Canada for 48 hours, or less, can bring back $25 worth of certain restricted merchandise.
14. This merchandise includes, perfume, 4 ounces of alcoholic beverages, 10 cigars, and 50 cigarettes.
15. US residents, who have been in Canada for more than 48 hours, may bring up to $400 back with them.
16. Restricted merchandise such as alcohol and tobacco, has limits.
17. US Customs, like its Canadian counterparts, has restrictions on transporting plants across the border.
18. Tourists who want to bring plants home with them should ask, what these restrictions are.
19. They could also learn that, "bringing whalebone and sealskin into the United States is illegal."
20. The US Customs Service in Washington, DC, will answer questions about American customs regulations.

EXERCISE 21-6
Commas: Editing Text

The following paragraphs contain unneeded commas and omit needed ones. Circle every unneeded comma and insert a comma wherever one is needed.

1   Argentina, the second largest country in South America extends 2300 miles from north to south. It is about one-third the size of the United States not counting Alaska and Hawaii. The land was settled by people from many European countries but, most Argentines are descendants of early Spanish settlers, and Spanish and Italian immigrants. The official language of the nation is Spanish. The Argentine people, most of whom live in the cities are generally better educated than people in other South American countries. About 90 percent can read and write. Some Argentines live in large modern apartment buildings and others live in Spanish-style buildings with adobe walls, tile roofs and wrought-iron grillwork on the windows. The homes of the poorer people, of course are not so grand.

2   Argentina is a major producer of cattle, sheep, wool and grain. On the pampa which is a fertile grassy area covering about a fifth of the country, cowboys called *gauchos*, tend large herds of cattle and farmers raise sheep, hogs and wheat. Farther south, in the windswept region of Patagonia people raise sheep, and pump oil. Because the country has such

exer
21

425

a wide range of elevation, and distance from the equator, it has a climate, that varies greatly. For example the north has heavy rainfall, the central area has moderate precipitation and parts of Patagonia are desert. Being in the Southern Hemisphere Argentina has seasons just the opposite of those in North America the hottest days occurring in January and February and the coldest in July and August.

3   Since its first settlement in the 1500s, when early explorers hoped to find silver in the land Argentina has found, that its real wealth is in its fertile soil and its lively people.

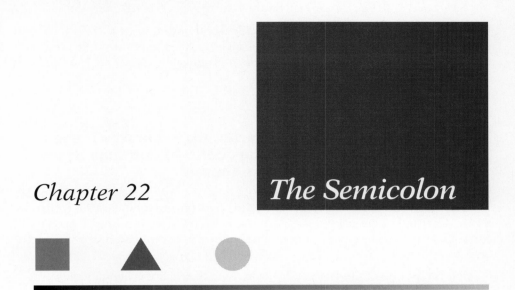

Chapter 22

The Semicolon

22a Use a semicolon between main clauses not joined by *and*, *but*, or another coordinating conjunction.

A **main clause** contains a subject and a predicate and does not begin with a subordinating word. When two main clauses in a sentence are not linked by a coordinating conjunction (*and, but, or, nor, for, so, yet*), they are separated by a semicolon.

> There are six museums in the city; the largest is the Museum of Fine Arts. The college motor pool has several cars; none is available for student activities.

Both clauses in these sentences could be written as separate sentences. If commas were used in place of the semicolons, the result would be a comma splice (see Chapter 11).

22b Use a semicolon to separate main clauses related by *however, thus, for example,* and so on.

Conjunctive adverbs such as *however, indeed, moreover, thus,* and *nonetheless* relate clauses but do not function as conjunctions.

> The reporters waited for an explanation of the policy change; *indeed,* they felt they were entitled to it.

Manufacturers each year recall more cars with defects; the number of faulty and even dangerous cars on the road, *however,* is still alarming.

Notice that the conjunctive adverb, unlike a conjunction, may fall in several places in its clause. If it follows the semicolon, it is generally followed by a comma. If it falls elsewhere in the clause, it is generally preceded and followed by commas.

22c Use a semicolon to separate main clauses if they are complicated or if they contain commas, even with a coordinating conjunction.

Though a comma is normally sufficient to separate main clauses joined by a coordinating conjunction (see 21a), a semicolon signals a longer pause and can make the clauses easier to read when they are complicated or are punctuated by commas.

The literacy rate in Indonesia, Malaysia, and Singapore is about 50 percent; *but* in Cambodia and Laos the rate is 70 and 80 percent, respectively.

The caterer arrived on time, and the food she served was delicious; *but* the guests had to drink from plastic cups because she forgot to bring glasses.

22d Use semicolons to separate items in a series if they are long or contain commas.

The staff especially wishes to thank N. M. Matson, mayor; "Lima Bean" Horton, deputy mayor; Axel Garcia, police chief; and Norma Smith, school provost.

Logan charged $370 for repairing the steps and the fence gate; Rogers charged $800 for painting the exterior of the house; and Morris charged $200 to replace the doors, $300 to fix the plumbing, and $250 to repair the patio.

22e Use the semicolon only where required.

 Delete or replace any semicolon that separates a subordinate clause or a phrase from a main clause.

A phrase or subordinate clause set off with a semicolon is a type of fragment.

FAULTY   American Sign Language is now seen as a full, expressive language; though it was once viewed as a poor substitute.

428

REVISED	American Sign Language is now seen as a full, expressive language, though it was once viewed as a poor substitute.
FAULTY	I do not see how I can get good grades; with such a heavy course load.
REVISED	I do not see how I can get good grades with such a heavy course load.

 ## Distinguishing the comma, the semicolon, and the colon

The **comma** chiefly separates both equal and unequal sentence elements.

- It separates main clauses when they are linked by a coordinating conjunction (21a).

  An airline once tried to boost sales by advertising the tense alertness of its crews, *but* nervous fliers did not want to hear about pilots' sweaty palms.

- It separates subordinate information that is part of or attached to a main clause, such as a nonrestrictive modifier or an introductory element (21b–21h).

  Although the airline campaign failed, many advertising agencies, including some clever ones, copied its underlying message.

The **semicolon** chiefly separates equal and balanced sentence elements.

- It separates complementary main clauses that are *not* linked by a coordinating conjunction (22a).

  The airline campaign had highlighted only half the story; the other half was buried in the copy.

- It separates complementary main clauses that are related by a conjunctive adverb (22b).

  The campaign should not have stressed the seller's insecurity; instead, the campaign should have stressed the improved performance resulting from that insecurity.

The **colon** chiefly separates unequal sentence elements.

- It separates a main clause from a following explanation or summary, which may or may not be a complete main clause (25a).

  Many successful advertising campaigns have used this message: the anxious seller is harder working and smarter than the competitor.

 ## Delete or replace any semicolon that introduces a series or an explanation.

FAULTY	Three of our team's players made the all-star team; the quarterback, the center, and the middle linebacker.

REVISED   Three of our team's players made the all-star team: the quarter-
                 back, the center, and the middle linebacker.

(See 25a and 25b for use of colons and dashes with lists.)

 Use the semicolon sparingly.

A series of sentences whose clauses are linked by semicolons often indicates repetitive sentence structure.

REPETITIVE   Several times they called to him; each time only their own echoes
                 answered back. They had expected to rescue him before nightfall;
                 now they hoped he could keep himself alive until morning.

REVISED   Several times they called to him; each time only their own echoes
                 answered back. Although they had expected to rescue him by
                 nightfall, now they hoped he could keep himself alive until morn-
                 ing.

See Exercises 22-1, 22-2, 25-2.

Related Exercises 5-15, 11-1, 11-2, 11-3, 11-4.

EXERCISE 22-1

Semicolon: Editing Sentences

Cross out misused commas and semicolons in these sentences, replacing them with appropriate punctuation if it is needed. If a sentence is already punctuated correctly, write *C* to the left of it.

Example: Some of the wonderful inventions of the past seem hopelessly outdated ⱼ however, the principles on which they were based are often still timely.

1. A 1915 cookbook predicts; "The fireless cooker will become recognized as one of the greatest achievements of the century."

2. "No home should be without one," it said, "every cook should use one."

3. Its primary advantages were that it saved fuel and prevented burning and scorching, it also kept cooking odors from spreading throughout the house.

4. The fireless cooker was little more than an insulated box; working on the principle that wood is a poor conductor of heat.

5. The box had depressions to hold cooking kettles, it was constructed of wood or some other poor conductor of heat.

6. Some fireless cookers had stone disks which could be removed and heated, then they were returned to the cooker for keeping food hot.

7. Several popular books of the time gave instructions on how to make a fireless cooker at home.

8. To use a fireless cooker, the cook would heat the food on a normal stove; until it was heated thoroughly.

exer
22

9. Foods that required long, slow, low-temperature cooking were suitable for fireless cooking, foods that required high temperatures were not suitable.

10. Foods such as cornmeal mush would be boiled on the stove for five minutes, then they were placed in the fireless cooker for five to ten hours.

11. If the fireless cooker was properly constructed; the mush would still be hot after ten hours.

12. Some homemade cookers, however, were not adequately insulated; and would allow food to become cool.

13. One of the dangers of fireless cookery is that food might not remain hot enough to prevent the growth of bacteria.

14. If food began to cool, the cook was advised to return it to the fire to reheat it, however, the cook was also advised not to open the cooker to see how the food was getting along.

15. Fireless cookers have gone the way of the dinosaurs; although, we still use some of the principles they were based on.

16. Our heavy cookware holds heat, conserving stove energy, our slow cookers extend cooking time to hours, using a minimum of electricity for heating, and our ovens are surrounded with insulating material, holding heat in.

17. Even though we don't ordinarily want to wait ten hours for our cereal to be cooked; with a fireless cooker we could start it the night before and have it ready when we get out of bed.

18. The fireless cooker could have advantages for the cook who works away from home; brown the roast before going to work, pop it into the fireless cooker, and have dinner ready on arriving home.

EXERCISE 22-2

The Comma and the Semicolon: Editing Text

In the following paragraphs insert commas and semicolons wherever they are needed.

1   The Aztec Indians inhabited the area around Mexico City from approximately 1200 until 1521 when they were conquered by Hernando Cortés. One of the most civilized groups of American Indians they lived in and around their capital city Tenochtitlán which was located at the site of the present Mexico City.

2   Families lived in simple adobe houses with thatched roofs. Some of their common foods were flat corn cakes which they called *tortillas* a drink called *chocolate* which they made out of cacao beans and corn beans tomatoes and chili. The men dressed in breechcloths capes and sandals the women wore skirts and sleeveless blouses.

3   Religion was central to the life of the Aztecs. They had many gods most of which they appeased with human sacrifices. As a consequence warfare was conducted largely for the purpose of taking prisoners who became objects of sacrifice. During the sacrificial rite the priests would often cut out the victim's heart with a knife made of obsidian. The Aztecs believed that human sacrifices were necessary to keep the sun rising every morning and to have success with the crops and warfare.

4   The Aztecs educated their children in history religious observances crafts and Aztec traditions. Outstanding boys and girls were trained in special schools so that someday they could perform religious duties.

5   Descendants of the Aztecs still live in the area around Mexico City still speaking their ancient language but practicing Spanish customs and religion.

Chapter 23

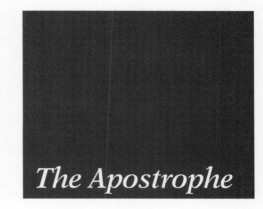

The Apostrophe

23a Use the apostrophe to indicate the possessive case for nouns and indefinite pronouns.

The **possessive case** indicates the possession or ownership of one person or thing by another (see Chapter 6).

Uses and misuses of the apostrophe

USES	**MISUSES**
Possessives of nouns and indefinite pronouns (23a)	Possessives of personal pronouns (23b)

Chip's	weeks'	**NOT**	it's	**BUT**	its
Park's	Parks'		your's		yours
everyone's					

Contractions (23c)		Third-person singulars of verbs			
won't	shouldn't	**NOT**	swim's	**BUT**	swims
they're	it's		goe's		goes

Plurals of letters, numbers, and words named as words (23d)		Plurals of nouns (23b)			
C's or *C*s 6's or 6s *if*'s or *if*s		**NOT**	book's	**BUT**	books
			Freed's		Freeds

1 **Add -'s to singular nouns and indefinite pronouns.**

That *person's* car was towed away.

Everyone's ears were ringing.

Dr. Hill's house is being painted.

Morris's career is prospering.

The *business's* files were confiscated.

EXCEPTION: Usage varies in a few nouns that end in *s* or *z* sounds, especially in names with more than one *s* sound (Cassius), names that sound like plurals (Gates), and other nouns when they are followed by a word beginning with an *s*. In these cases, some writers add only the apostrophe to show possession, while others use the apostrophe plus the *s*.

Cassius'	Cassius's
Gates'	Gates's
conscience' sake	conscience's sake

 2 **Add -'s to plural nouns *not* ending in -*s*.**

Men's suits are on sale until Saturday.

The coat is made of refined *sheep's* wool.

Children's minds are influenced by the violence they see on television.

 3 **Add only an apostrophe to plural nouns ending in -*s*.**

Students' rights are a big issue on this campus.

The *Sheldons'* stables caught fire.

 4 **Add -'s only to the last word of compound words or word groups.**

My *brother-in-law's* arguments bore me.

The *attorney general's* dismissal was overdue.

Everyone else's paper was late.

 5 **When two or more words show individual possession, add -'s to them all. If they show joint possession, add -'s only to the last word.**

Wyatt's and *Surrey's* contributions to the sonnet form have long been acknowledged. [The two writers made separate contributions to the sonnet form.]

23a

Fink and *Schlenk's* restaurant went bankrupt. [The restaurant was jointly owned.]

23b Delete or replace any apostrophe in a plural noun, a singular verb, or a possessive personal pronoun.

Only an *-s* is needed to indicate the plurals of most nouns.

FAULTY	The three *car's* were sold yesterday.
	The *Clarke's* are on vacation this week.
REVISED	The three *cars* were sold yesterday.
	The *Clarkes* are on vacation this week.

Third-person singular verbs end in *-s,* not *-'s.*

FAULTY	Marty *want's* to stop drinking excessively.
REVISED	Marty *wants* to stop drinking excessively.

His, hers, its, ours, yours, theirs, and *whose* are possessive forms and do not take apostrophes.

FAULTY	The victory was *their's.*
REVISED	The victory was *theirs.*

23c Use an apostrophe to indicate the omission in a standard contraction.

The apostrophe is inserted in place of the missing letter or letters.

doesn't	does not	'69	1969
who's	who is	o'clock	of the clock
it's	it is	they're	they are
you're	you are	let's	let us

NOTE: Don't confuse the personal pronouns *its, their, your,* and *whose* with the contractions *it's, they're, you're,* and *who's.*

FAULTY	On *who's* desk? *It's* members left *they're* votes on *you're* desk.
REVISED	On *whose* desk? *Its* members left *their* votes on *your* desk.

437

An apostrophe is often optional in forming the plurals of abbreviations, dates, and letters, numbers, and words named as words.

As a usual practice, include the apostrophe with abbreviations that contain periods but omit it in abbreviations without periods.

Ph.D.'s	CD-ROMs
B.A.'s	BAs

An exception is plural abbreviations for measurements: *ins. gals., lbs.*

In most cases you do not need an apostrophe to form the plural of a letter, number, or word you refer to as a word: *t*s or *t*'s, *21*s or *21*'s, *if*s or *if*'s, *1996*s or *1996*'s. Sometimes, however, the apostrophe adds clarity: *A's, I's.* (See 27d on the use of italics or underlining for letters, numbers, and words named as words.)

See Exercises 23-1, 23-2, 25-2.

Related Exercises 6-1, 6-2, 34-2.

EXERCISE 23-1

Apostrophes for Possessive Case: Changing Words

Form the possessive case of each noun and pronoun below by adding an apostrophe, adding an apostrophe and an *-s,* or changing the form as needed. Do not change singular to plural.

Example: Mike Smith   _Mike Smith's_

1. desks   _____

2. James   _____

3. everyone   _____

4. Ed Knox   _____

5. the Mileses   _____

6. fox   _____

7. community   _____

8. they   _____

9. women   _____

10. no one   _____

11. who   _____

12. St. Louis   _____

13. father-in-law   _____

14. Terre Haute   _____

15. sheep   _____

16. you   _____

exer
23

17. the Bahamas　　　　　　　　　　　_____

18. committee member　　　　　　　_____

19. oxen　　　　　　　　　　　　　　_____

20. *Denver Post*　　　　　　　　　　_____

EXERCISE 23-2

Apostrophe: Editing Text

Edit the following passage for use of apostrophes. Insert apostrophes where they are needed and cross out any that are unnecessary.

1   In my job delivering pizza's, I have learned a lot more about the city than I knew before. I have driven to many unfamiliar neighborhood's and have come to know many new people. I've also been lost many times, trying to find a house or an apartment or trying to read it's address in the dark—all, of course, while the pizzas grew cold.

2   My first weeks experience was one of the worst. I was delivering a large pepperoni supreme to the Swansons' on 49th Street SE I drove right out to 49th Street but couldn't find the Swanson's address. I found out the hard way that 49th Street stop's at the river and that 49th Street SE starts somewhere on the other side of the river, with no bridge connecting the two sections. Once I found the right section of the street, I drove to the house with no problem. Their name was on a board out in front: THE SWANSON'S, it said. "Its cold," they told me when they took the pizza, but they did'nt complain. They said they would warm it in their microwave oven.

3   Another time I had to deliver fifteen pizzas' to a large party on the north side of the city. I found the place without any trouble, and the piz-

exer
23

zas' were still hot when I got there, but the people who ordered could'nt decide who was going to pay me. The guy said the responsibility was her's because she had decided what kind to get and ordered them. But she said, "No, its his house so he should pay for them." It seem's that she did'nt have enough money to pay for fifteen pizzas'. They finally agreed to split the cost. That made me feel a lot better; I was getting worried about what to say to my boss when I brought all those pizzas' back.

4   Now that I know the city well, I'll probably have to quit my job because its taking too much of my time while I'm in school. At first I thought I would be able to reduce my hour's, but my boss does'nt want to hire two people to do the job of one. I wonder where I can find another job that will use the experience Ive gained from my pizza delivering but wont take too much time away from studying for my heavy load of class's.

Chapter 24

Quotation Marks

24a Use double quotation marks to enclose direct quotations.

Quotation marks primarily enclose **direct quotations** from speech and writing. They always come in pairs: one before the quotation and one after.

Shirer wrote that Hitler "remains, so far, the most remarkable of those who have used modern techniques to apply the classic formulas of tyranny."

The speaker said, "This year 350,000 Americans will use firearms to defend themselves."

NOTE: Indirect quotations—reporting what a speaker said but not in his or her exact words—are *not* enclosed in quotation marks:

NOT   He said, "that he would not be late again."
BUT   He said that he would not be late again.

24b Use single quotation marks to enclose a quotation within a quotation.

"Graham said 'No way!' each time the coach asked him to go into the game," the reporter for the *Messenger* wrote.

Handling quotations from speech or writing

(For explanations, consult the sections in parentheses.)

Direct and indirect quotation

DIRECT QUOTATION (24a)

According to Lewis Thomas⸃, "We are, perhaps uniquely among the earth's creatures, the worrying animal. We worry away our lives⸢."

QUOTATION WITHIN A QUOTATION (24b)

Quoting a phrase by Lewis Thomas, the author adds⸃, "We are ⸢'the worrying animal⸢.' "

INDIRECT QUOTATION (24a)

Lewis Thomas says that⸤ human beings are unique among animals in their worrying⸢.

Quotation marks with other punctuation marks

COMMAS AND PERIODS (24g-1)

Human beings are "the worrying animal⸢," says Thomas.

Thomas calls human beings "the worrying animal⸢."

SEMICOLONS AND COLONS (24g-2)

Machiavelli said that "the majority of men live content⸢"; in contrast, Thomas calls us "the worrying animal."

Thomas believes that we are "the worrying animal⸢": we spend our lives afraid and restless.

QUESTION MARKS, EXCLAMATION POINTS, DASHES (24g-3)

When part of your own sentence
Who said that human beings are "the worrying animal⸢"?

Imagine saying that we human beings "worry away our lives⸢"!

Thomas's phrase⸢—"the worrying animal⸢"—seems too narrow.

When part of the original quotation
"Will you discuss this with me⸢?" she asked.

"I demand that you discuss this with me⸢!" she yelled.

"Please, won't you⸢—"She paused.

Altering quotations

BRACKETS FOR ADDITIONS (25d)

"We ⸢[human beings⸢] worry away our lives," says Thomas.

BRACKETS FOR ALTERED CAPITALIZATION (26a)

"⸢[T⸢]he worrying animal" is what Thomas calls us. He says that "⸢[w⸢]e worry away our lives."

ELLIPSIS MARKS FOR OMISSIONS (25e)

"We are ⸢. . . the worrying animal," says Thomas.

Our worrying places us "uniquely among the earth's creatures. ⸢. . . We worry away our lives."

444

Punctuating identifying words with quotations

INTRODUCTORY IDENTIFYING WORDS (21h-1)

He says⟨,⟩ "We worry away our lives."

An answer is in these words by Lewis Thomas⟨:⟩ "We are, perhaps uniquely among the earth's creatures, the worrying animal."

Thomas says that ⟨"⟩the worrying animal⟨"⟩is afraid and restless.

CONCLUDING IDENTIFYING WORDS (21h-1)

We are "the worrying animal⟨,⟩" says Thomas.

"Who says⟨?⟩" she demanded.

"I do⟨!⟩" he shouted.

INTERRUPTING IDENTIFYING WORDS (21h-2)

"We are⟨,⟩" says Thomas⟨,⟩ "perhaps uniquely among the earth's creatures, the worrying animal."

"I do not like the idea⟨,⟩" she said⟨;⟩ "however, I agree with it."

We are "the worrying animal⟨,⟩" says Thomas⟨.⟩ "We worry away our lives."

See also:

SPECIAL KINDS OF QUOTED MATERIAL
Dialogue (3d-4, 24c)
Poetry (24c, 25f)
Prose passages of more than four lines (24c)

USING QUOTATIONS IN YOUR OWN TEXT
Quotations versus paraphrases and summaries (35a)
Avoiding plagiarism when quoting (35a)
Introducing quotations in your text (35a)
Citing sources for quotations (35a)

" "
24c

24c **Set off quotations of dialogue, poetry, and long prose passages according to standard practice.**

Dialogue

Begin a new paragraph for each speaker when quoting a conversation.

"Why did you come?" the instructor asked.

"Because the course is supposed to be easy," answered the student candidly. "And besides, the subject interests me."

When you quote a single speaker for more than one paragraph, place quotation marks at the beginning of each paragraph but at the end of only the last paragraph.

Poetry

Poetry quotations of one line are normally run into the text and enclosed by quotation marks. Poetry quotations of two or three lines may be run into the text and enclosed by quotation marks or set off on separate lines. If the quotation is run in, separate the lines with a slash (/).

> Coleridge's beginning places the poem in an exotic land: "In Xanadu did Kubla Khan / A stately pleasure-dome decree."

Always set off poetry quotations of more than three lines. To set off a poetry quotation, separate the lines from the text and indent them ten spaces from the left margin. Double-space above and below the quotation, and, in double-spaced papers, double-space the quotation itself. A quotation that is set off from the text needs no quotation marks.

> Emerson's poem opens with an indication of his worship of nature:
>
> > Think me not unkind and rude
> > That I walk alone in grove and glen;
> > I go to the god of the wood
> > To fetch his word to men.

Prose

Prose quotations of up to four lines should ordinarily be run into the text and enclosed in quotation marks. Quotations of four lines or more should be set off from the body of the paper and indented ten spaces from the left. Double-space above and below the quotation, and, in double-spaced papers, double-space the quotation itself. Don't enclose a set-off quotation in quotation marks. (See also Chapter 35.)

24d Put quotation marks around the titles of works that are parts of other works.

Use quotation marks to enclose the titles of songs, short poems, articles in periodicals, short stories, essays, episodes of television and radio programs, and the subdivisions of books. For all other titles, use italics (underlining) (see 27a).

 ### Titles to be enclosed in quotation marks

Other titles should be underlined (italicized). See 27a.

SONGS
"Lucy in the Sky with Diamonds"
"Mr. Bojangles"

ESSAYS
"Politics and the English Language"
"Joey: A 'Mechanical Boy'"

SHORT POEMS
"Stopping by Woods on a Snowy Evening"
"Sunday Morning"

ARTICLES IN PERIODICALS
"Comedy and Tragedy Transposed"
"Does 'Scaring' Work?"

SHORT STORIES
"The Battler"
"The Gift of the Magi"

EPISODES OF TELEVISION AND RADIO PROGRAMS
"The Mexican Connection" (on *60 Minutes*)
"Cooking with Clams" (on *Eating In*)

SUBDIVISION OF BOOKS
"Voyage to the Houyhnhnms" (Part IV of *Gulliver's Travels*)
"The Mast Head" (Chapter 35 of *Moby Dick*)

24e Quotation marks may be used to enclose words being defined or used in a special sense.

The "correct" version actually included fifteen errors.
Determining the meter of a line of poetry is called "scanning."

NOTE: Underlining (italics) is more common in definitions. (See 27d.)

24f Use quotation marks only where they are required.

" "
24g

Don't enclose the titles of your papers in quotation marks unless they contain or are themselves direct quotations.

NOT   "Rites of Passage in One Story by William Faulkner"
BUT   Rites of Passage in One Story by William Faulkner
OR   Rites of Passage in "The Bear"

Common nicknames, technical terms not being defined, slang, or trite expressions should not be enclosed in quotation marks. If slang or trite expressions are inappropriate, rewrite the sentence.

NOT   The government should "get its act together" on national health care.
BUT   The government should develop a comprehensive program for national health care.

24g Place other marks of punctuation inside or outside quotation marks according to standard practice.

 Place commas and periods inside quotation marks.

They sang "America the Beautiful."
It replaced "The Star-Spangled Banner," which no one could sing.

447

Place colons and semicolons outside quotation marks.

He said his footing was "precarious": he was on a high wire.

The label said "for relief of itching"; we bought two bottles.

 Place dashes, question marks, and exclamation points inside quotation marks only if they belong to the quotation.

The lawyer's one comment—"Immaterial"—sent a buzz through the courtroom.

Did I hear you say "No"?

BUT　　　Did I hear you ask "Why?"

Parentheses go inside the quotation marks or outside, depending on meaning. (See also 25c.)

Smith reports, "No one was able to predict with assurance what changes will take place in the earth's climate" (357). [Page number goes outside the quotation mark but within the period.]

Smith states further: "Warming occurs when carbon dioxide and other gases are prevented from escaping the earth (the greenhouse effect)" (358).

See Exercises 24-1, 24-2, 25-2.

Related Exercises 20-1, 21-4, 27-1.

" "

24g

EXERCISE 24-1

Quotation Marks: Editing Sentences

In the following sentences insert single or double quotation marks as required. Be sure to place the marks correctly in relation to other punctuation marks. If a sentence is already punctuated correctly, write *C* to the left of it.

> *Example:*   "How many of you," the instructor asked, "have read the assigned story, 'Araby'?"

1. Did Cohan write You're a Grand Old Flag?

2. The nucleus of a cell is its center, where its vital work goes on.

3. Did I hear you say, The show is sold out?

4. The committee declared, America would be a more appropriate national anthem than The Star-Spangled Banner is.

5. Never take Route 1 unless you like traffic jams, he stated.

6. African man, writes Mbiti, lives in a religious universe.

7. Dickinson's poem first sets the mood: A quietness distilled, / As twilight long begun.

8. Truman stated, I fired General MacArthur because he would not respect the authority of the President.

9. Remember the Alamo! was first used as a battle cry at San Jacinto.

10. Dandruff is the code name that CB operators give to snow.

11. Coleridge was ridiculed for writing I hail thee brother in his poem To a Young Ass.

exer
24

12. The Congo is a poem that experiments with rhythmic effects.

13. Why did you shout Eureka! as you left? she asked.

14. We spent a whole class discussing the word moral, yet we never agreed on its meaning.

15. The characters in the story are, in the author's words, antiheroes; however, none is realistic.

16. Her article, The Joy of Anguish, was reprinted in six languages.

17. Sotweed is a synonym for tobacco.

18. How many of you know the To be or not to be speech from *Hamlet?* asked the drama coach.

19. He said that the test would be challenging; he should have said that it would be impossible.

20. William Blake's poem The Fly includes this stanza:

> Am not I
> a fly like thee?
> Or art not thou
> A man like me?

EXERCISE 24-2

Quotations: Rewriting Text

In the following essays, use separate paper to rewrite all indirect quotations as direct quotations, revising as necessary and inserting quotation marks as appropriate.

A.

COOLING OFF

1   When I was twelve, I went swimming at St. Ben's College swimming pool with my good friend Paul, who is two years older than I. It was a steamy hot summer day when I suggested to Paul that we go for a dip. Chuckling, he told me that I had read his mind.

2   We left in the early afternoon, cruising down the road on our mud-covered bicycles. As we got to the pool, Paul yelled that the last one in was the biggest loser in the world. Naturally he won because I had to lock up the bikes.

3   Two walls of the indoor pool were enclosed in glass, affording a view of the entire campus and the sunny summer day. After we had been swimming for about an hour, I noticed that the sun was no longer shining. In fact, the sky was turning quite dark. I pointed to the leaden gray clouds moving toward us and asked Paul if he thought we should leave.

4   He exclaimed that we should—after one more dive.

5   As we dressed in the locker room, I told Paul that I was nervous about the weather, because I had never seen it change so quickly. When we pushed open the door, the wind pushed back. Rushing out, we ran toward our bikes, unlocked them, and headed in the direction of home.

6   About halfway home, we began to be hit by small pellets of hail. Paul yelled at me to hurry up, that I was falling behind. With lightning brightening the dark afternoon, thunder crashing around us, and hail bouncing off our chilled bodies, we pedaled furiously, seeing my driveway just ahead. As I turned in to the drive, Paul rode on to his house next door, yelling to me that he would see me later.

7   I dropped my bike on the lawn and dashed into the house, looking for a towel and some dry, warm clothes. I wasn't hot anymore.

exer
24

B.

SPOILED BRATS?

1   There is speculation that the People's Republic of China may become a nation of spoiled brats. In an article already several years old, *Time* magazine (7 Dec. 1987) estimates that there may be hundreds of thousands, perhaps millions, of children throwing tantrums throughout China (38). That is because of a law that China began enforcing in 1979 decreeing that each couple should have only one child. *Time* suggests that these children, called "little emperors" by the local press, have been swaddled in the love of their parents and grandparents and that as a result they are growing up spoiled, selfish, and lazy (38).

2   The *China Daily* provides an example of one of these little empresses. The article states that the girl's mother combs the little girl's hair, her grandmother feeds her breakfast, her grandfather is under the table putting her shoes on, and her father is getting her satchel ready (*Time* 38). *Time* quotes one little girl, who said that she rides on her daddy's shoulders and asks her parents to make a circle with their arms. Then she says to them that they are the sky and she is the little red sun (38).

3   The Chinese government is somewhat concerned about the long-term effects of the one-child-per-couple policy. When 21,000 children were asked to write a short paper on what they wanted to be when they grew up, only 5 percent said they wanted to be workers. *Time* reports that most wanted to become taxi drivers, hotel attendants, or Premier, because those occupations are perceived to be easy and comfortable (38). In a Communist country dependent upon workers, such an attitude is serious indeed.

4   Just as serious is the fear for the time when these pampered children grow up and their parents grow old. *Time* suggests that the new generation will be unwilling to care for aging parents and geriatric grandparents, forcing the elderly into the care of the state (38).

5   But perhaps the situation is being exaggerated. One Chinese psychologist says that single children seem to fare better than those with siblings in terms of intellectual development and that some children with siblings are even worse brats than those without them (*Time* 38). Some Chinese say that what is important is moral education at home, whether the family has one child or many (*Time* 38).

*Other
Punctuation
Marks*

Chapter 25

THE COLON

25a Use the colon to introduce and to separate.

The colon is mainly a mark of introduction, telling the reader that something, usually an explanation, will follow. In sentences it is always preceded by a **main clause,** one that contains a subject and verb and is not introduced by a subordinating word (see 5c-4). What follows the colon may be a series, a phrase, an appositive, or even another main clause. Colons frequently introduce long or formal quotations. Despite the similarity in their names, colons are usually not interchangeable with semicolons (see Chapter 22). However, in formal writing colons are sometimes used in place of the less formal dashes (see 25b).

NOTE: Do not use a colon more than once in a sentence, and do not resume an introductory clause after the explanation has been made.

 Use a colon to introduce a concluding explanation, series, appositive, or long or formal quotation.

SERIES

The winners could choose one of three prizes: a new car, a trip to Europe, or a lifetime supply of canned crabmeat.

453

Distinguishing the colon and the semicolon

- The **colon** is a mark of introduction that separates elements of **unequal** importance, such as statements and explanations or introductions and quotations.

  The first element must be a complete main clause; the second element need not be. (See 25a.)

  The business school caters to working students[:] it offers special evening courses in business writing, finance, and management.

  The school has one goal[:] to train students to be responsible, competent businesspeople.

- The **semicolon** separates elements of *equal* importance, almost always complete main clauses. (See 22a.)

  Few enrolling students know exactly what they want from the school[;] most hope generally for a managerial career.

FINAL APPOSITIVE

A good career has one essential quality: challenge.

LONG OR FORMAL QUOTATION

The senator issued his final statement: "I repudiate those who question my honesty, and I call on my constituents to do the same."

EXPLANATION INTRODUCED BY *THE FOLLOWING* **OR** *AS FOLLOWS*

The winners were as follows: Harriet Joyce, Bonnie Chapman, and Charleen Oliver.

 Use a colon to separate titles and subtitles, the subdivisions of time, and the parts of biblical citations.

TITLE AND SUBTITLE	*Poetry: Sound and Image*
TIME	5:45, 9:00
BIBLICAL CITATION	Luke 5:12

 Use the colon only where required.

Use the colon only at the end of a main clause. Don't put a colon between a verb and its object or complement, between a preposition and its object, or before an explanation lacking a formal introduction (such as *the following*).

FAULTY	The subjects of the painting were: a cow, a bear, and a zebra. [The colon separates the verb *were* from the subject complement.]
REVISED	The subjects of the painting were a cow, a bear, and a zebra.

454

FAULTY	Ships sailing the Amazon River carry raw materials such as: animal skins, Brazil nuts, lumber, and rubber. [The colon separates the preposition *such as* from its objects.]
REVISED	Ships sailing the Amazon River carry raw materials such as animal skins, Brazil nuts, lumber, and rubber.

THE DASH

 25b Use a dash or dashes to indicate sudden changes in tone or thought and to set off some sentence elements.

A dash is primarily a mark of interruption. To write it, use two hyphens (--) with no space before, between, or after them.

 Use a dash or dashes to indicate shifts and hesitations.

Jasper's sense of humor might appeal to you—if you are as witless as he is.

In response I said—well, my reply is unprintable.

"My father—" she blurted out and then stopped.

 Use a dash or dashes to emphasize nonrestrictive elements.

To set off nonrestrictive elements such as modifiers, appositives, and parenthetical expressions, dashes may be used in place of commas to achieve more emphasis and in place of parentheses to gain less separation.

Many animals—the elephant for one—are in danger of extinction.

The dash is particularly useful for setting off appositives that contain commas.

Some of the largest animals—elephants, rhinoceroses, and blue whales—are in danger of extinction.

 Use a dash to set off introductory series and concluding series and explanations.

Care, tenderness, a sense of humor—Gunther possessed all of these.

Reservoirs store water for several purposes—irrigation, power, water supply, and recreation. [Some writers would use a colon instead of the dash; the effect would be greater formality.]

Use the dash only where needed.

Don't use a dash when a comma, semicolon, or period is more appropriate. Keep in mind that too many dashes can give writing a choppy or jumpy quality.

FAULTY   The envelope—torn and scuffed—arrived on Tuesday—my birthday—and when I opened it, I found a bent birthday card—and a torn check.

REVISED   The envelope, torn and scuffed, arrived on Tuesday, my birthday. When I opened it, I found a bent birthday card and a torn check.

 Distinguishing dashes, commas, and parentheses

Dashes, commas, and parentheses may all set off nonessential information such as nonrestrictive modifiers and parenthetical expressions.

- **Dashes** give the information the greatest emphasis (25b-2):

  Many students—including some employed by the college—disapprove of the new work rules.

- **Commas** are less emphatic (21c):

  Many students, including some employed by the college, disapprove of the new work rules.

- **Parentheses,** the least emphatic, signal that the information is just worth a mention (25c-1):

  Many students (including some employed by the college) disapprove of the new work rules.

PARENTHESES

 Use parentheses to enclose nonessential elements within sentences.

 Use parentheses to enclose parenthetical expressions.

Parenthetical expressions include explanations, examples, and minor digressions that are not essential to meaning. Setting them off with parentheses rather than with commas or dashes separates them from the rest of the sentence and indicates their relative lack of importance to the sentence meaning.

456

The zoo places animals in settings that simulate their natural environments (forest, desert, swamp, and so forth).

William Butler Yeats (1865–1939) was not only a poet but also a playwright and an essayist.

Sometimes parenthetical expressions can be omitted. If they are so unimportant as to be included in parentheses, perhaps the piece of writing can get along without them.

When a sentence requires a comma in addition to the parentheses, the comma follows the final mark of parenthesis.

The writer of "The Lake Isle of Innisfree," William Butler Yeats (1865–1939), was not only a poet but also a playwright and an essayist.

Don't place a comma *before* the first mark of parenthesis.

FAULTY   The writer of "The Lake Isle of Innisfree," William Butler Yeats, (1865–1939) was not only a poet but also a playwright and an essayist.

REVISED   The writer of "The Lake Isle of Innisfree," William Butler Yeats (1865–1939), was not only a poet but also a playwright and an essayist.

 2 **Use parentheses to enclose letters and figures labeling items in lists within sentences.**

:—()[]…/
25d

Use a *pair* of parentheses:

The course has three requirements: (1) an oral report, (2) a midterm examination, and (3) a final examination.

BRACKETS

25d **Use brackets within quotations to indicate your own comments or changes.**

Brooke writes that "the essence of the religion [Islam] is legalism."

Use the word *sic* (Latin for "in this manner") in brackets to indicate that an error in a quotation appeared in the original and was not introduced by you.

The manual pointed out that "proofreading is an important job that must be performed caerfully [*sic*]."

THE ELLIPSIS MARK

25e Use the ellipsis mark to indicate omissions within quotations.

The **ellipsis mark** is three spaced periods (. . .).

ORIGINAL | "Riley's works must be read aloud for the reader to get the fullest possible enjoyment."

WITH ELLIPSIS | "Riley's works must be read aloud for . . . the fullest possible enjoyment."

When the ellipsis mark ends a sentence, it follows the sentence period: *"The plans went awry. . . . The 'perfect' crime was a failure."*

THE SLASH

25f Use the slash between options and to separate lines of poetry that are run in to the text.

OPTION | We faced an either/or situation: either sell or be taken to court.

POETRY | Wallace Stevens paints autumn differently: "The rain falls. The sky / Falls and lies with the worms."

Notice the spaces before and after the slash when it separates lines of poetry.

See Exercises 25-1, 25-2.

EXERCISE 25-1

The Colon, the Dash, Parentheses, Brackets, the Ellipsis Mark, and the Slash: Editing Sentences

Circle the place in each sentence where punctuation should be added or is used incorrectly, and write the correct punctuation, along with the adjacent words, on the line to the left. When more than one mark would be correct in a sentence, choose the mark that seems most appropriate. If a sentence is already punctuated correctly, write *C* on the line.

Example: _____*exhibit: the*_____ Adams was fascinated by one thing in the exhibit⊙the power of steam.

_____ 1. Of the nine regions surveyed, only one New England had a low suicide rate.

_____ 2. The ring was priced reasonably, ($200).

_____ 3. "Iamb," "trochee," "spondee" all are terms for poetry analysis.

_____ 4. "The penalty is a $500 fine and or a year in jail," the lawyer said.

_____ 5. There are two basic defenses: 1 the zone and 2 the man to man.

_____ 6. A good worker, he lacks only one quality tact.

_____ 7. Environmentalists find that incentives, (such as refunds) increase recycling.

_____ 8. The recipe my aunt's favorite calls for three eels.

_____ 9. The discount on the new car was insignificant only $50.

_____ 10. Two of the contestants (Perry and Hughy are my roommates.

exer
25

_____ 11. In two lines of the poem, Robinson portrays Richard Cory as "a gentleman from sole to crown,/Clean favored, and imperially slim."

_____ 12. The paper said, "People waved from the poopsite *(sic)* shore."

_____ 13. I got a high grade in only one course; Elementary Education 101.

_____ 14. The kit contained the following items, a flare, a wrench, two screwdrivers, one hammer, and a fan belt.

_____ 15. The life of Ernest Hemingway 1899—1961 was exciting by almost anyone's standards.

_____ 16. His new title [associate fireman] brought no increase in pay.

_____ 17. The hide—(alligator)—could not be imported.

_____ 18. The assignment for Friday was a long one pages 200–290.

_____ 19. The cathedral, built in 1295?, was open to tour groups.

_____ 20. "The state's largest drinking fountain" that is what Mayor Belotti called the new reservoir.

_____ 21. However, she then said, "Let's not forget how difficult it was to bring this water here and . . . how much it means to us."

_____ 22. Among the recruiters were IBM, Olivetti, and TRW.

_____ 23. Tolstoy's *Works* [volumes 2 and 3] was on sale for $7.95.

_____ 24. The course depended on only one assignment . . . the term paper.

_____ 25. The teacher, actually, his assistant wrote that my paper was "flabby and pointless."

EXERCISE 25-2

Punctuation: Review of Chapters 20–25

In the following passages insert correct punctuation wherever it is missing.

A.

THREAT TO THE EYES

[1]Sunlight is made up of three kinds of radiation 1 infrared rays which we cannot see 2 visible rays and 3 ultraviolet rays which also are invisible. [2]Especially in the ultraviolet range sunlight is harmful to the eyes. [3]Ultraviolet rays can damage the retina the area in the back of the eye and cause cataracts on the lens. [4]Wavelengths of light rays are measured in nanometers nm or millionths of a meter. [5]Infrared rays are the longest measuring 700 nm and longer and ultraviolet rays are the shortest measuring 400 nm and shorter. [6]The lens absorbs much of the ultraviolet radiation thus protecting the retina however in so doing it becomes a victim growing cloudy and blocking vision.

[7]You can protect your eyes by wearing sunglasses that screen out the ultraviolet rays. [8]To be effective sunglasses should block out at least 95 percent of the radiation. [9]Many lenses have been designed to do exactly this but many others are extremely ineffective. [10]When you are buying sunglasses you can test their effectiveness by putting them on and looking

exer
25

in a mirror while you stand in a bright light. [11]If you can see your eyes through the lenses the glasses will not screen out enough ultraviolet light to protect your eyes.

[12]People who spend much time outside in the sun really owe it to themselves to buy a pair of sunglasses that will shield their eyes.

B.

PARADISE NEXT DOOR

[1]Belize a small country on the eastern coast of Central America covers less than 9000 square miles. [2]Bordering Mexico on the north and Guatemala on the west and south this little nation has a population of approximately 154000. [3]The official language is English but Spanish and native Creole dialects are spoken as well. [4]The country which was formerly known as British Honduras achieved independence in 1981. [5]Home to Mayan Indians for centuries Belize was settled in the seventeenth century by pirates slavers and shipwrecked British seamen and was ruled by Great Britain until its independence it still maintains strong ties to the United Kingdom.

[6]While sugar is its primary export Belize is known mainly for diving fishing and swimming. [7]Divers come from all over the world to explore its coral reefs and limestone caves. [8]The reef offshore is 176 miles long exceeded in length only by Australias Great Barrier Reef. [9]Divers also like to explore the Blue Hole a chasm in the Caribbean that is 400 feet deep and 1000 feet wide it has stalactites and beautiful corals.

¹⁰Both the reef and the Blue Hole can be reached by boat from Belize City. ¹¹This city once the capital of the country is now a tourist attraction because of its location. ¹²Belize City is still the largest city in Belize but it has been replaced as capital by Belmopan which is located fifty miles inland. ¹³In this new location the government buildings are more secure from hurricanes.

¹⁴The tallest structure in the country is the ruins called El Castillo built about 1500 years ago by Mayan Indians. ¹⁵Other Mayan ruins are tucked within thick jungles and give spectacular evidence of the ancient civilization.

¹⁶A major aspect of the Belize economy is the tourist trade however investors and developers have been attracted to the country too. ¹⁷Its stable government and tropical climate both of which spur tourism have drawn foreign business as well. ¹⁸Only two hours by plane from New Orleans or Houston Belize is a near neighbor that approximates the romance of faraway places.

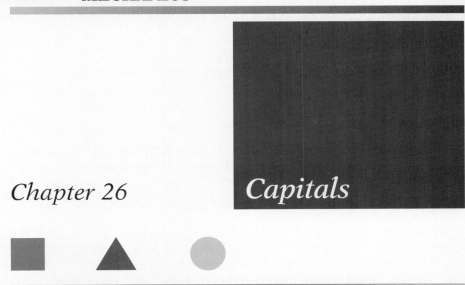

Chapter 26 *Capitals*

26a Capitalize the first word of every sentence.

The snows came early.
Why must we go?

26b Capitalize most words in titles and subtitles of works.

In titles and subtitles, capitalize the first and last words; any word after a colon or semicolon; and all other words except articles (*a, an, the*), *to* in infinitives, and connecting words (prepositions and conjunctions) of fewer than five letters.

"How a River Got Its Name"
"Sexist Language in Television Commercials"
All I Really Need to Know I Learned in Kindergarten

In hyphenated words, capitalize both parts if the second word is a noun or an adjective or is as important as the first word.

"New Sentence-Combining Exercises"
"Making Cut-out Dolls"

465

26c Always capitalize the pronoun *I* and the interjection *O*. Capitalize *oh* only when it begins a sentence.

"But O heart! heart! heart!" wrote Whitman on the death of Lincoln.

My interview was short, but, oh, did I have to answer hard questions.

26d Capitalize proper nouns, proper adjectives, and words used as essential parts of proper nouns.

1 Capitalize proper nouns and proper adjectives.

Common nouns name general classes of persons, places, and things. **Proper nouns** name specific persons, places, and things. **Proper adjectives** are formed from proper nouns. Capitalize all proper nouns and proper adjectives but not the articles (*a, an, the*) that precede them.

● Proper nouns and adjectives to be capitalized

SPECIFIC PERSONS AND THINGS

Stephen King	the Leaning Tower of Pisa
Napoleon Bonaparte	Boulder Dam
Doris Lessing	the Empire State Building

SPECIFIC PLACES AND GEOGRAPHICAL REGIONS

New York City	the Mediterranean Sea
China	Lake Victoria
Europe	the Northeast
North America	the Rocky Mountains

DAYS OF THE WEEK, MONTHS, HOLIDAYS

Monday	Yom Kippur
May	Christmas
Thanksgiving	Columbus Day

HISTORICAL EVENTS, DOCUMENTS, PERIODS, MOVEMENTS

World War II	the Middle Ages
the Vietnam War	the Age of Reason
the Boston Tea Party	the Renaissance
the Treaty of Ghent	the Great Depression
the Constitution	the Romantic Movement

GOVERNMENT OFFICES OR DEPARTMENTS AND INSTITUTIONS

House of Representatives   Polk Municipal Court
Department of Defense   Warren County Hospital
Appropriations Committee   Northeast High School
Postal Service   York Board of Education

POLITICAL, SOCIAL, ATHLETIC, AND OTHER ORGANIZATIONS AND ASSOCIATIONS AND THEIR MEMBERS

Democratic Party, Democrats   Rotary Club, Rotarians
Communist Party, Communist   Eastern Star
Sierra Club   League of Women Voters
Girl Scouts of America, Scout   Boston Celtics
B'nai B'rith   Chicago Symphony Orchestra

RACES, NATIONALITIES, AND THEIR LANGUAGES

Native American   Germans
African-American, Negro   Swahili
Caucasian   Italian
But: blacks, whites

RELIGIONS AND THEIR FOLLOWERS

Christianity, Christians   Judaism, Orthodox Jew
Protestantism, Protestants   Hinduism, Hindu
Catholicism, Catholics   Islam, Moslems *or* Muslims

RELIGIOUS TERMS FOR THE SACRED

God   Buddha
Allah   the Bible (*but* biblical)
Christ   the Koran

cap
26d

 Capitalize common nouns used as essential parts of proper nouns.

Center *Street*   *Mount* Rushmore
Lake Mead   Canadian *Embassy*
Williams *County*   Union *Station*

 Capitalize trade names.

Coca-Cola   Post-it
Xerox   Ford Mustang

Capitalize most titles only when they precede proper names.

Foreign Minister Khalil   Khalil, the foreign minister
Professor G. M. Dunning   G. M. Dunning, professor of history

Some writers capitalize a title denoting high rank even when it is not followed by a proper name, as in the sentence "The President has scheduled a news conference for this morning."

 Capitalize only when required.

 Use small letters for common nouns replacing proper nouns.

NOT   The Stadium was closed for repairs.
BUT   Landrum Stadium was closed for repairs.
OR   The stadium was closed for repairs.

NOT   The Committee decided to disband.
BUT   The Nominating Committee decided to disband.
OR   The committee decided to disband.

 Capitalize compass directions only when they refer to specific geographical areas.

Travel *east* for a visit, but live in the *West*.

 Use small letters for the names of seasons or the names of academic years or terms.

fall color   spring semester
winter rains   sophomore year

 Capitalize the names of relationships only when they form part of or substitute for proper names.

my uncle   Uncle John
my grandmother   Grandmother

NOTE: If you have any doubt about whether a particular word should be capitalized, consult a recently published dictionary.

See Exercise 26-1.

EXERCISE 26-1

Capitals: Rewriting Sentences

Substitute new words for all underlined words in the following sentences.

Example: The <u>Freedom of Information Act</u> has been costly to implement.

The <u>Refugee Act of 1980</u> has been costly to implement.

1. The governor gave a radio talk on <u>Christmas</u>.

2. Edith Farrara, president of <u>Grendel Corporation</u>, makes monsters for a living.

3. Carol titled her painting *All Alone in the Wheat*.

4. John still tells <u>World War II</u> stories on <u>Memorial Day</u>.

5. The waiter explained, "<u>The</u> soup changes every day."

6. Mike asked <u>Grandmother Collins</u> where she was born and heard a fascinating reply.

7. Heffeltooth is a local leader of the <u>Republican Party</u>.

8. Our family attends the <u>First Methodist Church</u> on <u>Main Street</u>.

exer
26

9. My grandfather always forgets to put in his teeth, and Granny then complains.

10. The anti-Islamic group distributed literature on Friday.

11. In English class yesterday, Professor Cohen was upset because Mia wrote her paper on how to make Jell-O.

12. My friend Joe lives on the east side of the park.

13. Ed was always in favor of having lights at Wrigley Field.

14. Both teammates are seniors this spring at Technical High School.

15. The book was titled *How to Deal with Stress*.

16. The U.S. Postal Service seems to make changes every year.

17. Next semester I want to take Industrial Studies 236.

18. Workers in the Netherlands have more vacation time than workers in the United States.

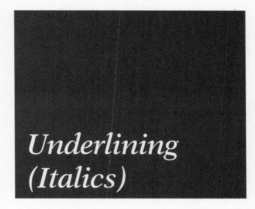

Chapter 27

Underlining (Italics)

Type that slants to the right is known as *italic* type and is used to distinguish or emphasize words. <u>Underlining</u> achieves the same purposes. In some situations, italics may be preferred; in others, underlining. Consult your teacher.

27a Underline the titles of works that appear independently.

Underline the titles of books, long poems, plays, periodicals, pamphlets, published speeches, long musical works, movies, television and radio programs, and works of visual art. Enclose all other titles in quotation marks (see 24d).

 Titles to be underlined (italicized)

Other titles should be placed in quotation marks. (See 24d.)

BOOKS
War and Peace
The Promise
The Bonfire of the Vanities

LONG POEMS
Beowulf
The Song of Roland
Paradise Lost

PLAYS	PERIODICALS
Equus	Time
Hamlet	Philadelphia Inquirer
Summer and Smoke	Yale Law Review
The Phantom of the Opera	Mechanical Engineering

PAMPHLETS	PUBLISHED SPEECHES
The Truth About Alcoholism	Lincoln's Gettysburg Address
On the Vindication of the Rights of Women	Pericles's Funeral Oration

LONG MUSICAL WORKS	MOVIES
Tchaikovsky's Swan Lake	Schindler's List
The Beatles' Revolver	Star Wars
But: Symphony in C	How to Relax

TELEVISION AND RADIO PROGRAMS	WORKS OF VISUAL ART
All Things Considered	Michelangelo's David
Seinfeld	the Mona Lisa
NBC Sports Hour	Picasso's Guernica

References to the Bible are generally not underlined: Bible, Genesis, Matthew.

27b Underline the names of ships, aircraft, spacecraft, and trains.

the USS Turner Joy   the US Enterprise
the Spirit of St. Louis   the Southern Crescent

27c Underline foreign words and phrases that have not been absorbed into English.

Deadly nightshade belongs to the genus Atropa.
Osborn's manners were très gauche.

27d Underline words, letters, numbers, and phrases named as words.

Why does sour grapes mean scorning something?
Even small children know there are four s's in Mississippi.

27e Occasionally, underlining may be used for emphasis.

When its trainer held out a chair, the lion <u>ate</u> it.

Be careful with this use of underlining, however. Too much underlining for emphasis makes writing sound immature or hysterical.

See Exercise 27-1.

Related Exercise 24-1.

ital
27e

EXERCISE 27-1

Underlining (Italics): Editing Sentences

In the following sentences underline any words that require underlining (i.e., italics).

Example: The word <u>emotion</u> pertains to feelings.

1. The tankers were blockaded for a week in the Persian Gulf.

2. TNT was used to demolish the building.

3. The Washington Star usually printed conservative views.

4. The yard became overgrown with Swedish ivy.

5. We took a tour of a ship, the North Carolina, for only $2.50.

6. Hamlet contains more violence than does any crime drama on television.

7. The clams were so gritty that we could not eat them.

8. Life magazine is a showcase for photography.

9. Shaw's Man and Superman is more often read than viewed on stage.

10. The Great Wall of China was completed in the third century BC.

11. The strange form was the mem of the Hebrew alphabet.

exer
27

12. She makes the dots on her i's so large that the page looks like an aerial view of the Charles County Balloon Festival.

13. We read the first five books of the Bible and discussed them in class.

14. We had to report on the P. W. Joyce book Old Celtic Romances.

15. Gree is an archaic word meaning "satisfaction."

16. A new journal, Fun with Caries, reprinted an article by Brady Hull, DDS.

17. The documentary program 60 Minutes continues to be quite profitable for CBS.

18. Miserere is the fiftieth psalm in the Douay Bible.

19. Eijkman won the Nobel Prize for medicine in 1929.

20. The expression c'est la vie never gave me much comfort.

21. The professor published her article in the sociology journal Studies in Poverty.

22. I was surprised to see that Wyeth's Christina's World is not a larger painting.

23. The foxglove belongs to the genus Digitalis.

24. My husband repeatedly mispronounces the word asterisk.

25. My twenty-year subscription to Boys' Life, given to me by my uncle, has finally expired.

Chapter 28 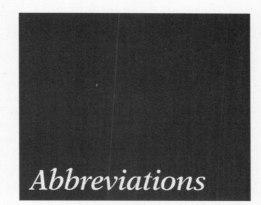 *Abbreviations*

The guidelines in this chapter apply to abbreviations in nontechnical writing. Science and engineering may use abbreviations differently.

 Abbreviations for nontechnical writing

- Titles before or after proper names: *Dr. Jorge Rodriguez; Jorge Rodriguez, Ph.D.* (28a).
- Familiar abbreviations and acronyms: *USA, AIDS* (28b).
- *BC, AD, AM, PM, no.,* and *$* with specific dates and numbers (28c).
- *I.e., e.g.,* and other Latin abbreviations within parentheses and in source citations (28d).
- *Inc., Bros., Co.,* and *&* with names of business firms (28e).

28a Use standard abbreviations for titles immediately before and after proper names.

BEFORE THE NAME
Dr. Peter Green
Mr., Mrs., Gen., Msgr.

AFTER THE NAME
Peter Green, MD
Ph.D., DDS, SJ, Sr., Jr.

The abbreviations *Mr., Mrs., the Rev., Hon., Prof., Rep., Sen., Dr.,* and *St.* (for *Saint*) are used only if they appear with a proper name. Spell them out in the absence of a proper name.

> **NOT**   The dr. was late.
>
> **BUT**   The doctor was late.
>
> **OR**   Dr. Smith was late.

Abbreviations of two or more words written in all-capital letters are increasingly written without periods. The title *Ms.* takes a period even though it is not an abbreviation (*Ms.* Shumway). The title *Miss* does not take a period (*Miss* Olmsted).

Abbreviations such as *Jr., Sr., Esq., MD, DD, Ph.D.,* and *SJ,* which generally appear after proper names, are rarely spelled out. Within a sentence they should be preceded and followed by commas. Abbreviations for academic degrees may be used without a proper name.

> Arthur Garcia, Sr., sold his business.
> Hester Mainz, MD, practices medicine in Detroit.
> He is still trying to earn an MA.

28b Familiar abbreviations and acronyms are acceptable in most writing.

An **acronym** is an abbreviation that spells a pronounceable word and is written without periods: NATO, UNESCO, AIDS. As long as they are well known, acronyms and abbreviations for the names of organizations, corporations, people, and some countries are acceptable in most writing. When the abbreviation consists of two or more all capital letters, it may be written without periods.

CIA	ABC	JFK	USA (or U.S.A.)
UAW	AFL-CIO	FDR	UK (or U.K.)

See also 20b.

28c Use *BC, AD, AM, PM, no.,* and *$* only with specific dates and numbers.

44 BC	AD 54	10:15 AM	no. 344	$3.60

Increasingly, BCE (Before Common Era) and CE (Common Era) are used in place of BC and AD. Both BCE and CE follow the date.

28d Generally, reserve Latin abbreviations for source citations and comments in parentheses.

i.e.	that is (*id est*)
cf.	compare (*confer*)
etc.	and so forth (*et cetera*) (referring to things in the same class)
et al.	and others (*et alii*) (referring to people)
e.g.	for example (*exempli gratia*)
N.B.	note well (*nota bene*)

Note that these abbreviations are not italicized (underlined).

The council (i.e., the three voting members of the committee) decided against the rule change.

Hardwoods (e.g., maple) make durable furniture.

The hardwoods (maple, oak, etc.) burn well in fireplaces.

28e Use *Inc., Bros., Co.,* or & (for *and*) only in official names of business firms.

NOT	The *Brown bros.* won the contract.
BUT	The *Brown brothers* won the contract.
OR	*Brown Bros.* won the contract.

ab
28f

28f Generally, spell out units of measurement and names of places, calendar designations, people, and courses.

NOT	The book, which was a fraction of an *in.* thick and had two *chs.,* was about *Robt.* Ash's struggles every *Tues.* to master *econ.* at the school he attended in *Mo.*
BUT	The book, which was a fraction of an *inch* thick and had two *chapters,* was about *Robert* Ash's struggles every *Tuesday* to master *economics* at the school he attended in *Missouri.*

See Exercise 28-1.

Related Exercise 20-1.

EXERCISE 28-1

Abbreviations: Editing Sentences

Cross out each abbreviation that is inappropriate and write the correct form above it. If the abbreviation is appropriate, write *C* in the left margin.

Example: Second ~~St~~ Street needs to be repaved.

1. The end of Jan. was the last time Alexi smoked a cigarette.

2. Econ. 145 will not be offered next semester.

3. The assignment for Tues. is to read the first ten pages of Ch. 8.

4. Wm. McDougall will address the campus community on Dec. 14.

5. The address will begin at 10:00 A.M.

6. Dan is considering transferring to the U. of Miami.

7. One psychological study suggests that people who are greatly self-involved—e.g., who talk about themselves a great deal—are more likely to have heart disease.

8. Joshua Stern, assoc. prof. of geography, will present the result of his research.

9. The U.S. Congress formally adjourned for Earth Day so members could attend teach-ins in their districts.

exer
28

10. Our conference will be held this year in St. Paul.

11. You can write to the Tex. Tourist Development Off. for winter travel information.

12. Or you can write to Jackson Hole, WY, for information about travel to the Grand Teton area.

13. Roots Research Bureau, Ltd., is one of the companies that offer family histories, ancestry charts, etc., for a price.

14. Three of the twelve Federal Reserve banks are located in Boston, N.Y., and Philadelphia.

15. The Count Dracula Society has its main office in Los Angeles, CA.

16. The no. of members exceeds one thousand.

17. Since its discovery in 1981, AIDS has spread to many nations.

18. The woman receiving the award was addressed as Ms Shumway, but she preferred to be called Clara.

Chapter 29

Numbers

The guidelines in this chapter apply to the use of numbers in nontechnical writing.

29a Use numerals according to standard practice in the field you are writing in.

Spell out most numbers of two words or less.

Last year my smallest class had *ninety-seven* students in it.

The administration expects enrollments to climb to *eleven thousand* and then level off.

When you use several numbers together, consistently spell them out or consistently express them in figures:

The broker bought *110* shares of mining stock at *$10* each, *15* shares of oil stock at *$50* each, and *4* municipal bonds at *$500* each.

29b Use numerals according to conventions for dates, addresses, and other information.

Even when a spelled-out number would be only one or two words, writers conventionally use figures in the following situations:

DAYS AND YEARS

January 10, 1975   AD 56   4 BC

NOTE: When the day of the month is not followed by a year, it may be expressed in words: *January tenth, April first; the first of April;* but not *April 1st or the 10th of January.*

PAGES, CHAPTERS, VOLUMES, ACTS, SCENES, AND LINES
volume 1, pages 67–68
Chapter 13
Act 3, Scene 2, lines 14–16

SCORES AND STATISTICS
a score of 18 to 3
an ACT composite score of 21
a mean of 87
a .305 batting average

DECIMALS, PERCENTAGES, AND FRACTIONS
1.2 liters
3½ years
62 percent (or 62%)

EXACT AMOUNTS OF MONEY
$6.28
$4.9 million (or $4,900,000)

ADDRESSES
327 Linden Avenue
3840 W. 148th Street *but*
315 First Street NW
Bloomington, Illinois 61701

NOTE: Round dollar or cent amounts may be expressed in words: *seven dollars, forty cents.*

THE TIME OF DAY
9:27   4:23 AM   12:00 M. (meridian) *or* 12:00 noon

NOTE: Express the time in words when using *o'clock: nine o'clock.*

**num
29c**

29c Always spell out numbers that begin sentences.

NOT	397 people attended the lecture.
BUT	The lecture was attended by 397 people.
OR	*Three hundred ninety-seven* people attended the lecture.

See Exercise 29-1.

Related Exercise 34-2.

EXERCISE 29-1

Using Numbers: Editing Sentences

Cross out any figure that should be spelled out in most writing, and write the spelled-out number above it. Cross out any spelled-out number that should be written in figures, and write the figures above it. If numbers are used appropriately, write *C* in the left margin.

> *Example:* Noted "Pogo" cartoonist Walt Kelly died in ~~nineteen seventy-three.~~ *1973*

1. The tallest building in Nashville is 452 feet high.

2. The UN Security Council adopted the resolution on June 1st.

3. "We need another forty cents for toll," said Alex.

4. Estimates of the death toll ranged from 550 to two thousand.

5. Oklahoma City's tallest building is 500 feet high.

6. Our instructor assigned Chapter Thirteen for tomorrow.

7. The unemployment rate rose to seven percent in June.

8. 7,800 athletes participated in the 1984 Olympic Games.

exer
29

9. The pact was signed at exactly 9 o'clock.

10. When the game was called on account of darkness, the score was still 7 to 4.

11. Hugo L. Black, Supreme Court Justice from Alabama, served on the Court for thirty-four years.

12. On December 29th, 1890, about 200 Native Americans and 29 soldiers died at Wounded Knee, South Dakota.

13. When the Cuban Giants baseball team was organized in 1885, players were paid an average of $15 a week plus expenses.

14. The Han Dynasty ruled China from 202 BC to AD 220.

15. 1 troy ounce is equivalent to 1.097 avoirdupois ounces.

16. You can write the National Education Association at 1201 Sixteenth Street NW, Washington, DC 20036.

17. Americans' eating habits were changed by a major study linking cholesterol and heart disease, released on the 12th of January, 1984.

18. The value of rice exports was estimated at $178 million.

Chapter 30

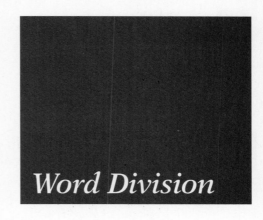

Word Division

These guidelines are mainly for writers who are not using a word-processing program, most of which do not divide words at the end of a line or, when so commanded, will divide words at appropriate places.

Whenever possible, avoid dividing words at the end of a line. If you find at times that you must break a word, do so only between syllables. Most dictionaries show syllabic divisions with dots in the main entry (e.g., *cash·ier*). Indicate your break with a single hyphen at the end of the line, never at the beginning of a line, and don't divide the last word on a page. Note that punctuation marks that follow the last word on a line go at the end of the line, not at the beginning of the next line, with the exception of beginning quotation marks.

30a Leave at least two letters at the end of a line and at least three letters at the beginning of a line.

NOT a-
    gree

NOT boot-
    y

NOT e-
    quip

NOT report-
    er

BUT agree

BUT booty

BUT equip

BUT reporter

30b One-syllable words should not be divided.

Not drop-		**Not** strai-	
ped		ght	
But dropped		**But** straight	

30c Divide compound words only between the words that form them or at fixed hyphens.

Compound words are made up of two or more words. If they are joined by a hyphen, the hyphen is called **fixed.**

Not for-		**Not** sec-		**Not** mid-		**Not** pseudosci-	
ty-two		ondhand		dle-aged		ence	
But forty-		**But** second-		**But** middle-		**But** pseudo-	
two		hand		aged		science	

30d Make sure a word division will not confuse readers.

Even when a word is correctly divided into syllables, the first or second half of the word may form a different word or a wrongly pronounced syllable that will momentarily confuse the reader.

Not poet-		**Not** rein-		**Not** the-		**Not** ide-	
ical		force		ory		alism	
But poetical		**But** reinforce		**But** theory		**But** idealism	

See Exercise 30-1.

Related Exercise 34-2.

Name _____ Date _____

EXERCISE 30-1

Dividing Words Correctly

Many of the following word divisions would be inappropriate in a final paper. Some words should not be divided, and some should be divided differently. If a word should not be divided, write the word on one line to the right. If a word should be divided differently, write the correct division on two lines. Write *C* on the line beside any word that is divided correctly.

Example: good-na-   ___*good-*___

tured   ___*natured*___

1. stew-   _____
   ed   _____

2. rel-   _____
   igious   _____

3. control-   _____
   led   _____

4. curr-   _____
   ent   _____

5. accomp-   _____
   lish   _____

6. Marx-   _____
   ist-Leninist   _____

7. ach-   _____
   ieve   _____

8. fin-   _____
   ished   _____

9. head-hunt-   _____
   ing   _____

10. gui-   _____
    ding   _____

11. poe-   _____
    try   _____

12. car-   _____
    nival   _____

13. pan-Afri-   _____
    can   _____

14. swarth-   _____
    y   _____

15. techniq-
ue   _____

16. usa-
ges   _____

17. cover-
ed   _____

18. drag-
ged   _____

19. self-in-
flicted   _____

20. res-
earch   _____

21. lit-
tle   _____

22. sig-
ner   _____

23. nutrit-
ion   _____

24. leng-
th   _____

25. divis-
ion   _____

26. litera-
ture   _____

27. bro-
ught   _____

28. assig-
ned   _____

29. rent-
ed   _____

30. regis-
ter   _____

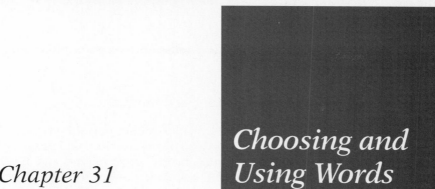

Chapter 31

Choosing and Using Words

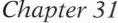

31a   Choosing the appropriate word

The words you use in any piece of writing depend on the situation. In much of our everyday, conversational language, we use the words our friends and colleagues expect and understand. That language may be **slang** or **colloquial**—appropriate only for that casual situation. However, most academic, business, and professional writing is serious and straightforward, meant to convey information, explain something, interpret facts or ideas, or defend a position. For most nonfiction writing in and after college, the appropriate vocabulary is the **standard English** commonly used and understood by educated writers and readers.

Diction in academic and business writing

ALWAYS APPROPRIATE

Standard English (31a)

SOMETIMES APPROPRIATE

Regional words and expressions (31a-2)

Slang (31a-3)

Colloquial language (31a-4)

Euphemisms (31a-7)

Neologisms (31a-5)

Technical language (31a-6)

491

RARELY OR NEVER APPROPRIATE

Dialect (31a-1)

Archaic and obsolete words
(31a-5)

Pretentious writing (31a-7)

Biased language: sexist, racist, etc.
(31a-8)

 ### Revising dialect and nonstandard language

It is common for people to use dialects and sometimes nonstandard language in their everyday speech—vocabulary, pronunciation, and grammar familiar within regional, social, or ethnic groups. In academic and business writing and in many speech situations, however, the appropriate dialect is standard English as described in this book. If you speak a dialect of English other than standard, you may need to give special attention to the language features you use in more formal situations.

 ### Using regionalisms only when appropriate

In writing for a general audience, avoid expressions that carry their intended meaning only in certain regions or that vary in meaning from one part of the country to another. Examples of local expressions are *redd up,* meaning "tidy or prepare," and *wheel,* meaning "bicycle"; an example of expressions that vary by region is *poke,* which means "sack" in some areas and "sum of money" in others. Dictionaries label such expressions *regional* or *dialect.*

 ### Using slang only when appropriate

Slang is a special conversational vocabulary of a particular group of people. To others its meaning may not be clear: a word may have different meanings or no meaning at all for different groups of people. The slang adjective *straight,* for instance, may mean "honest," "heterosexual," "inclined to wear a vest and tie," or "not on drugs," among other things. Moreover, since slang is generally short-lived, it can quickly become dated when committed to paper. Slang should therefore be avoided in formal writing.

 ### Using colloquial language only when appropriate

Another kind of conversational vocabulary is **colloquial language.** It is informal and entirely appropriate in everyday speech. We might say that we have *figured out* how to do something or that we *gave someone a hard time.* Colloquial words are generally clearly understood. In writing they give the im-

d
31a

pression of conversation. When writers want to convey a conversational tone, they will deliberately use colloquial words and expressions. Generally, however, such words are avoided in academic and professional writing because of their informality. Dictionaries label them *colloquial* or *informal*.

 ### Revising obsolete or archaic words and neologisms

You should also avoid words the dictionary labels *obsolete* or *archaic* because they are no longer part of the current American vocabulary. (An example is *dispensatory,* meaning "dispensary.") *Neologisms* are invented words that are not yet (and may never be) part of the common vocabulary; they are inappropriate unless you are sure your readers will understand them and appreciate them. (An example is *prioritize.*)

 ### Using technical words with care

In every academic or technical field, practitioners use certain terms to convey special, highly specific meanings. Sometimes, these words are newly invented or adapted from words in the general vocabulary. Botanists speak of an *etiolated* leaf, sociologists of the *ethos* of a culture, baseball players of a *fly* ball, psychologists of *reinforcing* a behavior, literary critics of an *intentional fallacy.* Such terms are useful for expressing common ideas precisely and economically. However, in writing for a general audience you should avoid such terms if possible because not all readers will understand them. When you must use specialized terms, explain them when you introduce them.

 ### Revising indirect or pretentious writing

A **euphemism** is an indirect, inoffensive substitute for a word that is potentially offensive or blunt. Examples are *human remains pouches* as a substitute for *body bags,* and *passed away* for *died.* Since euphemisms may be vague or misleading, use them only when direct, truthful words would needlessly offend members of your audience. Don't use them to hide your real meaning, such as calling a nuclear warhead a *reentry vehicle.*

Pretentious writing contains more words or longer words than are needed. For example, *She obtruded her presence into my realm of awareness* can be restated simply and unpretentiously as *I noticed her.*

 ### Revising sexist and other biased language

Avoiding biased language is a matter of reader awareness. Whenever you use terms that show prejudice toward groups of people, especially racial, ethnic, religious, age, and sexual groups, you reveal prejudice and may alienate

d
31a

your audience. Therefore, in the interests of fairness and clear communication, avoid such derogatory words as *nigger, honky, Polack, kike, geezer, fag,* and *broad.*

See Exercises 31-1, 31-2.

 ## Eliminating sexist language

- Avoid demeaning and patronizing language.

SEXIST	Ladies are entering almost every occupation.
REVISED	*Women* are entering almost every occupation.

SEXIST	I'll have my girl type the letter today.
REVISED	I'll ask my *assistant* to type the letter today.

- Avoid occupational or social stereotypes.

SEXIST	The considerate doctor commends his nurse when she does a good job.
REVISED	Considerate *doctors* commend *their nurses* on jobs well done.

SEXIST	The grocery shopper should save her coupons.
REVISED	*Grocery shoppers* should save *their* coupons.

- Avoid referring needlessly to gender.

SEXIST	Marie Curie, a woman chemist, discovered radium.
REVISED	Marie Curie, *a chemist,* discovered radium.

SEXIST	The patients were tended by a male nurse.
REVISED	The patients were tended by *a nurse.*

- Avoid using *man* or words containing *man* to refer to all human beings.

SEXIST	Man has not reached the limits of social justice.
REVISED	*Humankind* (or *Humanity*) has not reached the limits of social justice.

SEXIST	The furniture consists entirely of manmade materials.
REVISED	The furniture consists entirely of *synthetic* materials.

- Avoid using *he* to refer to both genders. (See also 8b-3.)

SEXIST	The person who studies history knows his roots.
REVISED	The person who studies history knows his or her roots.
REVISED	*People* who study history know *their* roots.

d
31a

Choosing the exact word

Because two words in English rarely mean exactly the same thing, a writer's choice of words affects the reader's understanding of the communication.

1 Using the right word for your meaning

A precise expression of meaning depends on the writer's awareness of the denotation and connotation of words. A word's **denotation** is its dictionary meaning. Confusion about denotation can cause a writer to make such mistakes as writing *depreciate* (to lower or underestimate the value of something) in place of *deprecate* (to show mild disapproval). A reader's problem with understanding what a writer means may result from a misspelling, as when someone writes *desert* when he means *dessert*. Always check a dictionary when you are uncertain about the meaning or spelling of the words you are using.

A word's **connotation** is what the word implies, the emotional associations it calls up in the reader. Reactions to words vary from one individual to another, depending on one's experiences; for example, the person who has had a family member die of cancer will have a different emotional reaction when hearing the word *cancer* from that of someone who has not been touched by the disease personally. However, people have many emotional associations in common. We react more positively to the words *love* and *home* and *mother* than to *affection* and *house* and *female parent*. Most of us react more favorably to being described as *trim* or *slender* than to being called *skinny*. We would rather call our new shirt *inexpensive* than *cheap*. Be sure that the connotations of the words you choose contribute to rather than clash with the impression you want to create.

There are ways you can help yourself choose the right word. When you are unsure of the nuances of a word you want to use, examine its synonyms and definitions in your dictionary. For example, if you looked up the verb *spy* in your dictionary, you might find that it involves furtive or hostile secret observation, whereas a synonym, *investigate*, suggests a systematic inquiry. Another way you can develop a sense for the right word is to read actively, observing how other writers use their words and how the words they use fit within the context of their writing.

2 Balancing the abstract and concrete, the general and specific

Words are your medium for getting your ideas and images transferred from your head into the mind of your reader. If you describe a dog as small, your reader can imagine any kind of dog and can picture it as being any size

d
31b

495

relative to his or her experience with dogs. By using a general term (*dog*) and an abstract one (*small*), you have probably failed to create in the mind of your reader the same image you have.

Abstract words name qualities or ideas: *small, beauty, anger, reality*. **Concrete words** name things you can touch or otherwise know by your senses: *typewriter, flower, cake, sweet*.

General words name classes or groups of things: *dog, tree, building, rain*. **Specific words** name particular members or varieties of a class: *dachshund, oak, Curtin Hall, drizzle*. In trying to make your writing more specific, you need to be aware that general and specific words are relative to the situation. *Dog*, for example, is more specific than *animal*, but *young brown and black dachshund with a tail that never stops moving* is more specific than *dachshund; pin oak* is more specific than *oak*.

Compare the following vague sentences made up of abstract and general words with the more exact revisions, which use words that are more concrete and specific.

VAGUE	Mites are small creatures that annoy people and animals.
EXACT	Mites are microscopic, spiderlike creatures that can burrow into the skin of people and animals, sucking the blood and causing itching.
VAGUE	A physician of ancient Rome made important contributions to medicine.
EXACT	The Greek physician Galen, who practiced medicine in Rome in the second century AD, formulated the first medical theories based on scientific experimentation.

In writing, abstract and general words often introduce and sum up concepts: *Apartheid is a policy of racial segregation*. Specific and concrete words then present the supporting details: what the policy is and how it works, what races are segregated, what the segregation consists of, and so forth.

 Using idioms

Idioms are expressions in our everyday language that often cannot be analyzed grammatically and whose meaning cannot necessarily be determined from the usual meanings of the words that make them up (for example, *out of his mind*, or *to make believe*). They make learning the language difficult for nonnative speakers; even people who have grown up with English have trouble with some idiomatic expressions. For this reason most dictionaries include many idiomatic usages. For example, look at the listings in your dictionary under the word *get*.

Many idioms include prepositions whose correct use is not always logical. For instance, we say that we *search for* something or are *in search of* it. But we do not say *in search for;* this expression is unidiomatic. A list of some common idioms with appropriate prepositions follows. If you are unsure of which preposition to use with an idiom, check your dictionary by looking up the preposition or the word that precedes it.

496

4 Using figurative language

Figures of speech add richness to writing by comparing the action or thing being described with some other action or thing, using vivid, specific qualities. A **simile** makes the comparison explicitly, using *like* or *as: She's like a rainbow. He's built like a panda.* A **metaphor** implies the comparison, omitting *like* or *as: Life is a carnival. When my soul was in the lost and found, you came along to claim it.* When using a metaphor, be sure to stick with it. A **mixed metaphor** combines incongruous figurative language, destroying the image the writer is trying to create.

MIXED   The Chinese and American ships of state march to different drummers.

REVISED   The Chinese and American ships of state are sailing in different directions.

 ## Idioms with prepositions

abide *by* a rule
abide *in* a place or state

accords *with*
according *to*

accuse *of* a crime

accustomed *to*

adapt *from* a source
adapt *to* a situation

afraid of

agree *with* a person
agree *to* a proposal
agree *on* a plan

angry *with*

aware *of*

based *on*

capable *of*

certain *of*

charge *for* a purchase
charge *with* a crime

concur *with* a person
concur *in* an opinion

contend *with* a person
contend *for* a principle

dependent *on*

differ *with* a person
differ *from* in some quality

differ *about* or *over* a question

disappointed *by* or *in* a person
disappointed in or *with* a thing

families *with*

identical *with* or *to*

impatient *at* her conduct
impatient *of* restraint
impatient *for* a raise
impatient *with* a person

independent *of*

inferior *to*

involved *in* a task
involved *with* a person

infer *from*

oblivious *of* something forgotten
oblivious *of* or *to* one's surroundings

occupied *by* a person
occupied *in* study
occupied *with* a thing

opposed *to*

part *from* a person
part *with* a possession

prior *to*

proud *of*

related *to*

rewarded *by* the judge

rewarded *for* something done	wait *at* a place
rewarded *with* a gift	wait *for* a train, a person
similar *to*	wait *on* a customer
superior *to*	

Personification treats an idea or object as if it were human: *Despair seized her in its merciless grip.* **Hyperbole** is an exaggeration for the sake of emphasis: *She was paralyzed by his stare.*

▲5 Using fresh expressions

Avoid *clichés*—trite expressions that have been used so often they have lost their freshness and impact.

TRITE   I had to *work like a dog.*

REVISED   I had to *work with all the concentration of a demolition expert.*

TRITE   In speaking up for his friends, Jorge *went the extra mile.*

REVISED   In speaking up for his friends, Jorge *did more than people would normally expect.*

See Exercises 31-3, 31-4, 31-5, 31-6.

Related Exercises 5-7, 5-8.

31c Writing concisely

Make sure that all your words contribute meaning to your sentences, and avoid those which simply fill up space or repeat what you have already said. Be careful, however, not to confuse conciseness with brevity. For concise writing you need to cut out all unnecessary words; but excessive brevity eliminates specific details and words that otherwise help explain what you mean.

● Principal ways of achieving conciseness

- Cut or shorten empty words and phrases (31c-1).

WORDY   The highly pressured nature of critical-care nursing is due to the patients' life-threatening illnesses.

REVISED   Critical-care nursing is *highly pressured because* the patients have life-threatening illnesses.

498

- Cut unnecessary repetition (31c-2).

> **WORDY**   Critical-care nurses must have steady nerves to care for patients who are critically ill.
>
> **REVISED**   Critical-care nurses must have steady nerves to *help very sick* patients.

- Simplify word groups and sentences (31c-3).

> **WORDY**   The nurses must have possession of interpersonal skills and combine them with medical skills.
>
> **REVISED**   The nurses must *possess* interpersonal *and medical* skills.

- Avoid jargon (31c-4).

> **WORDY**   It is considered by most health professionals that the critical-care nurse is an essential component in the improvement of the patient from the status of critical care to that of intermediate care or even that of home care.
>
> **REVISED**   Most health professionals *consider* the critical-care nurse *essential to the patient's improvement* from *critical to intermediate or even home care.*

 Cutting or shortening empty words and phrases

Avoid adding length to your writing without adding substance. Here are some filler phrases that take several words to say what one word can usually say just as well.

FOR	SUBSTITUTE
at all times	always
at the present time	now
at this point in time	now
in the nature of	like
for the purpose of	for
in order to	to
until such time as	until
for the reason that	because
due to the fact that	because
because of the fact that	because
by virtue of the fact that	because
in the event that	if
by means of	by
in the final analysis	finally

Padding can usually be cut without any loss in meaning.

> **PADDED**   Gray is of the opinion that at this point in time it is no longer acceptable to the American people that their government should lend its support to an agency specializing in activities that are by their very nature covert.

d
31c

499

REVISED   Gray believes that Americans no longer want their government to support an agency specializing in covert activities.

Many *qualifying phrases* can be shortened or deleted without affecting meaning. Use words such as the following only when qualifying is necessary.

in a manner of speaking   all things considered
as far as I'm concerned   more or less
for all intents and purposes   in my opinion
for the most part

Avoid *all-purpose* words such as those that follow. Substitute a more meaningful word, or delete the word altogether.

angle   character   kind   thing
area   element   manner   type
aspect   factor   nature
case   field   situation

 Cutting unnecessary repetition

Another form of padding is saying the same thing in two different ways. While writers use repetition effectively to emphasize main points and link important ideas (see 17b and 18b), thoughtless repetition can weaken writing.

WEAK   my theory that I have come up with

REVISED   my theory

WEAK   the program's purposes and goals

REVISED   the program's purposes

WEAK   at the corner where Main Street meets High Avenue

REVISED   at the corner of Main Street and High Avenue

 Simplifying word groups and sentences

Use the grammatical construction that states your meaning in the simplest and most direct way. Don't use a clause if a phrase will do; don't use a phrase if a word will do. Whenever you can, use direct, active verbs. Avoid passive verbs (see 18d) and noun constructions substituting for verbs. Also be wary of indirect sentence beginnings such as *there is* and *it is* (see 18e).

WORDY   The largest member of the deer family, *commonly known as the moose*, sometimes weighs as much as 1800 pounds.

REVISED   The largest member of the deer family, *the moose*, sometimes weighs as much as 1800 pounds. [Phrase reduced to two words.]

WORDY   Moose prefer to spend their summers in forest land *that contains willow swamps and lakes*.

REVISED   Moose prefer spending their summers in forest land *containing willow swamps and lakes*. [Clause reduced to phrase.]

WORDY	In the winter, protection from cold winds is found by the moose when they gather together in the woods and swamps.
REVISED	In the winter, moose find protection from cold winds by gathering together in the woods and swamps. [Passive voice revised to active. The subject now is the performer of the action.]
WORDY	There are moose living in northern regions throughout the world.
REVISED	Moose live in northern regions throughout the world. [*There are* construction eliminated to make the sentence begin with its subject.]

 Rewriting jargon

Jargon is the special vocabulary of a professional, academic, or technical group. (See 31a-6.) But the term also refers to any language used by writers trying to sound professional, academic, or technical by stating simple ideas in complicated ways.

JARGON	To be interdependent means to recognize that wholeness in human relationships depends on a giving and receiving dynamic.
REVISED	To be interdependent means that we help one another.

See Exercise 31-7.

Related Exercises 18-1, 18-2.

EXERCISE 31-1

Appropriate Words: Revising Text (31a)

Draw a line through each inappropriate expression and write a better term above it. Consult a dictionary as needed.

1.   When a person passes on to the next life, the mortal remains undergo specific changes. Hypoxia and the degradation of cells set in when there is no longer any synthesis of adenosine triphosphate (ATP). Once the death knell has actually sounded and there has been cessation of all cerebral function, the temperature of the carcase begins to drop. The amount is about one degree to one and a half degrees per hour—dependent on other factors, such as the temperature of the environment and the size of the corse. A manifest change is the one called *rigor mortis*. As all mystery fans know, this is the stiffening of the body that begins one or two hours after the goner passes on. The first to stiffen are the eyelids, then the rest of the face. For the next twelve hours, the rigor progresses downward until the entire body is affected. The stiffness begins to disappear and adipocere begins to form after about thirty-six hours.

2.   Political candidates have discovered that ladies make up over half of the eligible voting population. The trouble is that the little woman is cerebrating so much about her own irons in the fire that she is not totally sentient on what the issues are—or what these jokers think they are. Women

exer
31

with young children get more worked up about getting their kids off to school with both shoes on than they do about theirselves and which candidate promises them the most or looks the coolest on the tube. So the agonists rack their brains to figure out just how to get possession of the votes of this constituency.

EXERCISE 31-2

Biased Language: Revising Sentences (31a-8)

Revise the following sentences to eliminate biased language.

> *Example:*   Charlotte Battle was Norman Oates's girl Friday for seventeen years.
>
> *Charlotte Battle was Norman Oates's assistant for seventeen years.*

1. Pastor Olsen and his wife Barbara will be honored guests at the luncheon.

2. Each student should have his books by the first day of class.

3. The mailman was half an hour late today.

4. Under normal circumstances, wolves do not attack man.

5. Each employee should fill out his time card before the end of the day.

6. That old codger driving down the road looks as if he can hardly see over the steering wheel.

7. If you have any trouble with the washing machine, just call your serviceman.

8. I was stopped at a traffic light when a chick driving a Trans-Am rammed the rear of my car.

9. A nurse is always expected to put duty before her personal interests.

10. Has everybody put his name at the top of his paper?

exer
31

11. Every policeman in this city is equipped with a bulletproof vest.

12. Fisherman should check the wind forecast before going out in a boat.

13. The divers went deeper than man has ever gone before.

14. Every typist should type as fast as she can without making errors.

15. The old geezer is probably a member of AARP and writes his Congressman every week.

16. "Madam chairman," he said, "I'd like five minutes for answering the question."

17. We took the broken toy to the lady at the service desk.

18. My uncle wanted to know if I had met any cute coeds yet on campus.

19. A doctor has to hire someone to keep up on his paperwork for Medicare.

20. Anyone who wants to reserve a room has to use his credit card.

21. The Holy Rollers in the building down the street were practicing speaking in tongues.

22. The old fogy was helping his old lady up the steps so they could go in and vote.

23. It seemed as if every pharmacist at the convention was signing his name on the suppliers' lists.

24. A writer must always consider her readers.

25. Sylvia wondered if the tiger in the cage was a man-eater in its natural state.

EXERCISE 31-3

Denotation: Comparing Forms

Circle the word in parentheses whose established denotation fits the meaning of the sentence. Consult a dictionary as needed.

Example: The presiding judge listened intently but remained (*disinterested,* *uninterested*) in the libel case.

1. The president-elect was ready to (*accept, except*) the offer of support.

2. She was strongly (*affected, effected*) by the offer.

3. "It is not (*everyday, every day*) that your opposition comes to your side," she said.

4. "I take it as a (*complement, compliment*) to my integrity as a candidate," she concluded.

5. The building manager (*implied, inferred*) that we had broken the washing machine.

6. In making his accusation, he made (*allusions, illusions*) to other occurrences that had nothing to do with us.

7. Because it was untrue, his accusation (*aggravated, irritated*) us.

8. We are also upset by the (*amount, number*) of times he has been rude to us.

9. "I hope to be back (*sometime, some time*) soon," said our foreign exchange student as we took her to the airport.

10. "Who knows?" I said. "I (*maybe, may be*) in Spain one day myself."

11. "The time here has gone so much faster (*than, then*) I expected," she said.

12. "I'm (*all ready, already*) planning my next trip."

13. "And if I'm not careful, I'm (*liable, likely*) to be homesick for your home."

14. Jason was (*anxious, eager*) to start his new job at the car wash.

15. He was really (*conscience, conscious*) of the need to start off well.

16. He was hoping to work (*fewer, less*) hours than he did on his last job.

17. His (*idea, ideal*) in changing jobs was to have more time for study.

18. But he (*preceded, proceeded*) to work more hours so that he could spend more money on his car.

exer
31

EXERCISE 31-4

General and Specific Words, Abstract and Concrete Words: Revising Text (31b-2)

The paragraphs below contain words that are general or abstract. Revise each italicized word, writing in the space above it a word that is more specific or concrete.

1.   My *morning* class in *history* did not meet today because *the professor*

had to attend *a meeting*. So I spent the *time* in the cafeteria, eating a *bagel*,

drinking *coffee*, and studying for *my exam*.

2.   The candidate for *office said* to *the people* that he would support *family*

values, freedom, and *anticrime legislation*. He would bring *integrity* to the

position and would carry out its duties with *honor*.

3.   My favorite place in all the world is my family's cabin on *the lake*. Last

summer *my friend* and I spent *a few* days there, and they were *wonderful*.

We got up *late* in the morning, went for a walk in *the woods,* and then after

having *lunch* we'd stretch out on *a big rock* and snooze for a while before

taking a dip in the *water*. Afternoons we'd *go out* in *the boat*. Maybe we'd

fish and maybe just row around the shoreline. One day we caught a *big*

fish, so we *cooked* it for supper. Boy, did it taste *good*.

EXERCISE 31-5

Idioms: Comparing Forms (31b-3)

Drawing on the list on page 497 or consulting a dictionary as needed, circle the appropriate preposition in parentheses to complete the idioms in the following sentences.

Example: After much debate, we finally agreed (*with,* (*on*)) a new policy.

1. I was impatient (*for, with*) the class to end.

2. Differing (*from, with*) each other only over money, the couple nonetheless decided to divorce.

3. Though we were angry (*at, with*) each other, we continued to study together.

4. The dangers (*in, for*) someone learning to ski are slight.

5. The officer locked the suspect up and charged him (*for, with*) robbery.

6. College is different (*from, than*) high school in unexpected ways.

7. When the jury acquitted O'Reilly (*for, of*) murder, the townspeople were delighted.

8. During his visit the Pope stayed (*in, at*) Denver only briefly, but he electrified the city.

9. Although rewarded (*by, with*) increasingly flavorful foods, the pigeon would not learn any new tricks.

10. I waited impatiently (*on, for*) his arrival.

11. At the age of fourteen, Lucy was independent (*of, from*) her parents.

12. My courses vary (*in, from*) difficulty, so I have no trouble setting my priorities when I study.

13. Some researchers are impatient (*at, with*) the arguments of the theorists.

14. I was preoccupied (*with, by*) my work.

15. The shop charged me (*with, for*) a purchase that I had forgotten.

EXERCISE 31-6

Trite Expressions: Revising Sentences (31b-5)

Revise these sentences to eliminate trite expressions.

> *Example:* She was meek as a lamb, though she was a superb public speaker.
>
> *She was exceedingly shy, though she was a superb public speaker.*

1. He writes well, but he is no Shakespeare.

2. It just stands to reason that we need to balance our budget.

3. A budding genius, my little brother won a mathematics award and two science awards.

4. We could wait till hell freezes over to see a solution to hostilities in the Middle East.

5. The job of moving my grandfather to a nursing home was easier said than done.

6. I did not know for sure, but I had a sneaking suspicion that my friends were planning a surprise party.

7. Your message has come through loud and clear.

8. The sight of my old rival scared me out of my wits.

9. We may have to bite the bullet before we see an end to the budget crisis.

10. I nearly died when I saw the utility bill.

EXERCISE 31-7

Empty Words and Phrases: Revising Text (31c)

Revise the following paragraphs to eliminate empty words and phrases.

1   People who live in the "Frost Belt," otherwise known as the northern states, are, at this point in time, still moving toward the sun. According to the 1990 census, cities situated in the northern part of the United States decreased in size while cities located in the South increased. New York City, for example, decreased and diminished by 38,460 residents, Detroit decreased by 233,213, and Chicago decreased by 279,093. As a matter of fact, only two of the big and major cities in the Northeast and Midwest did not lose residents: Columbus, Ohio, and Indianapolis, Indiana. In contrast, every big city that is located in the areas of the South and the Southwest—with two exceptions—gained residents. The two exceptions that were noted are Memphis and New Orleans.

2   According to the new figures, New York City is still, at the present time, the largest city in the nation, but Los Angeles, a city situated in the area of the South, takes the place of Chicago, which is a city located in the northern area, as the second largest, and Houston, another southern city, replaces Philadelphia, a northern city, as fourth largest. Detroit moved down from sixth place to ninth, and San Antonio achieved the top ten.

exer
31

511

3   The point is that cities affected by changes and alterations in population will experience serious and dire consequences due to the fact that the census counted fewer people. The first and foremost consequence that exists is a decrease in federal funding, for the reason that it is based on population. Another is decreased political clout, due to the fact that representation, like funding, is based on numbers of residents.

4   It seems that some cities appealed the census count. They charged that many residents—thousands or even millions—were not counted. New York City, for example, charged that a million of its people were not counted, a loss of $1.5 billion for the city for a period extending throughout the 1990s. City officials said that among those not counted were minorities, homeless people, and illegal immigrants. For all intents and purposes, these are all people that cities provide services for but will not receive federal funding for under the new count.

5   But even with a more accurate count, and all things considered, the census still revealed a steady population trend toward the region of the South.

Using Dictionaries

Chapter 32

 32a Choosing a dictionary

◢ 1 Abridged dictionaries

Abridged dictionaries, while not exhaustive, contain most commonly used words and brief descriptions of their meaning and usage. The following abridged dictionaries (listed alphabetically) are recommended.

> *The American Heritage College Dictionary.* 3rd edition. 1993.
> *Merriam-Webster's Collegiate Dictionary.* 10th edition. (Available on diskette and CD-ROM as well as in print.)
> *The Random House Webster's College Dictionary.*
> *Webster's New World Dictionary.* 3rd college edition.

Dictionaries of greater help for ESL:

> Longman Dictionary of Contemporary English. (Available on diskette and CD-ROM as well as in print.)
> Oxford Advanced Learner's Dictionary.

2 Unabridged dictionaries

The most scholarly and comprehensive dictionaries, unabridged dictionaries emphasize the history of words and the range of their uses. When you need detailed information about a word or want to find an obscure word, consult one of the following.

> *The Oxford English Dictionary.* 2nd edition, 20 vols. (Available on CD-ROM as well as in print.)
> *The Random House Dictionary of the English Language.* 2nd ed. (Available on CD-ROM as well as in print.)
> *Webster's Third New International Dictionary of the English Language.*

Special dictionaries

Special dictionaries limit attention to a particular type of word, problem, or field. Especially helpful for writing are dictionaries of usage, which discuss common problematic words and constructions, and dictionaries of synonyms, which list together words that are similar in meaning. The following are recommended.

> Follett, Wilson. *Modern American Usage.* Ed. Jacques Barzun.
> Fowler, H. W. *A Dictionary of Modern English Usage.* 2nd edition. Revised and edited by Sir Ernest Gowers.
> *Roget's International Thesaurus.* 5th edition. Revised by Robert L. Chapman.
> Partridge, Eric. *Origins: A Short Etymological Dictionary of Modern English.* 4th edition.
> *Webster's New Dictionary of Synonyms.*
> Wentworth, Harold, and Stuart Berg Flexner. *Dictionary of American Slang.* 2nd supplemented edition.

If spelling is a problem for you and you are not writing with a word-processing program that has a spelling checker, you might find it helpful to have a speller's dictionary or one of the word lists prepared for typists. Because these books list only words, with their syllable breaks, some people can locate particular words in them more easily than in dictionaries.

 Working with a dictionary's contents

Finding general information

A dictionary can tell you how to spell and pronounce a word, give you the forms of irregular nouns and verbs, tell you the meaning of an unfamiliar word, and introduce you to new words. Besides containing an alphabetical list of words with their meanings, many dictionaries include synonyms, word origins, biographical and geographical listings, material on the history and grammar of English, and other useful supplements. In addition, most dictionaries indicate whether the words are slang, colloquial, regional, or otherwise restricted in their use.

Answering specific questions

A dictionary's function is to provide information about words. The main entry first shows spelling and word division—where to break the word if you have to divide it at the end of a line (see Chapter 30). Next comes the pronunciation, usually including all major variations. (Most dictionaries explain their pronunciation symbols in their opening pages and at the foot of every page or every other page.) The word is then identified by part of speech and its principal parts. Its **etymology**—its origin—may follow; in some dictionaries, etymology is given last. Meanings are given next, grouped by part of speech if the word can function as more than one. Sometimes major differences in meaning and usage are listed under separate entries. Various definitions may be labeled as obsolete, slang, foreign, and the like (see Chapter 31). Often a word's main **synonyms** (words with similar meaning) and **antonyms** (words with opposite meaning) are also given.

See Exercise 32-1.

32b

Name _____ Date _____

EXERCISE 32-1

Using the Dictionary

Use a college-level desk dictionary to answer the following questions.

Name of dictionary _____

Date of publication _____

A. Abbreviations and Symbols
Write out the meaning of the following abbreviations or symbols.

Example: *n. pl.* or *pl. n.* _____*plural noun*_____

a. *syn.* _____   d. *mil.* _____

b. *dial.* _____   e. *obs.* _____

c. *lit.* _____   f. *intr. v.* _____

B. Spelling
On the following lines, reproduce the way your dictionary lists the words given.

Example: dessertspoon _____*des·sert·spoon*_____

a. speakeasy _____   e. hayloft _____

b. backwater _____   f. freeze-dry _____

c. living room _____   g. Italy _____

d. catlike _____   h. self-government _____

C. Pronunciation

Copy out exactly the pronunciation given by your dictionary for the following words. If the dictionary gives more than one pronunciation for a word, provide both. Consulting the pronunciation key, sound out the word until you can pronounce it accurately and smoothly.

Example: beguile ____ bĭ·gīl' ____

a. pastoral _____

b. err _____

c. invalid _____

d. schism _____

e. often _____

f. Caribbean _____

g. kiln _____

h. irrelevant _____

D. Grammatical Functions and Forms

1. List and label the past-tense and past-participle forms of the following verbs exactly as provided in your dictionary.

Example: have ___ has (past tense and past participle) ___

a. prefer _____

b. work _____

c. break _____

d. echo _____

e. wring _____

f. see _____

2. List and label the comparative and superlative forms of the following adjectives and adverbs exactly as given in your dictionary.

Example: small ___ smaller (comparative), smallest (superlative) ___

beautiful ___ (no forms given) ___

inner _____

lovely _____

cross (*adj.*) _____

ill _____

median _____

E. Etymology

1. Trace the origins of the words listed below as they are given in your dictionary. List (1) the initial language and word from which our word is derived; (2) the meaning of the initial word (sometimes not listed separately if it is the same as the given word); and (3) the other languages through which the word has passed on its way to us. Use the full names of languages, not abbreviations (consult the key to the dictionary's abbreviations if necessary). The guide to the dictionary will tell you how to read the etymology of a word if you need help.

   Example: logic   (1) _____ *Greek logos* _____

                       (2) _____ *speech, reason* _____

                       (3) *Late Latin, Old French, Middle English*

   a. induce   (1) _____

                (2) _____

                (3) _____

   b. lieutenant   (1) _____

                (2) _____

                (3) _____

   c. shirt   (1) _____

                (2) _____

                (3) _____

exer
32

d. rhythm (1) _____

(2) _____

(3) _____

2. Provide the origins of the following words as they are given in your dictionary.

Example:

ohm ___*After Georg Simon Ohm (1787–1854), German*___

___*physicist*___

a. zipper _____

b. jargon _____

c. astronaut _____

d. jerk _____

e. quisling _____

F. Meanings

List two different meanings for each of the following words as they appear in your dictionary.

a. specie (*n.*) (1) _____

(2) _____

b. gall (*n.*) (1) _____

(2) _____

c. hound (*v.*) (1) _____

(2) _____

d. go (*v.*) (1) _____

(2) _____

G. Labels

Provide the label applied by your dictionary to each of the following words or meanings of words.

Example: ain't   <u>nonstandard (not appropriate for standard</u>

<u>written English)</u>

a. critter (noun meaning "animal") _____

_____

b. enthuse (verb meaning "to show enthusiasm") _____

_____

c. knock (verb meaning "to criticize") _____

_____

H. Other Information

1. Where does your dictionary provide biographical information on important persons: in the main alphabetical listing or in a separate section (give the page numbers if a separate section)?

_____

2. Where does your dictionary provide geographical information on countries, cities, rivers, mountains, and so on: in the main alphabetical listing or in a separate section (give the page numbers if a separate section)?

_____

3. Does your dictionary contain a history of the English language?

_____

4. Does your dictionary contain a guide to punctuation and mechanics?

_____

5. Does your dictionary contain a list of colleges and universities?

_____

exer
32

Chapter 33

Improving Your Vocabulary

Students are often frustrated at the size of their vocabulary when they are trying to express an idea. The thought is clear in their own heads, but when they try to write it on paper they cannot think of the right words. They correctly surmise that they need to increase the stock of words they can draw on. But they incorrectly think that this can be accomplished by doing some sort of relatively painless exercise. The truth is that vocabulary improvement takes time—a lifetime, in fact. You can improve your vocabulary not only by increasing the store of words you can draw on but by using your words more precisely as well.

This chapter offers no guaranteed vocabulary improvement. It does, however, show you ways to look at words and understand how they are used. It presents the background of English words and suggests ways for you to add new words to those you already know.

33a Understanding the sources of English

English is part of the Indo-European language family, whose origins go back perhaps seven thousand years. The earliest known language in England was Celtic. But the English we speak is descended from the language of Germanic tribes that conquered the Celts in the fifth and sixth centuries, leaving us with such common words as *heaven, earth, our, three,* and *day.* The vocabulary of Old English, as this early form of English is called, was later enriched by Danish invaders in the ninth and tenth centuries and by the French-speaking Normans who conquered England in 1066 and reigned for nearly

523

two hundred years. The resulting Middle English included large numbers of words derived from French, such as *catch*, *cattle*, and *cavalry*. In the fifteenth and sixteenth centuries, the Renaissance and the introduction of the printing press caused further changes in our language and vocabulary, introducing many Latin and Greek words and leading to Modern English. English continues to change today as we drop old words, coin new ones, and adopt others from languages throughout the world.

33b Learning the composition of words

Breaking a word into its component parts is often a good way to see where it came from and to work out what it means.

1 Learning roots

At least half the words in English have Latin or Greek roots. Here are some examples.

ROOT (SOURCE)	MEANING	ENGLISH WORDS
bene (L)	good, well	benefit, benevolent
bio (G)	life	biology, autobiography
demos (G)	people	democracy, epidemic
dic, dict (L)	to speak	dictate, dictionary
geo (G)	earth	geography, geology
graph (G)	to write	geography, photography
mater (L)	mother	maternal, matron
manu (L)	hand	manual, manuscript
pater (L)	father	paternal, patron
ped (G)	child	pediatrics
phys (G)	body, nature	physical, physics
scrib, script (L)	to write	scribble, manuscript
tele (G)	far off	telephone, television
verb (L)	word	verbal, verbose

2 Learning prefixes

A **prefix** is one or more syllables that can be added to the front of a word or root to change its meaning. Many standard prefixes come from Latin or Greek. A list of common prefixes follows.

PREFIX	MEANING	EXAMPLE
a-, an	without, not, away from	*atheist*
ad-	toward, next to	*adjacent*
ante-	before	*antecedent*

PREFIX	MEANING	EXAMPLE
anti-	against, opposite	*antisocial*
arch-	chief	*archduke*
auto-	self	*automobile*
col-, com-, con-	with	*concur*
demi-	half	*demitasse*
dis-	not	*dissatisfied*
ex-	from, out of	*exhaust*
extra-	beyond	*extrasensory*
hyper-	excessive	*hypertension*
il-, im-, in-, ir-	not	*immobile*
inter-	between, among	*international*
intra-	within	*intramural*
mal-	wrong, bad	*malcontent*
pan-	all	*pan-American*
poly-	many	*polygon*
post-	after	*postwar*
pre-	before	*premeditate*
pro-	before, forward, in favor of	*propose*
semi-	half	*semisweet*
sub-	under	*submarine*
super-	above	*supervisor*
sym-, syn-	together	*sympathy*
trans-	across	*transport*
un-	not	*unhealthy*

 Learning suffixes

A **suffix** is one or more syllables that can be added to the end of a word or root to change its meaning or function. Common noun suffixes include the following:

-*ity* (*community*)   -*er* or -*or* (*computer*)
-*ence* or -*ance* (*continuance*)   -*ship* (*hardship*)
-*sion* or -*tion* (*abortion*)   -*ist* (*meteorologist*)
-*hood* (*parenthood*)   -*ism* (*racism*)

Common verb suffixes include the following:

-*en* (*thicken*)   -*ify* (*qualify*)
-*ize* (*realize*)   -*ate* (*saturate*)

Common adjective suffixes include the following:

-*ful* (*plentiful*)   -*ish* (*reddish*)
-*less* (*painless*)   -*able* or -*ible* (*feasible*)
-*al* or -*ial* (*mechanical*)   -*ic* (*paramedic*)
-*ous* (*porous*)   -*ly* (*lovely*)
-*ant* or -*ent* (*different*)

33b

33c Learning to use new words

Examining a word's components and its context helps you understand its meaning. You can increase your vocabulary by increasing your sensitivity in hearing and reading words and in speaking and writing them.

 Examining context

To increase your vocabulary, first sharpen your perception. *Listen* to people whose vocabulary you admire to see how they use words. And *read.* How much do you read beyond what is assigned? When you read, pay attention to how writers use words. Try to grasp the meaning of new words within their context. Look up words that are not clear to you in context. Increasing your perception of words you hear and read improves your knowledge and understanding of them. Then, as you speak and write, make a conscious effort to use words you have added to your listening and reading vocabulary.

 Using the dictionary

The dictionary can give you the precise meaning of a word whose general sense you have guessed from its context. The dictionary may also help you fix the word in your memory by showing its spelling, pronunciation, grammatical functions and forms, etymology, and synonyms and antonyms. Check the meanings in your dictionary if you need to make sure you're using words correctly. By increasing your sensitivity to words, especially through frequent reading and writing, you'll see your vocabulary improve.

See Exercises 33-1, 33-2.

Related Exercises 32-1, 34-2.

EXERCISE 33-1

Roots, Prefixes, and Suffixes: Inferred Meanings

By referring to the lists of roots, prefixes, and suffixes given on pages 524–525, identify each word below as a noun (*n.*), verb (*v.*), or adjective (*adj.*) and guess at the meaning. If you are unable to guess, look the word up in your dictionary.

Example: antebellum _____ *before a war (adj.)*

1. belligerent _____

2. anterior _____

3. prorate _____

4. retroactive _____

5. advocate _____

6. Francophile _____

7. interdict _____

8. polymer _____

9. subvert _____

10. transceiver _____

11. kilocycle _____

12. intersperse _____

13. demagogue _____

14. amoral _____

15. transcend _____

exer
33

EXERCISE 33-2

Contextual Clues: Inferred Meanings

Use contextual clues to guess at the meanings of the italicized words in the passages below. Write out the meanings. Then check your definitions in your dictionary.

1. Because of the rapidly aging population, the *demographic imperative* is

   bringing about the prevention of long-term diseases.

   demographic _____

   imperative _____

2. The *disaffection* toward the present administration is a result of its *draconian* cuts in the budget.

   disaffection _____

   draconian _____

3. The investigative agency is requesting broad *latitude* to use *sophisticated*

   software in its *surveillance* projects.

   latitude _____

   sophisticated _____

   surveillance _____

4. Many people are *skeptical* about the *putative* benefits of vitamins in large

   doses.

   skeptical _____

   putative _____

exer
33

528

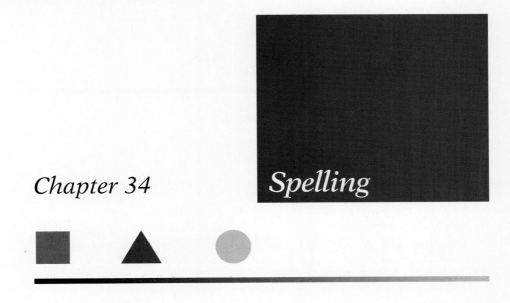

Chapter 34

Spelling

This chapter covers spelling problems and explains a few fairly dependable rules. Using these guidelines will make the spelling checker on your word-processing program more useful and reliable.

34a Recognizing typical spelling problems

Most spelling difficulties relate to differences between how a word sounds and how it is spelled. The same spelling may be pronounced more than one way, and the same pronunciation may have different spellings.

1 Being wary of pronunciation

George Bernard Shaw is said to have observed that the word *fish* could be spelled *ghoti: gh* as in *tough, o* as in *women*, and *ti* as in *action*. Shaw's point was that the pronunciations of English words can often lead us to misspell them. When in doubt about how to spell a word, look it up in your dictionary; and if you don't find it, try to think of other ways the word's sound might be spelled.

Frequent sources of confusion are *homonyms*, words that are pronounced the same but spelled differently, and near homonyms, which are pronounced

529

similarly but not identically. You cannot depend on your spelling checker to flag these words for you, because they are spelled correctly, even though they are not words you intended. Here are some examples:

 Words commonly confused

accept (to receive)
except (other than)

affect (to have an influence on)
effect (result)

all ready (prepared)
already (by this time)

allude (to refer to indirectly)
elude (to avoid)

allusion (indirect reference)
illusion (erroneous belief or perception)

ascent (a movement up)
assent (agreement)

bare (unclothed)
bear (to carry, or an animal)

board (a plane of wood)
bored (uninterested)

born (brought into life)
borne (carried)

brake (stop)
break (smash)

buy (purchase)
by (next to)

capital (the seat of a government)
capitol (the building where a legislature meets)

cite (to quote an authority)
sight (the ability to see)
site (a place)

desert (to abandon)
dessert (after-dinner course)

discreet (reserved, respectful)
discrete (individual or distinct)

elicit (to bring out)
illicit (illegal)

fair (average, or lovely)
fare (a fee for transportation)

forth (forward)
fourth (after *third*)

gorrilla (a large primate)
guerrilla (a kind of soldier)

hear (to perceive by ear)
here (in this place)

heard (past tense of *hear*)
herd (a group of animals)

hole (an opening)
whole (complete)

its (possessive of *it*)
it's (contraction of *it is*)

lead (heavy metal)
led (past tense of *lead*)

lessen (to make less)
lesson (something learned)

meat (flesh)
meet (encounter)

no (the opposite of *yes*)
know (to be certain)

passed (past tense of *pass*)
past (after, or a time gone by)

patience (forbearance)
patients (persons under medical care)

peace (the absence of war)
piece (a portion of something)

plain (clear)
plane (a carpenter's tool, or an airborne vehicle)

530

presence (the state of being at hand)

presents (gifts)

principal (most important, or the head of a school)

principle (a basic truth or law)

rain (precipitation)

reign (to rule)

rein (a strap for controlling an animal)

raise (to build up)

raze (to tear down)

right (correct)

rite (a religious ceremony)

write (to make letters)

road (a surface for driving)

rode (past tense of *ride*)

scene (where an action occurs)

seen (past participle of *see*)

straight (unbending)

strait (a water passageway)

stationary (unmoving)

stationery (writing paper)

their (possessive of *they*)

there (opposite of *here*)

they're (contraction of *they are*)

to (toward)

too (also)

two (following *one*)

waist (the middle of the body)

waste (discarded material)

weak (not strong)

week (Sunday through Saturday)

which (one of a group)

witch (a sorcerer)

who's (contraction of *who is*)

whose (possessive of *who*)

your (possessive of *you*)

you're (contraction of *you are*)

 Distinguishing between different forms of the same word

Often the root of a word changes slightly in spelling when the word's form and function change.

VERB	NOUN	ADJECTIVE	NOUN
advise	advice	brief	brevity
choose	choice	curious	curiosity
devise	device	deep	depth
envelop	envelope	long	length
proceed	procedure	wide	width
succeed	success	wise	wisdom

Many verbs form their principal parts irregularly: *choose, chose, chosen; drive, drove, driven; throw, threw, thrown; swim, swam, swum.* Some nouns also change their root spelling from singular to plural: *foot, feet; leaf, leaves; mouse, mice.*

 Using preferred spellings

Some words can be spelled more than one way. Often variants of the preferred spelling are British: *our* instead of *or* (*colour, color*); *ae* instead of *e*

sp
34a

(*anaemic, anemic*); *ise* instead of *ize* (*realise, realize*); *ll* instead of *l* (*travelled, traveled*). In your writing, use the form that the dictionary designates as preferred, usually the first form listed.

 34b Following spelling rules

Even though spelling rules always have exceptions, they're worth the trouble to learn because by practicing them you can avoid misspelling those words to which the rules apply.

 Distinguishing between *ie* and *ei*

The rule for *ie* and *ei* is "*i* before *e* except after *c* or when pronounced 'ay' as in *neighbor* and *weigh*": thus, *believe* (*i* before *e*) but *receive* (except after *c*). There are some exceptions: common ones are *caffeine, either, foreign, forfeit, height, leisure, neither, seize, seizure,* and *weird*.

 Keeping or dropping a final *e*

When adding an ending such as *-ing* or *-ly* to a word that ends in a silent *e,* drop the *e* if the ending begins with a vowel (*change + ing = changing; write + ing = writing*), but keep the *e* if the ending begins with a consonant (*brave + ly = bravely*). There are a few exceptions to this rule. Words that could be confusing if the *e* were dropped keep the *e* (*dye + ing* does not become *dying*). Words ending in a soft *c* or *g* keep the *e* when an ending is added that begins with *a, o,* or *u* (*notice + able = noticeable*). Sometimes when the *e* is preceded by another vowel, the *e* is dropped before an ending that begins with a consonant (*true + ly = truly*).

 Keeping or dropping a final *y*

When a final *y* is preceded by a consonant, the *y* changes to *i* when an ending is added (*baby + s = babies*), except if the ending is *-ing* (*babying*). When a final *y* is preceded by a vowel, or when it ends a proper name, the *y* stays as is (*say = s = says, play + ed = played, Kelly + s = Kellys*). Notable exceptions are *said* and *paid*.

Doubling consonants

Consonants at the ends of words are sometimes doubled when suffixes are added. Whether to double them depends on the sound of the vowels in the word: a doubled consonant gives a short sound to the vowel that precedes it: the vowel in *hopping* is short, the one in *hoping* long. When adding a suffix, double a final consonant if all of the following factors are present:

1. The word is one syllable or has stress on the final syllable.
2. The final consonant is preceded by a single vowel.
3. The suffix begins with a vowel.

In the following words, the final consonant is doubled.

admit, admitted	prefer, preferred
begin, beginning	ship, shipped
flat, flattened	sit, sitting
occur, occurred	stop, stopping

In the following words, the consonant is *not* doubled because the word does not have one of the factors listed above.

benefit, benefited (stress is not on final syllable)
differ, different (stress is not on final syllable)
equip, equipment (suffix does not begin with a vowel)
repair, repaired (final consonant is not preceded by a single vowel)

 Attaching prefixes

The addition of a prefix does not change the spelling of the word it is attached to: *un + necessary = unnecessary; un + able = unable; mis + spell = misspell; mis + adventure = misadventure.*

 Forming plurals

For most nouns, form the plural by adding *-s* to the singular form (*horse + s = horses; pea + s = peas*). For some nouns ending in *f* or *fe,* change the ending to *ve* before adding *-s* (*life + s = lives*). For singular nouns ending in *s, sh, ch,* or *x,* add *-es* (*mess + es = messes; bash + es = bashes; itch + es = itches; box + es = boxes*). For nouns ending in *o* preceded by a vowel, add *-s* (*scenario + s = scenarios*); but if the *o* is preceded by a consonant, add *-es* (*potato + es = potatoes*). A few nouns that were originally Italian, Greek, Latin, or French form the plural as in their original language (*solo* becomes *solos,* not *soloes; datum* becomes *data,* not *datums*).

533

Compound nouns form plurals in two ways. When two or more main words (usually nouns, verbs, or adjectives) form the compound, only the last word is plural (*streetwalker* = *streetwalkers; superman* = *supermen; strongbox* = *strongboxes*). When the parts of the compound are not equal—especially when a noun is followed by one or more other parts of speech—only the noun is plural (*sister-in-law* = *sisters-in-law*).

See Exercise 34-1.

Related Exercise 23-1.

34c Developing spelling skills

If you have a spelling checker, use it, because it not only will help you get the words right on a given paper but may also improve your spelling overall. But watch out for homonyms, words like those in the box on pages 530–531 and the wrong forms of words (such as *it's* for *it is*) because to your spelling checker they are right.

 Editing and proofreading carefully

Near the end of the writing process, all writers need to give high priority to checking for misspelled words. Once you have finished revising your draft and before making the final draft, check your spelling. You may have to try some kind of trick to make your eyes slow down and look at every word—reading aloud, for example, or reading backward word by word from the end to the beginning. If you're writing on a computer, use your cursor to stop at each word. With your final draft, you—like every other writer—must proofread for misspelled and mistyped words. If you find only one or two errors on a page, in most cases you can draw a line through the error and write the correction neatly in the space above it. If the errors are extensive, recopy the page and proofread again. If you're writing on a word processor, proofread a paper copy before printing your final draft.

 Using a dictionary

Go to your dictionary to check any words you are unsure of. To look up a word you can't spell, guess how to spell it. You'll probably come close, and the word is likely to be somewhere on the page. But check the meaning too to make sure you have the right word. If you're using a spelling checker, it will give you some choices of words, but you may need to refer to a dictionary before making the right choice.

 ## Pronouncing carefully

Many common misspellings come from inaccurate pronunciation. Be careful with words like *library, February, recognize, nuclear, mischievous, homogeneous,* and *athlete;* don't add or omit letters when either pronouncing or spelling them. For words that are particularly troublesome, you might try correcting the faulty syllable by stressing it; write on a piece of paper or note card: *FebRUary, reCOGnize, govERNment, envIRONment.*

 ## Tracking and analyzing your errors

Make your own "List of Commonly Misspelled Words." On an index card (handy for carrying with you) or in your notebook, make a list of all the words that you've overlooked in your editing and proofreading and that your teacher or someone else has marked. In parallel columns, show the correct spellings and your misspellings. Then study your list frequently. At first the list may seem to grow discouragingly long, but in time you will find it shrinking as you cross off words you've learned to spell.

 ## Using mnemonics

Mnemonics are tricks for memorizing. Some are standard: *stalactites* grow down from the *ceiling,* but *stalagmites* grow up from the *ground; stationery* has an *er* like *letter* and *paper.* But you can also make up your own.

 ## Studying spelling lists

Here is a list of some of the most commonly misspelled words in the English language. You probably know how to spell most of them. To find out which ones you *don't* know how to spell, have someone read the entire list to you while you write the words. Checking your words with the list will tell you which ones you need to work on. On a card or piece of paper write each word you don't know; on the reverse side write a sentence using the word. Then study the words a few at a time, testing yourself occasionally. You might also tape-record your own list and then play it back occasionally as you spell out the words.

sp
34c

absence
abundance
acceptable
accessible
accidentally
accommodate
accomplish
accumulate
accuracy
accustomed
achieve
acknowledge
acquire
across
actually
address
admission
adolescent
advice
advising
against
aggravate
aggressive
allegiance
all right
all together
almost
already
although
altogether
amateur
among
amount
analysis
analyze
angel
annual
answer
apology
apparent
appearance
appetite
appreciate
appropriate
approximately
argument
arrest
ascend
assassinate
assimilation

assistance
associate
atheist
athlete
attendance
audience
average

bargain
basically
because
beginning
belief
believe
beneficial
benefited
boundary
breath
breathe
Britain
bureaucracy
business

calculator
calendar
caricature
carrying
cede
ceiling
cells
cemetery
certain
changeable
changing
characteristic
chief
chocolate
choose
chose
climbed
coarse
column
coming
commercial
commitment
committed
committee
competent
competition
complement

compliment
conceive
concentrate
concert
condemn
conquer
conscience
conscious
consistency
consistent
continuous
controlled
controversial
convenience
convenient
coolly
course
courteous
criticism
criticize
crowd
cruelty
curiosity
curious
curriculum

deceive
deception
decide
decision
deductible
definitely
degree
dependent
descend
descendant
describe
description
desirable
despair
desperate
destroy
determine
develop
device
devise
dictionary
difference
dining
disagree

disappear
disappoint
disapprove
disastrous
discipline
discriminate
discussion
disease
dissatisfied
distinction
divide
divine
division
doctor
drawer

easily
ecstasy
efficiency
efficient
eighth
either
eligible
embarrass
emphasize
empty
enemy
English
entirely
entrepreneur
environment
equipped
especially
essential
every
exaggerate
exceed
excellent
exercise
exhaust
exhilarate
existence
expense
experience
experiment
explanation
extremely

familiar
fascinate

favorite
February
fiery
finally
forcibly
foreign
foresee
forty
forward
friend
frightening
fulfill
further

gauge
generally
government
grammar
grief
guarantee
guard
guidance

happily
harass
height
heroes
hideous
humorous
hungry
hurriedly
hurrying
hypocrisy
hypocrite

ideally
illogical
imaginary
imagine
imitation
immediately
immigrant
incidentally
incredible
independence
independent
individually
inevitably
influential
initiate

innocuous
inoculate
insistent
integrate
intelligence
interest
interference
interpret
irrelevant
irresistible
irritable
island

jealousy
judgment

kindergarten
knowledge

laboratory
leisure
length
library
license
lieutenant
lightning
likelihood
literally
livelihood
loneliness
loose
lose
luxury
lying

magazine
maintenance
manageable
marriage
mathematics
meant
medicine
miniature
minor
minutes
mirror
mischievous
missile
misspelled
morale

morals
mortgage
mournful
muscle
mysterious

naturally
necessary
neighbor
neither
nickel
niece
ninety
ninth
noticeable
nuclear
nuisance
numerous

obstacle
occasion
occasionally
occur
occurrence
official
omission
omit
omitted
opinion
opponent
opportunity
opposite
ordinary
originally

paid
panicky
paralleled
parliament
particularly
peaceable
peculiar
pedal
perceive
perception
performance
permanent
permissible
persistence
personnel

perspiration
persuade
persuasion
petal
physical
physiology
physique
pitiful
planning
playwright
pleasant
poison
politician
pollute
possession
possibly
practically
practice
prairie
precede
preference
preferred
prejudice
preparation
prevalent
primitive
privilege
probably
procedure
proceed
process
professor
prominent
pronunciation
psychology
purpose
pursue
pursuit

quandary
quantity
quarter
questionnaire
quiet
quizzes

realistically
realize
really
rebel

sp
34c

rebelled	scarcity	succeed	twelfth
recede	schedule	successful	tyranny
receipt	science	sufficient	
receive	secretary	summary	unanimous
recognize	seize	superintendent	unconscious
recommend	separate	supersede	undoubtedly
reference	sergeant	suppress	unnecessary
referred	several	surely	until
relief	sheriff	surprise	usable
relieve	shining	suspicious	usually
religious	shoulder		
remembrance	siege	teammate	vacuum
reminisce	significance	technical	vegetable
renown	similar	technique	vengeance
repetition	sincerely	temperature	vicious
representative	sophomore	tendency	villain
resemblance	source	than	visible
resistance	speak	then	
restaurant	speech	thorough	weather
rhythm	sponsor	though	Wednesday
ridiculous	stopping	throughout	weird
roommate	strategy	Thursday	wherever
	strength	together	whether
sacrifice	strenuous	tomorrow	wholly
sacrilegious	stretch	tragedy	woman
safety	strict	transferred	women
satellite	studying	truly	writing

34d Using the hyphen to form compound words

1 Forming compound adjectives

When two or more words function as a single adjective before a noun, hyphenate the words: *well-heeled benefactor,* a *decision-making problem.* When the same word group stands alone or follows the noun, hyphens are usually not needed: *We need a benefactor who is well heeled. Decision making is her main problem.*

2 Writing fractions and compound numbers

Fractions and compound numbers from twenty-one to ninety-nine are always hyphenated: *one-half; thirty-six.*

Forming coined compounds

Hyphenate a group of words you are linking to serve as a temporary (coined) adjective if they precede the word they modify: *The dog let out her there's-a-squirrel-in-that-tree bark.*

 Attaching some prefixes and suffixes

Most prefixes do not take a hyphen: *prewar, semiannual.* When a prefix consists of or precedes a capital letter, however, use a hyphen: *anti-British.* Prefixes that are complete words by themselves usually take hyphens: *self-indulgent, all-around.* Also hyphenate *ex-* meaning "former": *ex-president.*

Suffixes usually do not take hyphens, except *-elect: senator-elect.*

 Eliminating confusion

Use a hyphen after any prefix or in any compound when the resulting word might be misread without the hyphen (*re-echo, anti-intellectual*) or confused with another word (*re-create, un-ionized*). Also hyphenate adjective groups that could be misread: *new-gas prices* (meaning the prices for newly discovered gas).

See Exercise 34-2.

Related Exercises 29-1, 33-1.

EXERCISE 34-1

Commonly Confused Words (34a)

Circle the appropriate words in parentheses, referring to a dictionary as necessary.

1. The (*affect, effect*) of alcohol on (*ones, one's*) driving ability is often underestimated.

2. The boat (*passed, past*) us so fast that we rocked violently in (*its, it's*) wake.

3. When I open my own business, the first thing I'm going to do is order my own (*personal, personnel*) (*stationary, stationery*).

4. (*Its, It's*) often difficult to determine (*who's, whose*) to blame in fender-bender accidents.

5. Most people have a (*pore, poor*) understanding of the ecological (*roll, role*) of water snakes.

6. Scientists have (*lead, led*) a study of water snakes in Louisiana.

7. When scientists (*cite, site*) their findings, they must designate the (*cite, site*) of (*their, there, they're*) research.

8. The discoveries of scientists can (*affect, effect*) the way you view (*your, you're*) world.

9. For example, Hans Selye, a Canadian endocrinologist, showed how stress (*affects, effects*) the body.

10. His findings have (*lead, led*) to methods of (*baring, bearing*) the stress.

exer
34

541

11. Another scientist (*who's, whose*) discoveries may influence (*your, you're*) life is Ulf Von Euler.

12. In the 1950s, Von Euler discovered the hormones (*which, witch*) (*lead, led*) to birth control pills.

13. Von Euler also discovered the (*principal, principle*) neurotransmitter that controls the heartbeat.

14. Queen Victoria's (*rain, reign, rein*) in Great Britain lasted from 1837 (*to, too, two*) 1901.

15. Her royal (*decent, descent*) was from the ruling dynasty of Hanover, (*which, witch*) claimed five British kings.

EXERCISE 34-2

Spelling Rules: Practice (34b)

A. Insert *ie* or *ei* in the following blanks.

1. ach_____ve   6. h_____ght   11. forf_____t

2. w_____ght   7. rec_____ve   12. conc_____t

3. fr_____nd   8. n_____ther   13. s_____ze

4. ch_____f   9. bel_____ve   14. dec_____t

5. sl_____gh   10. hyg_____ne

B. Keep or drop the final *e* or *y* as necessary when adding endings to the following words. Consult your dictionary as necessary.

    Example: supply + -er _____ *supplier* _____

1. notice + -ing _____

   notice + -able _____

2. hate + -ing _____

   hate + -ful _____

3. sure + -ly _____

   sure + -est _____

4. agree + -ing _____

   agree + -able _____

5. duty + -ful _____

   duty + -s _____

6. true + -est _____

   true + -ly _____

exer
34

7. defy + -ing _____

   defy + -ance _____

8. study + -ing _____

   study + -ed _____

C. Write the correct forms for these words.

   Example: hop + ing <u>hopping</u>

   1. differ + ence _____
   2. travel + ed _____
   3. submit + ed _____
   4. refer + ed _____
   5. occur + ence _____
   6. permit + ed _____
   7. begin + ing _____
   8. stop + ing _____
   9. prefer + ence _____
   10. prefer + ing _____
   11. ship + ment _____
   12. beg + ing _____

D. Write the plurals of the following words and compounds, checking your dictionary as needed.

   Example: chief ___*chiefs*___

   1. buffalo _____
   2. tomato _____
   3. mother-in-law _____
   4. sheep _____
   5. shelf _____
   6. fox _____
   7. series _____
   8. index _____
   9. handful _____
   10. passerby _____
   11. analysis _____
   12. economy _____

EXERCISE 34-3

The Hyphen in Compound Words, Fractions, and Compound Numbers: Practice (34d)

A. Write out the following numbers, using hyphens when appropriate.

Example: 4500 *forty-five hundred*

1. 10¼ _____

2. ²¹⁄₂₂ _____

3. 39 _____

4. 102 _____

5. 3,000,152 _____

6. 92 _____

7. 25 _____

8. 25,095 _____

9. ³⁄₁₀ _____

10. 260 _____

B. As appropriate for correct spelling, leave each of the following groups of words as they are, insert a hyphen, or close up the space. Check your dictionary as needed.

Example: anti Soviet _____ *anti-Soviet* _____

1. ante bellum _____

2. pro American _____

3. self serving _____

© 1998 Addison-Wesley Educational Publishers Inc.

exer
34

4. car port _____

5. porch light _____

6. news stand _____

7. hot dog _____

8. non partisan _____

9. ninth century warfare _____

10. co author _____

11. post Victorian _____

12. red eyed rabbit _____

13. re shuffle _____

14. long handled _____

15. red handed _____

16. soft hearted _____

17. pre fabricated _____

18. life boat _____

19. life like _____

20. anti imperialist _____

Chapter 35

Writing a Short Documented Paper

Some writing assignments require you to refer to sources of information outside your own knowledge and to cite those sources appropriately and accurately. A major project of this kind is commonly called a research or term paper, often requiring you to summarize, report, interpret, analyze, synthesize, and evaluate facts, opinions, and problems (as described in the Introduction) and to document all your sources of information. Whenever you have such an assignment, you will find Chapters 35 to 37 in the handbook helpful in leading you through the project.

Some documented papers are shorter and simpler; though they are not full-blown research projects, they do cite information outside the writer's own knowledge and experience. Like the larger project, they require adherence to accepted conventions regarding the use of borrowed material. **Paraphrase, summary,** and **direct quotation** are handled in the same way as in the larger project, and all sources of information are cited accurately and completely. These papers may take the form of response to an assigned article, summary of a magazine or journal article, or a brief topical paper that is supported with evidence from books or articles. Often the instructor assigns the sources—such as a given article for summary—so the student doesn't need to work with indexes, catalogs, and other searches in order to collect information.

This chapter covers the special skills needed for a short documented paper. It deals mainly with summary, paraphrase, and direct quotation—what they are, how to use them, how to avoid misusing them, and how to document them. For skills and processes characteristic of all writing—such as **drafting, revising,** and **editing**—refer to earlier chapters. In particular, see the

547

Introduction for guidance on the critical thinking required of a project of this kind.

35a Using summary, paraphrase, and direct quotation

Whenever you write a paper that uses sources of information outside your own knowledge, you are very likely to use summary, paraphrase, and direct quotation. Each has its own characteristics and uses, and each requires documentation (see 35d).

1 Summary

Summaries condense and encapsulate another piece of writing. They tell in briefer form the main ideas of the original. A **summary** may be complete in itself, as is often true in academic writing, when an instructor wants evidence that you understand an assigned reading. This type of summary is discussed in I2-d. More often, summaries are part of a larger piece of writing, used as information or as support for an opinion. Both types are common in short documented papers.

As discussed in the Introduction, summaries are *objective, complete,* and *concise.* In telling your readers what someone else has said, be careful to read and interpret that idea in the context of the original, not according to what you want it to say. Being objective is not easy, because whatever you read is somewhat influenced by your own experience. Try to be true to the original. Being complete in your summary will help. Don't omit essential parts of the context, such as time, place, occasion, and purpose. While examples and descriptive details are usually omitted in summaries, your reader must be able to understand the context of the ideas you are borrowing. At the same time, you must be concise. Concentrate on the main ideas, those appropriate to your context, and omit everything peripheral. Use your own words and phrases, not those of the original, and never lift even partial sentences without enclosing them in quotation marks (see 35a-3). Omit all unnecessary words (see 31c).

For an example of a short summary, see p. 5.

2 Paraphrase

A **paraphrase** is an idea restated in someone else's words. It is not necessarily shorter than the original; more than likely it is as long as, or longer than, the original. Like summary, paraphrase does not distort the original nor rely too closely on the words of the original. To write an accurate paraphrase, you need to understand not only the idea you are paraphrasing but the surrounding ideas as well. Notice how the following paraphrase restates the original in new words yet remains true in meaning.

ORIGINAL

"A Gallup survey of New York shows that approximately ⅔ of the 1000 children born to persons on relief every month enter this world without the benefit of marriage between their parents."—Jonathan Kozol, *Death at an Early Age* (New York: Bantam, 1967), 224

PARAPHRASE

In 1967 Jonathan Kozol reported results of a Gallup poll showing that, of the 1000 babies born each month to welfare mothers in New York, at least 650 were to single parents (224).

This paraphrase is approximately the same length as the original. It uses the second writer's words, not Kozol's, although it keeps proper names and other words crucial to the meaning of the original. Note also that the historical context of the original is mentioned so that readers of the paraphrase will understand that the figures are not current at the time of the second writing.

If you are using *electronic sources* of information, be careful about reliability, especially on the Internet. Because anyone can post information for your retrieval, you must evaluate everything carefully:

- How does it compare to information you've found in print sources?
- What do you know about the author?
- Can you learn anything more about the author?
- Does the author reveal unexplained biases?
- Does the author cite sources you've encountered elsewhere?
- Have authors elsewhere cited this author?

Note, for example, the Peter Rule citation under "A World Wide Web Document" in "Documenting sources" (35d). Neither the article nor the Web address gives an indication that Rule is a student, not a professor, at "wsu," though finding his home page (using his http address without the last element) helps a reader evaluate the article. These questioning and searching methods can help you decide whether an electronic source provides reliable information.

 3 Direct quotation

When borrowing from other writers, use **direct quotation** sparingly, relying more often on summary and paraphrase. Reserve direct quotations for sentences in which the words cannot be changed without altering the meaning or the effect you want to produce. Examples are highly technical phrases, expert opinions, and ideas that are aptly phrased. The original writer may have written in a characteristic style or expressed controversial opinions or language that you don't want to appear as your own. Use direct quotation when

35a

the words of the original must be exact. But avoid long quotations. When you must refer to a long passage, summarize most of it and quote only those portions that must remain in the words of their originator.

Direct quotation must always be accurately transcribed and enclosed in quotation marks (see Chapter 24). When writing summaries and paraphrases, be particularly careful that you do not unintentionally use the writer's exact words. If you want to include an apt phrase or two in your summary or paraphrase, transcribe them exactly and enclose them in quotation marks. The following example shows a paraphrase, plus quotation, of another sentence from *Death at an Early Age:*

ORIGINAL

"And how are our schools to supply a needed father-image in teaching such half-homed and half-backed children?" (Kozol 224)

PARAPHRASE PLUS QUOTATION

Kozol wonders how schools can provide male role models for children of single mothers—children who, he says, are "half-homed and half-backed" (224).

When you quote directly, you may at times want to omit some of the original words, especially if they do not suit your context or the syntax of your sentence. Always indicate omitted material with the *ellipsis* mark—three spaced periods with spaces before and after (see 25e). Here are two examples:

ORIGINAL

"True education doesn't quiet things down; it stirs them up. It awakens consciousness. It destroys myths. It empowers people, as Dennison so well put it, to think and do for themselves."—John Holt, *Freedom and Beyond* (New York: Dell, 1972), 235

QUOTATIONS WITH ELLIPSES

"True education doesn't quiet things down; it stirs them up. It awakens consciousness. It destroys myths. It empowers people . . . to think and do for themselves" (Holt 235).

"True education doesn't quiet things down; it stirs them up. . . . It destroys myths. It empowers people, as Dennison so well put it, to think and do for themselves" (Holt 235).

Notice how the ellipsis mark is used in the second quotation. Because the omitted material follows a complete sentence, that sentence is ended with a period before the ellipsis is marked.

When it's necessary to use quoted material that runs more than four lines, set it off in block form, like the example in 35e, and omit quotation marks (see 24c).

35b Avoiding plagiarism

All borrowed material must be cited. Whether you use summary, paraphrase, or direct quotation, you must tell your readers where you found it.

This is a cardinal principle of scholarship. It is more than just a courtesy to the originator. When you write your ideas into words, you own those words, and someone who borrows them owes you the credit. When *you* cite borrowed sources, you as borrower gain some advantages. First, by observing the conventions of scholarship, you show yourself to be a member of a community of scholars—an advantage for anyone wanting to excel in a chosen field. Second, you borrow not only the words or ideas of an expert but the expert's authority as well. You are no longer only yourself trying to report some research; you now have the backing of an expert. And you show that you know who the experts are. Your reader also profits from your source citation. Accurate documentation allows interested readers to go directly to the source to learn more about the subject.

Plagiarism is the use of someone else's words or ideas as if they were one's own. It is a violation of the implicit contract between writer and reader that everything written under the writer's name was written by the writer. If you fail to document every summary, paraphrase, and direct quotation, you have committed plagiarism—a serious offense in most schools and in society as a whole. Carelessness and ignorance of the conventions are no excuse. You must therefore take your notes with care and be sure to list every source you have used.

If you're using *electronic sources* for some of your research, bear in mind that in some ways it's easier for a skeptical reader to find plagiarized material on the Internet than it is in the library. Just using a common search engine to locate a string of words can bring up every page on the World Wide Web that has that same string. Use care when you summarize, paraphrase, or quote; and cite online, Internet, and other electronic sources according to the basic rules of documentation (see "Documenting sources").

Two sources of information need not be documented: (1) your own thoughts and experiences and (2) common knowledge. Both may be a problem at times in deciding where to draw the lines. Your own thoughts generally derive from your own interpretation of your experiences; however, sometimes it may be necessary to mention where those thoughts originated—say, in a class lecture. Common knowledge, too, has some gray areas. Generally, you don't need to cite standard information such as historical facts and other information that can be found in any number of sources. Common-sense observations also, such as "the price of crude oil affects the economy," need not be cited. However, opinions and facts resulting from specialized research must be cited.

35b

Checklist for avoiding plagiarism

- What type of source are you using: your own independent material, common knowledge, or someone else's independent material? You must acknowledge someone else's material.
- If you are quoting someone else's material, is the quotation exact? Have you inserted quotation marks around quotations run into the text? Have

you shown omissions with ellipses and additions with brackets? (See 35a-3 and 25d.)

- If you are paraphrasing or summarizing someone else's material, have you used your own words and sentence structures? Does your paraphrase or summary employ quotation marks when you resort to the author's exact language? Have you represented the author's meaning without distortion?
- If you are using someone else's material in your own online publication, have you obtained any needed permission?
- Is each use of someone else's material acknowledged in your text? Are all your source citations complete and accurate? (See 35d.)
- Does your list of works cited include all the sources you have drawn from in writing your paper? (See 35d.)

35c Taking notes

The notes you take for a short documented paper will differ in amount and somewhat in kind from those you would take for a term paper. But as with note taking for the longer paper, it's advisable to read the article or chapter through before you begin taking notes, getting an overview of the topic and looking for ideas and insights. Mark points you want to return to, and underline central ideas.

The form your notes take will depend on the assignment and your own preferences. For some assignments, you may decide to highlight and annotate a photocopy or printout of the article in question, then record your own thoughts, thesis, and method of organization in a notebook. Or, especially if you're using more than one source, you may want to use 3″-by-5″ cards on which you record your notes and their source. Your notes may be summary, paraphrase, direct quotation, and your own commentary on what you have read. To ensure accuracy when you later use these notes, make certain that all direct quotations are accurate and enclosed in quotation marks. Always include the source of borrowed information, including page number, and label your own ideas as your own—perhaps with brackets and your initials. At the top of the card, write a key word heading so that later you can sort your cards according to subtopic. If you decide to take your notes at a computer, follow the same guidelines as for cards: be thorough and accurate, and use key locater words so that you can arrange your notes later with a *search* or *sort* function.

Your library may carry some of the articles you are looking for online (such as Expanded Academic Index) so that you can print a copy directly from the computer where you locate the article. This is a convenience, but you will notice that page numbers may be missing or don't coincide with those on the journal copy. In that case, you will be unable to cite page numbers for information you use, so in your list of works cited you should list the article as an online source (see "Full-text article in an online catalogue" in "Documenting sources" (35d)).

If you are working with a photocopy or printout of an article you must summarize, try highlighting or underlining. First read the article through. On the second reading, mark the sentence that expresses the main idea, then all other sentences that provide major support for that idea. Don't be waylaid by facts and examples that you find especially interesting unless they are crucial to an accurate summary or your purpose for summarizing. Write annotations in the margins, such as *T* for thesis sentence, numerals for major points, and question marks for statements you dispute or don't understand. Be careful not to use the exact wording of the sentences and phrases you have highlighted (see 35a-1).

35d Documenting sources

Unless your teacher has given you your sources of information, you probably need to do some research. In most college libraries, that search for information begins with a computer—to locate the library's holdings in books and journals, to provide access to online and CD-ROM information, and to read articles reprinted online from journals. Moreover, you may be able to print paper copies of the articles you find. Your librarian can probably give you help if you're new at this kind of research.

In scholarly writing, sources of information are cited according to disciplinary conventions, and as you progress in your chosen field you may learn to use a format other than the one illustrated here. The following examples illustrate the parenthetical MLA style (as described in the *MLA Handbook for Writers of Research Papers*, 4th ed., 1995, published by the Modern Language Association). MLA style is appropriate for courses and journals in composition, literature, foreign languages, and many other disciplines.

When you use MLA parenthetical citations, you don't need footnotes or endnotes. Instead, you briefly cite your source in parentheses, then give the full bibliographic information at the end of your paper. Here are two examples of parenthetical citations:

> In *The Guns of August*, historian Barbara Tuchman refers to the British defense plan at the beginning of World War I. "The method was plain," she says. "The muddle was in the British mind" (135–36).

> The British evidently had a plan for defense at the beginning of World War I, but they seemed incapable of carrying it out (Tuchman 135–36).

These examples illustrate two methods of citation. In the first, the source is named in the sentence, so only the page numbers are enclosed in parentheses. In the second, the author's name must be included in the parenthetical citation. Observe placement of the citation, punctuation, and the absence of *pp.* or other reference to the pages.

35d

At the end of the paper, the source would be named as follows:

Work Cited

Tuchman, Barbara. The Guns of August. New York: Dell, 1962.

Notice the basic format for a *book* named in a works cited list:

1. The author's full name, last name first.
2. The full title of the book, underlined or italicized (see 27a).
3. The publication information—city of publication, publisher, and date of publication.

Each of the three items is followed by a period.

The format for an article from a *periodical* (journals, magazines, and newspapers) differs somewhat:

1. The author's full name, last name first.
2. The full title of the article, enclosed in quotation marks (see 24d).
3. The publication information—underlined title of the periodical, the volume and/or issue number, the date of publication, and the inclusive page numbers.

Here's an example.

White, Robert M. "The Great Climate Debate." Scientific
    American 263.1 (1990): 36-43.

Notice the periods separating each of the three components—author, title, and publication information. In this citation, the issue number (1) is given in addition to the volume number (263), because each issue of *Scientific American* is paged separately. In some cases, the date would be given instead of volume and issue numbers (see examples below). In the list of works cited, second and succeeding lines of each entry are indented. The entries are arranged in one list alphabetically by author's last name or, in the case of unsigned articles, by the first main word of the title.

The format for an *electronic source* has the same basics as those for conventional sources: author, title, publishing information. Follow this pattern:

Author's last name, First name. "Title of work." Title of
    Complete Work. Publication medium. Address. Date of mes-
    sage or (visit).

See examples below. The three most common citations you are likely to want to use (assuming your teacher permits online sources or encyclopedias—either electronic or print) are to an encyclopedia, to a full-text article in your library's online catalog, and to a document on the World Wide Web. Because documentation of these sources, like the research itself, is still fluid, it's possible to find many variations in form. The most important thing to provide is the information a reader would need to locate the source you used.

The following examples of entries for a works cited list can serve as guides for documenting a short paper. If you need additional examples, refer to the handbook or to the *MLA Handbook*.

A BOOK WITH ONE AUTHOR

Sykes, Charles J. Dumbing Down Our Kids. New York: St.
     Martin's, 1995.

A BOOK WITH TWO OR THREE AUTHORS

Matsen, Patricia P., Philip Rollinson, and Marion Sousa.
     Readings from Classical Rhetoric. Carbondale, IL:
     Southern Illinois UP, 1990.

A BOOK WITH MORE THAN THREE AUTHORS

Lopez, Robert S., et al. Civilizations: Western and World.
     Boston: Little, 1975.

A BOOK WITH AN EDITOR

Ruitenbeek, Hendrik, ed. Freud as We Knew Him. Detroit: Wayne
     State UP, 1973.

A LATER EDITION

Bollinger, Dwight L. Aspects of Language. 2nd ed. New York:
     Harcourt, 1975.

A REFERENCE BOOK

"Tea." Encyclopedia Americana. 1985 ed.

A SIGNED ARTICLE IN A JOURNAL WITH CONTINUOUS PAGINATION THROUGHOUT THE ANNUAL VOLUME

Lever, Janet. "Sex Differences in the Games Children Play."
     Social Problems 23 (1976): 478-87.

A SIGNED ARTICLE IN A JOURNAL THAT PAGES ISSUES SEPARATELY OR THAT NUMBERS ONLY ISSUES, NOT VOLUMES

Boyd, Sarah. "Nuclear Terror." Adaptation to Change 7.4 (1981):
     20-23.

A SIGNED ARTICLE IN A MONTHLY OR BIMONTHLY PERIODICAL

Gottlieb, Annie. "Crisis of Consciousness." Utne Reader
     Jan.-Feb. 1997: 45-48+. [The + indicates that the article
     has discontinuous paging.]

35d

A SIGNED ARTICLE IN A WEEKLY OR BIWEEKLY PERIODICAL

Calvo, Dana. "Blood and Sand." The New Republic 17 March 1997:
19–20.

A SIGNED ARTICLE IN A DAILY NEWSPAPER

Gargan, Edward A. "Buffalo Concern Gives Pop Sound to Player
Pianos." New York Times 16 Feb. 1984: B1.

AN UNSIGNED ARTICLE

"The Right to Die." Time 11 Oct. 1976: 101.

AN ELECTRONIC REFERENCE WORK

"1896: Modern Olympic Games." Compton's Interactive
Encyclopedia. CD-ROM. Compton's NewMedia, 1994.
[Reference work on disk]

"Woodwarbler." Encyclopedia Britannica. Online. 1996.
[Reference work available online through library]

ARTICLE AVAILABLE ONLINE

Platisky, Roger. "Chopin's The Awakening." The Explicator 53
(1995): 99–102. Rpt. online. Expanded Academic Index
(January 1997). [The online article was printed in The
Explicator and was read on the EAI in January 1997.]

WORLD WIDE WEB DOCUMENT

Rule, Peter. "The Awakening: Not a Healthy Book." Online.
Internet. http://www.wsu.edu:8080/~peterr/awakening (6
January 1996). [Stand-alone document]

Landow, George P. "Ages of Technology." In The Victorian Web.
Online. Internet.
http://www.stg.brown.edu/projects/hypertext/landow/victo-
rian/science/sci3.html (14 December 1996). [Document belongs to The Victorian Web site at Brown University; the
article is unsigned but the phrase "added by GPL," when
clicked, identifies the author.]

35d

556

E-MAIL

Kenton, Carol F. "AP Writing Test." E-mail. ckenton-
    @asuvm.inre.asu.edu.

35e Sample Short Documented Paper

Observe how student writer Keri Bunkers has written a short documented paper based on the principles discussed in this chapter.

Keri Bunkers

English 163

                         Human Nature and Happiness
                    In Kate Chopin's <u>The Awakening</u>, Edna's awaken-
                ing happens naturally, unfortunately after she has
                married and borne children. Her actions are a natural
summary   result of someone awakening to her own sexuality and
                power over her own life. She is intrigued and
                thrilled by finding herself desirable by men and
                beautiful as a woman. She is stimulated by a sense of
                power to make her own choices. She has a new-found
                confidence and independence, not to mention a sensu-
                ality, that does not appear instantaneously but over
                time--a transformation she finds very gratifying as a
                woman with heart and soul longing to live.
                    For a long time, Edna has suppressed thoughts,
direct   feelings, ambitions, and desires. "Even as a child
quotation   she had lived her own small life all within herself"
                and as an adult she still holds her true feelings in-
                side (Chopin 14). Luckily, through her awakening Edna
                eventually finds a way to express these feelings. She
                is "beginning to realize her position in the universe
ellipsis   . . . and to recognize her relations as an individual
                to the world within and about her" (14). Edna begins
                to understand that not only is she a married woman

35e

with children, but she is a person with talents and interests who once had dreams for herself. She realizes that she will never be able to live her life as she wanted to. This realization, although shocking even to herself, is important and she can't ignore it. In short, Edna starts to validate her feelings and thoughts, and to take charge of her own happiness and satisfaction. She starts this process by simply speaking her mind more and expressing her feelings. Not only does she express them to the world but in a way she unveils them to herself by allowing herself to voice them at last.

Roger Platizky believes that Edna is suppressing having "been either the victim of or witness to sexual violation," childhood sexual abuse. Without

positive evidence from the novel, he makes his case from what he calls her extreme mood swings and her suicide at the end. He sees her awakening as depression and says:

> Her depressive thoughts seem to subside only when Edna feels she is in control of both her body and the men in her life, whether they be her father, her husband, her sons, or Robert and Alcee. (EAI on line)

I think it's wrong to assume that her oppression is so specific and that her unhappiness is depression. Due to her place in society and her family, she doesn't speak her mind, and this isolates her.

Not only was Edna unhappy because she didn't speak her mind, she was also unhappy because she got married young and without ever being in love. She didn't know what she wanted for herself in her life. How could she? She had not yet experienced life and what it had to offer her. The reason Edna's marriage was unhappy was that she was not in love with her husband when she married him. She had given up on romantic love for herself. She had adored so many unattainable men in her early years that she gave up on the idea that she should ever find anyone for herself who was exciting and whom she could love passionately. She "closed the portals forever behind her upon the realm of romance and dreams" (19).

So she resigned herself to marry a man she didn't love but who adored her. She reasoned that "as the devoted wife of a man who worshipped her, she would take her place with a certain dignity in the world of reality" (19). She thought that she could be happy with a man she didn't love and that she could settle down for the rest of her life without ever having been in love. She was wrong.

There were so many things she hadn't discovered yet about her tastes, her desires and her goals. And most importantly she hadn't discovered her choices. It didn't occur to her that there were other choices besides marrying Leonce Pontellier, a decision she later in life regrets. She made decisions in her youth that she later, as a woman who has finally come to grips with her true desires and ambitions for herself, realizes have severely limited her subsequent choices. Yet she was coerced by her youth and Nature into marrying, having a family and thereby limiting the choices she hadn't even realized yet. Doctor Mandelet understands her meaning and points out that "youth is given up to illusions" and "it seems to be a provision of Nature; a decoy to secure mothers for the race" (120). When she was young and inexperienced, she was under the illusion that all there was for her to do was start a family, and so she did. Later in her life she regrets it.

direct
quotation

page
citation

direct
quotation

35e

Dr. Mandelet is a well-respected doctor with a "reputation for wisdom" (64). As pointed out by one critic, Michael Hollister, Mandelet is sympathetic to Edna from the beginning and "sees Edna as a victim of neither her husband nor society, but of Nature" (91). Hollister goes on to point out that Edna is seen by the naturalistic physician as "some beautiful, sleek animal waking up in the sun" (Chopin 75). This observation says that Edna's "awakening" is similar to the

paraphrase

awakening of a reposing animal in nature. It is natural for her to have these new reflections on her life because she has so long been unconscious of them. The actions of her husband and her society are not the cause of her revelations, but they are "the sun" that wakes the sleeping animal. The sun has come out and Edna is waking, as is natural for her to do. People cannot live their lives with their souls asleep. Edna is simply allowing hers to awake.

I don't blame Edna for wanting to move out of her husband's house and live on her own. She feels that was what she needed to do to make herself happy. My point is that people make mistakes in youth, as a result of lack of experience and a limited perception of their own future opportunities. People want to try to correct these mistakes and modify their present unhappy and unsatisfying situations. They do this by making subsequent choices that they feel coincide with their desires as they now see them. Once they know what they want they then try to obtain it.

That's what Edna tries to do. It is human nature to try to improve one's own situation no matter what others think or what it costs them if the benefits are worthwhile. Unfortunately, "Nature has to account of moral consequences" sometimes (120). So if society deems it morally wrong to follow one's heart

thesis

and naturally act in their own best interest, then so
be it. It is her nature to try to obtain her happiness and it is her nature that leads her to start
making her own decisions no matter what her husband
or anyone thinks.

Works Cited

book   Chopin, Kate. The Awakening. New York: Signet
                  Classics, Penguin, 1976.

article   Hollister, Michael. "Chopin's The Awakening." The
                  Explicator 53.2 (1995): 90–92.

online   Platizky, Roger. "Chopin's The Awakening." The
article   Explicator 53.2 (1995):99–102. Rpt. online.
                  Expanded Academic Index (January 1997).

See Exercises 35-1, 35-2, 35-3.

Related Exercises I-1, I-2, I-3, I-4, 4-5, 24-1, 24-2, 27-1.

35e

Name _____ Date _____

EXERCISE 35-1

Writing Paraphrases

Write paraphrases of the following passages. Remember that paraphrases are often as long as the original. They do not use the phrasing of the original.

> *Example:* "The web of life in the oceans, perhaps more than any other part of the environment, is vulnerable to damage from increased ultraviolet radiation."—Jonathan Schell, *The Fate of the Earth* (New York: Knopf, 1982), 86.

> *In The Fate of the Earth, Jonathan Schell tells us that ocean life is particularly susceptible to harm from ultraviolet radiation (86).*

1. "Galileo had believed Copernican theory (that the planets orbited the sun) since early on, but it was only when he found the evidence needed to support the idea that he started to publicly support it."—Stephen W. Hawking, *A Brief History of Time: From the Big Bang to Black Holes* (New York: Bantam, 1988), 179.

2. "In April of 1919, in Paris, the President of the United States suffered, according to all evidence available after the fact, a thrombosis in his brain. His illness was diagnosed as influenza by his doctor—a logical diagnosis at a time when influenza outbreaks were sweeping the world."—Gene Smith, *When the Cheering Stopped: The Last Years of Woodrow Wilson* (New York: Time, 1964), 101.

exer
35

3. "It is certainly foolish to learn nothing from experience, but we can learn too much from it. Indeed, one way of defining a bureaucracy might be that it is an organization that has learned so much from the past that it can't learn anything from the present."—John Holt, *Freedom and Beyond* (New York: Dell, 1972), 45.

4. "Knowledge of human nature is the beginning and end of political education, but several years of arduous study in the neighborhood of Westminster led Henry Adams to think that knowledge of English human nature had little or no value outside of England. In Paris, such a habit stood in one's way; in America it roused all the instincts of native jealousy."—Henry Adams, *The Education of Henry Adams: An Autobiography,* Vol. I (New York: Time, 1964), 198.

5. "The law is constantly expanding and changing: it does not initiate social change, but does respond—slowly—to demands and pressures from the people it is supposed to serve. It follows the public consciousness into various levels of awareness about society and its institutions. It legitimizes or 'guarantees' specific rights only after those rights have been won on another battlefield."—Jean Strouse, *Up Against the Law: The Legal Rights of People Under Twenty-One* (New York: Signet, 1970), 20.

EXERCISE 35-2

Understanding Plagiarism

Examine the following paired passages to see if the paraphrase plagiarizes the original. Underline plagiarized words and rewrite the passages to eliminate the plagiarism. If there is no plagiarism, write OK in the space below the paraphrases.

Example: "The opportunity given to the Romans by their language was made the more compelling and inviting by the nature of Roman education. For all its faults, the pronouncedly linguistic and literary bent of the system seemed specially calculated to produce orators and writers."—Michael Grant, *The World of Rome* (New York: New American Library, 1960), 235.

Michael Grant claims that the Roman language and education seemed specially calculated for producing orators and writers (235).

Michael Grant claims that a special effect of the Roman language and education was the production of orators and writers (235).

1. "For centuries of ever-growing exaltation—the centuries when the Roman empire was at its zenith—the passionate Mystery religions supplied these wants, and also provided the cohesion, the community spirit, which was not available in so encouraging a form from any other source."—Michael Grant, *The World of Rome* (New York: New American Library, 1960), 185.

When the Roman empire was at its zenith, the passionate Mystery religions provided community spirit (Grant 185).

2. "Unlike the teaching of the Epicureans, the Stoic injunction *live consistently with nature* was meant ethically. Conscience and duty were the keynotes of Stoic ethics, and the prime duty of the soul was to realize its

exer
35

moral perfectability."—Michael Grant, *The World of Rome* (New York: New American Library, 1960), 218.

Stoics were concerned mainly with ethics and moral perfectability.

3. "On August 21 General de Castelnau heard that his son had been killed in the battle. To his staff who tried to express their sympathy, he said after a moment's silence, in a phrase that was to become something of a slogan for France, 'We will continue, gentlemen.'"—Barbara Tuchman, *The Guns of August* (New York, Dell: 1962), 264.

The World War I slogan "We will continue, gentlemen," has been attributed to General de Castelnau, expressed to his staff on the death of his son (Tuchman 264).

4. "There is no record what Asquith replied or what, in his almost mind, a region difficult to penetrate under the best of circumstances, he thought on this crucial question."—Barbara Tuchman, *The Guns of August* (New York, Dell: 1962), 72.

We don't know what Asquith's almost mind thought about this question (72).

5. "The records of paleontology provide evidence of the changing shapes of continents and the changing flow of the ocean currents, for these earlier earth patterns account for the otherwise mysterious present distribution of many plants and animals."—Rachel Carson, *The Edge of the Sea* (New York: New American Library, 1955), 30.

The mysterious distribution of animals and plants is accounted for by changing continent shapes and changing flow of ocean currents.

EXERCISE 35-3

Writing Bibliographic Entries

Write entries for an MLA list of works cited using the sets of bibliographic information below. (There may be more information than you need for some entries.) Then number your entries in the appropriate order for a works cited list.

Example: Michael Grant, New York, *The World of Rome*, New American Library, 1960.

Grant, Michael. The World of Rome. New York: New American Library, 1960.

1. Language, Gender, and Professional Writing: Theoretical Approaches and Guidelines for Nonsexist Usage, The Modern Language Society of America, New York, Francine Wattman Frank and Paula A. Treichler, 1989.

2. "Pluto," Scientific American, June 1990, pages 50–58, volume 262, number 6, Richard Binzel.

3. Janet Marinelli, "Packaging," May/June 1990, Garbage, pages 28–33.

4. Local Knowledge: Further Essays in Interpretive Anthropology, Clifford Geertz, Basic Books, New York, 1983.

exer
35

5. Calyx Books, Corvallis, Oregon, <u>The Forbidden Stitch: An Asian American Women's Anthology</u>, edited by Shirley Geok-lin, Mayumi Tsutakawa, and Margarita Donnelly, 1989.

6. Online. http://fledge.watson.org/rivendell/chopin%26gilman.html, "19th Century Women's Literature," <u>Rivendell's American Literature Page</u>, Leigh Denault, January 14, 1997.

7. Patricia Sharpe, Frances Mascia-Lees, and Colleen B. Cohen, <u>College English</u>, "White Women and Black Men: Differential Responses to Reading Black Women's Texts," volume 52, February 1990, pages 142–53.

8. "Conservation Update," B. L. Taylor, (4 February 1996), <u>Burlington Times</u>, Rpt. Online, Expanded Academic Index, B3, 2 February 1996.

9. Michael D. Lemonick, <u>Time</u>, "Those Computers Are Dummies," 1990, June 25, page 74.

10. "Stingy Is Best When Using Skin Medicine," Frank Bures, <u>St. Cloud (Minn.) Times</u>, page 4, section C, Sunday, August 12, 1990.

11. Steven H. Fritts, 1993, CD-ROM, "Wolves," <u>New Grolier Multimedia Encyclopedia</u>.

12. "Hypertext Today," 3 March 1997, Internet, <u>MUD History</u>, Online, http://www.nnt.cos.edu/mud-history.html, Carl Tenson.

ACKNOWLEDGMENTS

Allen, Frederick Lewis. Excerpt from *The Big Change: America Transforms Itself, 1900–1950*. New York: HarperCollins Publishers, Inc.

Angelou, Maya. Excerpts from *I Know Why the Caged Bird Sings*, p. 166. New York: Random House, Inc.

Bowen, Ezra. From "New Life for a Dead Language" by Ezra Bowen from *Time*, December 24, 1984, p. 61. Copyright © 1984 by Time Inc. Reprinted by permission.

Carson, Rachel L. Excerpt from *The Sea Around Us*. New York: Oxford University Press, Inc.

Dingwell, Anne. Excerpt from a letter written by Anne Dingwell, Campaign Director of Greenpeace.

Ehrenreich, Barbara. "Sorry, Sisters, This Is Not the Revolution" by Barbara Ehrenreich from *Time Special Issue*, Fall 1990, p. 15. Copyright © 1990 by Time Inc. Reprinted by permission.

Elbow, Peter. Excerpt from "The Open-ended Writing Process" from *Writing with Power* by Peter Elbow, pp. 50–51. New York: Oxford University Press, Inc.

Excerpt from "Lip-Flop" from *The New Republic*, July 23, 1990, p. 9. Copyright © 1990 by The New Republic. Reprinted by permission.

Excerpt from "Why They Choose Separate Tables" from *Newsweek On Campus*, March 1983, p. 4. Copyright © 1984 by Newsweek, Inc. Reprinted by permission.

Goodman, Ellen. Excerpt from *Close to Home*. New York: Simon & Schuster, Inc. Reprinted by permission.

Hodgkinson, Tom. "The 7 Deadly Virtues." *Utne Reader*, September-October 1996, p. 50.

Holt, John. Excerpt from "The Problem of Choice" from *Freedom and Beyond* by John Holt, pp. 77–78. New York: Holt Associates, Inc.

hooks, bell. "Overcoming White Supremacy" by bell hooks from *Zeta Magazine*, January 1987, pp. 24–27. Reprinted by permission.

Lacayo, Richard. Excerpt from "A Hero's Welcome" by Richard Lacayo from *Time*, July 2, 1990, pp. 14, 16. Copyright © 1990 by Time Inc. Reprinted by permission.

McGeary, Johanna. Excerpt from "Challenge in the East" by Johanna McGeary from *Time Special Issue*, Fall 1990, p. 30. Copyright © 1990 by Time Inc. Reprinted by permission.

Pitt, John S. "Don't Call Me Red." *Newsweek*, October 14, 1996, p. 16.

Stewart, D. L. Excerpt from "New (Old) House Beckons 'Visitors'" by D. L. Stewart as appeared in *St. Cloud Times*, October 13, 1990, p. 5. Copyright © 1990 Tribune Media Services. All rights reserved. Reprinted by permission.

Strouse, Jean. Excerpt from "Dress Codes" from *Up Against the Law* by Jean Strouse, p. 45. New York: Penguin USA.

Trueheart, Charles. "Welcome to the Next Church." *The Atlantic Monthly*, August 1996, p. 47.

Wallis, Claudia. From "The Fatty Diet Under Attack" by Claudia Wallis from *Time*, December 24, 1984, p. 58. Copyright © 1984 by Time Inc. Reprinted by permission.

INDEX

Note: **Boldface** page numbers indicate exercises.

572

gerund phrases as, 142
gerunds as, 142
identifying, 132–133, **157–160**
infinitive phrases as, 142–143
infinitives as, 142
possessive form with gerunds, 194–195
proper forms of, 466–467
in sentence patterns, 134–137
verb agreement with, 251
Number, 245
consistency in, 70, **91–92**, 331–322,
325–327
pronoun-antecedent agreement in,
251–254, **263–266**
subject and verb agreement in,
245–251, **255–262, 267**
Numbers, 483–484, **485–486**

O, capitalizing, 466
Object complements, 135, 137, **161–164**
Objective case, 189–195, **195–200**
and compound objects, 190–191
for pronoun subjects/objects of infinitives, 192
and *whom*, 193–194, **197–198**
Objects, 135–137
complementary form of, 135, 137
direct form of, 135–137
indirect form of, 135, 137
of prepositions, 140
repeated, 342
of verbal phrases, 142–143
Online research, 549, 551, 554–557,
567–568
Opening paragraphs, 78–79, **97–98**
Opinion, 104
or, 248
pronoun-antecedent agreement with,
252
Organization, 31–35, 67–68, **85–89, 93**
Organizing tools, 32–34
Outlines, 32–34, **44–46**
parallelism with, 369
Oversimplification, recognizing,
108–111, **125–126**

Paragraphs, 63–82, **83–101**
central idea in, 64–65, **83**
climactic order, 68, **89**
for closing essay, 80–81, **97–98**
coherence in, 63–64, 66–72, **99–101**
consistency in, 70, **91–92**

defined, 63
developing, 72–78, **94**
and dialogue, 81
dramatic order in, 68, **89**
irrelevant details in, 64, **83**
length of, 77–78
linking in essays, 82, **95–96**
for opening essay, 78–80, **97–98**
organizing, 67–68, **85–89**
parallelism, 68, **95–96**
repetition in, 69, **95–96**
special kinds of, 78–81
topic sentence in, 64, **83–84**
transitional, 81
transitional expressions in, 71, **95–96**
unity in, 64–66, **83**
varying sentences in, **391**
Parallelism, 367–370, **371–376**
for coherence, 68, **99–101**, 369–370
for coordinate elements, 368–369,
371–376
for emphasis, 378, **381–384**
in paragraphs, 68, **95–96**
patterns of, 367–368
Paraphrase, 547, 548–549, **563–564**
Parentheses, 456–457, **459–460**
Parenthetical citation, 553–554
Parenthetical expressions, 406, 456–457
Participial phrases, 142–143, **171–174**
Participles, 141, 143–144, **170**
with helping verbs, 207–209,
229–230
present and past forms of, **170**,
202–203, 204–206, **223–224**,
273–274
tense sequence with, 213
Particles, 220–221, **243–244**
Parts of speech, 132
Passive sentences, 152, **185**, 216–219,
239–240
Passive voice, 152, **185,** 208, 216–219,
239–240, 379
Past participle, 141, **170**, 202–203, 213,
223–224
Past perfect tense, 209–211, 213–214,
230–234
Past tense, 215–217, 218–221, **239–242**
Patterns of development, 26–27
in paragraphs, 73–77, **94**
Perfect infinitive, 213
Perfect tenses, 209–215, **231–234**

580

Useful Lists and Summaries